GRAMMAR IN PHILOSOPHY

GRAMMAR
IN
PHILOSOPHY

BEDE RUNDLE

Fellow of Trinity College, Oxford

CLARENDON PRESS, OXFORD
1979

Oxford University Press, Walton Street, Oxford OX2 6DP

OXFORD LONDON GLASGOW
NEW YORK TORONTO MELBOURNE WELLINGTON
KUALA LUMPUR SINGAPORE JAKARTA HONG KONG TOKYO
DELHI BOMBAY CALCUTTA MADRAS KARACHI
NAIROBI DAR ES SALAAM CAPE TOWN

Published in the United States by Oxford University Press, New York

© *Bede Rundle 1979*

British Library Cataloguing in Publication Data
Rundle, Bede
    Grammar in philosophy.

    1. Languages—Philosophy
    I. Title
    401   P106   79-40345

    ISBN 0-19-824612-9

P151
R78

*Set in IBM Baskerville by Graphic Services, Oxford
Printed in Great Britain
at the University Press, Oxford
by Eric Buckley
Printer to the University*

To My Parents

PREFACE

Philosophy may begin with wonder, but it soon ends up in confusion. Some of the confusion simply reflects the difficulty of the subject; much of it is self-inflicted, of the practitioners' own making rather than anything for which a mysterious universe could take the credit. Both forms, as they arise in the philosophy of language, furnish material for the negative side of this study, where I seek to remove misconceptions that are grammatical in nature, not just in the broad Wittgensteinian sense of the term, but in a more literal sense as well. To an extent that is perhaps surprising, it proves possible to clarify questions concerning existence, meaning, facts, and truth by appeal to syntactical and semantical considerations of an elementary kind, avoiding altogether the elaborate theorizing at present in vogue and which so often makes for grammar as a fitting subject for therapy rather than as an aid to analysis.

In so far as there are confusions, or just opposing views, this negative aspect is inevitable, but my main concern is with a more positive understanding of the workings of language. The challenge presented by philosophy is to state and support something that is true but not trivial, something that can be reckoned as falling within the province of the subject but is not merely destructive of a misconception. Those who favour a close association of philosophy with formal semantics and logic in their present stages of development may hold that the challenge has already been met. I reluctantly dissent, but here and more generally on the grounds of their indifferent showing to date rather than on the basis of arguments about the expectations we can rationally have of the subject. I believe that there is scope for constructive analysis of a philosophical character, for actually learning matters of substance rather than merely eliminating distortions and assembling reminders of what we already know.

I confess, indeed, to a craving for generality. In philosophy as much as in other disciplines it is satisfying to light upon patterns and regularities, to succeed in accommodating to one another a small number of principles and a larger number of seemingly disparate facts. This satisfaction can even be expected to go with a gain in understanding, for it is as instances of broader truths that individual findings are seen to be both significant and explicable. However, I intend this appeal to generality and explanation in an undemanding way; not so as to put me on the side of those who think in terms of the construction of 'theories', as that pursuit is understood in much contemporary philosophy and linguistics. In particular, I wish to reject the theorizing which proclaims that in philosophy, as in physics, we progress by postulating various unobservables, entities which can never finally be shown to exist, but which we may justifiably invoke on the basis of their explanatory value. I have little regard for this as an account of what takes place in the sciences; I have no regard whatsoever for such an approach in philosophy, where it constitutes a regression to a more primitive state of the subject, an abandonment of one of the major gains for which we can thank the philosophical revolution of this century. Generality is one thing, the appeal to transcendent explanations another: with the former we risk falling into error, with the latter we make error a certainty.

If philosophy has in recent times begun to look more like a science, this appearance is, in my view, largely illusory. However, I do not wish to deny the continuity of philosophy with science. This I tend to see as an involvement of philosophical questions within the sciences, rather than as an assimilation of any branch of philosophy to the latter, but there certainly are methodological considerations of a scientific nature which are crucial to the philosophy of language, and these, together with other general preliminaries, form the subject matter of chapter 1. This methodology is applied in the next two chapters to accounts of the definite and indefinite articles, in conjunction with familiar topics relating to reference and an analysis of the subject–predicate distinction. Chapter 4 surveys various departures from the subject–predicate form, including intentional and existential sentences, my aim being to dissolve the puzzlement which such departures have caused and to discourage the drastic remedies which have been able to flourish so long as confusion has reigned in this quarter. In similar spirit the next two chapters defend the claim that so-called 'abstract objects', such as numbers, harbour no mysteries, but that common attitudes to questions of existence harbour gross misconceptions. Forms of words which are genuinely more challenging in this respect are considered in some detail in chapter 7, such units as clauses and participial constructions calling for a radical departure from what is suggested by the superficial grammar. I am grateful to the Editor of the Aristotelian Society Proceedings for permission to include here material which originally appeared in my 'Transitivity and Indirect Speech' [1968]. The unorthodox semantics to which I have recourse at this point constitutes a crucial stage in the development of the argument, and once freed from certain natural preconceptions we are in a position to make headway with an understanding of facts and truth, topics for chapter 8. By now puzzles about meanings as entities need little attention, but the issue is rounded off in chapter 9 and questions revolving upon the relation of meaning to use, tone, and force are then pursued, to the advantage of an account of meaning currently in some disrepute. A final chapter ties up a number of loose ends, none too securely, with discussions of synonymy, analyticity, and verification.

My thanks go to Dr P. M. S. Hacker for helpful comments on the text, and to my wife, Ros, without whose patient understanding this book would not have been possible; not to mention those many writers in the tradition of Frege and Russell without whose excesses much of it would not have been necessary.

BEDE RUNDLE

Trinity College, Oxford
July 1978

CONTENTS

1 MEANING AND METHOD   1

   1 Reference, and a problem posed by its absence   4
   2 The intended object of analysis   8
   3 A trivial condition of adequacy for an analysis   12
   4 False determinants of meaning   18
   5 Conditions for an adequate analysis: the examples
     of existence and number   30

2 METHOD AND REFERENCE   41

   6 Token-reflexivity   42
   7 The definite article   50
   8 Reference and identification   66
   9 Proper names   71

3 REFERENCE AND SUBJECTS   83

   10 The indefinite article and covert reference   84
   11 Plural nouns and mass terms   92
   12 Strawson on subject and predicate   95
   13 Negatability as a mark of predicates   102
   14 Predication and assertion   105
   15 Completeness and incompleteness   109
   16 The universality of the subject–predicate
     distinction   115
   17 Relations of dependence within a sentence   120

4 SUBJECTS AND EXISTENCE   133

   18 Existence   136
   19 Logical subjects and oratio obliqua   145
   20 The possibility of opacity   163
   21 Modality and substitutivity   175
   22 The Frege argument   179

5 EXISTENCE AND ABSTRACTIONS 187

23 *Ontological commitment* 187
24 *Reductive analyses* 200
25 *Generic 'the'* 204
26 *Identity* 209
27 *Mass and count nouns* 218

6 ABSTRACTIONS AND NOMINALIZATIONS 231

28 *Sameness and difference with abstract nouns* 231
29 *Identity and identifying reference* 239
30 *Words and propositions* 250
31 *Numbers* 254
32 *Possibility and infinity* 271

7 NOMINALIZATIONS AND FACTS 278

33 *Intransitivity and verbs characterizing
    speech acts* 280
34 *Transitivity and the origins of the noun clause* 283
35 *Clauses as subjects* 289
36 *Propositions and indirect speech* 293
37 *Psychological verbs* 298
38 *Other nominal forms* 306
39 *Facts* 312

8 FACTS AND TRUTH 324

40 *Facts, states of affairs, and propositions* 324
41 *'Fact' and adverbial qualifications* 332
42 *Truth and correspondence* 339
43 *Further cases of 'making true'* 348
44 *Truth and redundancy* 358
45 *Near-synonyms of 'true'* 365
46 *The analysis of 'true'* 369

9 TRUTH AND MEANING 377

47 *Meanings and entities* 377
48 *Meaning and use* 383
49 *Meaning and tone* 389
50 *Meaning and intentions* 403

51 Parts of speech and their meanings   409
52 Force   415
53 Sentence meaning   423

10 MEANING AND VERIFICATION   432

54 Sameness of meaning   432
55 Meaning and application   441
56 Analyticity   444
57 Indeterminacy of translation   452
58 Verifiability   457
59 Verification and generality   468
60 Verification and observability   472

Bibliography   481

Index   487

1
MEANING AND METHOD

In the tradition which Wittgenstein wished to correct, if not to terminate, the distinctive character of philosophical propositions was not appreciated, such propositions often being presented very much as if they were highly general or abstract empirical hypotheses, hypotheses for which, their meaning being supposed clear, the essential question was that of their truth. So it was asked: do universals exist? Some were of the opinion that they did, others of the opinion that they did not. Still others were uncertain as to the facts. But at least there was, it could be supposed, a definite question with a definite answer, even if that answer was not merely not known, but perhaps not even humanly knowable. Or, it may have been recognized that questions of meaning were of some importance, but not thought that the resolution of the problem went only trivially beyond the clarification of meaning—as if, to take another example, we could be quite clear as to the interpretation of 'Women have souls', but still be far from knowing whether this was true or false. Hence the likeness to empirical hypotheses.

This tradition continues into the present, but with an emphasis on the affinity of philosophical theses with the more theoretical propositions of the sciences and a correspondingly more pragmatic approach to questions of existence. With respect to universals, for instance, we may find the more tough-minded urging that, in a purified language for science, we dispense with such 'posits' as numbers and propositions, entities which have a place only within the mythology of the subject. The bolder, by contrast, may throw caution to the winds and embrace such entities; not without some discomfort, perhaps, but able at least to draw solace from the scientific parallel: the nature of universals may be elusive, but they have indispensable practical value, or value as explanatory constructs.

Philosophers may find themselves moving from the one

general position to the other, or being sceptical about propositions, let us say, but 'realists' with respect to numbers. These
vacillations are understandable. On the one hand, we happily
say that there are numbers of various kinds—whole numbers,
irrationals, and so forth—on the other hand, there are many
terms, from the 'Absolute' to the 'id', whose interpretation is
sufficiently uncertain for us to find the question of existence
only marginally intelligible. With regard to the former possibility, it is a fact of obvious relevance that non-philosophical
knowledge dictates an answer, even if the question of analysis
remains. However, the reasons for the opposing views all too
frequently do not rely on this distinctive difference: the answer
which common knowledge furnishes to the more intelligible
query may simply be discounted, while the suspect formulations are treated as on a par with ordinary requests for information, such as 'Is there a cure for the common cold?', rather
than as standing in urgent need of clarification, and indeed as
containing their solution in their eventual analysis. The shift
from an incorrect to a verbally correct view on a particular such
question of existence is no sure sign of even partial enlightenment: the underlying misconception—that intelligibility can
take second place to utility—just comes to be associated now
with one, now with another of the possible alternatives.

It would be going too far to reject altogether the possibility
of a significant comparison between philosophical and scientific propositions. Just in so far as they are not conclusively
established, both can be thought of as conjectural or speculative, for instance, and even in logic there is a sense in which
we may accumulate evidence for a generalization. However,
this negative characteristic—falling short of constituting an
established truth—is hardly indicative of a virtue which specifically philosophical propositions may share with certain
scientific claims, and in general it is the contrast with the latter
that is most striking: if a philosophical proposition proves
unacceptable, this will typically be because it is eventually
exposed as incoherent; we shall not be able to say that it states
a genuine possibility, but one which just happens to be edged
out by a superior competitor. To take an example which we
shall be discussing further, Frege has an account of indirect
speech, exceedingly elaborate when worked out in detail,

according to which the words used therein have as their reference what is customarily their sense. If I am right, this commonly accepted account is not simply wrong in part, adequate only in some cases; it is, along with later versions inspired by it, quite bluntly, *absurd*—and the truth correspondingly plain and simple. Unfortunately, error can, in a sense, be more creative than the truth, the complex manoeuvrings which avoidance of obvious falsehood requires resulting in a structure which may be superficially far more impressive than the mundane observations which go to make up a correct account.

But is it not at least conceivable that we should have important generalizations which are properly called 'philosophical' though neither nonsensical nor trivial? This possibility might be resisted on definitional grounds: anything which could be presented as a genuine hypothesis with a coherent alternative will hardly rate as philosophical, but will have a home in one of the sciences, or in common knowledge. Again this is further than I wish to go. Perhaps it is not an unreasonable stand, given that any proposition which does allow of an alternative can hardly fail to belong to some other area of knowledge, even if it can at the same time be reckoned to fall within the province of philosophy. However, it is the characteristically philosophical thesis that, in my view, invites this contrast with empirical propositions. To repeat, with the latter meaning is generally clear, even if truth is difficult to decide; with philosophical propositions the balance alters, the major task being one of fixing a coherent interpretation, the assignment of truth value being then by comparison a minor matter. But there is a spectrum of cases here, and I do not wish to exclude any overlap between the two categories. Many traditional philosophical positions harbour recognizably empirical propositions along with propositions of uncertain sense, and I acknowledge that what may emerge on probing the latter is something close to the former, or on other occasions, a proposition which can be accounted true or false on logical grounds. Philosophical pronouncements which are as they stand just plain false, or, conversely, empty platitudes, are familiar enough, as much of the literature on time testifies. When C. D. Broad wrote, 'There is no such thing as *ceasing* to exist' (Broad [1923], p. 69), it should have been clear enough into which class that contention fell. My claim is merely that we must look to forms of words for which the question of interpretation has priority if we are to find what has been characteristic of philosophical propositions. Conversely, I do not deny that one may meet with such propositions in scientific theorizing. Indeed, as I have already indicated, I see the continuity of philosophy with science as residing in just such an overlap, rather than in the assimilation of philosophy to a science.

The philosophers with whom I am most in dispute are those who fail to accord a central place to the question of analysis and who consider a pragmatic approach appropriate. In some cases, I claim, the question of existence may be straightforward enough, so, as with many of the things we say about numbers, not a philosophical matter at all. In other cases, obscurity of sense may make talk of postulation quite inappropriate. We could look more favourably upon the pragmatic approach if there were room for a choice, if the analysis of the meaning of, say, sentences seemingly alluding to certain abstractions, left the question of existence undecided. There are reasons for thinking that this cannot be so, and the arguments to come will, I hope, bear out the general objection in particular cases.

1. Reference, and a problem posed by its absence

There is a limit to the usefulness of generalizations about the nature of philosophy unaccompanied by a detailed examination of specific issues, a limit which I have probably already overstepped with these few observations. Moving nearer to the particular, but with matters of meaning still to the fore, I shall focus for the rest of this chapter on specific sources of error for which philosophical investigations offer such scope, as when we misidentify the precise source of implications carried by a sentence, see a multiplicity of meanings where there is really only one, misconceive of the factors which determine meaning, and so forth. Our approach to these familiar pitfalls will be via a brief consideration of reference.

General accounts of the workings of language reveal philosophers under considerable pressure to find matching items for words, phrases, and even whole sentences: proper names are mapped onto persons or things named, adjectival and verbal phrases onto properties and states, and declarative sentences, when true, onto their corresponding facts. Sometimes it is not so much worldly correlates that appear to offer themselves: concepts and propositions, for instance, may be assigned a matching role but denied location, at least in the spatio-temporal universe. However, the pressure is similar in either case, and readily understandable. Language surely has significance through relating to a reality which is, for the most part, outside it, a reality which, in its differing aspects, may be thought in turn to explain various features of language: facts, for instance, are said to make true statements true, and it is because of the existence of particulars and universals that our use of singular and general terms respectively has been thought to be warranted.

Although the general view just sketched embodies considerable confusions, the truth is in part, and in an important way, in keeping with it. In learning the meaning of a word we learn something relational, a connection between word and something quite different. The idea of such a duality may be viewed with some misgivings, no doubt because the specific relation between a name and its bearer has so often been taken as a model for the understanding of words of very different kinds. However, the breakdown of that model should not lead us to abandon any and every conception of a duality. It is surely by learning to make some kind of association between words and what is in evidence when they are spoken that we come to an understanding of our language. In some cases, as with statements and facts, the picture will prove to be a dangerous distortion, but at the level of individual words the general conception is plausible enough to be treated with sympathy as the basis for an account of meaning and understanding.

There are two strands here: words connect with non-words, and the latter are items which, since we learn of their correlation with words, must presumably in some way fall within our knowledge or experience. This latter strand, which clearly ties up with questions concerning verification, will receive attention at a much later stage; our principal concern will be with whether and how different types of term relate to the world, what 'ontological commitments' are enjoyed by, for instance, such units as clauses. Here our starting-point is the notion of *reference,* and in particular the notion of 'identifying' reference which is commonly associated with the use of proper names and kindred expressions.

Reference thus understood is central to a pattern of sentence close to the hearts of philosophers: that, namely, in which a proper name is linked by some part of the verb 'to be' to either an adjective or a noun phrase, as in 'Galois was impetuous' and 'Galois was a mathematician', or in which a name is followed by a verb or verb phrase, as in 'Galois died in a duel'. Here we find the favoured role of the name being complemented by that of the predicate, the two combining in a sentence form which is felt to be particularly satisfying if we are concerned with the way words both fit together and 'fit the world', a sentence form for which truth and falsity are simply explicable in terms of the predicate's being true or false of what is named by the subject term.

The chosen formula allows of wide application. A grammarian may not recognize the name 'Devon' as a grammatical subject in 'We visited Devon last summer', but this sentence—transposed from the page to a live context—can be thought of as asserting something of what is named by 'Devon', and to that extent can be regarded as a variant of the basic form. Recognition of the similarity of pattern is sometimes shown by calling the name a 'logical subject', a usage which will be followed here and which is to be distinguished from that in which it is said that a term is the logical subject of a sentence through specifying the agent or actor. In this sense, the name 'Suzie' is subject in 'The flowers were arranged by Suzie', superficial grammar notwithstanding. I also make a possible contrast with what grammar prescribes, but my use of 'logical subject' does not imply fulfilment of this specific role. In applying the phrase 'identifying reference' in connection with the use of logical subjects, I shall intend not merely that the reference be of a kind appropriate to names and certain other noun phrases, but that it shall be conveyed explicitly by the words used. The contrast is with a less familiar notion of 'covert' reference to be introduced in chapter 3.

While proper names can be joined by such phrases as 'the goat', 'that shadow', and 'our lawn' in giving instances of the subject-predicate sentence form, not every use of a noun phrase involves the referential or designatory role which would justify the description, 'logical subject', and it is easy to find sentences containing phrases which, because they do not fit comfortably into the favoured pattern, threaten to defeat the general procedures which rely upon locating that pattern within a sentence. To take a familiar example, the word 'nothing' fills a place in a sentence which can also be occupied by a logical subject, as in 'Nothing was in the cupboard', yet we are not using 'nothing' to designate something of which the rest of the sentence is affirmed.

That words like 'nothing' and 'nobody' are not namelike is plain enough, but there are many phrases whose categorization is less obvious. How are we to classify the grammatical subjects in 'Crime pays' and 'Contributions will be gratefully received'? With these and many other examples we may simply be unsure as to what should be our guide in deciding whether to speak of reference, and hence unsure of the consequences of agreeing or disagreeing to speak thus. Again, what of the indefinite article? Is such a phrase as 'a city' ever to be said to have a referential use? In some cases, as with 'A city was destroyed', we might feel that some kind of naming function was purportedly in evidence, but what of such sentences as 'A foolproof lock does not exist' or 'A new school is urgently needed'? Here, surely, nothing akin to naming is involved; but in that case, just what is the logical structure of the sentence? In asserting the former we are not to be represented as saying of some foolproof lock that it does not exist, and in asserting the latter we are unlikely to be saying of an actual school that it is needed; but how, then, do the grammatical subject and predicate of either sentence fit together?

Priority here would seem to go to the clarification of the notion of reference, but even in advance of this it might be wondered why a departure from the subject-predicate pattern should be of any account. Language can hardly be required to conform to the expectations of logicians and philosophers, and there are many everyday sentences which fail to fit the favoured categories, much as there are grammatical features of the English language that are not best described in terms of the categories of Latin grammar. In saying 'It is raining', we are not saying of something designated by 'it' that it is raining, yet the sentence is perfectly intelligible: we know when it is correctly asserted and correctly denied, and that surely is the prime consideration. The need to force it into a chosen logical form or the puzzlement which may result from the failure of any such attempt merely reflects, it may be said, the inappropriateness of the preconceptions which we bring to a study of the language.

Certainly, it is not uncommon to find a philosopher showing an exaggerated respect for what he describes as the 'logical form' of a class of sentences, seeing in his own artifice a fundamental linguistic or logical pattern when in practice the process of extracting it from actual sentences more often than not results in their distortion. However, even with such a familiar sentence as 'It is raining' there is at least a topic for further enquiry: it is not entirely obvious what the role of the pronoun is, how it compares with other uses of 'it', and so forth. We may grant that, from one perspective, what is fundamental is our mastery of the sentence as a whole, our knowledge of when its assertion is warranted, but it is reasonable to expect that we should be able to give some finer analysis of the sentence, indicating the contributions of the component parts. Even in the 'divergent' sentences there is, after all, pattern: the use of the pronoun as in 'It is raining' is not confined to this sentence, so there is a presumption that we can isolate a common function in the relevant class of sentences and not simply treat them as unanalysable units. What the objection highlights generally is the importance of an accurate characterization of any use considered fundamental and a justification for assigning it that status. Then perhaps we can appreciate how a different use is to some degree anomalous and possibly problematic.

2. The intended object of analysis

In characterizing the logical form of a sentence the concern is to lay bare those features which are relevant to the deductive interconnections of that sentence with others. Such a task is not remote from the present enquiry, but it is worth emphasizing that my interest is primarily in the language as it is, undoctored, and hence that there are severe limits to the extent to which I can or should wish to avail myself of any logical 'regimentation' which does not remain very close to the language which I am concerned to elucidate. This point is crucial in what follows, and I shall now devote some space to making it clearer and drawing attention to its methodological implications.

In the sentence, 'A new school is urgently needed', we can certainly suppose that no reference to a school is intended. Might it not be possible to bring this out by a paraphrase which assigns 'a new school' the role, not of a name or the like, but of a general term which, with some suitable qualification, is said to be true or false of something? Here, as with 'a child' in 'He is only a child', we meet with the standard complement to the referential use of a term, namely, the (first-order) *predicative* use, and the model which comes to mind for the kind of analysis to be given in the present case is that provided by a certain common analysis of statements of existence. When we say 'A quasar exists' we are not attributing anything to some indefinitely designated quasar, it is said, but we are saying something about the concept *quasar,* viz. that something answers to or falls under it; hence the translation, 'Something is a quasar', in which the predicative status of 'a quasar' is made explicit.

The general objection to such a procedure is obvious enough. We may readily grant that a given sentence allows of a paraphrase in which a problematic term comes to function in a way that is no longer problematic, or in which the problematic term has been replaced altogether, but this may or may not serve to explain the behaviour of the term as it occurred in the original. Clearly, that question will remain untouched if it is admitted that the original use was problematic and that this is not the use invoked in the translation, and it is certainly possible that this is the situation if we are relying on the notion of a predicative occurrence. That, as indicated, is an occurrence of a common noun, N, in the context 'S is an N'—or with some other part of the verb 'to be' (or 'become')—where S is a logical subject. This is the kind of example with which, in the first instance, both the noun 'predicate' and the adjective 'predicative' are associated, but it is clear that if that is all there is to the definition of the latter then there is nothing left of the idea of a predicative occurrence once we take away the accompanying copula, so no question of discerning such an occurrence in 'A new school is urgently needed' or 'A quasar exists'—unless we can show that the copula is somehow implicit in 'exists'.

I am not saying that this definition is the only one possible; indeed, I support a more general conception of general terms as having a primary use in application to objects, in being affirmed or denied of them, the use in which an understanding of such a term may be manifested and its meaning conveyed. However, there is this risk: that the operative element in the notion of a predicative occurrence should be locatable in the copula to such an extent that when the common noun is removed from this context and transferred to subject position it will bring with it nothing that can still be identified by this term. In passing from 'A quasar exists' to 'Something is a quasar', we are adopting a form of words which is thought to be less misleading or in some sense more perspicuous than the original, and for some purposes, e.g. putting sentences into a canonical notation, that may be as much as we require. But *one* problem presented by statements of existence, along with the example with 'need', is that of how the grammatical subject is to be construed, and it is no answer to this to abandon that form of words for a translation which is deemed successful by dint of its avoidance of what made for the difficulty in the original. If, because of an implicit copula in the verb, or because of a characterization which makes no essential appeal to a copula, there is the continuity between the two versions which would warrant the common label 'predicative' with respect to the noun phrase, then the analysis may have something to offer; but, failing such continuity, no light is shed on the question how the words fit together in the original proposition.

But perhaps this condition is too demanding. Might not the translation fail to satisfy it, yet somehow serve to make clear the true structure of the original? Why shouldn't grammar be misleading as to logical form? Indeed, why shouldn't 'surface' grammar be misleading as to 'deep' grammar? We could, it is true, define a particular logical or grammatical function in such a way that whether or not a term had that function

depended on there being the possibility of certain transformations of the sentence in which it occurred, so on moves which
took us away from the original form of words. Thus, if we
wished to know whether 'ravishing' was intended verbally or
adjectivally in 'He likes ravishing women', we might well ask
whether the formulation, 'He likes women who are ravishing',
would be a close approximation to the sense of the original.
Not merely are definitions of grammatical function which
demand consideration of further related sentences allowable,
they are likely to be especially useful, since if it is no more
than the immediately identifiable features of the phrase in its
setting that determine the applicability of a certain characterization, there is some likelihood that the characterization will
relate to comparatively superficial features.

There is nothing amiss with definitions of this kind; it is
just that it must be possible to say, given these transformations,
that the term has the function in question in the original, and
not just in a related sentence in which it may occur, since
otherwise its role in the former is so far uncharacterized.
Whether or not a noun is a grammatical object in a given sentence may depend on the legitimacy of a passive rendering of
that sentence, but it is precisely the role in the original sentence
that the possibility of the transformation establishes. In the
case of existence there will not, as I say, be the same objection
if it is possible to maintain that 'a quasar' is used in the same
way in each of 'A quasar exists' and 'Something is a quasar',
for in this event the translation may be illuminating through
making clear some aspect of the use of the noun phrase which
is obscured in the former context. For instance, if it were
maintained merely that 'predicative' meant 'non-referential',
there would be at least this much correspondence between the
two forms. Alternatively, if it could be argued that the problematic sentence was elliptical, the prospects would be brighter
for an application of 'predicative' which required an implicit
copula. However, the synonymy claim does not appear to be
what is usually intended, and any absent copula can be introduced only by a radical rewriting, not by simply inserting it
in the sentence as it stands, or with a minor modification. That
'predicative' does not, on the definition given, equate with
'non-referential' is shown, incidentally, by such a sentence as

'What I could do with is a hammer': if 'what I could do with' is not used referentially, as it certainly need not be, then 'is a hammer' is not used predicatively, though it is non-referential.

3. A trivial condition of adequacy for an analysis

Having decided that our goal is an understanding of the behaviour of a given term, the next problem is to ensure that what is offered as a characterization of that behaviour does indeed relate precisely to that term. Nothing could be plainer, but then nothing could be more familiar in this area than mislocations or misidentifications of meaning or function. For illustrations we may usefully turn to analyses of the logical particles, such as 'or' and 'and'. Here attempts are regularly made to read into the words factors which are properly located in other features of the context, and not such as to justify attributing different senses to the words themselves. So, for instance, an exclusive sense of 'or' is not demonstrated by such examples as 'The ship will float or it will sink', but the incompatability of the disjuncts is sufficient to account for any exclusion of the one alternative by the other. To establish the alleged sense of 'or' it would be necessary to find a disjunction with *compatible* disjuncts which could be said to be ambiguous between an exclusive and a non-exclusive interpretation. To take another example, the convention that we narrate events in the order in which we suppose them to have occurred has come to find expression in the mistaken claim that 'and' sometimes has a temporal sense, being equivalent to 'and then'. We might add that on these grounds it would be hard to deny a like reading of the comma which may often replace the conjunction: we differentiate between 'I telephoned, crossed the room, and looked out the window' and 'I crossed the room, telephoned, and looked out the window', but not, surely, by ascribing a temporal sense to the punctuation marks.

Again, there is the common misconception that in phrases like 'the house' the article indicates that it is a matter of just one house, when it is the singularity of the accompanying noun that is responsible for this implication. There is, too, the appeal to sentences like 'All John's children are asleep' to show that 'all' may presuppose non-emptiness of the subject class, when one would naturally look to the phrase 'John's children'—i.e. '*the* children of John'—to furnish this implication. Finally, and close to our present concern, we may mention the claim that 'is' has a number of different senses: an 'is' of predication, one of identity, and even an 'is' of constitution. What in fact we find is a single, constant 'is' coming into association with terms which differ among themselves in pertinent ways. Consider 'The colour of sulphur is yellow'. We are not here describing the colour, as we might describe sulphur as yellow, but we are identifying the colour, so, allegedly, using an 'is' of identity, not of predication; compare the symmetrical 'Yellow is the colour of sulphur'. But since we know anyhow that 'yellow' allows of the two uses, what grounds have we for seeing a further difference in the verb? In order to ascribe differing senses to 'is' we should have to find contexts in which the overall variation in meaning could be accounted for in this way only. We should require, that is, that all the other terms be held constant through either interpretation, and hence that differing readings of 'is' should finally be indicated as the source of the two interpretations.

Philosophers are not alone in proliferating errors of this kind, but in writings in linguistics the practice is threatening to reach epidemical proportions. Other related errors are also worth warning against, perhaps the most obvious being the assimilation of *covering more than one case* to *having more than one meaning*. Mumps and measles are both describable as 'illnesses', and snakes and lizards are equally reptiles, but in neither case do the differences induce distinct interpretations of the common description. Again, 'dog' is not ambiguous because it applies to both the male and the female of the species, but because, as well as this use, there is a use in which it is exclusive of the latter possibility, where 'dog' is explicitly opposed to 'bitch'.

As with misassignments of meaning, so too with multiplications it may be the extensiveness of our knowledge that encourages the error. Consider the claim made by Geoffrey Leech that 'by' has three locative meanings, on a scale of descending generality, as evidenced by the sentences:

> The shell exploded by the wing of the aeroplane
> An oak tree stood by the farmhouse

The red car was parked by the green one

The meaning of 'by' allegedly varies according as mere spatial proximity is conveyed, or the more specific relation of proximity on a horizontal plane, or finally that of proximity only on the 'side-to-side' axis (Leech [1974], pp. 131-2). The spatial relations could indeed be expected to take these forms, but it is common knowledge concerning the relevant objects and not suitably circumscribed meanings of 'by' that underpins any inference we might draw concerning relative position.

One case in which we might be prepared to speak of different meanings or senses, even though a single specification of the meaning of the word may apply to all of the relevant contexts, is that in which the meaning of surrounding words, rather than knowledge of matters of non-linguistic fact, determines a reading for the phrase as a whole. Thus, while we might well expect a single paraphrase for 'good' to be applicable to the word as it occurs in each of 'a good fit' and 'a good argument', we might also be prepared to say that 'good' means 'close' as used of a fit, and 'sound' as used of an argument. Certainly, these characterizations of particular uses do not clash with the possibility of a more general account: we should expect that the specific characterizations would be predictable from such an account taken in conjunction with an understanding of the surrounding contexts. There would accordingly be no objectionable multiplication of meanings, in the sense that it would become unclear how a person could appreciate what 'good' came to in a particular context without having to be specifically taught its meaning in that context. Similar remarks apply to the use of 'have' in the rather different phrases, 'have a cold' and 'have an uncle'. In either case, however, we might prefer to say that it is the phrase as a whole that has as a part the meaning suggested, that it is 'a good fit' that means 'a close fit'. This is my preference, though since it is only as it occurs in this or a similar phrase that 'good' may be replaced by 'close', no damage is done if we speak of the latter as giving the sense there of the former.

To show that a word has two different meanings we look for paraphrases which make this clear, but as well as shifting the problem onto the paraphrases, this leaves us with the difficulty of ensuring that we have not simply formulated our paraphrase at the wrong level of generality. So, for instance, 'mite' surely means something different when used of a coin of little value, a tiny child, or a kind of arachnid, but what are we to say to someone who regards our demands for three separate classifications as simply reflecting our failure to come up with a definition which applies equally to all three? Again, it could be held that 'affair' had a specialized meaning when used of amorous encounters, as opposed to its more general use in such phrases as 'business affairs' and 'affairs of state', but once more the objection is possible.

In particular cases there can be considerable uncertainty whether we are dealing with a difference in word meaning or a difference of another kind, the example of 'by' being hardly typical in this respect. One approach, though not the only one, is to consider the behaviour of the given word—'mite', say—in general statements. If such statements featuring 'mite' were never made unless they were supposed true of all three types of object, then we should be dealing with a word having a single broad meaning. Otherwise not. Suppose, that is, that while allowing that 'mite' applied to things which were in certain respects very different, we treated them as forming a single kind, saying such things as 'Some mites are to be found in cheese, others are to be found in people's pockets', and never taking the term to apply just to, say, the arachnids, so not allowing the unqualified 'Mites live in cheese'. In that case we could say that 'mite' meant something like 'small thing' as applied to coins, children, and certain arachnids. It is clear, however, that in actual usage a difference of meaning is prescribed for 'mite' by the occurrence of true generalizations which would be contradictory if the word had only one meaning. Thus, 'Mites are arthropods' and 'Mites are coins' are both true. As suitably intended, we can of course add. And it is not enough that the intention should be that of a single individual. For us to be able to say that the word has one of the meanings in question, we must be able to invoke an established pattern of usage in which that intention is to be discerned and to which a given individual can appeal when he says he is using the word in that sense.

As a further example, take the verb 'run'. Sheep, shows, motors, and mascara can all be said to run; do we have here a single phenomenon univocally described, or do we have to do with a range of activities or processes whose non-identity is reflected in distinct, if related, senses of the verb? A plurality of senses is forced if the same thing can be said to be running, in the way this applies to sheep, but not to be running, in the way this applies to mascara. However, it may be claimed that this test requires that the putative senses should at least be possible with respect to a single subject, and such a subject may be hard to find, in which case might it not be the inter-action of the word with two very different types of noun that generates the overall difference? Perhaps the general meaning of 'run' is to be explained in terms of rapid movement, which comes to 'flows' in the company of 'her mascara', but not when united with 'the sheep', for which it implies the posses-sion of legs. On the other hand, the difference between the two cases is one that we find striking, and which we may well wish to explain in terms of different, if related, criteria for the two uses of the word. That having legs is one criterion would emerge once more in the unqualified character of such a state-ment as 'If a thing runs, it must have legs'. To allow that this is true, whilst recognizing that there are some legless things that can be said to run, is to ascribe at least two senses to the verb. However, it is hard to see how anything of substance could hang on the distinction: you can say, 'If a thing runs, it must have legs—at least for certain kinds of thing', or 'If a thing runs, it must have legs—at least in one sense of "run"'. The distinction can find its way in at one point or the other, and which it is is of no great moment—fortunately, since it is frequently far from clear which one we should opt for.

These observations may be used to illustrate the thesis that differences in word meaning must *show* themselves in actual usage—the difficulty being one of getting a clearly defined opposition that has just this effect. Thus, suppose it is main-tained that the Latin *altus* must, since it translates both 'high' and 'deep', have at least two distinct senses. This is not shown by the non-equivalence of our pair of words, but it would have to be backed by the production of sentences in Latin in which differences in truth value of the same form of words obliged us to recognize a difference in meaning at this point. In default of a pattern of differing implications which can be taken as conferring distinct identities upon a given word, we are left with, at best, differences in speaker's meaning rather than in word meaning. This at least is generally true. What we begin from is the thesis that a word *w* has *v* as one of its particular meanings if and only if there is a generally recognized intention to use it as thus confined. Such an intention is likely to emerge in the way indicated, but so long as it reveals itself in *some* way in the usage of the word, this thesis remains intact.

The distinction just mentioned between speaker's meaning and word meaning is worth a more definite illustration. To take an example of a familiar kind, the sentence, 'You're late', might be uttered as a rebuke or merely to inform. We should not, however, introduce reference to the former role in giving an account of the meaning of the words; rather, we should appeal to their meaning, among other factors, in explaining the possibility of enlisting them in this role. This is not to say that we are totally debarred from speaking here in terms of a difference in meaning; on the contrary, the relevant difference is a difference in what is meant by the speaker. Similarly, the word 'he' has but one meaning, not several, and not one which is as specific as that of 'my cousin'. But this does not mean that my cousin cannot be the person I mean when I say 'he'.

Examples such as these may make the point seem trivial, but there is no shortage of controversial cases. Here are two, though with an emphasis on whether or not we have a difference in word meaning rather than, if not that, that what we have is a difference in speaker's meaning. If I say 'I shall sneeze', I may be merely making a prediction or I may be expressing an intention. If I say 'I cannot tell him that', I may clarify my remark in terms of very different considerations: I say 'cannot' since the whereabouts of the person in question is unknown to me, or I say it because I think the matter too disturbing to pass on to him. Do these examples establish differences in word meaning, or, at best, differences in speaker's meaning?

Once more I wish to proceed by emphasizing the common content, only acknowledging a subdivision of senses if this is somehow forced upon us, or seen not to constitute a significantly different alternative. To take the first example, expressions of intention are often contrasted with predictions, but

when the future tense is used I claim that a prediction is involved in either case: 'I shall sneeze' will be asserted on a
different basis when an expression of intention is involved as
opposed to a 'mere' prediction, but in each case a prediction
is made. Given this common element, with its common associated notion of fulfilment, we have good grounds for denying
a difference in word meaning, even if in other languages distinct auxiliaries are used in the two cases; the conclusion is as
yet hardly compelling, but it is further reinforced by considering substitution of the explicit 'intend' for 'shall', a substitution which makes for a statement that is quite diffe erent
assessable, and not to be regarded as one of the reading. s of
the original.

In the modal example we have again a common idea underlying the use of 'cannot' in either case, a matter of the presence
of inhibiting factors, of whatever kind, and given that the
remaining context does not impose any more specific reading,
it is the speaker's intention, it would seem, or the different
basis on which he might say what he says, that makes for any
differences in the inferences we might draw. This is not unlike
the case where we have an incomplete form of words completable in more than one way, as with 'I have'; again a circumstance to be distinguished from difference in word meaning.

4. *False determinants of meaning*

There is undeniable uncertainty with regard to many questions
of sameness and difference in meaning, and we shall make
something further of this topic when we come to discuss the
analytic/synthetic distinction. For the present I wish merely
to emphasize that, however fluid and complex, it is the pattern
of usage that determines meaning, so sameness and difference
thereof, and I emphasize this simply because seemingly rival
accounts of the determinants of meaning are currently in vogue.

I have in mind here, *inter alia,* attempts at explaining certain linguistic incongruities by having regard to supposed
features of 'deep structure', attempts which exclude, or at
least bypass, the more familiar and accessible realm of actual
usage. For instance, it is suggested by Charles J. Fillmore that

the acceptability of 'please leave the room' as opposed to 'Fred please left the room' can be explained by supposing that there occurs in the deep structure a silent performative verb of ordering (Fillmore [1970], p. 271). We may well have doubts about the notion of deep structure, but in any case we do not have to go beyond the given words to explain why 'Fred please left the room' is nonsense: we need simply observe that the sense of 'please' requires that it be associated with a request rather than a report. There is room for an expansion of this observation in the direction of an elucidation of the general issue involved, together with a detailed tracing of the linguistic connections, but no room for a rival explanation from elsewhere.

Again, it has been suggested that sentences containing noun clauses as seeming object or subject are to be ascribed different deep structures depending on whether or not the speaker pre-supposes that the embedded clause expressses a true proposition (Kiparsky [1970]). Thus the contrast between 'Edward knew that he was about to die' and 'Edward hoped that he was about to die'. If, as with 'knew', there is this presupposition, then 'fact' is supposed to occur in the deep structure, otherwise not. However, if the sense of the verb *entails* that the remainder is asserted as factual, no further explanation of how the one reading rather than the other is secured is neces-sary. It is not because it somehow 'comes from' a sentence containing 'fact' that a statement of something known carries a commitment to truth, but, given the established usage, this would be so whatever the derivation. If there is a genuine alternative, then an explanation is required why one particular reading was chosen, but if the sense of the verb excludes any such choice then any purported explanation is otiose.

The general area into which we have entered is one in which redescriptions are commonly passed off as explanations, and it is worth pausing to consider further misconceptions of this kind. In their *English Transformational Grammar,* Roderick A. Jacobs and Peter S. Rosenbaum note that verbs and adjec-tives are thought by some not to be distinct constituents in deep structure, certain characteristics common to either word class providing evidence for this belief. For instance, there is a comparison between the verb 'kick' and the adjective 'honest', in that both can appear in imperatives—'Kick the ball!', 'Be honest!'—and hence in reports of these—'I told the girl to kick the ball', 'I told the girl to be honest'. Here verb and adjective unite in their contrast to other verbs and adjectives: we do not have 'Own the house!' or 'Be short!' (in stature), nor, of course, their reports.

There is nothing surprising in these groupings—we should not expect verbs and adjectives to be invariably opposed in their classifications—and the common thread is easily seen: imperatival occurrence is proper to the case where we have to do with an activity or state which is under one's control; that it should be described by verb or by adjective is in this regard quite irrelevant. Jacobs and Rosenbaum claim that 'the common characteristics of verbs and adjectives are at least partially explained on the assumption that both are instances of the same kind of constituent' (op. cit., p. 64). This appears to hover uncertainly between an intelligible redescription and an unsuccessful explanation. If anything like a common underlying source in the deep structure is being held to explain the likeness—and the appeal to explanation suggests such a reading—we have an unsuccessful rival to the elementary explanation just offered. On the other hand, being an instance of the same constituent is hardly a matter of a shared genetic relation, and what is said could be held to be true just in so far as it alleges the existence of a categorization which is sufficiently general as to be indifferent to the specifically verbal or adjectival character of phrases to which it applies—though any explanation of the common characteristics is now at a minimum.

More generally, if the notion of a deep-structural description is thought of in this way—as a very general description of a sentence, cast perhaps in such terms that sentences which were superficially quite different could none the less fall under the same description—we should not be confronted with the difficulties which the current notion of deep structure presents; and since that notion lacks explanatory virtues, we should not be losing anything by this shift. The difficulties arise when talk of deep structure involves not simply a more abstract way of looking at a sentence, but the introduction of a new entity, an entity whose nature, and relation to the sentence, the surface structure, are exceedingly problematic.

Consider these points in turn. We have already seen that, whatever its exact interpretation, the notion of *coming* or *deriving from* will have no place in explanations of the desired kind. When it is suggested that, in the deep structure, 'kill' comes from 'cause to die', it is not of course being supposed that some process of phonological development generated the former from the latter—the most likely interpretation when *words* are at issue. If a historical derivation were at stake, we could have some use for the notion, as when we explain how the present meaning of 'silly' unfolded from its past meanings, though, when it is a matter of a development from a past to a present usage, the connection between the former and current meaning is only contingent: what essentially is determinative of present meaning is present usage. In tracing the connection of a word with an earlier form we are not moving towards a description of greater generality, but the movement is in an *actual* dimension, with the temporal separation of the earlier and later forms ensuring the contingency of any relation between them. The notion of deep structure suggests a separation in some other dimension, but once more any real separation would leave the connections between deep and surface elements only contingent; no more than past usage could deep structure usurp the place of current usage and determine current meaning.

The nature of the deep-structure forms is equally problematic, especially if the spatial metaphor is thought to reflect a region in which actual linguistic items, including our familiar words, are taken to enjoy some kind of existence, but an existence known of only by argument. It is not enough simply to characterize deep-structure derivations and their constituents as 'theoretical', as if this label could somehow make amends for the inapplicability of the descriptions which our ordinary understanding of linguistic forms would have us expect to hold. We may avoid falsification by prising these notions off anything that might constitute a concrete realization, but only at the risk of leaving them without any clear interpretation. The mind has been turned to as the home for these constructs, but the mind is hardly hospitable towards anything of which we lack awareness: our understanding of mental phenomena is such that we attach no sense to a claim that, say, we were thinking about medieval ship-building, if a full and sincere statement of what was going through our mind would show us to be totally preoccupied with the football results. We can *give* a sense to the notion of unconscious mental events or states by appealing either to behaviour or to neural happenings. The former is hardly a suitable location for deep structure, so the only hope would seem to lie with the latter, though again the kinds of consideration which those who invoke deep structure are bent on explaining continue to be elusive, questions of meaning being questions of the connection of words with world, not of intracranial connections.

So far I have been focusing on examples from semantic syntax or generative semantics, but similar observations apply when more straightforwardly syntactical relations are at stake; when, for instance, deep-structural derivations are invoked in explaining the different structural relations, and therewith interpretations, of such pairs as Noam Chomsky's 'John is eager to please' and 'John is easy to please'. The belief that we must look beyond surface structure to deep structure in accounting for the undoubted differences between such sentences is supported by the consideration that we seemingly must in *some* sense go beyond the given sentences. At one level of description we see only likenesses. To see where we have moved to when we are in a position to account for a difference of the relevant kind, consider a simple case of structural ambiguity, as with (1) 'She asked him to call every day'. This is ambiguous, the temporal qualification being capable of attaching either to 'asked' or to 'call' and the ambiguity is of course resolved by discovering which attachment the speaker intended. Here, as often, a simple rearrangement may make clear the intended meaning, as with (2) 'Every day she asked him to call', and in having recourse to this form we obviously go beyond the original sentence.

What is the significance of this transition? Bringing in only familiar linguistic forms, it takes us to a sentence which may unambiguously give the intended meaning of the original. Because it provides such a stopping-point, and does not itself stand in need of clarification by a further rephrasal, (2) can be said to enjoy priority over (1) with respect to the interpretation in question. Similarly, while we do not have actual ambiguity with 'John is eager to please' or 'John is easy to please', the structural difference between them is shown by the different ways in which either can be expanded or recast. The similarity of the former to 'John is eager to come', where the verb is patently intransitive, and its expansion to 'John is eager to please others', reveal 'John' as subject of the verb—after a suitable preliminary elucidation—while the versions, 'John is easy for one to please' and 'It is easy to please John', show more plainly the different relation involved in 'John is easy to please', 'John' here being describable as object of the verb 'please'.

All this is plain sailing; not so the claim that neither sentence can have the meaning it has unless that meaning is conferred upon it by an underlying deep structure. It is held that, since we have identity at the surface level, considerations which confine us to that level will not account for the differences in structure and meaning. The retort is obvious: any shortcomings in our structural descriptions will be of our own making; the senses of the adjectives 'eager' and 'easy' ensure that 'John' will be now subject, now object of 'please'; there is enough information for any speaker of the language to arrive at the appropriate readings and for any grammarian to give an account of the structural relations. Still, while this retort is in place in this instance, it does not take us to the heart of the matter; other familiar examples, such as 'The shooting of the hunters was terrible', present the same general issue, but with a single form of words which does allow of two distinct parsings.

At all events, given a sentence form which, if it is not actually called upon to remove an ambiguity, at least presents the construction in a plainer form, the question arises as to how they are related. Are we to regard the less straightforward sentence, one in which the differences between the two distinct constructions have perhaps become obliterated, as the result of a transformation based upon the preferred form? The most that can be said, I suggest, is that for any of the relevant constructions there should be sentences in which that construction can be unambiguously discerned. Certainly, if there is to be a grammatical form in which a name is subject of a verb, and a distinct form in which the name is object, then the difference must sometimes be recognizable, and it is hardly likely—though not impossible—that it will always be left to the context of utterance to provide the basis for assigning the one interpretation rather than the other. This gives us a sense in which the more perspicuous formulations can be said not merely to make a particular reading of the ambiguous sentence clearer, but to make it possible. They ensure that there is an identifiable reading of the kind required.

Let me explain this further. Structural ambiguities involve uncertainty about the way in which two or more words or phrases are related to one another. Typically, there is uncertainty as to whether a given noun phrase is intended as subject or as object of a verb phrase, as when 'the shooting of the hunters' may represent a subjective or an objective genitive. For a given structural analysis to be a real possibility, there must be such a thing as intending the words as related in the way in question—not a matter of individual whim, but a generally recognized interpretation which the words can bear. When two interpretations are possible the differences must show themselves at least in the different implications generated, and when the ambiguity is structural we should expect the alternatives to be made plain by a different arrangement, a different juxtaposition of relevant phrases. So it is that certain unambiguous formulations can be considered primary.

So is there a derivation? Once more, the connections being traced are logical rather than genetic. Furthermore, they are within the language, and not in a realm of which we can have only indirect knowledge. On the first point, we allow that the less straightforward form, the form in which distinct constructions coalesce, is derivative. However, to grant that each of two conflated constructions must allow of an unambiguous representation or identification is not necessarily to see these forms, or more abstract reflections of them, as starting-points for the application of deletion, substitution, or any other transformational procedures. The existence of the unambiguous form is at best required if we are to make sense of a possible description of a construction; it is not a hypothesized link in a generative chain. For the ambiguous form to have one of the readings made possible in this way, it will be sufficient that

the speaker *intend* it thus, since, so long as the language provides a vehicle for that reading which is in general recognizable,
it makes sense to ascribe such an intention. Something in
addition to what is given at the level of surface structure is
required, but at this point it is only an intention, and behind
this there is simply a general practice. Similar observations
apply to other instances of structural ambiguity, as with 'It's
too hot to eat', 'The assistant was not dismissed because of
his relation to the proprietor', and 'He caught sight of the
witness alighting from a bus'. Questions of uncertain antece-
dents, misplaced adverbs, unattached participles, and the rest,
have long had a place in manuals of correct usage. They should
have stayed there.

My second point was that the connections considered were
within language, that it is in familiar sentence forms that we
shall discern clear instances of the constructions in question.
Questions of meaning will, of course, arise with these. Our
sentence, (2) 'Every day she asked him to call', presents us
with a stopping-point, in so far as the attachment of the
temporal qualification is not now in doubt. We can ask why
it is that such a phrase is thus taken to qualify the verb with
which it is in immediate temporal or spatial association, but,
whatever our answer to that, we know in general terms that
usage dictates such an interpretation in this instance. Now,
however, think of (2) as the form which represents the deep
structure. Here similar questions must be faced. We do not
have to regard the deep structures as bearing more than a
structural similarity to the actual items of language for the
question to arise, the question of what it is that prescribes
that a given combination of elements in them should have the
meaning it has; the components of the abstract structure will
not automatically interact in the required way. But now,
whereas we have usage to impose one reading to the exclusion
of another, what can achieve this in mind or brain? Of course
nothing can, any more than something in my head might
somehow be a name of the Taj Mahal, despite the total ignorance that I and others have of it as standing in that relation.

I say that for deep as well as for surface structures, the
question would arise as to why a combination of elements
should have the meaning it has. That there is such a question

is perhaps overlooked because of the common assumption that the meaning of a phrase is something mental, an idea perhaps, which is required merely to occur in association with either a word or a deep-structural element. A desperate Fregean expedient might also be imagined: it is simply *of the nature* of the deep-structural elements to issue in a form with the relevant meaning. At all events, to attempt to explain the synonymy of two sentences by saying that they have identical deep structures—cf. Jacobs and Rosenbaum, op.cit., p. 73—is to turn away from the real problem. It is sometimes said that a phrase-structure grammar cannot do justice to the close relation which holds between an active sentence and its passive form, but the transformational account is no substitute for an explanation of how the two constructions issue in sentences so close in meaning.

Although the notion is novel, the misconceptions involved in the appeal to deep structure are venerable enough. We shall find analogues when we turn to consider abstract entities, the problem of universals being a fertile source of descriptions masquerading as explanations, with ascent to a higher level of generality being construed as 'creative', rather than as providing an alternative form of description for more familiar objects. Here, and in other connections, however, I shall be making use of something *like* the notion of deep structure. Thus, certain complex forms of words, such as those involving an abstract term, come, on my analysis, to be rewritable in a different form, the abstract term being replaced by a cognate adjective in a predicative construction, for instance. However, I do not wish to say that there is a sense in which the former can be said to 'come from' the latter—as nominalizations might be said by a transformational grammarian to 'come from' the corresponding verbal phrases. It is rather a simple equivalence of meaning that is in question, or, more generally, a matter of a deductive equivalence between two forms of words. Similarly, if I speak of *ellipsis,* it will only be where considerations of meaning and context ensure that the ellipted form is uniquely recoverable, as with 'He will come if she will'. Even then, it is not so much that a term has been *dropped,* as that there is thought to be no need in that context to make it explicit. At all events, the constraints to which I regard legitimate appeal to ellipsis as subject would not allow us to follow those who would say that 'I wonder who can see' comes from the form 'I wonder it who can see', by deletion of the 'it'. Again see Jacobs and Rosenbaum, op. cit., p. 27.

In so far as I have a quarrel with approaches to language currently in vogue with linguists and logicians, my objections tend to bear on this one point: the explanations offered simply do not appear to be of such a kind as even to begin to explain what they are intended to explain. Though this is of less importance, it also appears that the more fruitful approaches are also more straightforward—disappointingly unadventurous, perhaps, when viewed against elaborate formal analyses. Let me illustrate with two such trivia, this time from the side of logical theory rather than linguistics.

How are we to justify the inference from 'Jones buttered a piece of toast in the bathroom' to 'Jones buttered a piece of toast'? It may be wondered how this could possibly be a question for serious discussion, but for those who think we have a secure grip on such inferences only in so far as we can view them as exemplifying patterns dealt with in modern logic, there is a problem. One way of resolving this problem has been put forward by Donald Davidson, who suggests that we extract reference to an event, something x which is both a buttering of a piece of toast and is in the bathroom; given that there is something with both these properties, the statement that there is an x with the former is a simple consequence in first-order logic (Davidson [1967]).

There is no reason to object to this procedure on the grounds that a suspect category, that of events, has been invoked. It is quite unexceptionable to point out that if a man buttered toast then a buttering occurred; the step from 'butter' as a verb to 'buttering' as a noun is a small one, with the difference residing only in the grammar—the activity warranting use of the one being identical with what warrants use of the other—though some care may be called for with certain locutions. For instance, does the 'it' in 'Jones did it' do duty for a more specific reference to an event? Perhaps, but in general I should not regard such phrases as 'do it' or 'do something' as so divisible, as having a variable for a verb and another that 'ranges over' events or deeds, since the generalizations in question can be made with respect to intransitive verbs, as 'Jones spoke'. Still, the problem is not with events, but with any claim that the original pattern of inference is clarified by transition to this form. I allow that what separates the two is quite minor, at least on the point discussed, but further rules would be needed to explain how we move to and fro between the two formulations, and there is no reason whatsoever to suppose that anyone's reasoning ever takes this roundabout route. Given its detachment from actual practice, that route is at best an improbable possibility, explaining nothing in that practice.

And if we had succeeded in reducing the original inference to, primarily, an instance of conjunction elimination, where would that have left us? Not with an inference that has been satisfactorily explained, given the misconceptions which we shall find the truth-functional approach to embody. Instead, something like the following appears to be called for. A form of words which can be classed as an assertion is regarded as in force, as still adhered too, so long as it is not withdrawn or qualified. But additions may be made to an assertion, and they may result in an expansion or a retraction thereof, partial or total. The adverb 'almost' has a qualifying effect, but adding 'and Q' to P leaves the latter in full force; it is just like asserting Q having asserted P: in either case we may not quite know how to take the speaker if P and Q clash, but unless we can speak of the former as having been cancelled, rather than as remaining to form part of a contradiction, P will still stand. Certainly, 'and' does not of itself offer any qualification. Similarly, we could explain the legitimacy of the inference from 'I'm afraid I must be going' to 'I must be going' by pointing to the non-restrictive character of the qualification, 'I'm afraid', which contributes an affective comment, but without diminishing the assertive force—though this is not the only pattern of explanation for the construction generally.

Spatial and temporal phrases may have some qualifying effect. If the remainder of the assertion is suitably general, they can restrict its scope, though in other cases they may constitute expansions which leave that remainder intact: addition of 'in the bathroom' to 'Jones buttered a piece of toast' is an instance of the latter, whereas in 'He rarely does what he is told', 'rarely' may be taken to qualify the remainder in such a way as to prohibit inference to the bare 'He does what he is told'. What is of interest is that it is the same style of explanation as seems required for 'and': we may infer P from the larger context in which it occurs depending on whether that context does not or does make for a qualification or retraction of P.

My second example is similar. Sometimes combinations of noun plus adjective can be given conjunctival form, as when 'Minet is a greedy cat' becomes 'Minet is greedy and Minet is a cat'. Sometimes, however, this breakdown is questioned. If Lulu is a large mouse, does it follow that Lulu is large and that Lulu is a mouse? If Minet is a good companion, does it follow that Minet is good and that Minet is a companion? Given that the beloved conjunctive form is, or is considered to be inapplicable, it is sometimes thought that we do not have a secure understanding of these attributive constructions; that will come only when we have a proper *theory* to explain them. In fact, it is not so clear that the shortened forms are to be rejected; it depends on how the sentence with just the adjective is understood. It could be quite plain that 'Minet is good' was to be understood as 'Minet is a good companion' in one context, and as 'Minet is good at catching mice' in another, though in the absence of an explicit complementary phrase, or of further information, we tend to suppose a more general completion intended—'Minet is a good cat'—and in some cases would not allow that anything more specific could be left understood: 'He is perfect' will not abbreviate 'He is a perfect idiot'. There is, of course, no problem as to how one and the same thing can be a good F but a poor G, the difference in the respects in which goodness is being judged giving an obvious defence against inconsistency. Needless to say, any comprehensive taxonomy will distinguish further possibilities among adjectival phrases—see Bolinger [1967] for relevant data—but so long as we merely seek to spell out the understanding we have of our familiar adjectives, nothing at all elaborate, profound, or speculative appears to be called for. Certainly, there is nothing in the claim that our actual understanding is somehow defective so long as the constructions are anomalous from the point of view of current formalizations of logic.

Michael Dummet has dismissed as 'so plainly silly' Wittgenstein's claim that mathematical logic has completely distorted the thinking of philosophers (Dummett [1959b], p. 330; Wittgenstein [1956], iv. 48). Perhaps 'completely' makes for an overstatement in Wittgenstein's condemnation, but it is certainly far easier to find instances in which mathematical logic has been an obstructive rather than a constructive influence. At best, perhaps, we can say that there is no necessity that this should be so: formal languages do not look to be promising models for the understanding of natural languages, but many of the misconceptions which originate in a concern with the former—those just considered, for instance, or the claim that a truth predicate cannot be consistently defined within the language to which it belongs—are fortunately not essential to a formal approach.

5. Conditions for an adequate analysis: the examples of existence and number

One of my main concerns—that we should elucidate the forms of words which generate puzzlement, rather than simply abandon them for others—was illustrated in terms of statements of existence, and I shall now take the illustration further, with particular attention to the kind of analysis put forward by Frege. As a preliminary, I offer a number of mundane observations on the doctrine that 'exists' is not a predicate. This doctrine has been interpreted in more than one way, but it is the current interpretation, not that of Kant, for instance, that is most relevant here. According to this interpretation, the thesis is interchangeable with the claim that the grammatical subject of a statement of existence is not a logical subject: in saying 'S exists' or 'S does not exist', we cannot be affirming or denying existence of something named by the grammatical subject, S, since to couple reference with such affirmation or denial is to render the statement either redundant or contradictory. 'Exists' is not a predicate, then, in that the grammatical subject is not a logical subject, and, *a fortiori*, 'exists' is not true or false of something designated by the subject.

As it stands, this statement of the doctrine is unsatisfactory, and would generally be acknowledged as such. In the first place, it is rarely the single proposition, '*S* exists', that is to be described as redundant or pleonastic—or its negation as contradictory—since whatever the speaker may take himself to be doing in terms of reference, this is unlikely to be something which finds explicit expression in the grammatical subject used. If redundancy and contradiction are to be unearthed we should look not just to the statement of existence but to its conjunction with the supposition concerning reference: 'When I say "*S* exists" I am referring to *S*' is one appropriate form to examine for undesirable features. Second, it is clear that, if the doctrine is understood in reasonably comprehensive terms, there is no shortage of counter-examples. I can refer to the 'existing façade' of a building, and I can readily say such things as 'This library would not have existed but for the generosity of our benefactor' and 'The first church which he designed is still in existence'. There is a threat of redundancy or inconsistency only if the statement of existence constitutes an affirmation or a denial of the condition for the subject term's having reference, but since there are many propositions which count as existential without expressing such a condition, there is no lack of falsifying cases for the thesis in its simpler formulations. After all, the condition that the subject term have reference is not necessarily that the referent should exist, only—or perhaps at most—that it should have existed at some time or other. The Pharos of Alexandria is no longer in existence, but I am still referring to it when I say that it was one of the seven wonders of the ancient world, and indeed when I say that it does not now exist. There is, it is true, room for further discussion of how the notion of a property of something might be understood, but so long as it is this very formal interpretation that is at stake, an interpretation requiring no more than a correlative logical predicate, we have good grounds for insisting on a qualification of the doctrine.

One case in which the doctrine appears correct, if for rather more general reasons, is that in which the grammatical subject contains the indefinite article, as in 'A solution does not exist'. How is such a sentence to be understood? What are the roles here of the grammatical subject and predicate? If we are determined to preserve the logical subject–predicate pattern as far as possible, we may be tempted to appeal to *concepts* as providing what an appeal to objects cannot provide: an assertion of existence is an assertion about a concept, not an object. However, just what is involved in this complex claim is not altogether clear. First, while it may be suggested that, just as 'has green feathers' is a predicate which may be affirmed of a designated object, as in 'Our budgie has green feathers', so 'exists' is a second-order predicate assertible of what is signified by the concept expression, 'a solution', there are reasons for supposing that, for Frege at least, this interpretation would be inaccurate. It is true that Frege speaks of concept words where he might equally have spoken, as he also does, of general terms, but in view of his insistence on the essential incompleteness which characterizes concepts, we must regard such a way of speaking as secondary; it is primarily via such incomplete expressions as '... is a walrus', '... walked off in a huff', and '. . . likes toffee', that concepts are introduced, rather than via a noun or adjective occurring within these phrases—with the emphasis on the presence of the gap or argument place rather than on the copula, which Frege regarded as logically superfluous.

However, since a sentence such as 'A solution does not exist' does not appear to be in any way a completion of the incomplete '... is a solution', it is difficult to know how to interpret the suggestion that the expression for the concept, strictly understood, occurs here. We might be able to say that it did occur, albeit with its argument place suppressed, if it were possible to regard the sentence as elliptical for a version of the desired form, but the departure from this form is quite radical: nothing as minor as, say, a rectifiable omission of the copula. It would, then, seem fair to say that 'A solution does not exist' will represent an assertion about a concept only, at best, in the sense that there will be some way of rewriting these words so that something comes to be said about a concept. But that, I wish to say, is no sense at all. It is all very well to say, as Frege would, that grammatical form may be no guide to logical form, that 'A solution does not exist' may constitute an assertion about a concept, contrary appearances notwithstanding. The objection is that concepts have been introduced in such a way that talk of them is possible only

when a particular verbal form is evident, so Frege risks denying himself the right to make use of this flexible view. It is
possible that 'A solution does not exist' is equivalent to a
version in which that form is to be found, but that tells us
nothing about the way in which either 'a solution' or 'exists'
is to be understood here. From the perspective of our present
concern, it is no advance over saying that the sentence as a
whole must be taken as the unit.

This is just a repetition of the earlier argument with respect
to the notion of a predicative occurrence of a noun: if our
initial definition is in terms of the actual occurrence of a copula
in conjunction with the noun, we can make nothing of the
suggestion that a noun occurs predicatively in the absence of
the copula unless we can argue that ellipsis has occurred, and
a similar conclusion follows in the present instance if identification of a concept expression calls for identification of an
argument place. In either case, furthermore, even if we can
allow that a translation featuring a genuinely predicative occurrence of that noun is possible, this may be quite uninformative
with respect to its behaviour in the original. So, 'A solution does
not exist' may allow of a Fregean translation in which reference
to a concept is manifest, but it would be a mistake to assume
that we may transfer to the original the descriptions which hold
for this translation. Thus, acceptance of 'The concept *is a solution* applies to nothing', or 'Nothing falls under the concept *is
a solution*', as translations of 'A solution does not exist', yields
no enlightenment with respect to the individual terms in the
latter, in the sense that we could turn around and say that, e.g.,
'does not exist' is thereby shown to be a second-order predicate.
'Applies to nothing', or 'has no instances', might appear to be
such predicates, attaching as they do to the expression, 'the
concept *is a solution',* but neither, patently, is a synonym of
'does not exist'. They form part of sentences which as a whole
may be (stipulated to be) equivalent to the original, but there is
no correspondence of a kind which would allow substitutivity,
either with respect to the subject—'The concept *is a solution*
does not exist'—nor with respect to the predicate—'A solution
applies to nothing'. Neither is an acceptable rephrasal of 'A
solution does not exist'. (Compare Russell's muddled claim
that existence is a property of propositional functions.)

Although he sometimes expressed himself carelessly in these matters, Frege was well aware that 'exists' is not interchangeable with 'has an instance', or with any of the other terms which might figure in such an analysis. If, for example, we rewrite 'There is at least one square root of 4' as 'The concept *square root of 4* is realized', then, he says, the first six words of the latter form the proper name of an object (Frege [1892b], p. 49). And in general, the more we approximate to a form of words featuring the concept as what we are speaking of, the more likely we are to find that our assertion is now about an object, not a concept. None the less, with respect to the present example, Frege is still happy to say that the original constitutes an assertion 'about a concept, *square root of 4*; viz., that it is not empty'. Clearly, this way of putting it is subject to just the same difficulties, and we are left no wiser about the sense in which the original contains an assertion about a concept. 'The assertion that suits the concept does not suit the object'. True, but what *does* suit the concept? If we are right in saying that the statement of existence is not as it stands an assertion about a concept, and if the rephrasal aimed at making clear how there might be such an assertion turns out to be nothing of the kind, we are not as yet assured that there can even be any consistent way of speaking about concepts.

If, waiving our earlier argument, we try to understand 'A solution does not exist' in Fregean terms without rewriting it in any of these ways, then, if the reference of 'a solution' is held to be a concept, or the meaning of the phrase—perhaps the most natural gloss—we are obliged to say that this is being asserted not to exist, and this obviously will not do. To deny that this is implied seems to amount to denying the only point that could be involved in saying that 'does not exist' is affirmed of what 'a solution' stands for, that one is actually referring to a concept when one uses 'a solution', rather than merely that 'a solution' has a meaning—without the implication that it is also used to refer to this meaning. Nor, incidentally, can we argue that concept words must stand for something if sentences in which they occur are to be true; not, at least, if 'stand for' is thought of as a variant of 'refer to'; if it is just a matter of such words having a meaning—which, indeed, may be all that the existence of concepts comes to—then of course the claim can be granted. Similarly, we should also abandon the idea that the reference of a name in certain contexts, e.g. within clauses subordinate to a verb such as 'believe', may be to the sense of that name: 'not used with its customary reference' is a far cry from 'refers to its sense', and in the relevant context amounts to 'has a sense but does not refer to anything'. Supposing that we can at least speak of the sense of a name, there is no call to take this as a subject of predicates which might in another context be ascribed to the bearer of that name, yet this seems to be what is involved if it is not simply a matter of insisting that the name must *have* a sense—and perhaps be intended in that sense—in these contexts. Or, we might say, in the sense in which words may be said to stand for their sense in *oratio obliqua,* they stand for that sense in *oratio recta:* in either there is the constant factor of having meaning.

We are led to a similar observation by considering Frege's contention that 'the singular definite article always indicates an object, whereas the indefinite article accompanies a concept-word' (op. cit., p. 45), a contention which does not appear to do justice to the identity of the contribution made by the noun in such pairs as 'a dove' and 'the dove', along with 'some dove', 'our dove', and the rest: it is surely to differences in the accompanying words, and not to the general term, that we look in accounting for differences in the meaning and use of such phrases. This constancy on the part of the noun is to be borne in mind when it is suggested, as a possible qualification of Frege's dictum, that a phrase like 'the emperor' can be used either referentially or predicatively—as in 'The emperor was glad to be the emperor'—so standing now for an object, now for a concept. Indeed, if 'standing for a concept' comes to no more than 'having a meaning', there need be nothing amiss with saying that 'the emperor' may stand both for a concept and for an object at the same time—nothing amiss, that is, apart from the misleadingness of using 'stand for' in such different senses—though this is a possibility which Frege quite emphatically would not allow. Cf. 'Only when conjoined with the definite article or a demonstrative pronoun can a general concept-word be counted as the proper name of a thing, but in that case it ceases to count as a concept-word' (Frege [1884], § 51).

Returning to the question of existence, we may note that there is a parallel with the provision of an 'intentional object' for certain psychological verbs. We preserve the supposedly customary function of the noun in 'I want a drink' if we take it to name an object which exists in the understanding, even if not in reality. However, while there is the (grammatical) fact that one who wants wants something, it is clear that no real advance is made by interpreting this as a less definite characterization of something which enjoys 'immanent' or 'intentional' existence, if the puzzle was how one could want something which did not exist. This object does not constitute what is wanted, but, just as what exists when a solution exists is not a concept, so what is wanted when I want a drink is a real, not a mental, liquid.

Still, it may be insisted, I am surely saying of *something* that it does not exist when I say that a solution does not exist, and we should like to know what this is. Saying *of* something that it does not exist or merely saying that something does not exist? There seems to be a difference, and it seems to be the latter that is at stake if the generalization derives from my saying that a solution does not exist, when there is no question of my having in mind or referring to an actual solution. Certainly, there is a sense in which I do not say of some solution that it does not exist, and in this sense do not say this of anything; but I do say something does not exist and you can legitimately ask what. And of course I can answer: when I say that a solution does not exist I am saying that a satisfactory answer does not exist—not, e.g., that a fluid produced by the action of a solvent does not exist; or, when I say that a solution does not exist I mean a solution to the four colour problem. Such accounts would qualify as specifications of what I meant, but it may be felt that I am avoiding the issue; what is wanted is some sort of account of what, in general terms, is named by such an expression, rather than a mere citation of another phrase which shares the same problematic use. But if 'a solution' names anything it names a solution. There is nothing to be gained by introducing the meaning of the phrase as its referent when there is otherwise nothing to fill this role. However difficult it may make our understanding of the grammar—and I am not denying that there is a genuine question here—it simply must be recognized that nothing whatsoever is being referred to in such cases. Not on the grounds that the referents proposed are suspect abstract entities which a rigorously scientific philosophy should not tolerate, but simply on the grounds that provision of a referent of any sort is at odds with the sense of the assertion. The provision of concepts, say, as appropriate referents, may seem to preserve the pattern of asserting something of what is named, in some sense, by the subject, but only at the price of preventing us from saying that what is being denied existence is a solution.

But what of this possibility: in saying 'A black hole exists', I am saying that a strange kind of physical phenomenon exists; if a kea exists, then it is a kind or type of bird that exists. Might it not be, then, that 'exists' is a predicate of *kinds*? This use of 'kind', along with 'type' and related words, is to be treated with care. First, nothing peculiar to 'exists' is involved, but an expansion along these lines is more generally possible. A star may explode or be observed; so too may a kind of star, but it is not something physical that is concerned in the one case, and merely a concept in the other. In these instances, moreover, and in those with 'exists', we may well feel that a certain displacement in sense has taken place with respect to a version in which 'kind' figures differently: 'A star of a certain kind exists (was observed)'. Certainly, it seems to be in accordance with this latter formulation that the context surrounding 'a kind of *N*' is determined. We can say, 'The most useful kind of spanners are adjustable', with the plural 'spanners' attracting the verb, even if omitted—'The most useful kind are adjustable', not 'The most useful kind is adjustable—and a similar phenomenon is seen in other relations which 'a kind of *N*' may bear to a verbal phrase: I can sit on a kind of settee, but I cannot sit on a kind.

So much, for the present, for kinds. To round off this discussion let us consider briefly Frege's account of statements of number, an account which raises again some of the points already touched upon. That is, as with statements of existence, the main objection is simply that what he presents is not an analysis of, and does not cast light on, the language as it is, the language which initially gives rise to a problem of interpretation.

Frege's central contention is that a statement of number contains an assertion about a concept. The choice of concepts in this role is arrived at by eliminating their rivals, objects, and the arguments which are thought to bring about this elimination will be examined later. According to the resultant analysis, to say 'The King's carriage is drawn by four horses', is to assign the number four to the concept, 'horse that draws the King's carriage' (Frege [1884], § 46). It is difficult to see how this formulation could be explained without invoking the kind of use of a number word which Frege considers logically secondary, the use which he calls 'adjectival', as in 'Four things fall under the concept *horse that draws the King's carriage*', and there is the further familiar difficulty that he is now seemingly obliged to talk about an object in place of the desired concept. But this is not where our problem lies. For us what is pressing is the question how we might make use of the proposed translation in elucidating the role of the terms in the original, 'The King's carriage is drawn by four horses', and here the kinds of objection provoked by the analysis of existence crowd in on us again. In particular, the very fact that the 'adjectival' use of 'four' gives way to its use as a 'proper name' would seem to ensure that our understanding of the original is not going to profit from this analysis.

Suppose that, with respect to the original, we ask 'Of what are we here saying there are four?'—as in Fregean spirit we well might. The appeal to concepts appears to provide an answer to this question when, as Frege has argued, there is no possibility of citing objects or groups of objects as the subjects, in a non-linguistic sense, of numerical predications. So we have 'The number 9 is the number of the planets', 'The number 12 is the number of the apostles', and so forth, and we seek a more general description of what it is that number is being ascribed to in such cases. But now it soon becomes clear that the sense in which number is ascribed to planets and apostles is not the sense in which it can be ascribed to concepts. If you ask to what I am ascribing the number 9 when I say there are nine planets, I may give some more general term in answer: 'heavenly bodies', say, or some synonymous or more general description. The question can be repeated and met with successively more general specifications of what the number here is being ascribed to, but we shall never in this way reach the answer, 'a concept'; 'a concept' is not a terminus of generalizations along this route, but the terminus is reached when our descriptions give way to something as general as 'things'. Once again it will be said that an ascription of number is not to be understood in such a way that it has this consequence, but once again we can protest that in that event we are no further ahead with our question, to what is number ascribed? I do not wish to imply that this is a question we should be raising—unless, perhaps, as a way of requesting clarification of the grammar of numerical statements, or of asking what 'being ascribed to' comes to here—but it represents the kind of preoccupation with the subject–predicate model which might initially appear to be satisfied by the Fregean analysis.

I do not attach great weight to all of the preceding considerations, and any details that are important for me will be examined further when the more positive accounts of existence and number are given. These are what matter, since there is often the possibility that a seemingly misguided analysis may, if it depends on appeal to analogies, be interpretable with sufficient ingenuity to bring it unexpectedly close to the correct account. But it should at least be clear what I want: an analysis of certain elements of the language as we find it, rather than as it might appear when rewritten in accordance with some preferred model. This requirement could be presented merely as an expression of a particular interest, but it is an interest which I think it difficult for a philosopher to disown. Philosophers who have concentrated their attention on 'ordinary' language have often been accused of demeaning the subject. I should have thought that the dominant concern has been with the language in which the problems have been stated and discussed—which does not of necessity mean ordinary language—rather than with an analysis of ordinary language for its own sake, and in these terms the present approach is inevitable, the real problem being, e.g., that of knowing what degree of detail is required in order to formulate reliable generalizations. On the one hand, niceties of usage may not feature significantly in our understanding of a given concept; on the other hand, it is in general not possible to ignore the complexities of actual language, to proclaim a dispensating concern with the higher reaches of theory in the face of recalcitrant details, if at the same time it is hoped to make a contribution to our understanding of a traditional philosophical problem. Analyses which are at odds with actual usage, but which blithely retain the same words, have stood in the way of enlightenment and simply added to the confusion, and even if their dismal record to date is to some extent accidental, I should have thought that, furnished with the correct account of a troublesome concept, we should for the most part have little use for an analysis which applied at best to a philosophical surrogate for that concept.

It may be reasonably clear what I want, but it is less clear how I am to get it, and my second methodological point has been elaborated in order to offer guidance here. In attempting to be more scrupulous than is customary in identifying the precise terms to which a certain semantic contribution is to be assigned, the principle to be observed is much the same as that which should govern the identification of causes in science: since a variety of conditions will be realized when the factor which interests us is in evidence, isolation of a relevant condition is unlikely to be immediate; roughly speaking, the problem is one of engineering the conditions in such a way that a single condition comes to co-vary with the factor in question— a principle for which, curiously enough, scientifically minded philosophers show no more regard than do others. Thus, we recognize that, say, existence is somehow implied in sentences of a given type, but which among the several possible conditions can be identified as that or those responsible? Of course, in the present case the problem is further complicated by questions of meaning: it is not always clear just what the function is that we are trying to localize. The extra extent to which considerations of meaning or definition form part of the problem is what makes for the difference with an established science.

2

METHOD AND REFERENCE

Simple subject-predicate sentences, such as 'Her father died', may be silent on pertinent questions of time, place and manner without being linguistically unacceptable, the words enjoying a minimal completeness despite this lack of specificity. However, there are respects in which it is difficult, if not impossible, for a sentence to fail to be specific without being incomplete. What is important here may vary from language group to language group. In some American Indian languages, for instance, an indication of time—as we speak of an 'erstwhile bandleader'—may be as obligatory for nouns as an indication of number is in English. Thus, just as in English any completion of an incomplete noun phrase automatically makes it determinate as to singularity or plurality, ambiguity aside, so in these Indian languages a comparable requirement is made with respect to the question of past, present or future existence. Number, by contrast, may be considered of less moment, the same form of words serving to render either of 'There is an F' or 'There are Fs' indifferently (cf. Boas [1911], pp. 37-9).

Such examples of exotic languages can show that intelligible word forms need not mark distinctions which we regard as fundamental, and reflection on an Indo-European language should in any case reveal that, given a term which is stripped of a particle associated with such a distinction, it would be possible to assign a meaning appropriate to this lack of determination, and not necessary to consider the partial word as completable only by returning to it a feature of the kind which we have envisaged as removed. For instance, while tense is in English, as opposed to Eskimo, a non-optional feature of finite verb forms, a verb deprived of any tense inflection, as in 'Her father die', could be read as covering all the possibilities that might complete it, so as equivalent to 'Her father either is dying, has died, or will die'. It is to some extent an accident that linguistic practice has not conferred an interpretation upon anything less than the verb with its tense determination when it occurs in such a combination. On the other hand, this consideration is not telling if our aim is to find categories which a given language recognizes as fundamental. With this in view we should look to those features absence of which does in fact make for incompleteness, and in English, as in many other languages, what is soon thus disclosed is a concern with number and identification, tense and mood, and at the level of the sentence, with the union of subject and predicate.

The essential characteristics of noun phrases have been investigated in some detail, though not always with sufficient regard to the methodological principles which I consider important, and I shall spend some time in this and the following chapter trying to give an account of certain notable nominals which is sufficiently accurate to protect us from error when we come to consider problems of scope and intentionality into which they enter. Here and elsewhere, much of what I have to say is quite familiar, its presence being dictated by its relevance to an overall picture rather than by its novelty. Less familiar will be the gradually developing emphasis on a distinction between indicative and subjunctive uses of verbs. The verb has taken very much second place to the noun in philosophical writings, but the distinction which I invoke seems to me to be critical for an understanding of the behaviour of certain noun phrases, as well as of language more generally.

6. Token-reflexivity

We begin with a topic which brings in both noun and verb phrases. The question *how* a given word or morpheme functions often has a ready application when there is an association with a specific speech act. If, for instance, it is said that 'good' is used to commend, it is natural to ask how utterance of the word may achieve this purpose. With tense, the parallel query is less clear in its purport, even if we can see that there is a question as to what is the precise contribution made by a tense inflection. Still, it does not take long for the significance of the question of function to emerge.

If we are told, 'The wedding will take place in six weeks time', we are able to fix a time reference for the planned event by taking as the starting-point for our calculation the time at which these words are spoken. Similarly, if someone says, 'The doctor will be along soon' or 'We haven't seen you around recently', it is with respect to the time of utterance that we determine the point or period of time signified by 'soon' or 'recently'. Spatial relations are likewise often established by having regard to the location of the speaker, 'here' indicating an area, of varying extent, in the proximity of the one who utters the word, 'abroad' referring us to countries at some distance from that in which the speaker finds himself, or at least to countries different from his own.

These terms, or certain among them, have been described as 'token-reflexives', 'token' being used in recognition of the role of an actual spoken or written occurrence of the word in fixing its reference. However, the reflexivity is sometimes thought of in terms of reference by the words to themselves, and since this is a mistaken account of their role, I prefer the less misleading label, 'indexical expression', or simply 'indexical', the latter being more in place when, as with tense inflections, we have to do with something less than a full word. As more usual illustrations we may cite 'I', 'now', and 'this'. Thus, 'I' identifies the producer of the token 'I', 'now' relates—in the relevant use—to a point or period of time simultaneous with or embracing the utterance of 'now', and 'this', reinforced perhaps by pointing, may be used to indicate something in the vicinity of the one who says 'this', some containing space or place, as 'this island', or some proximate period of time, as 'this year'. In general, we can say that something is determined as the reference of an indexical in virtue of standing in a certain spatial and/or temporal relation to the utterance of the indexical. In some cases it may be more natural to think of the utterer rather than the utterance as providing the point of reference, but since identification of the speaker will be via the utterance, that is no real difference.

From even these few words the way in which indexical expressions engage in the actual context of their utterance and secure reference seems clear and fundamental. And economical. A general knowledge of the language, so an appreciation of the specific relation which defines the indexical, may require supplementation by no more that the utterance of the word for the reference to be grasped. Proper names are sometimes thought to be basic among terms with a referential role, but what they gain in independence of context they lose on this more general count: in using a name we do not bring to bear on particular circumstances our general knowledge of the language, but such a use relies upon an already known association, generally of a logically arbitrary kind, between the name and its bearer. Certainly, indexicals are important, not because they are terms which happen to display referential function in a particularly convenient and straightforward fashion; with the exception of proper names, they are the *only* terms which have such a function.

Leaving aside the written word, which calls for obvious modification—especially as regards the degree of abstraction with which we are to conceive of the token of a word type—it is clear that it is the actual utterance of an indexical, sometimes in conjunction with gestures, and frequently in conjunction with a descriptive phrase, that can be said to secure reference, but it is not just in *any* way that this is to be achieved if it is to be achieved in virtue of the indexical's standard linguistic role. Take the example of the first-person pronoun, 'I'. Uttering 'I' serves, of course, to draw attention to a particular person, to wit, the speaker, but then any audible sound made by him might be expected to do that. We are not interested in the case in which production of 'I' has this effect in the way that any other sound might; similarly, we are not interested in the case where utterance of 'this' is merely causally instrumental, *qua* arresting but uninterpreted sound, in directing a person's attention to the right object. If it is to be the workings of language that concern us, we want it to be at least partly in virtue of his understanding of the meaning of these words that a person is enabled to grasp their reference on a given occasion.

The causal virtues of 'this', say, have their part in our training in the language, utterance of the word taken in the company of an appropriate gesture serving to attract the child's attention and focus it on the intended object, though it is no doubt early on that an intention to refer comes to be discerned, failures of the child to attend to the right object being greeted by further attempts at directing his attention to it and cessation of such further attempts following on success in this respect. In order for 'this' to secure reference *qua* linguistic sign, the audience's knowledge of the relation between word and object proper to 'this' must be brought into play. That is, the knowledge of which the understanding listener makes use is knowledge that production of the sound is typically used to draw attention to an object, person, or whatever, that stands in a certain relation to the utterance or utterer, a relation which is definitive of the sense of the indexical.

As far as such demonstrative relations go, the Indo-European languages tend to be particularly simple: the Eskimos would have to render 'this man' differently depending on whether the man in question was near the speaker, near the person spoken to, near a third person, behind, in front of, to the right of, to the left of, above, or below the speaker (see Boas, op. cit., pp. 40-1). The principles, however, are in general terms the same as with our 'this' and 'that'. It is clear that, even when a language deploys such a complex system of indexicals, knowledge of the meaning of such an expression is not necessarily sufficient to enable a listener to determine the intended reference, nor is the speaker automatically assured of securing reference to anything by his use of the indexical; not at least with most such expressions, though the contrasting behaviour of 'I' in this latter respect is of interest, a contrast which has led some to associate it with an infallible form of acquaintance, and others even to deny it an identifying or referential function altogether. Should we say that merely to understand what one is saying ensures that in using 'I' one is referring to oneself? Or should we refrain from speaking of reference here at all? It can be granted that normal circumstances offer no scope for saying I may have misidentified the person in question when I say 'I am tired' or 'I hope it snows', but it is the contrast with identifying another—or indeed, with failing to identify oneself, in the sense of refraining from doing so—that gives point to saying that 'I' identifies the speaker, or that he thereby identifies or refers to himself. As far as any reservations might go about the use of these notions, there is no more to be said than this: I do not have to identify the person who is tired, in the sense of find out who he is, when I say 'I am tired'. This has no repercussions for the propriety of saying that I identify myself, i.e. tell you (one person) who is tired, when I utter these words.

But is it not extraordinary that the mere utterance of a word should guarantee its possession of a reference? Are there not precedents, and general arguments, which should lead us to suspect the inapplicability, or at least the vacuousness, of talk of reference, when such reference is thought to be infallible? There is nothing in the least extraordinary in the consideration that from a description of a given situation we should be able to extract a condition which we have explicitly written into that description. We, anticipated by Descartes, are struck by the fact that someone's utterance of 'I' cannot but identify the speaker, but we had to suppose that there *was* a speaker —a person to whom the utterance could be referred and a person making a genuine use of language. Without this assumption the utterance would not have had the same significance: 'I' somehow produced from the mouth of a dead man or by an electronic device is not the basis for any such inference.

Of course, the assumption that there is a speaker making a genuine use of language is common to all the uses of language under discussion, so against that background the use of 'I' may be special. But not unique. Since utterances are in time, there is a comparable standing condition which guarantees that utterance of 'now' will fix a time reference, however ill defined. Again, there is nothing magical about this inevitable success, nor any cause to deny the word its obvious role because of its faultless performance. The same point holds for tense inflections of verbs, the indexicals with which we began and to which we now return. In 'The lady vanished', the termination '-ed' fixes the time of occurrence as prior to the time of its utterance; in 'By then the lady had vanished' we have a verbal form, 'had *V*d', which locates the time, not only as prior to the time of speaking, but as earlier than another past time, that which in this instance the indexical 'then' determines. This temporal element is not, of course, the only contribution which these terminations and auxiliaries introduce, but the mood and aspect of the verb—as perfective or progressive— are also conveyed. The ease with which the temporal indication is effected, without reliance upon pointing or other extralinguistic aids to identification, coupled with the inseparability of the inflection from the verb, perhaps account for the frequent absence of tense inflections from discussions of indexicals, an oversight which leads, as we shall see, to neglect of an interesting symmetry between noun and verb phrase.

The meaning of an indexical does not necessarily fully determine its reference on a given occasion, but more precise knowledge of the speaker's intention is often called for: I may be quite clear as to the meaning of 'this card', but still unclear as to which card is meant. Furthermore, it is not necessary that the information required should be given by a more refined description; the intended reference can sometimes shine through efforts at further description which fall wide of the mark. The notion of *sense,* as understood by Frege, can be usefully brought into the discussion at this point, since we appear to have just assigned its role to somewhat different factors. Frege's 'sense' is not the same as our 'meaning', not because 'meaning' may sometimes mean 'reference', which it may never, but because Frege reckons a difference in sense differently from the way we reckon one of meaning. He would say, for instance, that the sense of 'This patient needs attention urgently' differed from occasion to occasion of its utterance, as it came to be applied to different people at different times, and he would say that 'That patient needed attention urgently' could have the same sense as the former, in one of its senses (Frege [1918]). Here it looks very much as if individual intentions are being imported into the sense; we may certainly suppose that 'this patient' has but one meaning, irrespective of the number of distinct individuals to whom it might come in time to apply, and the difference which thus arises from one occasion to another would appear to be a matter either of a difference in who is being referred to or a difference in the speaker's intentions. However, neither of these, nor meaning, appears to coincide with Frege's notion of sense as that whereby the reference is determined.

How might sense apply to an indexical such as 'this'? It may seem odd to ask in virtue of what it was that 'this' secured reference on a given occasion, since this suggests that an object must satisfy a certain description, be of a certain kind, before we can refer to it by the demonstrative, whereas anything whatever can be thus designated. Sense as that whereby reference is determined appears to relate to something on the side of the object, some set of features in virtue of which the designation fits, yet in the case of 'this' it would seem that it is the speaker's intention, communicated often through gestures, that determines what is meant.

It is true that anything can come to be picked out by 'this', but only—considering just physical objects—in so far as it comes to stand in a certain relation to the speaker; to be, roughly, in proximity to him. Here we have something which counts as a condition for the applicability of the demonstrative, a condition which is not all the time satisfied by every object. On the other hand, there is a gap between being a potential candidate for ostension and being the object in fact intended. As already indicated, many things could be singled out by 'this', with none inevitably determined as referent by dint of satisfying the condition of proximity to the speaker. Frege would presumably wish to say that the sense of 'this' was not fully determinate on such an occasion, but if supplementation of word meaning, as ordinarily understood, is called for, it seems plain that nothing more than an appeal to the speaker's intention is necessary. Russell thought that the meaning of 'this' was constantly changing. It is not, but different things are meant by speakers using the word on different occasions.

The meaning of an indexical is not conveyed by a listing of its referents, but understanding involves a grasp of some principle whereby an object is reckoned as being such a referent. It might be suggested that 'sense' is to be understood as whatever proves to be thus determinative of reference, so as word meaning, intentions, or a combination of the two. I doubt that what Frege says of sense leaves it sufficiently open in this way, but it is the adequacy of the combination that I wish to stress.

Consider the pronoun 'you'. A person comes to an understanding of 'you' by learning a particular association of the word with, for the most part, persons, but it is the form of association that matters rather than the character of the term's 'extension'. We could not convey the meaning of 'you' simply by detailing the various referents which it has had over the years, and even specifying its possible referents—namely, all those persons who ever have existed or will exist—takes us no further ahead. The pronoun is obviously applied in virtue of the satisfaction of some condition on the part of the person of whom it is used, and the condition is simply that of being the one to whom the speaker is addressing what he says. And what is involved in an appreciation of this as being the relevant condition? An ability to articulate the relation, to state what it is, reveals that understanding, but all that is actually necessary is that the person's behaviour, verbal and otherwise, should show him to make the right identifications on hearing 'you', whether addressed to himself or another, and that he in turn should use it in accordance with the condition stated.

More generally, we have that an indexical, i, is defined in terms of a relation which holds between the utterance or utterer of i and some object, person, point of time, or whatever; so, ideally, a speaker learns to use i of x only when x stands in the given relation to him or to his utterance. As stated, proof that he appreciates the defining relation for i may reside simply in his use of i in conformity with what is prescribed by that relation, there being no need that he should be able to formulate the relation in question. What determines the meaning of i is the regular association with, in general, just those objects or whatever which stand in the relevant relation to the speaker. The reason why this account has to be supplemented is clear: on a given occasion there can be more than one thing which satisfies the relation in question. But it seems equally clear that an intention to apply the term to one such thing rather than another is all that need be added.

But could it not be argued that, far from dispensing with sense, an appeal to intention has to make implicit use of the notion? After all, in saying 'this card', say, I shall intend an object which I take to be so-and-so, and this looks very much like introducing a condition whereby the sense might be specified. However, sense, as in some way continuous with or a refinement of word meaning, does not force itself upon us here. Thus, if we think of reference as determined by sense— or meaning—we think of the referent as what *answers* to certain conditions, but even when I can readily furnish a further condition which makes clear the intended reference of 'this card'— as, e.g., 'beside the blotter'—the intended reference is not such *because* it answers to that condition. Frege's picture is best suited to a consideration of expressions of a language in abstraction from their users—as we should expect, given his general concerns. So, we ask what, if anything, is determined as the reference of a phrase in the light of the meanings of its component expressions. Or, if we introduce a person, we think of him as one who might 'trace the route' from sense to reference, rather than the user of the words. With the user comes a different perspective. His problem is not to proceed from a given sense to an appropriate referent; he does not start with a description like 'this card, beside the blotter', and then look to see what satisfies it, but, wishing to refer us to an object, he seeks descriptions which are appropriate to that end. It is primarily the person, and not the sense of the words, that determines the reference. This is particularly clear when, as with a bare 'this', or even 'this card', the words used may not be adequate to that task, and it is also clear when the words misdescribe the intended referent. A person can refer to an orange even though what he says is 'that grapefruit'.

7. *The definite article*

Continuing with indexical expressions, I turn now to consider in some detail the definite article. That 'the' should receive particular attention is to be expected. It can occur in combination with almost every common noun in the language, whether concrete or abstract, and it is the most general of the indexical terms with which it comes into comparison. And, of course, it has been the focus of much philosophical controversy.

Definite descriptions, phrases combining 'the' with a noun phrase, as 'the post office', are not generally explained by making clear their indexical character, but the possibility has only to be mentioned for its relevance to become apparent, given the evident affinity, in sense and etymology, which 'the' bears to 'this', 'then', 'that', and 'thou', and the frequent contrast with proper names on the score of context dependence. The role enjoyed by 'the' may be located in rather different elements in different languages: the noun may itself assume it, exploiting context and/or making use of intonation or word order, and it is even possible to find the article's contribution assigned to verbs and adjectives. For a survey of the possibilities see Krámský [1972]. In all cases, however, it seems possible to discern an indexical element.

One account which decidedly does not favour this approach is that provided by Russell in his 'theory of descriptions': here no explanation is given of the definite article taken in isolation, nor even of the phrase formed by combining it with a general term, as in 'the hurricane', but the analysis deals with such definite descriptions by prescribing translations for a range of larger contexts within which they occur (Russell [1905]). The sentences to which, following Russell, commentators on the theory have given most attention are those in which the description occurs in subject place, as in 'The King of France is bald'. Here the theory prescribes the reading: 'There is one and only one king of France and he is bald'. That, at least, is a verbal rendering of the breakdown suggested; the further representation in symbolic terms gives rise to complications which do not bear upon our present purpose.

Russell's analysis is to be assessed in terms of the demands which it is intended to meet, and with one aim in mind—the representation within the logic of predicates, with identity, of such sentences as 'The square of -1 is positive'—it gives a workable translation. Technical reservations concerning its handling of improper descriptive phrases are possible, but it is arguable that we have an accurate enough statement of necessary and sufficient truth conditions for such sentences. The success of the theory in resolving philosophical questions of meaning and existence in the way Russell thought is another matter altogether, but again not one with which we shall be directly concerned. The problems which do engage us are those which arise once we try to apply the theory quite generally, or claim for it the virtues of a literal translation in those contexts in which it can render a useful technical service. It is clear that, at best, the theory will cope with only a restricted number of uses of 'the': it is inadequate to mass nouns, as in 'The butter is rancid', to abstract nouns, as in 'the existence of God', and it has nothing to say about the article followed by a plural noun, as in 'the stars', a combination which is obviously standard and which any comprehensive account is obliged to accommodate. Further, even when we are dealing with the comparatively straightforward case in which the definite description embodies a singular count noun in the subject position of a declarative sentence—rather than a troublesome imperative or interrogative—there are well-known difficulties, difficulties relating to the two major conditions which figure explicitly in the analysis; those, namely, of existence and uniqueness.

One objection is obvious. When we say something of the form, 'The F is G', there is an implication that a single F is at stake, and this Russell represents in terms of the existence of exactly one thing which is F. In many cases, however, it is not so much that there is at least and at most one F as that we have in mind only one such thing. In saying 'The light went out', I shall doubtless be referring to just one light, but I should not wish what I say to be taken as a claim that just one light exists and it went out. Of course, not only is there just one light that I mean, but there will presumably be some other more specific description—'light in the next room'—which will, if still with some reliance on context, relate only to the intended item and warrant the use of 'the', but it would seem that Russell regards the description which actually features in the sentence, and not some such unexpressed refinement, as furnishing the uniqueness condition. The majority of definite descriptions will not be so obliging as to embody a characterization which, as a matter of logic or empirical fact, will apply to at most one thing, and if Russell's account does apply it will be only by good fortune.

But if Russell does not sufficiently acknowledge the extent to which unexpressed uniqueness conditions have to be called upon, that surely amounts to no more than an oversight, not a condemnation of the whole theory? Surely the sense of 'The light went out', uttered on a particular occasion, is indeterminate until further individuating descriptions are introduced, so as long as the theory can handle the expanded version, it is adequate to what is demanded of it. The question here is: what *is* demanded of the theory? If we are concerned with getting the closest possible translation of a sentence of the relevant form which can be directly transcribed into first-order logic, then the theory of descriptions obviously rates highly. If, on the other hand, we seek a translation which could be accounted the same in meaning as the original, then it is clear that, once unexpressed conditions have to be introduced into the former, there can be no question of meeting this requirement. Part of the point about 'the' just *is* that it may give only an oblique indication of identifying conditions. This is not merely incidental to its use, it is definitive of it.

Are we to suppose that, so long as the characterization actually given applies uniquely, the translation which the theory dictates is to be reckoned satisfactory? Not, we may recall, on one prominent view. Criticism of the theory has generally been directed at the existence rather than the uniqueness condition; most notably, we have P. F. Strawson's objection that such a statment as 'The King of France is bald' presupposes rather than entails the existence of a unique king of France. This objection can be understood in at least two different ways, depending on the interpretation given to the term 'presuppose'. As originally intended by Strawson, and also by P. T. Geach, the existence of the King of France is presupposed in the sense that it is a precondition for the truth-or-falsity of the statement: if there is no king of France then the proposition ostensibly asserting that he is bald is neither true nor false (see Strawson [1950a] and Geach [1950a]). On the other hand, there is another interpretation, also invoked by Strawson, according to which the existence of a unique king of France is presupposed by the speaker in the sense that it is something that he takes for granted. In saying 'The King of France is bald', one does not as much as say that there is a king of France, but one draws upon the assumed knowledge of this on the part of one's audience. In this latter sense we may speak of existence as presupposed without committing ourselves on the question of truth value when the presupposition is not fulfilled. For this tack see Strawson [1964].

Consider first the relation of presupposition as associated with a truth value gap. This is thought to differ from entailment—or from implication, understood here as equivalent—on the grounds that if P entails or implies Q, then if Q is false, so too is P, while if P presupposes Q, the falsity of Q does not make for that of P, which will be without truth value. Thus, 'The King of France is bald' presupposes rather than entails

'There is a unique king of France', since if there is not a unique king of France we cannot say that 'The King of France is bald' is false. However, it is clear that this distinction, and therewith the need for introducing presupposition in addition to entailment or implication, depends on associating falsity with the so-called 'internal' rather than the 'external' negation of the proposition, 'The King of France is bald'. If there is not a unique king of France, we cannot say 'The King of France is not bald', understanding this as a denial of the predicate with respect to an individual named by the subject, and if describing 'The King of France is bald' as *false* has this implication, then it is to be ruled out. What this calls for is a more general interpretation of the negations in the contraposed conditional which, it is said, does not hold: if P implies Q, then if it is not the case that Q, it is not the case that P, the negations, or at least that in the latter, now being external.

In terms of 'not true' rather than 'false', we can surely say that if there is not a unique king of France, then 'The King of France is bald' is not true. Indeed, one who holds that the proposition is neither true nor false must be prepared to say that it is not true, and so distinguish between 'not true' and 'false'. He must, that is, allow that the proposition in question is not true, since what he has said, viz. that it is neither true nor false, implies this, and he must not equate 'not true' with 'false', since he has denied falsity. But could it not be held that calling the proposition 'not true' carried the same unwanted implication as did calling it 'false', the implication that the sentence with the negation construed as internal is assertible? To preserve consistency it could then be proposed that 'neither true nor false' be read as meaning that neither 'true' nor 'false' applied, and *'true' does not apply* be distinguished from *'not true' applies*.

This supposition is not absurd. If someone says 'Ahem' or 'Aha!', we might be as reluctant to say 'That is not true' as 'That is false', but we should certainly agree that 'true' did not apply. However, none of this should lead us to ignore the fact that there is a perfectly good sense in which, if there is no king of France, then the proposition, 'The King of France is bald', simply is not true. We hesitate to treat 'Ahem' or 'Aha!' in the same way, since to say that these are not true suggests that we are rejecting a possibility which at least makes sense. It does not, but then 'The King of France is bald' is not comparable in this respect: it is at least of a form suited to expressing a truth in appropriate circumstances. In passing, it may be noted that sentences which are said to involve a 'category mistake' may be intermediate in this respect, sentences such as 'Indecision is octagonal'. Here again, one who regards such a sentence as neither true nor false cannot automatically appeal to this exclusion of alternatives to deflect any of the consequences which derive from such a sentence's being true or not true. Indeed, since we may well find ourselves offering such elucidatory remarks as 'Indecision is not the sort of thing that can be octagonal', we should think twice before excluding 'false'.

Returning to 'The King of France is bald', it is not clear that 'false' is invariably inappropriate. As Strawson subsequently observed, if the assertion of these words is aimed at providing a value for 'x is bald' which would make this true, rather than adding to our information about a known person, we might well reject the proposition as simply false (Strawson [1964]). At all events, it would appear that there is no necessity to introduce the notion of presupposition, since the notions of entailment and external negation, or 'true' and 'not true' rather than 'true' and 'false', can satisfactorily characterize the use of sentences of the form in question. To repeat, but with a change of example, contraposition need not be taken to show that the implication of 'No one saw the intruder' by 'It is surprising that no one saw the intruder' does not hold, for all that is yielded by that move is the acceptable conclusion that, if the former is not true, neither is the latter; the illegitimate step is taken if we further infer that the existence of someone who saw the intruder implies the truth of 'It is not surprising that no one saw the intruder'. As this example suggests, replacement of presupposition by implication makes for a more straightforward treatment of the many supposed instances of the former investigated by linguists. There is everything to be said for, and nothing against the naïve view that such an assertion as 'They regretted that they had lied' *implies* the truth of its embedded clause, 'they had lied'. Similarly if the sentence is non-declarative. We can say that one who asks, 'Why are we waiting?', presupposes that certain people have been waiting, but 'implies' would be equally at home in place of 'presupposes'.

What does remain to be described is the standard use of a descriptive phrase as it occurs in an affirmative sentence or a sentence in which any negation is internal, and here we might feel that there is room for a distinction between explicitly asserted and merely presupposed existence. That is, the second suggested sense of 'presuppose' might be considered more promising—though in this sense it is not a matter of 'presupposes' *rather than* 'implies', the existence of a unique king of France being both presupposed and implied by 'The King of France is bald'. Similarly, we could say that 'He saw a pretty girl' both presupposed and implied 'Some girl was pretty'.

It would be unusual to say, right out of the blue, 'The tennis racquet has been stolen'; without, that is, any previous indication being given of *which* tennis racquet is in question. But if we think of the utterance as inappropriate because of an unfulfilled presuppostion of knowledge of existence, why is there not a similar infelicity attending 'My tennis racquet has been stolen'? Here too it may be the first the audience has heard of the racquet in question, yet such ignorance presents no obstacle to a standard use of this form of words. Rather than look to a different relation to the matter of presupposed existence, would it not be more natural to suppose that what is wrong with 'The tennis racquet has been stolen', in contrast to 'My tennis racquet has been stolen', is simply the absence of a description which is sufficiently specific to enable us to identify the object in question? Contrast 'The cousin of our next-door neighbour has been to Brazil'. This is something that can be said without first indicating that one's neighbour has a cousin, and the reason it is in order is, it may be suggested, simply that the subject term is specific enough to make identification possible, in contrast to the indeterminate 'the tennis racquet'.

There are examples such as these, but, it may be argued, we can set against them sentences which, since they are in no way lacking in specificity, appear to leave existence as the only item of presupposed knowledge. Consider 'The mouse which Sally used to keep was poisoned' and 'The meteorite which landed in the meadow last week contained traces of rare elements'.

Despite the specificity of the subject phrases, it is surely inappropriate to use such sentences in speaking to someone who is ignorant of the existential facts. Lack of specificity may constitute an additional reason for not employing a definite description in communicating a totally new item of information, but adequacy in this respect is still not enough; there will continue to be, as these examples show, the kind of reliance on known existence which makes talk of reidentification possible. What is true is that if the existence condition is one that can be expected or seen to hold, then if nothing is wanting on the side of specificity, use of 'the' may not require a preliminary indication of existence. This is what distinguishes the two sentences just given from the example of the neighbour's cousin, or from such sentences as 'The foreign department of the bank will deal with that' and 'The activities of the students have won them few friends'. Furthermore, phrases with possessive pronouns such as 'my' may also ring oddly if the existence in question is out of the ordinary. In this respect, 'My brother's orang-outang is off his food', compares with 'The orang-outang belonging to my brother is off his food'.

It might be argued that uniqueness is assured only if a qualification such as 'only' is introduced, but even with 'The only meteorite which landed in the meadow last week contained traces of rare elements', the fact of existence is one which the speaker would commonly take as known, or in other cases as obvious or at least in no way out of the ordinary. What must be granted is the extensiveness of these latter categories. Definite descriptions can, if the context or subject allows, be used to identify as well as to reidentify: in saying 'The edge of this plate is jagged' or 'The car ahead has a faulty brake light', we can be as much pointing something out as redirecting attention to it, and without any preliminary indication of existence we might say 'The radio in my car has ceased to work', the existence of the radio being not unexpected, even if not already known.

In all these cases we could say that existence is presupposed rather than directly asserted, in that we do not as much as say 'There is a . . . and it . . .', but there is no necessary presupposition of knowledge of existence and no call to deny that existence is implied as well as presupposed. However, I should wish to characterize what is distinctive of descriptive phrases, and their near relations, not so much by simply denying their equivalence with explicit statements of existence as by pointing to the asymmetry which the contained noun shows *vis-à-vis* a noun in predicative position. In 'The author was a former pilot' and 'Her teacher is an idealist', the phrases 'a former pilot' and 'an idealist' are explicitly affirmed of whatever the subjects identify, but the nouns in these subjects are not in turn presented in a form which invites our acceptance or rejection. Not merely do they not occur in explicit existential fashion, as in the context 'There is a . . .'; they also fail to occur as part of a phrase joined by a copula to a subject. In neither way do they form the focus of an explicit affirmation, of a construction that is negatable or otherwise subject to adverbial qualification. Because the general term is not presented as negatable, we are not given an opportunity to contradict the implied fact of existence by simply introducing a 'not' into the sentence. That is why 'false' is in turn inappropriate, ascribed on the grounds that nothing describable by the subject term exists, and why we naturally reserve the construction for cases where the matter of existence is not problematic. Likewise with such non-declarative examples as 'Why are we waiting?' and 'Keep walking'. It is not that the speaker does not *imply* that people have been waiting or walking, but the matter is not presented in such a way that a simple 'true' or 'false' will convey our agreement or disagreement.

This account is of some generality. It is obviously applicable to phrases containing demonstratives, and even to phrases with numerical qualifications. The sentence, 'Three attacks were unsuccessful', does not put the matter of existence in the straightforward form given by 'There were three attacks', and is thus better suited to the case in which existence presents no problem—though of course the implication of existence can be generated without having to have recourse to the explicit form. As a contrast, consider 'A castle was built'. There are combinations of noun phrase and verb phrase which, like this, can be directly denied by one who denies the matter of existence, combinations which it will accordingly be possible to think of as species of existential propositions.

Let us return briefly to the theory of descriptions. There is a sense in which a Russellian translation may, if it incorporates sufficient individuating information, amount to a statement of truth conditions for, say, 'The band has stopped playing'. However, aside from the possible difficulties occasioned by the repetition of 'the' or like expressions in the clause giving this information, there is the undeniable difference between securing identification by the explicit introduction of individuating information and invoking a term which may exploit the context into which it is introduced to refer an audience to the band in question, short-circuiting any such presentation of detail. None of the preceding remarks is to be taken as minimizing the importance of this aspect of the use of the article.

This possible recurrence of 'the' and similar terms is also of importance. If 'the band' becomes 'a unique band in the pavilion', we still have 'the pavilion' to cope with, and at some point we shall find ourselves using expressions which, like 'over there', fix reference with respect to the speaker's location, or terms which, while more general in this respect, depend ultimately on identifications of this kind, as names of parks, buildings, bridges, and so forth. So long as we are speaking of a spatio-temporally individuated object, so of something which might, logically, be duplicated in all but its space–time co-ordinates, there is no relying on descriptive detail to ensure identification and no eliminating contextual dependence. We can, of course, simply affirm that the object in question is unique, distinct from anything else in some respect, but this uniqueness will have to be, at least theoretically, in its space–time location.

In passing, I might mention that a relation to a speaker appears to be involved as much in our spatial as in our temporal descriptions. It is sometimes said that one could give as full a description as one wished of things in their spatial relations without having to envisage oneself as standing in any spatial relation to those things, whereas with time this is not so, an ordering of events in terms of *before* and *after* being incomplete so long as it gives no indication of what is happening at the time of speaking. However, excluding any spatial perspective means excluding sentences of the form 'x is in front of y', 'y is to the left of z', and so on, and if we are entitled to do that we are entitled to remain silent on the question of the speaker's temporal relation to the sequence of events of which he is speaking. What is true is that some artifice will have to be used to avoid giving away this information—a timeless verb form, perhaps, representing a disjunction of the past, present, and future tenses.

We have seen that a Russellian translation does not retain for the components of a descriptive phrase the roles which they normally enjoy, but we have not yet emerged with an explicit characterization of the definite article. Indeed, if we stay with such examples as 'The King of France is bald', we may find it hard to think of an alternative to an analysis along Russellian lines. Certainly, this proposition would appear to be true when and only when there is just one king of France and he is bald. However, we are at some distance from a general explanation of the article if we merely say that it is used because there is taken to be just one king of France, since it is equally possible to use 'the' with a plural, as in 'The kings of France have all been wise'. The analysis is of no help here, and even with a singular count noun we are left in the dark as to the role of 'the F', which is not mapped onto any corresponding unit in the proposed analysis, yet appears to be fairly constant throughout the various contexts of its occurrence.

It has already been indicated that the meaning of a definite description might be explained in something like the terms appropriate to phrases containing the demonstratives with which the definite article has an affinity. In these terms we might say that 'the F' enjoys a very general identificatory or specificatory role, in accordance with conditions (usually) furnished by the context, a role which both compares and contrasts with that of the demonstratives 'this' and 'that'. With both 'That F is G' and 'The F is G' we have phrases which purport to identify an F, but while with 'That F is G' the emphasis is often on the singling out of one F from among other Fs, with 'The F is G' the concern is more to draw attention to a certain F rather than to something of another kind; there is not an implied contrast with other Fs, not the same emphasis on the identity of the F selected. Compare 'We can solve that problem' with 'We can solve the problem'. With 'that', and more especially 'those', it is accordingly likely that a fuller knowledge of identity is involved: 'those kings of France' will seek to pick out certain kings of France; 'the kings of France' is, unless some further condition is understood, less selective. Let me repeat the point with an example of another kind. Because of the unspecific character of the individuation provided by 'the'—as against 'this', say, with its connection with proximity—any contrasts made by 'the F' tend to focus on F. A story which led off with 'Once there was a woodcutter who lived on the edge of a large forest', would be unlikely to have an immediate continuation beginning 'The woodcutter . . .', but 'This woodcutter . . .' or simply 'He . . .' are more to be expected. If, on the other hand, the first sentence ran 'Once there was a woodcutter who lived with his wife on the edge of a large forest', we could more comfortably continue with 'The woodcutter . . .', presence of 'his wife' making for the possibility of the requisite contrast.

Among the terms with which it compares, 'the' is the most general, requiring no more than *determinacy*, actual or envisaged, and not the more specialized conditions characteristic of the demonstratives. This determinacy calls for a closer look. The definite article is often explained in terms of an association with a restrictive condition, but not just any condition will do. An adjectival phrase may restrict the application of the noun which it modifies, but it need not on that account attract 'the'. We can say 'He likes old books', but not, in the same sense, 'He likes the old books', and if 'the' can be used it will relate to a further condition, not the one that is explicit. There is a certain openness or indeterminacy about 'He likes old books' or 'Students are eligible for benefits', a contrasting determinacy, a pinning down to the particular, in 'He looked through the old books' or 'She introduced herself to the students'. Our assertion about students is not, in the first case, confined to a particular group of such, nor, on the other hand, does it relate to a fixed totality, but we are thinking in terms of arbitrary instances; or, if we wish to speak of a totality, it is a totality which is not envisaged as fixed, but is continually gaining and losing elements.

To see what is involved in the relevant determinacy we might look at the contrast provided by the article in French, which would be used in each of 'He likes old books' and 'Students are eligible for benefits'. Old books and students comprise things and persons united in their contrast with the complementary classes; they form single types or are determinate in point of kind, and it is this unity that the article reflects. Without further qualification, a sentence like *Il aime les bouquins* could accordingly be taken in two ways: *les* could be introduced because a determinate set is intended in the way which would lead to English 'the'—as when the sentence continues with *qu'il a hérités de son oncle*; on the other hand, old books quite generally being thought of as forming a restricted or determinate class—not, as it were, open sortally—the article could find its way in on this basis. In both cases the article imports universality: where kinds are at stake this may be expressed in terms of arbitrariness, a matter of liking old books generally, with, in French, the partitive article providing the appropriate contrast. In the other case it will be a matter of all the individuals in question, all the old books which he has inherited from his uncle. Again, with a mass term, like 'butter', English uses the definite article to identify a particular amount or portion, as in 'The butter is going off', whereas French, while using the article in such cases, also retains it in generalizations, such as that translatable as 'Butter is high in cholesterol', determinacy or singularity of type here dictating its occurrence.

Use of so-called 'generic' 'the', as in 'the internal combustion engine', is closer to the French model, but in general the definite article in English implies definiteness at the level of individuals rather than of types: 'the *F*' occurs in association with an individuating condition, when it is a matter of an *F* with a determinate *identity,* whether actual or merely envisaged, a condition which the provision of further descriptive detail does not make redundant. The contrast is with terms which do not signify determinacy in this respect—notably 'a'—rather than with terms which, like demonstratives, pick something out on the basis of some more specific condition.

This characterization applies readily enough to uses of plural nouns and mass terms, as well as to singular count nouns. So, when I say, 'Then add the butter', I may be speaking with a determinate quantity in mind, or thinking of a situation in which there will be such a quantity, and even when it is only a matter of a hypothetical situation, there is a corresponding distinction between the implications of this phrase and those of the simple 'Then add butter'. Similarly with 'Add cherries' and 'Add the cherries'. The latter, but not the former, supposes cherries to have been set aside, say, cherries with an identity which could be characterized by their location at that time.

What of abstract terms, as with 'the size of his shoes' or 'the existence of God'? Once more, we must look further than the simple formula in terms of uniqueness. It is not helpful to say that we use 'the' in 'the size of his shoes' because the person's shoes are supposed to be of a single size, but uniqueness is to the point only through its connexion with determinacy, the more general notion applicable to the equally possible 'the sizes of his shoes'. Note again that in general it need not be the accompanying phrase that furnishes the condition on which use of the article is based, such a condition being able to occur both when we do and when we do not have the necessary determinacy. However, with abstract 'mass' terms, almost any qualification on the noun F will bring 'the' with it. We do not speak in general terms of 'the existence' or 'the immortality', as with German *das Sein* or French *l'immortalité*, but we have 'the existence of God' and 'the immortality of the soul', the associated phrases providing the minimal determinacy demanded.

My characterization of definite descriptions has been sufficiently broad as to imply no necessary connection with actual existence—nor with reference, or knowledge of identity—so the question arises as to what precisely underlies any existential implications that can be drawn in particular cases. In saying 'I couldn't marry you even if you were the only girl in the world', I do not imply anything as to the existence or identity of a solitary girl, nor is the existence of a future Prime Minister implied nor reference to him involved in 'His aim is to be the next Prime Minister'. By contrast, with 'I'm glad you're not the girl I saw in the bus', existence and reference are more likely to be as with 'The girl I saw in the bus had red hair'. What makes for the difference? With 'I'm glad you're not the girl I saw in the bus', we surely turn to the verb 'saw' to determine the implications of the phrase as a whole. In English the indicative is here likely to retain its full force, to allow us the extract 'I saw a girl in the bus' as an implication of the sentence. If, on the other hand, we had a suitable use of a subjunctive for 'saw', then we could have a reading which made it clear that no reference was intended by the description, so that what I was ostensibly glad about was not a non-identity, but simply the failure of the person addressed to satisfy the description. However, even when features of the description—notably the verb—do not dictate the interpretation to this extent, we tend to impose or extract a referential use. This, I imagine, is the reading we should most readily associate with 'I wish you were the girl next door'. With titles, certainly, we may feel there is need for the article only if reference is intended; otherwise it can be omitted, as regularly happens with such sentences as 'He has his heart set on being Prime Minister (secretary, captain, best man)', and is often obligatory in other Indo-European languages. We might even ascribe a varying force to descriptive phrases, distinguishing them as 'indicative' and 'subjunctive' in accordance with their possible expansions: 'He wished he was the child's teacher' becomes 'He wished he was the one who taught (indicative) the child'—i.e. that actual person—or 'He wished he was the one who taught (subjunctive) the child'—no identity intended. It would clearly be possible for a language to locate the difference in the article itself, and in Malagasy we find that something like this has taken place. The language has two definite articles, one of which covers a wide range of functions, while the other is restricted to phrases purporting to pick out something which the speaker has already specifically identified. The latter article—which is an article rather than a demonstrative—always has a referential force, whereas the former may be used in either way. Cf. Keenan and Ebert [1973], pp. 421-4, and Krámský, op. cit., p. 109.

Although factors other than 'the' conspire to generate any existential implications of definite descriptions, it is likely that it is actual existence that makes for determinacy, and there may be some awkwardness in the use of the article in denials of existence, such as 'The largest number does not exist' or 'The King of France does not exist'. We should prefer,

I suggest, 'A largest number does not exist' and 'There is no king of France'. Even with 'There is no such person as the King of France', we perhaps feel that the title is under some strain, to be rescued by a rewording in which the phrase 'the King of France' comes to be merely mentioned, rather than used in seemingly referential fashion. Furthermore, with certain other examples, such as 'The Colossus at Rhodes does not exist', there is both a possible use and, without inconsistency, a possible reference; here something which did once exist, and so can be referred to, is being denied present existence. What of such a sentence as 'The man in the moon does not exist'? Once more we may feel some uneasiness about this form of words, but we might also hold that there are in this instance grounds for speaking of an attenuated existential implication, one at least that is sufficient for the demands made by the description: the man in the moon may be familiar to us from children's stories, so to that extent and in that sense we may consider we have to do with *something* whose real existence may be denied. We do have some use for a notion of there being some things which do not exist, and occurrence in fiction or in myth is one of the conditions which could be regarded as sufficient for reference—though we shall see a rather different way of looking at this question later on.

What holds for 'the' holds too for 'that'. We might suppose that wishing to be 'that person' would inevitably have one wishing to be a person whom the speaker actually designated or purported to designate. This is no doubt generally so, but 'that' may also stand in for a condition which fails to imply existence, as with 'Joan's husband', suitably understood, or 'the first man to set foot on Mars'. Some languages, such as Spanish, may make the absence of reference clear by invoking a subjunctive in the appropriate verbal expansion. This, as I say, is not generally open to us with English verbs, but finite forms of these verbs often cover both possibilities, as evidenced by such a sentence as 'I should like to be the man who has the last say on these matters'—though the referential case would usually be eliminated on weakening 'the man' to 'the one', and the infinitive may cancel the unwanted implication of the indicative, as with 'I should like to be the first man to set foot on Mars'.

There are cases in which the existential implications of the sentence featuring the definite description are uncertain. Consider 'The man who marries the butcher's daughter will be well provided for'. Do I imply that there will be such a man, in my opinion? This is, again, a question which leads us to focus on the verb figuring in the description as much as on the definite article. The form 'marries' is not as committal as would be 'will marry', nor, of course, as 'is going to marry', but it is not quite as weak as a subjunctive, and we need to insert 'if any' to cancel its residual indicative force.

8. Reference and identification

Still staying with 'the', I wish to give preliminary attention to some broader issues. It is worth noting that, while existence of an F may be implied by a sentence in which 'the F' occurs, this does not necessarily reflect any intended reference to an F. We have the former implication with each of 'The cat's name might not have been "Ginger"', 'The Mayor's address is no longer 25 Park Drive', and 'The answer would not have been "No" had you asked earlier'. However, in asserting the first I am not asserting of that name which is in fact the cat's that it might not have been as it is, and in asserting the last I am not hinting at a conceivable non-identity of the given answer with itself. Disregard this feature of such subjects and you will doubtless be well on the way to inferring all manner of sceptical conclusions concerning the intelligibility of modal, temporal, and conditional sentences.

When it is a question of giving or stating a person's name, address, and so forth, there is a departure from the pattern of identifying reference coupled with a further identification or predication, even though the existence of the item in question is an immediate consequence. In saying 'The answer is "No"', for instance, there need be no preceding identification of an answer followed by the identification of it as 'No'. Similarly, when I say 'The height of the tower is 125 feet', I do not give a further specification of something initially identified as 'the height of the tower'. This absence of identification is a feature of sentences containing descriptions of an abstract character, sentences which can in consequence often be reworded in

such a way that the description vanishes. If there is no identifying reference to anything, nothing need be lost by forgoing
use of a phrase which, while of a form appropriate to that role,
does not in fact enjoy it in the given case. So, 'The height of
the tower is 125 feet' becomes 'The tower is 125 feet high',
'The versatility of this model is amazing' becomes 'This model
is amazingly versatile', or 'It is amazing how versatile this
model is', and so on. In any sense in which existence can be
implied by the description, it can continue to find expression
in such variants. We shall come back to these numerous cases.

As a less complex kind of example, consider 'The girl's
name is "Jean"'. This might represent an identification of
a name coupled with an actual specification of it, as when
someone deciphers a signature which he knows to be of the
name. In such a case we have an identity, and therewith the
possibility of an error which could be reported as 'He thought
"Joan" was "Jean"', say—i.e. thought on that occasion, with
respect to a particular token, not thought quite generally—as
well as by 'He thought the girl's name was "Jean"'. However,
as a more likely interpretation, imagine that the person hears
the name 'Jean' being spoken in the presence of a certain girl
and accordingly concludes that that is her name. If her name
is in fact 'Joan', he is mistaken in saying that it is 'Jean', but
his error is not one of confusing 'Joan' with 'Jean', even
though the former is her name. It is not that there is something which he knows to be her name, but which he then mis-
identifies, takes to be other than it is: he incorrectly applies
the description, 'the girl's name', to the name he hears; he
does not link up 'Jean' with an identification of the person's
name made on another occasion.

This notion of identification is important to that of an
identity. Statements such as 'He is the owner of a yacht',
'Howard is the best bridge player here', or 'The man to ask
about that is Ron', are sometimes put forward as examples of
identity statements, but it is precisely because, in their more
usual readings, there is no reference involved except on the
part of the names or pronoun, that this label is ill chosen.
Thus, in terms of a familiar example, the supposed identity,
'Scott is the author of *Waverley*', would generally have the
force of 'Scott (alone) wrote *Waverley*', just as 'He is the

owner of a yacht' imports no more reference than does 'He owns a yacht'. Suppose, however, that on a certain occasion someone was introduced to George VI as 'Scott', and on another occasion a person was pointed out to him as being the author of *Waverley*. Realizing that he had to do with one and the same person on each occasion, King George might have expressed this in the identity, 'Scott is the author of *Waverley*', or 'The author of *Waverley* is Scott'—a form which tends to discourage a predicational interpretation. Here the rephrasal as 'Scott wrote *Waverley*' would not be apposite, since it would lose sight of the two independent identifications which he was concerned to link together. If we are to speak of an *identity*, we should expect some talk of *sameness* to be in place, and it is only when we combine two phrases which are both used to make an identifying reference in that context that we have the possible rephrasals, 'Scott is the same person as the author of *Waverley*' and 'Scott and the author of *Waverley* are one and the same person'.

My main concern here is to resist the assimilation of identities to mere predications, but an intermediate position is a possibility. It could be held that we might speak in terms of an 'identity' provided only that we knew that *someone* was the author of *Waverley*, even if we had no idea who. Despite our ignorance in this respect, the knowledge we have of existence can survive the falsity of the particular identification given by 'Scott is the author of *Waverley*', so there is no collapse into the kind of predication which provided our original contrast. By way of such contrast, consider the sentences, 'Hunt is the holder of a British passport' and 'Maxwell is the owner of a yacht', sentences in which the definite article is used because passport and yacht are supposed to have just one holder or owner, not because there is only one holder of a British passport or only one person who owns a yacht, individuals which the phrases might then pick out. Not only is there no identification, but if I am in error in saying 'Hunt is the holder of a British passport', there is no independent fact of existence on which use of the description rests and which can be extracted from the denial, 'Hunt is not the holder of a British passport', so that we might infer: someone else is.

We could speak of an *identity* given only the weaker condition, knowledge of existence, but I do not wish to say that this weaker condition is sufficient for us to be able to speak of *reference* with respect to a use of 'the *F*'. For that I require that we should have taken something to be the *F*, in such a sense that our characterization or identification of the thing in these terms can meaningfully be said to be a mischaracterization or misidentification. So, we can readily see how there may be no question of misidentification with respect to the grammatical subject in 'The architect who designed this house should be sued', there being no one whom the speaker takes to be, rightly or wrongly, the architect, and in this case I wish to say that there is no identifying reference either. The distinction here is reminiscent of that drawn in Donnellan [1964] between referential and attributive uses of definite descriptions, though I intend the contrast to the former use to be given not merely by phrases which can be accompanied by a rider disclaiming knowledge of identity, as 'The architect, whoever he is . . .', but also by phrases for which such a disclaimer makes no sense, as with 'the need for care', 'the absence of friends', or 'the possibility of a storm'.

To interpret *reference* in this now familiar way involves a degree of legislation, but it is only if there is something which we can still be said to have intended to pick out, despite the possible inappropriateness of the word or words used for this purpose, that our judgement can be taken to be *about* that object in such a way that the principle of extensionality for names and similar referential phrases can be applied in reporting it. That is, such sentences as 'He took x to be F' are true for every substitution for x if true for any, provided only that we substitute co-referential terms. If, on the other hand, the speaker does not have an intention to refer which is thus independent of the terms he uses, such freedom of substitution is not invariably permissible. This may happen when I purport to say something about, let us say, the largest city in the world, not knowing what city that is. My belief, expressed as 'The largest city in the world is in Europe', cannot then be reported by use of a name of that city, so as to have me believing that Tokyo is in Europe.

To take another example, in stating 'The girl's name is

a common one', a person may be identifying some name as being that of the girl in question and saying of it that it is common, in which case, supposing that he correctly identifies a name as being that of the girl, we can say indifferently 'He thought the girl's name was a common one' or 'He thought "Jean" was a common name'. Suppose, however, that he has no knowledge of the girl's name. He will no doubt say that she has a name and he might even be in a position to say, relying on hearsay or on vague memories, 'The girl's name is a common one'. However, given his ignorance of the name in question, we should not wish to say that he held any opinions as to the commonness or otherwise of the name 'Jean'. He thinks the girl has a common name, but what it is he does not know. Similarly, if he surmises that the girl's name is Scandinavian, it does not follow that he surmises that 'Jean' is Scandinavian.

Again, a person might conjecture, 'The place where this wine came from is east of Bordeaux', and in saying this mean no more than: this wine came from some place east of Bordeaux. In this case it is not necessarily true that he thought that Cahors was east of Bordeaux, supposing that to be the place in question, though if he had intended his statement to be true of a place he could identify—if there was a certain place east of Bordeaux which he thought the wine to come from—then, provided he was correct in his identification, we could truly say, 'He thought Cahors was east of Bordeaux'. And, for our report to take this form, it is not necessary that he should know of the place as 'Cahors'; he need never have heard of its name.

This is not to say that, in the absence of knowledge of identity, inferences based on the substitution of terms applicable to the same person or thing will never hold. There can be more than one pattern of inference involving such descriptions: if the police say they wish to interview the man who last saw the doctor alive, and that man is you, then we might say that the police wish to interview you—certainly, that you are the man whom the police wish to interview—though not necessarily that they *said* they wished to interview you. We can make this rephrasal without having to ascribe to the police any knowledge of the identity of the man who last saw the doctor alive.

Similarly, if the police want to interview anyone who witnessed the accident, then they want to interview you if you did. The inference does not fail because 'anyone' is not a referential term in my sense.

My sense is not, of course, one that has to be accepted. It may be thought preferable to place emphasis on a less demanding notion of singling out one thing from among others, where a description is said to have that function so long as its sense is, perhaps with help from the context, sufficiently determinate, and so long as there is, or comes to be, a corresponding person or thing. In this use we could speak of reference even with 'The loser will be given a month's holiday in Blackpool', since the description is, or can be made, sufficiently specific to indicate which individual—in a certain sense—will meet the fate in question. Here I have in mind the kind of further specification which could be given by such an explanation as 'I mean the loser of the competition we were just discussing'. With such a use there is a symmetry with the past case in that we judge the prediction to be true depending on whether or not it comes to hold with respect to the person who turns out to satisfy the description. I opt for the reading I do, not because the alternatives are unreasonable—though this last is an extreme case—but because that reading is better geared to statements of principles of inference which make significant use of terms of the relevant kinds.

9. Proper names

In discussions of referential terms, proper names are accustomed to receiving the lion's share of the attention. Undeservedly, perhaps, but they do introduce points of interest, some of which I shall now approach by way of the question, can proper names be said to have a sense? If talk of sense requires that talk of meaning be at least possible, the prospects for an affirmative answer are not bright. Asked by a foreigner the meaning of 'Arthur Clarke', we might well explain: it doesn't have a meaning, it is someone's name. Furthermore, our reluctance to speak here of meaning is surely significant, since this is hardly a matter about which we might be silent through lack of knowledge. There is a similar hesitance in our use of *understanding* with respect to names. Should we speak of understanding the name 'Arthur Clarke'? What there is to understand is that the name is a name, and, in a slightly different sense, that it is the name of such-and-such a person, but using 'understand' in this way does not require that the name have a meaning.

It might be suggested that recognition of the sense or meaning of names is forced upon us by the consideration that we often understand a sentence even if we do not know whether anything is referred to by a name in the sentence, what we understand at the point where the name occurs being the sense of that name. To this the only alternative might appear to be the construal of such a name as a surd which makes no contribution to our understanding of the sentence. But again the answer is clear: we may readily appreciate what a sentence is about, grasp the gist of the words, if we simply recognize the name as a name—or, perhaps, say, as a person's name. True, there is more specific knowledge which may then elude us, knowledge of the identity of the person whose name it is, or, if the name occurs in fiction, knowledge of the fictional character with which it is associated. But to deny, as we must, that such details have a place in an account of the meaning of a name, is not to deny them a place in our knowledge more generally. It would be silly to say that, for instance, only if we could speak of the sense or meaning of a name could we know what it was for a sentence containing that name to be true.

With the common noun 'scorpion' we have a meaning fixed in advance of any application to a particular instance, and any putative instance must satisfy the relevant defining conditions before we speak of it using the noun. However, a person does not have to conform to a certain description before we christen him 'Ralph', not at least at the level of generality at which sense supposedly enters: in searching among the stock of names for one to give to a child, we are not constrained by any possible discrepancy between the character of the bearer and the meaning of the given name, nor might we prefer one name to another—irrelevant etymological considerations aside— on the basis of its meaning. Again, a woman may change her name on marriage, but the name does not have to undergo a change or an extension of meaning in order to accommodate its new bearer. This is not, of course, to say that we are free to use names in an altogether arbitrary fashion. Before a child has been christened the choice is open, but once a name has been conferred upon him it *is* his name and it is not correct, by and large, to call him by another. But again, correctness in the use of a name is not to be explained in terms of a correct fit as determined by the name's meaning.

In so far as there are constraints on personal names they relate to the division between first names and surnames and to the association with gender. We do not use first names and surnames interchangeably, but use of the former generally testifies to a closer relationship with the bearer of the name. Exactly what dimension of use is thus involved is a question worth pursuing; here I simply note that it is not connected with a difference on the side of the bearer, unlike the connection with gender, which is accordingly more relevant to sense. Thus, 'Jack' is a boy's name, 'Jill' a girl's, and 'Pat' is used of either. The association with gender can, however, be overriden. 'Jack' could retain its essential function, the function proper to names, even if it were used of a female newt. Certain classes of names, such as those of cats, dogs, racehorses or ships, may be fairly distinctive, but however incongruous it may be to christen one's child 'Tabby' or 'Fido', a subsequent identification, 'This is Tabby', will not involve the falsity or deception incurred when we misdescribe with a general term. The proper name can still be used in its central role, viz. as a name—the name 'Tabby' can still be used to *identify* the child—whereas with a general term such as 'cat' the word is unable to survive such a change in its use: its whole being lies in its precise descriptive force or meaning. Even a nickname can continue to be used after the bearer has lost the characteristics which prompted the name, again because it survives as an established form of identification, rather than description, of the person.

Further to the first-name/surname distinction, we may observe that while gender is not relevant to the latter, kinship is, with not the same scope for choice in determining one's surname (in Western society). Again a consideration relevant to sense, but again very much a matter of custom incidental to the function of proper names generally. In the same vein we note that familial ties are implicit in such a phrase as 'the

Grays', and the Grays of this world can be said to form a kind, if only as the bearers of that name, so there is to that extent a uniform condition, satisfaction of which makes for the applicability of '*a* Gray'. There is also a use with the indefinite article to mark different phases in the history of a single individual, as with 'An unhappy Gray broke the bad news', but in neither case do we have repercussions for the unqualified name, 'Gray'. We cannot infer that, for instance, the name has a whole range of meanings, so that we might say: one meaning of 'Gray' is 'the man who wrote the poem *On the Death of a Favourite Cat*'.

But for one who knows a person named 'Gray', will that name not have a meaning? After all, there will be something distinctive about the bearer of the name to which the speaker will implicitly appeal in deciding whether to address a person as 'Gray', and if we should put this into words what we should have is surely something which would count as specifying the sense which the name has for the speaker. It is true that we cannot in general speak of *the* meaning of a proper name, since there may be as many meanings associated with the name as there are users of it, given the likelihood that the criteria which guide one man in his use of a name with respect to a given person do not coincide with the criteria used by another with respect to the same name and person. But whether one or many, meaning can be admitted on this basis.

My present objection to speaking of the meaning of a proper name does not rest on the consideration that the singular is out of place. To say that 'Gray' has a multitude of meanings prompts the same misgivings. Nor do I deny that a person may be guided by features of the object or individual in question when he applies a name. Names are not applied blindly, but in accordance with knowledge of the bearer which the speaker possesses. The question is one as to the nature of this knowledge and its proper location in the use of a name. If a citizen of eighteenth-century Königsberg knew as 'Immanuel Kant' a man of a certain appearance accustomed to emerge from a particular house for his daily walk at a regular time, that citizen would identify a figure as that of Kant in accordance with his ascertainment of these familiar features and behaviour. What is crucial is the question which this information would put him in a position to answer: the question, as indicated, of the identity of the figure; he knows *who* it is. The name 'Immanuel Kant' was that of a person who had a certain history, was encountered by various people at various times and places, presenting a variety of appearances and making a variety of impressions. In the most useful sense, two people can be said to have the same understanding of the name, not if and only if they associate the same descriptions with it, are guided by the same considerations in fixing its reference, but if and only if they understand it as the name of the same person.

Knowledge of identity need not, of course, extend to the ability to recognize the person at all times: the distinguishing characteristics of which one knows may be duplicated in another and one is unlikely to have kept track of the space–time path connecting the individual encountered at some time in the past with the individual currently observed. However, even if I have been in a person's presence for only a matter of seconds, and could not now distinguish him from a large number of similar-looking people, let alone from an identical twin, I can still use his name to speak of him and grasp the intended reference of the name as used by others. It is correspondingly clear that knowing a person by two different names is consistent with ignorance of the identity, the informativeness of a statement of identity resting on this fact. Even though a man may possess sufficient identificatory knowledge to use the names 'George Orwell' and 'Eric Blair', neither item of knowledge need provide a basis from which the other could be inferred, subsequent spatio-temporal history not being predictable from known history to date.

Joining two names in a statement of identity does not make for a departure from the standard use of those names. I say this in opposition to a view that may be found tempting, the view that the knowledge involved in such a statement can be more accurately formulated in a statement about the names, as Frege originally thought. Not 'George Orwell and Eric Blair were one and the same person', but '"George Orwell" and "Eric Blair" were names of the same person'. However, if the former involves linking together two identifications or sets of identifications, then the names are actually being *used*, just as if one said, with the appropriate knowledge, 'George

Orwell's vision of the future was not encouraging'. In either case the form of words is appropriate to possession of knowledge of who George Orwell was. On the other hand, I can know that the names are names of a single person without having the remotest idea who that person is, in which case the form which merely mentions the names is more in place.

More accurately, it may be possible to give a paraphrase in which we mention rather than use the names, but if that is so the relevant identifications should reappear at another point, as with 'The man who was known as "George Orwell" was identical with the man who went by the name "Eric Blair"'. Conversely, I do not wish to suggest that absence of quotes invariably purports to signify knowledge of identity. It is rather that, when such knowledge is lacking, no more is asserted than when quotes are used. Thus, 'George Orwell was Eric Blair' might in such a case come to 'George Orwell's real name was "Eric Blair"'. Similarly, when we say, 'In real life *N.N.* was *M.M.*', this could often be rephrased as 'In real life *N.N.* was known as "*M.M.*"'. Again, even though I might know no more about Francesco Redi than that he was the first man to appreciate that maggots were formed from flies' eggs, and not by spontaneous generation, I might conceivably find occasion to write 'The first man to appreciate that maggots were formed from flies' eggs was Francesco Redi'. Given, however, that this is the extent of my knowledge of the man, there will be no loss to me in rephrasing this as 'The first man to appreciate that maggots were formed from flies' eggs was called "Francesco Redi"'. I should have thought, indeed, that the latter would be preferable, and in general we tend to avoid the unqualified name if we are unaware of the person's identity: we speak of 'a certain John Smith' doing such-and-such, or 'one John Smith'; we ask 'Is this person Smith to be trusted?', rather than simply 'Is Smith to be trusted?', and we employ less presumptive phrases, such as 'some man', in lieu of the name when reporting a person's words about the man. Compare too the presumption in the announcement, 'I am *N.N.*' as against 'My name is *N.N.*', the presumption that *N.N.* is someone whose identity can be expected to be known.

It is sometimes suggested that our ability to use a person's name to refer to him is not impaired by the falsity of all the beliefs which we should be prepared to express using that name. Such a suggestion may be advanced as an uncompromising objection to the view that a proper name has a sense that can be given by some description or cluster of descriptions: if I am prepared to expand the name $N.N.$ in terms of some description, then that gives me the material for at least one proposition of the form '$N.N.$ is F' which I take to be true; conversely, if the falsity of any and every such proposition that I am willing to assert is consistent with my referring to $N.N.$, then, at least as far as my usage is concerned, the name does not allow of any such expansion.

Suppose, then, that the extent of a person's beliefs about Redi is confined to the discovery cited, and suppose that this attribution proves to be in error. Could it then be said of that person that he 'mistakenly thinks that Francesco Redi was the first to appreciate that maggots were formed from flies' eggs'? It could, if it were meant merely that the person mistakenly believed 'Francesco Redi' to be the name of someone responsible for this discovery, but it might be held that more than this could be involved, that, despite the mistaken belief, there could be a referential use to which this rewriting did not do justice. Here we must take seriously the hypothesis that this is—apart from its entailments—the only relevant belief that the person has. After all, the man will presumably have encountered the name in the speech or writings of others, and while the only item of information which he has retained may be as stated, he could often reasonably assume that those from whom he had gained this information were better placed, that they had in mind someone whom they knew to be responsible for deeds other than the putative discovery. In such a case he could at least say that Redi was a man spoken of by so-and-so in such-and-such a work, let us say, and could then appeal to this fact when asked who Redi was. Not very helpful information, but it does individuate: the man's conjectures about Redi are now not just about anyone who might have gone by that name, but he can narrow down the possible bearers by appeal to this further condition—supposing there is no confusion in the authorities' use of the name.

If the person's individuating knowledge is as scant as this, we may still prefer to see the name mentioned rather than used in unqualified fashion in a report of the belief, but in any event our interest is in the case where the man is quite ignorant of any works in which the authors use the name in knowledge of the bearer's identity, where indeed he has no further beliefs concerning the bearer that are determinative of identity, however indirectly. Now, surely, it is not possible to give substance to the alleged reference. It is suggested that, despite the severance of all such links, 'Francesco Redi was the first to appreciate that maggots were formed from flies' eggs' will mean more coming from him than '"Francesco Redi" is the name of a person who was the first to appreciate that maggots were formed from flies' eggs'; accordingly, we are entitled to ask which of the people thus named is intended. There could, after all, be many; the speaker has not been given the item of individuating information: there was only one person by that name. How, then, can he answer? Not by saying that it is the person meant by *N.N.*, where *N.N.* is someone who had some knowledge of the relevant Francesco Redi; he cannot say that what he has said is true if the person meant by 'Francesco Redi' is as he claims or conjectures, since 'the person meant by "Francesco Redi"' does not individuate. Someone will be the person meant by the name only when it is a question of the use of that name by someone on some occasion; by hypothesis, no such use is known of, and any conjectures the man may make in such a state of ignorance allow him to suppose that many people may have been intended by the use of the name at different times.

This, then, is not the right way to show that proper names are not just definite descriptions in disguise. Should we have recourse to differences in behaviour between names and descriptions with respect to modality? It might be argued that 'Röntgen' could not be taken to mean 'the discoverer of X-rays', since Röntgen might have existed yet failed to make that discovery. But the question to ask is whether Röntgen might have failed to be the person who discovered X-rays, and there is a clear sense in which he could not but have been that person. Even if Röntgen had not discovered X-rays, he would still have been the man who, as it happened, did just that. Again, while we may attach a different reading to 'The discoverer of X-rays could not possibly have been a Scot', depending on whether an identifying reference is or is not made by the description, the same difference is reflected in the two uses which the name may involve in 'Röntgen could not possibly have been a Scot'. This, too, may or may not be about Röntgen in the stricter of the senses indicated.

Of course, that names are not to be equated with definite descriptions is a trivial consequence of the fact that only the latter can be said to have a meaning. However, we also find a corresponding difference in usage in that descriptions allow of a purely predicative use denied to names. A boy may say, 'I wish I were the head prefect', expressing either a wish to hold that office or a wish to have been a certain individual. Put a proper name in place of the description and any such choice is eliminated, the referential uses—meaning by this the less as well as the more strict—exhausting the possibilities, precisely because the name does not expand into any realizable condition. What of names which occur only in fiction? Could it be claimed that, lacking a real referent, such a name must be understood in terms of some condition, a condition which a person could then wish to satisfy? Only legislation could bring us to this conclusion. Taken literally, someone who said he wished he were Pickwick would be wishing to be a product of Dickens's imagination, which would be quite absurd. I suppose we might accordingly take him to wish to have had the kind of character displayed by Pickwick, rather than to have enjoyed only a fictional existence, but this is to introduce a special reading.

Have we shown that names are not to be ascribed senses? If a supporter of sense for names is committed to defending the ascription of meaning to them, his cause is lost, and while Frege is not to be taken as identifying his sense with our meaning, it is not unlikely that his understanding of the former places him in that losing position. Let me repeat the main reason for rejecting this ascription. Unlike a general term, a proper name does not have a meaning which must be respected when we are proposing to confer that name on a person or thing, a meaning fixed in advance of any such christening. Allowance must be made for certain common associations, notably those of gender, but the use of names is in this respect essentially arbitrary, function as a *name*—a non-indexical form of identification—not being threatened by disregard for these associations. Lack of meaning—the fact that we must have non-linguistic knowledge of what is intended, and cannot derive this from an interpretation of the name—explains the inclination to say that names are not part of the language; the existence of a stock of standard names—words which can at least be recognized as names—explains the contrary inclination.

What are we to make of the question: what decides whether N is this man's name? Well, it will be his name if it is an inherited surname, if it was conferred at a christening, or by deedpoll, or if it is at least a name whose attachment to him has been sanctioned by common practice. This is what makes N the person's name, so, in a sense, what ultimately justifies use of N with respect to that person. A name is not someone's name simply because someone chooses to use it of him, we may note. There is, however, a less general question of justification, the question how someone recognizes a person as the bearer of the name, i.e. as the person with whom the name has been associated in the ways mentioned, or as the intended referent of a name that is not in fact his. I find room for something like the notion of sense in so far as I grant that there will be something in virtue of which a person applies a name to some person or thing, but I do not accept that information of this nature can be reckoned to anything like the meaning of a proper name. If our concern is with the common currency of language, with a general account of the use of a name, appeal to sense threatens to introduce an unwanted, idiosyncratic element, to take us away from the common denominator of what is understood in a sentence containing a given name. Identity of reference is all that is required at this point to ensure a common understanding, and in specifying what is understood, the content of a sentence containing the name, we cut through any differences associated with different individuals' criteria for the application of the name.

However, once a name has been conferred upon an individual, a question of reapplication arises to which the answer is not at all arbitrary. Is there any possibility of reinstating the notion of sense in this connection? So, 'Zoe' contrasts with 'zinc', in that one could give anyone or anything the former name without misdescription. Since it does not mean anything it does not convey anything: not, at least, in any essential way. Unlike 'zinc', it is just a name, even if, because it is usually a female name, we are surprised to find it used of a hurricane. However, once 'Zoe' has become someone's name, the question whether a given person is Zoe is more like the question whether a given piece of metal is zinc. Of course, there is a sense in which 'zinc' too could have been given to anything, but this is not such as to destroy either the contrast or the comparison: the contrast remains in the way the use of the proper name with respect to other individuals is not determined by a given christening; the comparison is in the non-arbitrary question of reidentification which arises for the proper name.

The sense of a name, then, will be a condition or criterion whereby its reapplication, rather than its initial application, is determined, How is such a criterion to be understood? I have spoken of conditions in terms of which a person might be recognized as the bearer of a name, and that would appear to be what Frege had in mind with his characterization of sense in terms of 'mode of presentation'. However, this suggests conditions which are lacking in a temporal dimension, conditions relating to facial characteristics, voice, gait, and so forth. It is certainly by such features that we recognize a person, but they are features which may change over the years, and, more important, which may conceivably be duplicated in another. Our concern should be not so much with *clues* to a person's identity, as with a condition that is definitive of that identity, a condition which will perforce extend back into the past, beyond what we are given at any time after we have learned who the name is a name of.

For this purpose, any condition true *only* of the bearer will suffice, so, most naturally, any suitable condition of a spatio-temporal kind. However, what is now threatened is the connection with recognition. The idea of sense as relating to a condition whereby someone might be recognized as the bearer of a given name seems important, so perhaps the demand that the condition should actually guarantee the applicability of the name should be relaxed, given the difficulty in satisfying such a condition—though we should surely wish to keep as close to it as possible.

Whatever exactly is decided on this point, we are still no closer to sense as an 'ingredient' in meaning. But perhaps this does not matter. However we describe it, we are not denying the possibility of speaking of an association of a name with individuating knowledge of the intended referent. Sometimes people use names knowing whom or what they are talking about, sometimes they do not; how could this be challenged? Again, the connections with meaning and understanding may not be as thought by a defender of Frege, but we continue to explain the significance of identities in much the same terms.

So long as he is not feigning ignorance or is otherwise insincere, a person shows that he associates names N and M with different identifications—if any—merely by raising the question whether N is M or by denying the identity, and the difference may also emerge more directly in his statement as to who N and M are, specifications which differ in meaning being used of either, never of both. What we must not do is follow those who appeal to seemingly 'intentional' or 'opaque' contexts in an effort to expose a difference in sense between two names of a single individual, arguing that since for instance, we may take someone to be N but not to be M, this shows a difference in our understanding of the two names. This, we shall find, goes the same way as most appeals of its kind. Indeed, in so far as the strategy proves persuasive, it will have us acknowledging what may be reckoned a difference in *reference* between the names in question—a curious development which we shall later pursue.

3

REFERENCE AND SUBJECTS

Much of the difficulty in giving an accurate account of philo-sophically interesting terms has a simple source: words or phrases of the language are not explicitly or uniformly marked for the feature which concerns us. Accordingly, there can be considerable scope for misidentification when trying to esta-blish how that feature is conveyed. The problem was well illustrated with the definite article. If distinct articles are in use for descriptions which are, and those which are not intended to make an identifying reference, there is both absence of ambiguity in practice and greater ease in identi-fying and characterizing the two cases. If, as in English, the article is unvarying, it may be far from clear where we are to look to find the source of these differences.

Another example is presented by phrases consisting of a noun preceded by the indefinite article, as 'a prince' or 'a pauper'. In some languages there is more than one form of words which might be rendered in English by such a phrase. For instance, in ChiBemba, a Bantu language of Zambia, the sentences, 'The woman allowed the child to read a book' and 'The child will read a book tomorrow', translate differently depending on whether the speaker has in mind a definite book or not (see Givón [1973]). When the distinction is explicitly marked in this way, localization of function tends to be straightforward, but in English, which follows a different pattern, we have a potentially complex question concerning meaning. How many meanings can we ascribe to 'a' on the strength of this pair of sentences? Is there perhaps a further reading to be extracted from such sentences as 'A change is as good as a rest' or 'A straight beats a flush'? How, after all, do these sentences come to have the general readings which we should so readily infer? What of such notorious contexts as the intentional and the existential? How does the phrase with the indefinite article function in 'They fear a reprisal' or 'A wealth tax does not yet exist'?

The definite and indefinite articles are among the ten most frequently used words in English. The distinguished position of 'the' is acknowledged by philosophers in the quantities of ink spilled over it, but 'a' has been by comparison quite neglected. I should like to do something towards redressing the balance, and I shall fasten on the indefinite article in following up questions of meaning and reference, turning then to a consideration of the subject–predicate distinction in order to see further how the factors which we shall isolate combine. Again we find that resolute adherence to our methodology pays dividends, opening up a fresh perspective on the interplay between particular and general in the workings of language.

10. The indefinite article and covert reference

Let us begin by asking whether the combination of noun with indefinite article furnishes us with a potential referring expression. There is a familiar contrast, already glimpsed, which to some extent favours an affirmative answer. Thus, we find a number of verbs, such as 'want' and 'look for', which, when they have such a phrase as their grammatical object, may yield a sentence which can be taken in two ways, one of which might be thought to feature the noun phrase in a referential capacity. So, if someone says, 'I am looking for a dictionary', it may be that he has in mind a particular dictionary, one that he has mislaid, say, or it may be that he has not: just any dictionary will do. In the latter case we should not say that the speaker was referring to some dictionary, in the former we might. Here at least we have the commitment to existence which reference demands and which to a large extent constitutes the interest of the notion. Somewhat similarly, we are more inclined to speak of reference in the case of 'A salesman telephoned' than we should with 'He is not a salesman'.

However, there are complications. First, we note that the involvement of existence must be treated with care. We happily say that a man wants something just on the strength of knowing that he wants a receipt, let us say, and without any assumptions as to the existence of such; indeed, with the same lack of assumptions we shall even say that *there is* something that he wants, viz. a receipt. There is more than one kind of 'existential commitment' if we choose to associate this notion with what there is as well as with what exists; what is intended in this case, for reference to be possible, is that what the man wants should exist, not merely that there should be something wanted. In this latter case we have only the weaker demand that there should be such a thing as a receipt— to make the desire intelligible; and, if that is just to say that 'a receipt' should have a meaning, this is not to introduce the meaning of the phrase as a non-material surrogate for what is wanted when the more demanding existence condition goes unsatisfied.

Second, we have a complication relating to the nature of what is wanted. You say you are looking for a dictionary and I enquire whether you mean any one in particular. To answer 'Yes' you do not need to have been looking for a particular copy of a dictionary, but particularity can come in with respect to the type: *The Shorter Oxford English Dictionary* is in the required sense a particular dictionary just as much as is your copy of that work. The appropriateness of inserting 'particular' still leaves open the question of what precisely it is that is being referred to. It is also just worth pointing out the mistaken way in which such a phrase as 'a particular dictionary' is sometimes construed, as if 'particular' itself expressed a restriction of the type indicated by the noun, so that a 'particular' dictionary meant a kind of dictionary. This distortion occasionally finds expression in such sentences as 'There are no dictionaries that are not particular dictionaries', or in the more general 'Whatever exists is particular', and it is risked by the use of the term as a noun, as in 'a concrete particular'. The difference between the presence and absence of 'particular' in the phrase 'a dictionary' is, roughly, a matter of the difference between the case in which one does and the case in which one does not make it known that one has in mind one dictionary rather than another—at either level of generality—though it is true that the grammar makes it look as if it were a difference in *kinds* of dictionary.

Does insertability of 'certain' give a better indication that reference, in some sense, is intended? The suggestion which its use carries—that the speaker has a knowledge of the object or individual in question which extends beyond the context to which his assertion relates—does make for a relevant likeness to proper names, the possible paradigms for a philosophical usage of 'reference'. On the other hand, it can still be said that the failure of the indefinite description to definitely pick out or identify one person or thing from others of the kind in question stands in the way of its classification as a potential referring expression. True, if I say 'A newspaper reported the bishop's death', or 'An actress had been seen leaving his house', you can ask, and I may be able to answer, 'Which newspaper?' and 'Who was the actress?', but in making these statements I do not actually specify which or who, not even in the oblique way characteristic of the definite article, so certainly do not refer you to the newspaper or actress in question. Moreover, it may be urged, even though I can be said to have in mind a certain newspaper or actress as I say these things, this is not a fact that is felt when it comes to considering the truth of what I say. I may be reckoned to have spoken truly even if a newspaper and an actress other than the ones I was thinking of satisfied the relevant descriptions.

There is clearly a close connection between the ideas of referring to a person or thing and specifying which person or thing, but the force of the preceding observation is not so much to reject altogether any notion of reference in connection with the indefinite article—after all, it is allowed that we can speak of *having in mind* a certain newspaper or actress as the one that is as stated—as to give priority to the case in which a more explicit indication of the reference is given by the actual words used, the case in which some attempt is made, by linguistic means, to refer one's audience to the relevant object. We might mark the distinction by reserving 'identifying reference' for this case, and speaking of a 'covertly referential' use of an indefinite description when it is at least backed by knowledge of identity. This, then, will be our characterization of the use involved in 'I am going to telephone a plumber', say, when we do have some cause to speak of reference, and it will contrast both with the use of the indefinite description when the speaker has no idea which plumber he is going to telephone, and with the use of definite descriptions and proper names when these are involved in an explicit or identifying reference.

Consider now the contrast between the use of a proper name and that of an indefinite description, as in 'Stevens went onto the bridge' and 'An officer went onto the bridge'. I may be wrong in saying of a particular person, Stevens, that he went onto the bridge, but in that event there will be a complementary predicate that I can assert of him, e.g. that he stayed below. If, on the other hand, I am mistaken when I say simply, 'An officer went onto the bridge', I am not assured of a subject of whom some alternative is similarly assertible. Or so it might be argued. But there is not this asymmetry if I use 'an officer' where I might have used 'Stevens', or at least had sufficient identifying knowledge for my intended reference to survive the falsity of the given statement. In each of 'An officer went onto the bridge' and 'An officer did not go onto the bridge' we shall have constancy in what the use of the subject terms implies, and in either case we can discern something of the pattern of recounting an episode in the history of a named individual.

As another illustration, take the sentence, 'A house in the next street is being demolished'. A person who asserts this may have been in a position to be more specific—knowing that the house in question is the one on the corner, for instance—but he may have little or no idea which house is being demolished; he knows, or can reasonably conjecture, that some house or other is being demolished—he can tell from the noise and the dust—but that is all. Again, I may be able to say 'A book is missing from this shelf', but not be in a position to say which book. I have no idea of its identity, I just know there should be one more than there is. If we wish to speak of, in some sense, a 'referential' use of phrases like 'a house' or 'a book', it will most naturally apply when there is this further knowledge; if I am to be referring to a book when I say 'A book is missing from this shelf', I surely must have some idea which book it is that is missing. As with identifying reference, so here there is more than one way in which we might make the specification of this further knowledge more precise, and for the sake of continuity it would seem best to have the two forms of reference agree in this respect; so, there will be covert reference with a use of 'an F' only if something is taken to be an F, in such a way that it makes sense to say that something was thereby mischaracterized.

Even when we should not say we knew which person or thing was in question, there may be a determinacy which makes for a contrast with sentences like 'Do bring a map of the area if you have one', or 'It would not be sensible of them to have a child'. In these instances there is no question of an identity which is determinate, but possibly known, possibly unknown. An example which presents all three possibilities is given by 'She wants to marry a millionaire'. When speaking in these terms I may know the identity of the millionaire in question; I may, on the other hand, know that there is a certain millionaire whom the woman wishes to marry, but have no idea who he is; finally, her wish may not be to marry any millionaire in particular, in which case identity is quite indeterminate, and *a fortiori* unknown.

Consider now a sentence containing an indefinite description which may or may not be used to make a covert reference, as with 'I am going to telephone a plumber'. In the absence of further information, we may be more inclined to take this in the less determinate form, requiring covert reference to be signalled by, say, an introductory 'there is'—'There is a plumber whom I am going to telephone'. However, both readings are possibilities, and it would appear reasonable to fasten on the phrase with the indefinite article as the source of the alternatives. Would it be correct to say that the article had two meanings, sometimes paraphrasing as 'a certain' or 'a particular', sometimes not? Should we, that is, introduce covert reference into the domain of word meaning?

It may seem hard to resist the claim that the indefinite article is capable of more than one sense. How else could such a distinction as this be accommodated? However, a difference in sense is only one possible hypothesis, and a hypothesis that is not without its difficulties. Suppose that 'a' did have more than one sense or meaning, one of which was given by the expansion 'a certain' or 'a particular', let us say. (These are, of course, two alternatives, not one, but we have no cause to treat them differently here.) The question immmediately arises as to how 'a' is to be dealt with in these contexts, but

I shall not pursue this point. The observation I wish to make is simply this: if one meaning of 'a' is given by 'a certain', then surely we could claim to be using the article with this meaning in 'A change is as good as a rest' or 'Never hit a man when he is down'. There is allegedly, that is, an ambiguity in 'a plumber' in our example, and one which we might resolve by saying that we did or did not have in mind a certain or a particular plumber, but if the difference is to be found in the two interpretations of the article, why do we not have 'A particular change is as good as a rest' or 'Never hit a certain man when he is down' as possible readings of the versions without the explicit 'certain' or 'particular'? Clearly, however, these versions will not bear such interpretations; even if the context provides us with an individual with respect to whom what we are saying is eminently applicable, the more general reading of 'Never hit a man when he is down' will stand firm. Nor will 'Even a child could do it' or 'It is no bigger than a mouse' allow of the readings, 'Even a certain child could do it' and 'It is no bigger than a certain mouse'—or 'There is a certain child such that even he could do it' and 'There is a certain mouse than which it is no bigger'.

If in such cases it is not open to use the article with one of the senses or meanings which it supposedly has, then we should surely not be thinking in terms of different meanings. After all, it is not as if the sense of the remainder of the sentence—of, say, 'It is no bigger than . . .'—precluded its attachment to a phrase thought of as characterizing a single determinate thing. A further qualification can have the effect of tying down 'a mouse' in this way, as with 'It is no bigger than a mouse which the cat brought in last night'; it is just that there is not a sense of 'a' which will have this effect. But how, then, are we to explain the evident differences between the possible interpretations of the various sentences, and if the contribution of the article does not vary, how is its meaning to be characterized?

On the second of these questions, we might suggest the following. The indefinite article is no more than an index of singularity for a noun which pluralizes. That, we might say, is the extent of the contribution which the article makes to the phrases in which it occurs. The emphasis should not be so much on the singularity of the accompanying noun—nothing may be made of the singular-plural contrast, and singularity could be adequately indicated by the absence of a plural inflection—as on the *capacity* of the noun for forming a plural, and so on the sort of noun which it is thus shown to be. In 'This is a gas', for instance, the article is not redundant, since in indicating that it is a question of a use of 'gas' in which it pluralizes, it serves to mark this off from the different use shown by 'This is gas'; to mark, clearly, a different range of contrasts. The article tags along with the noun as a reminder of the character of the noun, or as conveying the intended interpretation of the noun if it has, as with 'gas', more than one use.

What has just been suggested is not entirely correct, since there are, however rare, uses of nouns which take 'a' but which do not form a plural. Think of such phrases as 'a detailed knowledge' and 'a thorough understanding'. Here it is because of a contrast between different forms or degrees of knowledge or understanding that we have a use for 'a', so there is at least plurality of a kind. Also, the contrast with the use as a mass noun does not of necessity require that the noun be capable of forming a plural. Contrast the uses of 'a pity', which does not pluralize (outside such phrases as 'a thousand pities'), with the simple 'pity'. However, these refinements are incidental. The important question is whether 'a' allows of enlistment in a role which is more positive than that of unstressed numeral. If its contribution is no more than indicated, then the interpretation which we might hope to identify by the expansion to 'a certain' is one which by itself the article is simply too weak to bear. If the context does not make it clear that the speaker must be in possession of the kind of identificatory knowledge which would warrant the insertion of 'certain', and so entitle us to read 'an *F*' as if it had been 'a certain *F*', then the article must be helped out by the specific inclusion of this or a comparable word.

Our second question concerned the source of the two different interpretations of such a sentence as 'I am going to telephone a plumber', and here it seems clear enough that an appeal to speaker's meaning is what is demanded. But could it not be said that these words were genuinely ambiguous? It is certainly true that, without further information, we cannot be sure of the speaker's intention in the relevant respect, but the question is whether the possibilities in that area are reflected in two distinct interpretations of the article. We can ask the speaker whether he has in mind a particular plumber, but this is plainly a question about what *he* means, and not a question about the meaning of the article. He can indeed mean a particular plumber, but not be using 'a plumber' with a correspondingly restricted meaning. Again, while a girl who says 'I hope to marry a millionaire' may leave us uncertain as to her intentions, I should wish to say that the article receives a common interpretation whether or not she has her eyes set on a particular millionaire. It is more a question of the article's covering two cases rather than of its having two meanings—just as 'child' applies to either a girl or a boy, meaning the same in either case. The fact that in some languages the difference may be marked by a different article does not affect this point about English; in such cases we presumably can, by an appropriate choice of article, strengthen 'It is no bigger than a mouse' to 'It is no bigger than a certain mouse', a reading which, as I say, is just not possible for the English sentence, but which should be if the article did have 'a certain' as one of its senses.

The argument does not concern only 'a', nor is it restricted to the possible contrast between having and not having in mind, conceived of with respect to the lowest level—i.e., with respect to individuals rather than to types or kinds. It does not concern just 'a', since other determiners may raise the same question, as 'some' in 'I am looking for some glasses'. The consequent doubling of senses for a number of words becomes even less plausible, but if it holds for 'a' it can hardly be resisted elsewhere. Second, there is a parallel indeterminacy relating to the meaning, rather than to the possible reference, of an indefinite descriptive phrase. Consider again 'I am looking for a dictionary'. Presented with a dictionary, the speaker may reject it as not of the sort intended; it is not that he had in mind a particular copy, one other than this, but he was looking for an Italian–English, not an English–Italian dictionary. It is possible for him to say that by 'a dictionary' *he* meant 'an Italian–English dictionary', but not possible to say that the latter gives one meaning of the former. Whether we are considering the contrast between a particular and an arbitrary copy, or that between one kind of dictionary and another, we have ambiguity only in the sense that the speaker's meaning has not been adequately specified and can be specified in incompatible ways. The fact that, from either point of view, there is a possible incompleteness with respect to 'a dictionary' does not mean that this phrase has a number of different meanings, rather than merely covers distinct possibilities.

11. Plural nouns and mass terms

It is reasonable to allow phrases employed in the making of a covert reference to count as logical subjects, since with nominal status and referential use to invoke we can give substance to the underlying idea of 'saying of S that it is P'. So, we could have the subject-predicate pattern with 'A river broke its banks' and a contrasting use in 'A defeat would be disappointing'. Or consider 'Some people will be disturbed by this programme'. On one reading, this may paraphrase as 'There will be some people who are disturbed by this programme', but if the speaker has in mind certain people as sure to be disturbed by the programme, and might indeed have said 'certain' instead of 'some', we shall have an instance of the subject-predicate form. There is also the case where 'some' and 'certain' do duty for a sortal determination—'Some people, namely people who are sensitive to scenes of violence, will be disturbed by this programme'. Since the notion of misidentification does not appear to apply, either to the expanded or to the unexpanded form, I do not reckon these as instances of covert reference.

The topic of plurals merits a closer look. It is evident that the minimal role which I ascribe to the indefinite article is matched by a similar parsing of the plural: the '-s' termination, to take the usual form, indicates no more than simple plurality. The staggering obviousness of this observation may be excused by this further clarification: a simple plural, such as 'emus', is not in general to be identified with any more specifically quantified term such as 'some emus' or 'all emus'. Further features of the context sometimes make it clear that insertion of one or other of these quantifying expressions will introduce nothing that is not already implied, but in other contexts such an addition may well result in a distortion of the intended sense.

Consider the sentences, 'Fred keeps pigeons', 'Elizabeth smokes cigars', and 'Raymond designs hats'. There would normally be no question of 'all' being understood, and 'some' is likely to alter the sense: with 'Fred keeps some pigeons' we must think in terms of an unspecified but determinate number of birds or kinds of bird, whereas the simple 'pigeons' allows for the variability which the habitual 'keeps' requires. Similarly, 'Elizabeth smokes cigars' will hardly take an 'all' or a 'some' as qualifiying a plurality of individual cigars, and if either can be meaningfully inserted, it may result in a specificity that is far from the speaker's mind. Thus, 'some cigars', with 'some' stressed, would most naturally relate here to *kinds* of cigars—Elizabeth discriminates with respect to brands—which need not have been intended, and with 'some' unstressed we still have a determinacy at odds with the openness of the assertion.

Generalizations are often made from the perspective of a changing situation, and the interpretation appropriate to them will reflect this. The quantifiers 'some' and 'all' are in place when, by contrast, there is some form of determinacy, actual or anticipated—when, that is, the identity of the relevant things is fixed, or envisaged as fixed—a determinacy which may be at the level of individuals or of types. When expressing generality in first-order logic we are forced to choose between 'at least one' and 'all', but the reason this choice may be insufficient does not lie so much in the narrowness of the options from a numerical point of view—we can, after all, construct numerically definite quantifiers such as 'there are exactly three . . .' starting from the given quantifiers—but in the determinacy that is of the essence of the sytem. There is no way of adequately representing sentences of the forms just considered, nor of those in which the unquantified plural is in subject position, nor of such phrases as 'in centimetres' and 'by degrees', though mangled analogues are frequently offered as accurate formalizations; indeed, in some minds 'all' and the notion of generality appear to be quite inextricably tied.

The points just made with respect to count nouns could also be made for mass nouns. There is an indeterminacy about 'Plastic is not biodegradable' in that there is room for further precision about both kinds and circumstances. We shall later have occasion to look closely at such terms; for the moment let me simply indicate the points of contrast which define the two classes of noun. Count nouns, nouns which may take the indefinite article and form a plural, are often contrasted with mass nouns or names of stuffs, such as 'water', 'gas', and 'gold'. In the relevant sense we cannot speak of 'a gold', for instance. These are the terms in which the contrast is commonly drawn, but if it is basically the formal criterion, that concerning the presence or absence of article modification and pluralizability, that is decisive, then the appeal to the notion of *stuff* makes for a needless restriction. Words such as 'fun', 'laughter', and 'magic' compare with 'water' rather than, say, 'prism' or 'doll', in not taking the indefinite article or plural; and, to take a further, if derivative test, they allow of modification by 'much' and, in the relevant sense, 'some'; however, they have nothing to do with anything material. Conversely, such words as 'jelly', 'egg', 'chalk', and 'cheese' may signify stuffs, even when they are classifiable as count nouns. These are, we may note, words which allow of either use—a not uncommon feature: 'He had egg on his lapel' and 'He had an egg for breakfast'. The term 'mass noun' is likewise misleading, but since it is so entrenched I shall retain it, with the understanding that its application is as prescribed by the formal criterion mentioned. Pronouns and proper names aside, the only nouns which elude classification as either count or mass are those which, like 'earnings' and 'outskirts', are plurals with no singular, and those which, like 'knowledge' and 'understanding', can be singulars—'a full understanding'—with no plural. Taken together, these classes are not negligible, but they raise no special problems for us.

Do mass terms qualify as logical subjects? Intuitively, a term such as 'hydrogen' seems very close to a proper name, an impression that is strengthened by considering the kinds of phrase to which it may occur in apposition: a certain substance, hydrogen . . .; hydrogen, the lightest element . . . However, it is less clear that 'hydrogen' can qualify as a possible

logical subject in my more demanding sense unless it is reinforced by a term such as 'the'. Phrases such as ' the hydrogen
in the balloon', phrases which may pick out a particular
volume or quantity, can be used in the requisite identificatory
way, but the simple mass term shows a greater resistance to
the substitutions which status as a logical subject requires. I
am inclined to think that the mass terms can qualify, but a
non-referential use is more likely.

12. Strawson on subject and predicate

I pass now to a general consideration of the subject–predicate
distinction, with an eye to the contrast between subject and
predicate rather than to that between terms which do and
terms which do not qualify as subjects, whether strictly or
less strictly understood. With respect to the broader division
the difficulties may appear slight; certainly, if our task is
simply to provide a basis for distinquishing subject and predicate in such a sentence as 'Socrates was condemned to death',
we may be forgiven for feeling confident that success will require no great ingenuity. However, different though 'Socrates'
and 'was condemned to death' assuredly are, there are equally
large differences in views as to the naure of the distinction.
It is worth repeating that the 'logical' subject–predicate distinction here at issue is not identical with that drawn by the
grammarian, though the two do overlap: the category of
referential corresponds fairly closely with the grammarian's
category of *definiteness,* the latter being commonly, and in
some languages inevitably, associated with subjects. Apart
from this feature, and consequences derivable from it, perhaps
the most salient characteristic of subjects, grammatically construed, concerns the selectional relations which they bear to
verbal phrases, relations which tie subjects to other elements
of a sentence and which make for their involvement in such
syntactic operations as those of passivization and reflexiviza-
tion—for details of which see Keenan [1976]. And, at a semantic level, we have the connection of subjects with such notions
as that of *agent.*
These familiar observations take on greater significance

when we look for a contrast to languages for which a topic-comment contrast is prominent. Thus, in Li and Thompson [1976], the authors instance sentences of Mandarin Chinese which translate crudely as

> Animals, I advocate a conservation policy
> That fire, fortunately the fire-brigade came quickly
> This matter, you can't just bother one person

along with sentences from Japanese and Lahu rendered respectively as

> School, I was busy
> Elephants, noses are long

In the original sentences, the initial noun phrases are said to indicate a *topic*—a role that is sometimes morphemically marked, optionally or obligatorily—such phrases serving to present an item or items, a domain or area, about which a more specific comment or observation is then made. In translation, such a phrase as 'with respect to' is often in place with the topic.

This construction provides a useful contrast to the subject-predicate combination, the term or terms signifying the topic lacking the requisite syntactic connection to a verbal phrase which would confer upon it the status of a subject. The notion of reference has application to topical phrases, but it is the complementary union of reference with predication that concerns us with subject and predicate, a concern which, incidentally, the existence of topicalizing languages does not reveal as parochial. In the examples cited we find subject–predicate constructions invoked in furnishing specific information in respect of the general topic initially introduced.

If a logical subject is as stipulated and a predicate whatever remains on deletion of a subject in a sentence, it might seem that the distinction has been adequately drawn. However, there are, as I say, varying conceptions of the rationale underlying this division, and varying views as to the nature of the linkage uniting the two parts of the sentence. The most thoroughly worked out account of these matters is that provided by Strawson, and it is to his analysis that I now turn.

In Part II of *Individuals*, Strawson characterizes subjects and predicates both on the basis of the respective *ways* in which they introduce their terms and on the basis of the *kinds* of term that each introduces, 'term' here being used of extra-linguistic items rather than of words or phrases: the propositional style of introduction characterizes predicates in opposition to subjects, and the universals which occur as terms introduced by the former differ from the spatio-temporal particulars which, in the basic case, are the terms introduced by the latter. The introduction of terms, in either mode and of either kind, essentially involves the idea of identification, but while a subject identifies its term through some empirical fact, a predicate in general makes no such demand. So, for instance, the speaker's identifying use of the name in 'Socrates was condemned to death' will rest on his knowledge of the existence and identity of the bearer of that name, but it requires no more than a general grasp of the language to introduce the universal corresponding to 'was condemned to death', or, from the audience's point of view, to appreciate what universal is intended. For Strawson it is this asymmetry that is fundamental and that accounts for our feeling that subjects are 'complete' or 'saturated', predicates 'incomplete' or 'unsaturated'.

Initially, at least, this appears to constitute a fitting characterization of the difference in the demands made by each of the two parts of the sentence, demands to be met if we are to have a proper grasp of the role or meaning of either: unstated knowledge of the particular is frequently exploited by the user of a name, pronoun, or other logical subject, whereas in fitting a predicate to someone or something thus identified we draw upon the stock of words or phrases in the language whose meanings are assured independently of any particular such facts of existence.

However, we may have misgivings about the supposed likeness and the supposed difference between subject and predicate. The supposed likeness is seen in the use of the terms 'identify' and 'introduce' with respect to each, both subject and predicate being said to identify or introduce their respective terms. Is this coherent? Is there a relevant sense of 'identify' explicable in such a way that its association with a phrase functioning specifically as a subject, or at least as a noun phrase, is not demanded, a sense in which it allows of transference to predicate terms as well, leaving the basic difference to be located in the *kinds* of term identified? Indeed, is there any question of there being a *term*, a non-linguistic item, which such a phrase as 'was condemned to death' could be said to identify or introduce? In the second place, is the predicate really so detached from the particular, so very different in this respect from the subject? For, just as a subject may consist of a general term together with a determiner of one kind or another, so too the predicate may channel a factual commitment through the verb. Take 'The train stopped'. The ostensible involvement in the particular on the part of 'the train' may be acknowledged, but to regard the verb 'stopped' *merely* as specifying a concept is to ignore the presence of the indicative tense inflection, a morpheme which involves a particularizing element in a way which compares with the individuating role of the definite article. Since we can, conversely, discern a concept-specifying expression within the phrase, 'the train', we have a fair measure of symmetry between subject and predicate, the combination of general concept and particularizing element being present in each. Is it possible that, buried as it is in the verb, the inflection '-d' has been overlooked, the separable determiners in noun phrases, such as 'the', attracting unjustifiably exclusive attention? How should we regard the division if, as in Norwegian, article and noun united in a comparable fashion, our sentence 'The train stopped' being rendered as *Toget stoppet*?

On the other hand, it might be argued that there is a relevant difference in the two kinds of contribution made by these two possible components of subject and predicate. For one thing, use of 'the' is very much context-dependent. It serves to identify only through its engagement with the particular extralinguistic circumstances, whereas it takes no more than knowledge of the language to appreciate that the time indicated by the past-tense determination is prior to the time of utterance. That, as we have seen, is true, but to know with respect to what time the event in question is said to be past you must know when, if at all, the sentence is being spoken. The utterance itself, as something that occurs in time, is the basis for an appreciation of the intended time reference. It is trivial to say that one who understands the language will, on hearing the utterance, be provided with all he needs in order to grasp that reference, but the engagement with the particular is none the less real. It could rightly be said that the line from past tense to pastness of event is in general more certain than the line from description or name to object or person intended, but a division on that scale hardly seems suited to marking the radical distinction between such pairs as 'Socrates' and 'was condemned to death'.

For Strawson, then, a subject identifies a particular, at least in the basic case, whereas a predicate identifies a universal, a concept, or a general characteristic. Grammatical features of subject and predicate are not to be dismissed, but they take second place to the extralinguistic division; indeed, Strawson appears anxious to avoid tying either species of non-linguistic item to any one grammatical form, and would, I gather, be willing to speak of the same concept with respect to both subject and predicate of such a sentence as 'The dance was danced'. There is, of course, more than such specification in either case, and it is to the additional elements that we should look to find what is distinctive of either, even if there is symmetry on the point just discussed, but if in characterizing the predicate we are allowed to reduce it to the role of concept-specification, a similarly undifferentiated description of the subject would appear to be in order.

I have questioned whether the predicate *merely* introduces a concept, but this aside we might, as I say, ask what 'introduce' or 'identify' come to in either case, given that Strawson is prepared to speak of both subject and predicate as introducing or identifying their respective terms. In the case of a subject term, the word 'designate' provides an appropriate gloss; not so with respect to the predicate, where the interpretation is far from clear, at least if anything more is intended than that the predicate should have a distinctive meaning. Furthermore, once we start to distinguish relevant senses of 'identify', allowing that it betokens reference in the case of the subject only, we are making the question of role as important as that of the nature of any items identified. Indeed, if S can be assigned a designatory function, then it is *ipso facto* fitted to being a subject term, whatever the nature of its referent.

An invocation of role seems inevitable, given the vast difference in the syntactical character of 'Socrates' and 'was condemned to death', and more generally, the differences which separate noun and verb. In distinguishing these parts of speech, the crucial step is surely away from a differentiation in terms of the species of item to which each supposedly applies, and towards a differentiation on the basis of the kind of determination appropriate to each and the functions that go therewith. Thus, nouns combine with indices of number and individuation, verbs with indices of tense, mood, aspect, and person. Proper names and mass terms do not necessarily enter into phrases with the complexity of general term and accompanying determiner, but both serve to identify, either systematically, in accordance with their meaning (mass terms), or in accordance with a largely arbitrary, known association with their bearer (proper names).

In some languages—e.g. those of the Far East—it is easier for a word to do duty either as a noun or a verb, and even with Indo-European languages it would seem that what essentially makes for nominal or verbal character is to be located in the appropriate determinability rather than in any feature of the noun or verb radical. Contrast this with the traditional idea that nouns are names of persons, places or things, whereas verbs stand for activities, events, changes, and the like. If this looks to a difference between extralinguistic referents of nouns and verbs respectively, it is clearly misguided, since activities, events, and so forth, are not themselves excluded from the items to which nouns may be applied. The sun sets and night falls; both events, but 'sunset' and 'nightfall' are none the less nouns. Once more a supposedly uniform notion of *standing for* may lead us to seek the difference outside language when we should be thinking in terms of the distinctive roles which this conflates.

In his more recent work, *Subject and Predicate in Logic and Grammar,* Strawson again takes as fundamental the distinction between spatio-temporal particulars and general concepts, linking this with language in the proposal to correlate sentence parts specifying particulars with subject terms and those specifying concepts with predicate terms (p. 23). Particulars and concepts are distinguished in terms of their differing compatability relations; we cannot consistently relate all of a range of concepts to a single individual, though we can relate all of a range of individuals to a single concept: 'For every general character there is another general character such that no particular can exemplify them both at once; but for no particular is there another particular such that there is no general character they can both exemplify' (p. 126). If you are talkative, that does not preclude anyone else from being talkative, but it does preclude you from being taciturn.

By appealing to this underlying difference between particulars and concepts, it is thought that we can account for certain common distinctions between subject and predicate. In particular, it is held that the negatability of predicates and the corresponding resistance of subjects to negation can be explained on this basis; since, furthermore, it is natural to associate propositional combination with negation, applicability of the latter to the predicate confirms the usual location in the predicate of the linkage or mutual assignment through which the two parts of the sentence are brought together.

Once more I am unhappy about the way in which the crucial differences are concealed under the common term *specify* and the comparative indifference shown towards grammatical form. We might also note that the affinity for each other of the concept-specifying function and the function of indicating propositional combination can only exceptionally give us something to explain, since it is only exceptionally that they are separable. The exception arises with the appearance of the copula, but this is not a constituent of predicates in general. I should prefer to reverse Strawson's priorities, regarding subject and predicate as identifiable through their general roles in a way that does not require us to ascertain the character of the terms which they might be said to specify—or even to make sense of that requirement—but suppose we grant that, despite my objections, it is still right to see a general association of subjects with individuals, predicates with what is repeatable. The different roles of the two types of expression still appear to be to the fore, in that the enormous difference which we have remarked upon with respect to the two parts of 'Socrates was condemned to death' is equally striking when the subject is one that would be regarded as a universal, as with 'Smallpox has almost been eradicated', or the predicate one which carries a reference to the particular, as with 'Philby was a Cambridge graduate'.

13. Negatability as a mark of predicates

If my priorities are accepted, it would seem fitting to focus on the more formal condition of *negatability*; this is a condition thought by many to provide the fundamental distinguishing mark of predicates, and while for Strawson it is secondary, it does furnish an important link in his chain of explanations, being invoked to show why the predicate has the form of a verbal phrase and thence why it has the double function of concept-specification and propositional indication.

Negatability is not, of course, the sole prerogative of the predicate. In 'Not many people came', the 'not' bears upon the 'many' rather than upon 'came', just as 'almost' qualifies 'every' in 'Almost every seat was taken'. What of proper names? Can we not at least say that these are not negatable? Certainly, there is only a limited scope for coupling a name with 'not' in English. We can say 'Plato, not Socrates, was the teacher of Aristotle', but not the simple 'Not Socrates was the teacher of Aristotle'. The closest we come to this is with 'It was not Socrates who was the teacher of Aristotle', or 'Someone other than Socrates was the teacher of Aristotle', to take a form which compares syntactically more closely with the version with the name and without the negation.

We do not wish the supposed asymmetry between subject and predicate to reflect no more than a linguistic accident concerning the use of negation. Suppose, then, that we had the form, 'Not S is P', and that this had the sense of 'Something other than S is P'. Does the asymmetry remain? Note first that we do not have here simply a reformulation of predicate negation. 'Not John was late' implies 'John was not late' in the reading proposed, since it involves denying the identification made in the affirmative version, but 'John was not late' does not imply 'Not John was late', since it is an implication of the latter, as opposed to the former, that someone or other was late. It is important to recognize this divergence, since the occasional 'proof' that names cannot be negated tends to assume the opposite; indeed, those who indulge in this exercise regularly ignore the pertinent question of what negation could plausibly be taken to involve if we did extend its use to names.

There is more than one way in which 'Not S is P' might be understood. We could take it as equivalent to 'It is not S that is P', where it is not implied that anything is P, or we could take it as having that implication. The latter is the more natural reading, and is certainly called for with respect to the form 'Something other than S is P', the form which for present purposes is the more suitable. With this reading of 'Not S is P', there is no collapse into 'S is not P', but we find an obvious symmetry with the latter: with the predicate negation we imply that S is something other than P; with the subject negation we imply that something other than S is P. So, if the plums are not ripe, then they are something other than ripe; trivially, they are unripe. With 'Not the plums are ripe', as I interpret it, we have a declaration that some thing or things other than the plums are ripe.

Once we allow the possibility that names might coherently occur in different frameworks from those familiar to us as speakers of English, other possibilities suggest themselves. We could, for instance, make sense of the notion of a disjunctive name. Phrases of the form of 'either Joan or Jean' are held not to constitute a truly compound term, since such a sentence as 'Either Joan or Jean both acts and sings' is equivalent to 'Either Joan both acts and sings or Jean both acts and sings', whereas a genuine term would require an equivalence with 'Either Joan or Jean acts and either Joan or Jean sings' (cf. Strawson [1974], p. 8). But suppose we had a use of 'either Joan or Jean' in which it behaved as 'it is either Joan or Jean who', or 'someone identical with either Joan or Jean'; we may think here of the use of 'he or she' as a designation of a person whose sex is unknown. Then, it is clear, the interpretation appropriate to the use of the phrase as a genuine term would be as with the rejected equivalence: if it is either Joan or Jean who both acts and sings, then it is either Joan or Jean who acts and it is either Joan or Jean who sings.

More revealing is the generalization to other adverbials. The force of 'Perhaps John is in our room' may be customarily that of 'John is perhaps in our room', rather than that of 'It is perhaps John that is in our room', but the latter interpretation defines a conceivable usage. Similarly, we could have the form, 'Probably the neighbour's child is crying', with the sense of 'It is probably the neighbour's child that is crying'. And so on. It is surely only to be expected that the role proper to a subject term is one which might allow of suspension or qualification, that an identification, like a predication, could be rejected or qualified. Indeed, even if no such qualification is expressed, we might conceivably have two uses of a name to go with the relevant difference in 'fit'. This difference is marked in Japanese, where the subject of the sentence translated as 'Tokyo is the largest city in the world', would be followed by *ga* or *wa*, depending on whether the speaker's concern was to identify as Tokyo the largest city in the world, or whether he was simply saying something further about Tokyo, that city already being under discussion (cf. Kuno [1972]).

In English, a particular stress is sometimes associated with a name in that use in which, I am suggesting, it might make sense to negate it. Thus, a word in a sentence has the significance it has through its distinctness from the other words that might have occurred at that point, and giving greater stress to a given word emphasizes the contrast with these other possibilities. So, with the stress on the name in 'Andrew cleaned out the cage', we emphasize that it was Andrew, not someone else, who cleaned out the cage; shift the stress onto the verb and we draw attention to what it was that was done: Andrew actually cleaned out the cage, nothing less than that. However, stressing the name does not invariably give rise to the use in question. If, in answer to the question, 'Has anyone signed the form?', I say, laying emphasis on the name, 'Enid has signed the form', this is not like saying 'It is Enid who has signed the form', or 'Enid is the one who has signed the form', with the implication that, even if I have got the identification wrong, still *someone* has signed the form.

Although it is perhaps not possible to negate a name in English, we have seen that such an operation could be made intelligible. What does that show? Does it simply confirm the thesis that subjects are to be distinguished from predicates on grounds of unnegatability, or does it show that thesis to be too parochial, too accidental in its truth to be assigned much significance? If the thesis is that names are of their nature resistant to negation, that we could make no sense of the combination, then it is mistaken. Coupling 'not' with 'Fido' may conjure up bizarre pictures of negative objects, of matching 'anti-dogs', but we have seen that it is possible to impose upon the combination a use which is symmetrical with that involved in a negated predicate. But the negation of a name is not a name, whereas the negation of a predicate is still a predicate, an expression of the same general type. I do not know whether Strawson regards a predicate and its negation as on a par, 'is not wise' introducing a general character, 'unwisdom', in the way that 'is wise' is said to introduce wisdom, but in any case the fact that we are still prepared to call a negated predicate a predicate may be of less importance than the consideration that negation can qualify the identificatory role of the subject just as much as the characterizing role of the predicate; in these terms, we have seen, there is a striking symmetry between subject and predicate, a symmetry which does not, I repeat, call for the introduction of a new type of individual, 'not-Fido'. On the other hand, it does seem true to say that if a name could be negated in the way suggested, then it would be a significantly different use of the name that was involved, and indeed it does appear that conversion to a predicational form is necessary for the operation of negation and other adverbial qualifications.

14. Predication and assertion

This still leaves the question of the significance of the unnegatability of subjects very much up in the air, and for the moment that is where I shall leave it while I turn to another feature of the subject–predicate distinction which Strawson connects with negation, namely, the association with the predicate of the function of indicating propositional combination, an association which for me is prior to negatability and indeed definitive of predicates. What is at issue here is the traditional conception of the predicate as that part of the sentence that is affirmed or asserted of what is identified by the subject. There have been vigorous protests against this conception, put most forcefully in Geach [1965], on the grounds that we can readily make sense of the notion of an unasserted predicate. Strawson's formulation in terms of *propositional* rather than *assertoric* combination gives him a defence against such an attack, but in any case the attack is, in a sense, misguided.

It is easy enough to see how the noun 'predicate' might be held to apply independently of an assertoric use, but if the role to be associated with the notion of predication is to have any significance for us, it will surely be with an understanding that an actual use of the sentence is being envisaged. Consider the parallel with proper names and definite descriptions. If we describe 'Iceland' as a 'referring expression', this will be with an eye to an actual use of the name, just as if we say that in 'The moon is full', 'the moon' is used to identify a heavenly body, we mean 'in any live use of these words'. Imagine now someone saying that when 'The moon is full' is uttered merely, say, for its phonetic value, the speaker is none the less *predicating* the phrase 'is full' of the moon. What could predicating come to here beyond the mere mouthing of the words? If it is an act consistent with complete absence of intention or even of understanding on the part of the speaker, it hardly embodies any kind of linguistic function. We can readily appreciate how a form of words can be described as a 'predicate' when it occurs unasserted, since it will have a potential for this latter use. It is much more difficult to find a parallel interpretation for the verb 'to predicate', and yet for Geach, 'predication is effected just as much in moods other than the indicative, in questions, in unasserted clauses of asserted propositions' (Geach [1975], p. 143).

However, the above example is not of the kind upon which we should be resting our argument. More challenging and more to the usual point are occurrences of a predicate within seriously intended language, and in particular within a disjunction or a conditional. In 'Either the moon is full or it is into its last quarter', there is no asserting 'is full' of the moon—supposing the whole disjunction to be affirmed—but it is surely being predicated thereof. But again, I do not know what 'is predicated' could mean, or how it could be worth interpreting, in this connection, though once more I see well enough that the phrase 'is full' may be described as a predicate;

it is not actually being affirmed of anything, but it is clearly fitted to such a role. However exactly 'predication' is understood, it surely relates to a speech act that might be suspended, and it is in any case reasonable to class 'if' and 'or' among terms that can have a qualifying effect.

But, it may be objected, that is to ignore the fact that some kind of use is being made of 'is full' in this disjunction: it is not on a par with the mindless utterance of a parrot. Certainly, I affirm the disjunction, stating, in effect, that one or other of 'is full' and 'is into its last quarter' applies to the moon. There is no affirmation or predication of either, but a claim that one or other is affirmable or predicable. This looks trivial, but it does indicate how the kind of use involved, while more than the parrot can aspire to, is conceivable in terms of a qualified predicational use. Similarly with 'if': in 'If the moon is not full then it is into its last quarter', we make no actual predication, but affirm the predicability of 'into its last quarter' on condition that 'is not full' is predicable of the moon.

What of unasserted clauses of asserted propositions? This brings us to the subjunctive, and here too I should think it more conducive to clarity to deny predication. There is, of course, only a limited use of such a mood in English, where we have for the most part to make do with such modal terms as 'may' and 'should', forms which are rather more specific than the subjunctive, conceived of merely as the form in which assertoric force has been neutralized. Or we make use of the infinitive. Compare English 'I shall tell him to go away' with Spanish *Le diré que se vaya*. However, while grammarians never tire of telling us that modern English is largely, if not entirely, lacking in a subjunctive form, this lack proves nothing about the propriety of differentiating a reading in which the verb carries an assertive commitment from a reading in which it does not. Thus, with 'I shall let my committee consider the latest offer before it is rejected', we can reasonably speak of a subjunctive reading when there is no intention to imply the eventual fulfilment of the temporal clause, and in this case, I maintain, there is no reason to insist that we have at least to do with a predication. If, as has often been said, the subjunctive were used to express hope, fear, joy, sorrow, or surprise, we might see some content to predication, but this claim is wrong: it is the specific verb that expresses hope, say, the subjunctive being merely a consequentially appropriate form invoked to cancel the unwanted commitment of the indicative.

On Geach's way of speaking, predication is just as much present in 'Is Florence fond of Dougall?' as in 'Florence is fond of Dougall'. It is surely more useful to place questions in a separate category, indeed to distinguish between an actual interrogative use—which would correspond to actual predication—and the suspended interrogative use which would apply when, for example, a question was being cited rather than posed, as with 'No one tackled the question, "Was Wittgenstein a behaviourist?"'. Throw all four forms together and the prospects of finding anything which 'predication' might usefully identify are about as bright as with attempts at discerning a common *proposition* in declarative, interrogative, and imperative word forms. That, certainly, is not a move which leaves 'proposition' in close connection with any kind of speech act, such as that of propounding. Abstracting from particular speech acts is not a way of specifying some form of universal speech act. I should add that Geach appears to recognize that predication becomes, on his broad reading, a pretty contentless notion, the subject–predicate form reducing to no more than juxtaposition of a name with another term of unspecified role. Thus, in 'Names and Identity' he writes: 'I have described the difference between the two terms in "Raleigh smokes" by saying that "Raleigh" has the role of a name, whereas "smokes" has significance merely as serving to form this pattern: a name followed by "smokes"' (Geach [1975], p. 143). What significance that is we have yet to learn.

The centrality of assertion is, of course, a presumption of attempts at explaining a word w in terms of what it is to call something w, as with R. M. Hare's claim that to call something 'good' is to commend it (Hare [1952]). The natural belief that a grasp of the meaning of certain parts of speech is shown primarily in the use of sentences in which words are affirmed (or denied) of things is sometimes countered by observing that there are many standard uses of a word w in which nothing is actually called w (or denied to be w). So, 'I wonder if this is w' and 'Is this w?'. In the case of 'good', the thesis under attack is not to be defended by substituting a description of the relevant speech act, so as to give such sentences as 'I wonder if I commend this' or 'Do I commend this?', but the connection with the basic case is preserved by such paraphrases as 'I wonder if this is what would be called "good"' and 'Is this what would be called "good"?'. The equivalence between w and 'what would be called w', or 'what is called w', is generally unilluminating, but it is useful here as a reminder of how the central case reappears in the allegedly problematic departures from it—whatever other difficulties remain for the proposed analysis of 'good'.

15. Completeness and incompleteness

From the preceding arguments it would appear that the way is clear for one who would associate predication with assertion; if we have to make any concession, it will be only to allow that the predicate is that part of a sentence which is affirmable or assertible, rather than affirmed or asserted, of what is named by the subject. This approach has at least the merit of keeping close to our initial impression of the vast difference between, say, 'Socrates' and 'was condemned to death', and, as is surely fitting, it is directed at clarifying the distinctive *roles* of each. On the other hand, this is not the only approach that is possible at the level of language, and it is worth considering what an analysis of completeness and incompleteness can add to the discussion, especially as this appears relevant to the matter of union or linkage which is often thought important.

Subject and predicate combine to form a unity, a sentence. One conception of this fit is that expressed in Frege's notion of the completeness of objects, the referents of proper names, and the complementary incomplete or unsaturated character of concepts, the referents of predicates. The unitary character of a sentence reflects the slotting together, as it were, of concept and object, the former being by its nature suited to just such completion. In Dummett's words the concept 'is an entity whose being is to be true of some objects and false of others' (Dummett [1967], p. 231).

In 'Socrates was wise', 'Socrates' picks out something to

which 'was wise' is applied, of which it is affirmed. 'Was wise' does not in turn pick out anything. If it did, what sense could we make of predication? Should we not be landed with something closer to an identity, and an identity of an impossible kind? That is one way of looking at the matter, but Frege would see this threat of the 'two-name' theory as showing the need for a special kind of entity, the concept. We might hope to back up this view in the following way. When I state 'His car is maroon', or 'His car is 14 feet long', I can be said to have stated that the car in question is a certain colour or a certain length. We can say *of* a certain colour or length, but we need not; if we choose the former idiom, a colour or length reveals itself as just the kind of predicative entity that Frege took it to be, having perforce the kind of incompleteness that befits it for this role, rather than something that is forced into an impossible identity with a car. More generally, we can appeal to the similar use of a word such as 'type': if I say 'This tree is a laburnum', I can be said to have stated that the tree is a certain type—though omission of the 'of' is less natural here.

There are innocent ways of speaking which lend themselves to something like Frege's view, but this approach does not take us far enough for his purposes. The notion of a type, while perfectly legitimate in this connection, applies only to part of the predicate. For Frege it is the phrase 'is a laburnum' that signifies a concept, not just the noun within it. If appeal is made to the superfluity of the copula, we can simply change our example. There is no scope for speaking of a type, or of anything else which behaves in a similar way, with respect to the predicates in 'Socrates was condemned to death' or 'Walter has become a recluse'. Even without this objection we might challenge the significance of the possibility of introducing 'type' into certain of these contexts; talking of a type of tree is, after all, merely talking of trees of a certain type. It is also worth mentioning that the attempt to introduce Frege's concepts via existential generalization may fall short in the same way. We can certainly pass from 'This tree is a laburnum' to 'This tree is something or other', or 'There is something which this tree is'. However, if it is strictly the expression, '. . . is a laburnum', that 'stands for' the concept, then the generalization will surely have to be with respect to this, not just to a part of it, and despite the ease with which we may in general substitute 'something', it would seem that even this substitution is subject to strain it cannot bear in 'This tree is a laburnum, so there is something such that this tree something'. Very well, then, let us make 'something' into a verb at its second occurrence: 'This tree is a laburnum, so there is something such that this tree somethings'. This leaves us with the problem of connecting the two uses of 'something', but even larger difficulties await us with, for instance, a sentence in the passive, as 'Socrates was condemned to death'. Certainly, the supposed inference to 'There is something such that Socrates something(ed)' is not likely to win over those who are hesitant about endorsing Frege's position.

While I do not think it correct to speak of a predicate, 'is P', as having a referent, let alone as having some kind of incomplete entity as its referent, I do claim that, given a true predication, 'S is P', we have the materials for the construction of an expression which can in some cases be said to name something, and something outside the realm of spatio-temporal individuals. The possible awkwardness noted with respect to existential generalization is a reflection of differences in the kinds of expression which may be yielded, not all of which can be meaningfully assigned referents, as we shall eventually see when we come to examine the differing grammars involved.

In passing, there is one well-known difficulty in this area which is worth revealing as no more than that. If, from 'His car is 14 feet long', we can infer '$(\exists F)$ (his car is F)', how are we to read 'F'? There is thought to be a difficulty here, in that the letter is a dummy for an adjectival expression at its second occurrence, and yet this role does not mesh with its reading in '$(\exists F)$,—not, certainly, if that is to be thought of as 'for some property, F'. (cf. Sellars [1960].) But let us suppose we have a use of 'property' in which it is geared to nouns like 'length', 'temperature', 'colour', 'size', 'sex', and so forth. So, just as we can say, 'There is some length such that his car is that length', and 'There is some colour such that his car is that colour', so we shall now be able to add the more general 'There is some property such that his car is that property', with, in this use, no more of an absurd identification than is to be read into the currently possible sentences. What are the implications of this new locution—which we can take as a basis for interpreting our '*F*'? These last few sentences have not seen the creation of something from nothing, but in using 'property' in the way proposed we should be committing ourselves to no more than was already demanded by the sentences which would count as its particular instances, and the latter in turn commit us to no more than do the particular predications whose generalizations they represent. If Evans and Jones are both Welsh, then they are the same nationality, whence we conclude, in our new use, that there is some property which they both are. In thus ascending we lose in informativeness, but, as we shall later see, we come no closer to identifying entities of a troublesome kind.

In what sense if any, then, is it appropriate to speak of completeness and incompleteness with respect to subjects and predicates? The following is a possibility. An intuitive account of the subject–predicate distinction is likely to state that the subject purports to identify something of which the predicate is affirmed, and in expanding on this we shall doubtless fasten on the terms indicative of the different roles, viz. 'identify' and 'affirm'. There is, however, another asymmetry, easily overlooked: in characterizing the predicate, reference is made to what the subject has furnished, but in characterizing the subject, we make no reference whatsoever to what the predicate has contributed.

What might we extract from this asymmetry? Could we say that it points us to a sense in which a name such as 'Socrates' can be considered complete through already having done its job before the sentence is finished? By itself the subject does not constitute an assertion, but in drawing attention to or referring an audience to an individual, it has already done all that it will have done when the sentence is completed. With the predicate, by contrast, *nothing* is done until the sentence has taken further steps towards completion.

That is perhaps suggestive, but it is also an overstatement. More accurate is the following. The application of the predicate is determined by that of the subject, whereas the subject owes nothing in this respect to any other element in the sentence. In '*S* is *P*', *P* is affirmed of whatever *S* designates, but in general the converse characterization is not appropriate.

There is an ordering here, the reference of the subject having
first to be fixed before it can be determined what the predicate
applies to, and a consequent dependence of the predicate on
the subject which is not reciprocated, the subject having its
designation fixed without regard to the remainder of the
sentence. This asymmetry is obscured if it is thought that
subject and predicate must each have its own distinct referent,
differences at this level—as between individuals and concepts—
being taken as the basis for the distinction between the terms
applicable to either. I do not say that the predicate has a
referent, but I do say that it can be applied to or affirmed of
something, the very thing which the subject initially discloses:
quite simply, in 'Socrates was wise', 'was wise' is affirmed of
whatever has been introduced by the subject, so of Socrates,
not of wisdom. Even without a namelike subject we may find
a similar asymmetrical relation of dependence. In 'A crocodile
is a reptile', we have that 'a reptile' applies to whatever 'a
crocodile' applies to, so once more determination of the
intended application of the predicate awaits a prior determination of the subject. We have, then, a sense of 'incompleteness' at the level of words, but nothing to give support to a
conception of the concept as an entity with gaps.

The incompleteness with which I have been concerned is
not that which might be ascribed to just any term which fell
short of constituting a complete sentence, so to a name as
much as to a predicate. Nor have I been concerned with the
further form of incompleteness exhibited by predicates which
can be represented as having more than one gap, and where
a proper grasp of the predicate is thought to require knowledge of how those gaps are to be filled. So, an incomplete
expression such as '. . . likes . . .' is sometimes thought to
specify a different predicate depending on whether the gaps
are to be filled with the same name—'Harold likes Harold'—
or with two different names—'Marcia likes Joe'. Even if
'Harold likes Harold' were a natural alternative to 'Harold
likes himself', rather than an awkward rendering of this or of
'(One) Harold likes (another) Harold', I should not think it
appropriate to speak of the language as containing two different predicates, ambiguously represented by '. . . likes . . .'.
There is but the one predicate, doubly incomplete, on my

account, and variously completable, any differences being on the side of the speaker's intentions from occasion to occasion. Philosophers and logicians tend to hold predicates and the number of their argument places in curious awe: as though the conventions of logical theory had it in their power to render nonsensical, and not to merely reveal as an inconvenience, the proposal that, let us say, 'Jack hunted' and 'Jack hunted the moose' featured the same predicate.

The account of completeness and incompleteness which I have offered is in terms of the kind of relation of dependence which anyone concerned with structural features of language should expect to unearth. It is also in harmony with the traditional subject–predicate distinction, and accordingly with the claim that negatability defines an important feature of predicates. Thus, in the normal reading of the sentence, 'Andrew agreed', as opposed to that which would equate it with 'It was Andrew that agreed', the name takes the first and last step in identifying an individual about whom something is then asserted; there is no question of a fit of the name with someone who has been identified in other terms, hence no way that such a fit might be questioned or qualified, but it is left to the name alone to furnish the identification. So long, then, as the predicate remains the focus of any additional qualification, the subject remains undisturbed in its role, as we see in the usual readings of 'Andrew did not agree', 'Andrew perhaps agreed', 'Andrew supposedly agreed', and so forth. Suppose, however, that it became possible to attach such qualifications to the subject, resulting in sentences to be read, quite unequivocally, as 'It was not Andrew that agreed', 'Perhaps (it was) Andrew (that) agreed' and 'Supposedly (it was) Andrew (that) agreed'. Here the predicate remains constant, unaffected by the qualifications, in the sense that there is a continuing implication that someone agreed, any doubts or uncertainties attaching to the identity of the person. On such a reading, the name has relinquished its function of furnishing a direct identification, some other identification being presupposed, and to that extent the behaviour of the name becomes more symmetrical with that of the predicate, to the point that we could cease to regard it as a subject at all. 'S is P' is now true if what is P is S, it being supposed that something is P, rather than that 'S is P' is true if P is true of what is named by S, it being supposed that something is named by S.

To the extent, then, that S is envisaged as negatable, it is reasonable to deny it the role of subject. It would be a mistake, however, to suppose that negation had some unique role in this respect. It is relevant because its applicability is indicative of verbal function, but there are other adverbial terms which provide equally good indications of that function. But if that is the significance of negation, why not start from a characterization of the predicate as a verbal phrase, with a suitably contrasting characterization of the subject? Why not indeed? That, after all, is just what the naïve account of the distinction furnishes, with something like the following as the implied contrast. The choice we have with respect to a subject term is simple: we either use it or we do not. Having used it we have, as far as it is concerned, no further choices to make. A predicate, by contrast, can engage with a subject in more than one way; we do not have to choose simply between its presence and its absence, but though present it can appear with various qualifications, the qualifications being, of course, qualifications in its mode of attachment, i.e. in its basic semantic role, the role which complements that of the subject, for which some form of identification is primary.

16. The universality of the subject–predicate distinction

To what extent is the subject–predicate form a universal of language? Those philosophers who, like Russell, have thought that our predilection for thinking in terms of substances and their accidents rests on no more than an accident of syntax can derive no support from actual languages, which appear quite generally to make use of terms having particular persons and things as their referents. On the other hand, from a grammatical perspective there can be problems in identifying subjects with respect to some languages, problems which may lead us to characterize subjects in terms of a cluster of concepts, with no guarantee that all will apply whenever one is satisfied. For instance, in Schachter [1976] it is argued that with the Philippine languages the properties of subjects are distributed among *two* types of term, those in the category

of *topic*, and those in the category of *actor*, and there are
certain ergative languages, such as Tibetan, Tongan, and
Eskimo, in which a subject is not indispensable in the way we
find it in English. Thus, along with a Tongan sentence translatable as 'David killed Goliath', Edward L. Keenan cites a
sentence which omits the first name, leaving a form of words
which is not incomplete but which has the sense of 'Goliath
was killed' (Keenan [1976], p. 313). There are also languages
which make more extensive use of impersonal passive constructions, as does Dutch with sentences like *Er kan door alle
jongens gezwommen worden*—'There can be swimming by all
the boys' (cf. Kirsner [1976], p. 404)—though even with the
Tongan example, the very liberal *logical* subject–predicate
form can be discerned. There is even a language, Lisu, in which,
while topics are identifiable, subject and object cannot be
differentiated. Thus, in Li and Thompson [1976], p. 472, we
find a Lisu sentence, apparently quite representative, in which
a word meaning 'people' occurs unmistakably as topic, but
which is followed by words that can be rendered either as
'they bite dogs' or as 'dogs bite them', factors other than form
being left to decide the likely interpretation intended.

If it is said that the subject–predicate form characterizes
sentences used in saying of something that it is so-and-so, it is
difficult to see how anyone could talk about anything without
making use of that form. It is being supposed, however, that
what we are talking about is verbally identified, so the possibility arises that we should still affirm an expression of a
generally predicative character, but leave it to the context, or
some other factor, to indicate what that expression is being
affirmed of. Or perhaps that we should forgo that identifying
role altogether. Here sentences like 'There was a fire' come to
mind, where we have affirmation without complementary
identification.

This existential form is often at the centre of attempts at
showing the general dispensability of the subject–predicate
construction. However, it retains enough of the latter to dis-
qualify it as a reduction if it relies on pronouns or variables
having that function. 'There was a fire' is one thing, the
continuation, 'and it was hot', another. Here a complex verbal
phrase, as in 'There was a hot fire', can eliminate the subject

which intruded with the pronoun 'it', but we often have occasion to affirm the distinctness of individuals, and it is less easy to see how this can be accomplished without making use of forms which, like '$x \neq y$', appear to feature terms in an ineliminable pronominal role.

To consider further the possibilities, let us imagine a language having a construction which accepted both noun and verb phrase, but dispensed with the link. That, after all, would be one way of avoiding the subject–predicate form as here defined. So, suppose we are to accommodate the sentence, 'The rooms were untidy', and suppose the language has an impersonal form translatable as 'it was untidy', where the pronoun is meant to compare with that in 'it is raining', and not to allow of replacement by a more specific term. There is, clearly, a likeness with the 'there is . . .' construction. We now suppose that this impersonal form can be juxtaposed with a phrase which specifies a topic, giving us 'The rooms, it was untidy'. Here the mismatch between the number of noun and verb would indicate absence of the subject–predicate relation, yet a reading as 'The rooms were untidy' would remain a possibility.

However, such a description would appear to depend on the language's having, contrary to hypothesis, sentences of the subject–predicate type. For, what right have we to speak of a dummy subject, rendered by our pronoun 'it'? Might not a particle which we were inclined to translate in this way be merely a constant component of a verb, now without meaning—or at least without the meaning which we discern? And how might we arrive at an identification of number for verbs which did not connect with subjects? Perhaps some appeal to an existential form is possible on the last point, but to think of the ostensible dummy pronoun as one which attracts the verb away from the noun we must surely see it as appearing where a genuine subject might also occur, which requires that we be able to identify such a construction in the language. So, whether or not we see difficulties in the style of translation proposed, it would seem that the language must contain some sentences characterizable in the proscribed terms if there are to be cases in which that characterization is to be resisted on the grounds given. Incidentally, it has been interestingly suggested that 'subjects are essentially grammaticalized topics' (Li and Thompson [1976], p. 484) and even (Givón [1976], pp. 154-5) that we have in language a general movement from topics to subjects whereby a combination like 'The man, he come', with 'the man' as topic, becomes reanalysable as 'The man he-come', with the pronoun being morphologically bound to the verb—as is apparent in some languages.

If a language has both noun and verb phrases, it needs no more than their juxtaposition to guarantee the possibility of the subject–predicate combination. To exclude this, a more drastic departure is necessary, the elimination, perhaps, of one of the parts of speech essential to that combination. Since the noun is at least as dispensable as the verb, let us get rid of it. In such a language it could fall to the verb to provide the contribution made by the absent nouns, and indeed an illustration of this possibility is already to hand in the way we speak of smells. From 'smell' as a noun to 'smell' as a verb is often a short step: 'The smell in the cellar was disgusting' is close in sense to 'It smelled disgusting in the cellar', and for 'That smell was also in the loft' we have 'It also smelled that way in the loft', or 'It smelled the same in the loft'. In general, the construction with a transitive verb is difficult to dispense with, since if the object of the verb is to go—which as a logical subject it must—the verb can no longer be transitive, which leaves us with a problem of reintroducing in some other way the original connection between verb and object. In the present instance, however, the problem is less formidable. For 'I like the smell of lavender', we can say 'I like it when it smells of lavender', and for 'We smelled a faint smell' we have 'It smelled faintly to us'. Note that in either case the 'it' is a dummy 'it', not a stand-in for any more specific term.

But suppose we are called upon to capture a proposition expressive of identity; not in kind, where the same smell is merely a matter of its smelling the same, but identity with respect to an individual smell, a smell which is identifiable in terms of its location or origin (as well as by its other characteristics). It may smell the same to you in your garage as to me in mine, but we could reckon the smell produced from the rubber burning in your garage as a distinct smell from that in mine—a procedure which we certainly follow in the more realistic case of sounds. Of course, we could say that a certain article smelled to you and another smelled to me, but that is to abandon the form with the dummy subject, 'it smelled . . .', for the subject–predicate combination which we are trying to avoid. To keep the favoured form yet not lose the identity it seems we must make use of a spatial term. So, we can say we both smell the same smell, in the required sense, if it smells to you *where* it smells to me—adding perhaps 'in the same way' if there is still some uncertainty. And plurals? A plurality of smells will presumably have to be a matter of its smelling repeatedly, which, suitably understood, seems a plausible enough equivalent.

It is clear that, as with Russell's theory of descriptions, the distinction between explicitly affirmed and presupposed existence has been obliterated. 'The smell pervaded the room' becomes 'It smelled pervadingly throughout the room', or 'It smelled pervadingly where it roomed'—to give 'the room' the same treatment—which fails to indicate that we are harking back to an already mentioned smell. Moreover, the transformations result in bizarre reconstruals of our familiar terms when we take arbitrary nouns in place of the accommodating 'smell', and since in any event we have shown only how 'smell' as noun can become 'smell' as verb within a broader subject–predicate framework, it is far from clear that we could rewrite the language so as to achieve in another way what subject and predicate now accomplish. Still, there are the beginnings of a formula here. We understand identity and difference in either locational or sortal terms—taking the latter broadly enough—and it is perhaps conceivable that adverbs of time and place should be capable of taking upon themselves this all-important individuating role. As we shall have occasion to observe in some detail, the language as it stands generally allows us to redistribute the functions of noun phrases through very different parts of speech, so long as sameness is understood on a sortal rather than a locational basis; the difficulty which we have in providing alternatives for the remaining contexts no doubt helps explain why the category of physical object has been considered so fundamental.

17. Relations of dependence within a sentence

The subject–predicate distinction is, as I interpret it, an instance of a relation of dependence of one part of a sentence on another relevant to the interpretation of the sentence as a whole. More generally, I think of sentences as involving certain functional relations among their components, so that one element determines another in its application, and the subject–predicate form is a particularly important instance of this phenomenon. There is a complementary relation of dependence between noun and verb which may hold when the noun is not a logical subject, and to this less familiar topic I now turn, going back to the discussion of the indefinite article for my starting-point.

I claimed earlier that 'a' has only one meaning, which commits me to looking elsewhere for any differences which we might discern in sentences containing an indefinite description. I cannot follow W. V. Quine, for instance, who declares 'a lion' to be ambiguous as between 'some lion' and 'every lion', the former being appropriate to 'A lion escaped', the latter to 'A lion likes red meat' (Quine [1960], p. 133). But it is puzzling if I am right, since it is far from clear where the undoubted difference in meaning is to be sought. As argued above, it cannot lie in an appropriate difference in speaker's meaning, for instance.

Our first inclination may be to take as basic the use of the article in such a sentence as 'A spider made its web in the cupboard', and to consider its use in, say, 'A spider has eight legs', as a deviation from this norm. However, in line with my remarks on the meaning of 'a', it would seem that this conception of what is prior must be reversed: 'a' has, as indicated, a single meaning, and unless 'a lion' or 'a spider' is compelled by the remainder of the sentence to apply to a single thing, if to anything, or to satisfy some other such restrictive condition, the application of the phrase will remain as unspecific as is consistent with its general sense, as characterized earlier.

The article is, as has been said, a very weak word; it is unable by itself to determine a particular one of several readings of the phrase in which it occurs, but, in a certain sense, it lends itself to a number of readings dictated by other elements in the sentence. Even this is inaccurate, since the other readings relate to the sentence overall, but the main point is this: there is no need to explain why 'a spider' is not to be understood as characterizing a single, actual spider in 'A spider has eight legs'; since the sense of the article does not require this reading, and since there is nothing else in the sentence capable of imposing it, the sentence receives the interpretation appropriate to this lack of further determination. By contrast, the predicate, 'made its web in the cupboard', does make demands not made by 'has eight legs', demands which account for the legitimacy of the inference that some actual spider made its web in the cupboard. Since the phrase with the article will receive that interpretation which accords it maximum generality or indeterminacy, the onus shifts: it is the particular implications that have to be accounted for, 'a spider' being no more than a *general term*—with an index of singularity.

Again, compare 'I know a man who thinks he knows everything' with 'I dislike a man who thinks he knows everything'. 'Dislike' makes sense here without restricting 'a man' to a particular man, and so it is powerless to impose this interpretation. We thus tend to read the sentence in a way which does not match the version with 'know', a verb which clearly does require just such a restriction. If, in the former case, the speaker wishes to make it known that he has in mind a single individual, he would normally recast or expand the sentence. For instance, 'A man whom I dislike thinks he knows everything', or 'There is a man I dislike who thinks he knows everything'. Similarly, the preferred reading of 'She looks like a horse' would be the non-specific reading; if comparison with an actual horse is intended, a formulation along the lines of 'There is a horse which she looks like' is called for.

It is not, then, as if the indefinite article had a number of meanings—'a certain', 'any', 'a single', 'some or other'—so that, having assigned to it the reading in which it equates with 'any', for instance, we could then proceed to combine it with suitably general predicates. Rather, we look first to other elements in the sentence to find out how, if at all, they result in a more determinate *application* of the indefinite description. If the application of the description remains indeterminate, the article will still be in place as an index of singularity, because, typically, it will be a mater of the application of the description to a single thing on any of the occasions which fall under the characterization given by the verbal phrase: with the repeated or arbitrary applicability of that phrase goes a like applicability on the part of the indefinite description.

In a language in which, like Turkish or Malayan, a general term, N, can occur without a determiner, having the force now of 'an N', now of 'the N', there will not be two meanings of N, any more than there are two meanings of the corresponding noun in English, but in such a case it is simply left to other parts of the sentence, or context, to provide the determining information. By way of contrast, consider the pronoun 'you', which can be straightforwardly described as ambiguous. If someone says, 'You should see a doctor if you are always breathless', there may be some uncertainty in his audience's mind: does he mean *me*, or just that anyone so afflicted should see a doctor? Sometimes the sense will impose one or other interpretation—for instance, 'You're looking well today' can have only the more restricted reading—but there are sufficiently many contexts in which either interpretation is consistent with the rest of the sentence for us to be able to locate the ambiguity in 'you' itself.

The main line of my argument verges on the trivial. If we detach from a general term everything other than an index of number, then of course we must look elsewhere if we are to find factors which determine the application of that term more narrowly—as applying to a single thing at some past time, for instance. However, as with any such near-tautology, there are the underlying matters of fact that give it point: in the present case, the fact that this is the extent of the indefinite article's contribution coupled with the fact that there are general terms in this sense and that we can appropriately look to the remainder of the sentence to find this information. We are accustomed to the idea that a determiner such as 'the' can combine with a general term, but we are less likely to see the verb as having an analogous effect. Perhaps if the verb preceded the noun, as in a *VSO* language, we should be more receptive to this possibility. There would seem to be some logic in this order when the subject is indefinite, since we have in that case a term which narrows the choice coming first, whereas initial occurrence of the indefinite phrase leaves open a number of alternatives which have subsequently to be eliminated. In English we obtain this order with the use of the terms 'there' and 'it', along with various phrases, mainly locational, which are felt to be particularly in place when the identification conveyed by the noun phrase does not antedate awareness of the setting or activity in which the person or thing to which it is applied is found or engaged, as with 'Out of the hole came a large rat'. In many languages there is a tendency for more definite terms to occur near the beginning of the sentence, less definite terms towards the end, and sometimes a different positioning in this respect may actually make for the relevant reading. Thus in Finnish, the sentence, *Hevonen on pihalla*, is rendered 'The horse is in the yard', whereas *Pihalla on hevonen* translates as 'There is a horse in the yard'. Similarly in Mandarin Chinese, where it is necessary to remove the subject of a transitive verb from initial position if an indefinite reading is desired for it. This can be achieved by prefacing the noun with a verb, *yŏu*, meaning 'exists' (cf. Li and Thompson [1975].)

It is worth combining the point about the dependence of indefinite descriptive phrases with the earlier observations concerning covert reference and the indefinite article. The two forms of determination come close to one another in some cases, but we can still see a difference in the different sources from which they derive. In the sentence, 'A candidate was summoned', the predicate 'was summoned' introduces a degree of determinacy, in so far as it implies that it is a matter of the past existence of an individual. This is not enough to ensure that the speaker has in mind one candidate rather than another, though it is not unlikely that one who is in a position to use this form of words should be in possession of the requisite knowledge. A covertly referential use presupposes a suitable degree of determinacy, but since that use may or may not then be made, it enjoys an independence not shared by an indefinite description when some other element in the sentence confers determinacy upon it, there being in the latter case no choice as to how the description is to be construed.

With respect to the sentence, 'She wants to marry a millionaire', I suggested that there might be two readings in contrast with the one in which it is a matter of just any millionaire: the speaker might know of the millionaire's identity, or he might know only that the woman did have a particular such person in mind. I associated covert reference with the former possibility, but it might well be extended to cover the latter; indeed, it is quite useful to have a uniform treatment of the case where we at least have independent knowledge of existence, so where the rephrasal as 'There is a millionaire whom she wants to marry' would be in order.

With this more general interpretation in mind, let us look again briefly at the question of the number of meanings of the indefinite article. Take the sentence, 'A cat could not squeeze through this opening'. If 'could not' is to be read as 'would be unable to', then the reading is correspondingly general for the noun and the sentence rephrases as 'No cat could squeeze through this opening'; if, on the other hand, 'could not' is to be taken as a past definite, 'was unable', then the application of 'a cat' is correspondingly determinate; here again there is symmetry of the affirmation and negation in respect of the implication of existence, 'could not' making the same specific demands as the affirmative 'could'. What we do not have is the former use of the verb with the latter use of the noun. As our analysis stipulates.

Such explanations confirm the thesis that an indefinite description has the indeterminacy of a general term, and if there may or may not be covert reference in a given case, that appears to be a matter of two possibilities being covered by a single form of words, but not possibilities which define distinct meanings of the words. This is indicated by the absence of impact upon truth: the sentence, 'I am looking for a dictionary', would not be held to be true in one sense, false in another, depending on whether a particular book was intended. But there are more difficult cases. Consider 'Every morning a nurse came to the house' and 'A neighbour occasionally helped out', where the speaker may be thinking of repeated acts on the part of a single person, or allowing the possibility of different persons being involved on the various occasions. Here we might wish to assign covert reference a determining role, in that the predicate will in that event have the first of the two readings imposed upon it, while if there is no knowledge of a single individual, the sentences will be true in their intended interpretations just so long as some individual or individuals behave in the ways stated.

If covert reference did feature here as a determiner of scope, then it certainly would take on greater semantic significance, but once more I think we have to do with a form of words that is indifferent between the two cases, rather than words for which we have a shift in meaning matching a possible change in truth value. I should also say the same with respect to such a sentence as 'We both saw an alligator', which covers the case in which a single alligator is intended as well as that in which it is not. Again, the assessment, true in one sense, false in another, does not seem to be correct. However, it must be acknowledged that there are instances in which we come close to being forced to admit two readings of the indefinite article, simply because we are hard pressed to locate the ambiguity elsewhere. Such a case would be 'A disobedient child will be punished'. I suggest that the source of the ambiguity lies in 'disobedient' rather than in 'a'—is it a matter of *has disobeyed* or of *will disobey*?—and in general I know of no contexts which definitely overturn the univocality thesis, but here and elsewhere, if only peripherally, that thesis can become difficult to defend.

If we wish to extend the subject–predicate pattern to take in more than the types of logical subject considered, the extension is likely to be in terms of covert reference. So, it is only if we have such reference that such an assertion as 'A guide will accompany you' can count as 'saying of some guide that he will accompany you'—vague though this conception admittedly is. Again, consider phrases of the form 'some *F*s'. It does not in general appear correct to regard these as logical subjects, since we tend to meet with the reverse dependence, where it is the predicate that determines applicability. In 'Some crystals may have formed', for instance, there is no implication that there are or were any crystals, but the uncertainty implicit in the modal qualification is transmitted to the implication of existence. On the other hand, with 'Some crystals may soon disintegrate', we can, if we have the relevant knowledge, be affirming this possibility of certain crystals, in which case we may characterize the assertion as being of subject–predicate form.

There is an interesting comparison and contrast here with Geach's treatment of sentences containing 'some' in his illuminating 'Subject and Predicate'. The comparison is in the way Geach detaches terms like 'some' from their accompanying noun, regarding them as combining with the predicate in specifying the kind of identity of reference intended with respect to subject and predicate (Geach [1950b], pp. 478-9). This is perhaps not far from the way in which I see the predicate functioning *vis-à-vis* a general term, but it is only when 'some' can form an appropriate referential unit with its noun, or behaves as such unaccompanied, that I classify the sentence as subject–predicate in form, whereas Geach appears not to allow this case but to treat the general term as itself the subject. In part this is a matter merely of definition, though the question of what is named by a general term is difficult, and is acknowledged as such by Geach (op. cit., p. 471).

In general, it would seem to be the predicate that counts in determining the behaviour of universal affirmative propositions. There are several cases to consider under this heading, and a proper treatment calls for an analysis of, at least, 'all', 'any', and 'every', but I shall confine myself to some brief remarks on just 'all'. First, if the subject phrase contains a determiner apart from 'all', this determiner, perhaps in conjunction with the remainder of the sentence, may generate an implication of existence. There is such an implication with 'Five children were rescued' and 'The children were rescued', and it remains in force if we preface either by 'all'. Suppose now that 'all' is joined with a bare plural, as in 'All candidates for honours must take an extra year'. Again I think we look to the version without 'all'; indeed, we may bypass the noun altogether and consider what the predicate dictates, concluding in this instance that existence, either present or future, is not implied, though with another predicate another inference may be in order. Thus, 'All candidates have been informed of the examination time-table' will imply the existence of candidates in a way which matches 'Candidates have been informed of the examination time-table'. Or *very* nearly so. It must be allowed that it may make some sense to hold the former to be true despite, or indeed because of the non-existence of candidates, and perhaps the same could be said even in the example with 'the'. However, although there may be some uncertainty as to what it implies, I think it is essentially to the sentence minus the 'all' that we must look to settle implications of existence with respect to the subject term.

Determination by the verb extends to noun phrases at other points in the sentence. Thus, the sentences, 'He was a four-star general' and 'A general was forcibly retired' represent very different operations, as it were, on the common term 'general', but they result in the same determination as regards existence. If we wish to make a further distinction we can appeal to covert reference, or knowledge of identity at second hand, but as long as we take into account no more than what can be read off the actual words used, we shall light upon this shared character. This should not come as a surprise. I have claimed that we are to look to the verb to discover how the application of an indefinite description is to be understood. This is appropriate if the description is in either subject or object position, there being an obvious symmetry in this respect between both noun phrases in such sentences as 'A straight beats a flush' and 'A boy caught a fish'. That is, 'beats' and 'caught' have similar repercussions on each member of the associated pair of nouns. It would be strange if the verb 'to be' were an exception here, having implications only for the subject term—though of course it is true that the term which follows is to be described as a 'complement' rather than as an 'object'.

The assimilation just suggested is of some interest in connection with other attempts to see uniformity in the behaviour of general terms which, grammatically, enter into sentences in very different ways. For instance, with 'He was a four-star general' and 'A general was forcibly retired', Frege would see a common role, but would be thinking in terms of a suppressed copula in the latter. Given the generality of the verb 'to be' and its connection with the basic idea of application, this is a step in the right direction, but there is no call to read in any particular verb to justify the assimilation which I propose. That is, I regard the notion of application as fundamental in any account of the use of general terms, a practical grasp of when such a term applies and when it is to be withheld surely being essential to an understanding of words of this kind. It is just such application that the verb 'to be' may convey, but the same determination can be provided by more specific verbs, if less directly.

The point bears repeating. We seek to characterize the behaviour of certain noun phrases which, on the surface, have a range of very different roles. Frege shows us one way in which a consistent pattern may be discerned, but at the cost of requiring us to pretend that the sentences have a structure which they lack. However, we find that the basic notion of application is sufficiently general to transcend the relevant differences, so long as verbal phrases generally can be enlisted as determinants of application. This is to credit such phrases with a role more naturally associated with terms which, like demonstratives, appear more intimately associated with nouns, but we have already seen how the two forms of deixis present a common contrast to the general nouns and verb stems with which they respectively combine. And, of course, there is no complete assimilation, the subject–predicate distinction, as we have drawn it, showing one important difference.

As a final application of the analysis, consider the following phenomenon. While there is nothing amiss with the sentences, 'A cry was heard' and 'A street has been closed to traffic', there is a disconcerting incompleteness about 'A cry was loud' and 'A street is wide'. To explain the difference we might naturally think to assign 'a street', say, the same role in each of 'A street was closed to traffic' and 'A street is wide', and then look for grounds for excluding the latter combination, or in general for excluding verbs with the non-episodic reading. This, however, is to suppose that 'a street' does enjoy the relevant independent use, that having assigned it such a use we can then consider possible completions into a sentence. In the light of the preceding discussion, a very different observation is called for, at least as a starting-point: the sentence, 'A street is wide', perforce has the general sense and is false.

To expand on this, we have seen that a sentence such as 'A house is not a home' will, because of the lack of an appropriately restrictive condition, automatically assume the more general reading. However, the sense of the predicate must allow this. With 'A street is wide', our common knowledge leads us to resist the general reading, in which it would parallel 'A street is a road in a built-up area', and on which it would be false, and yet there is insufficient specificity for a reading in terms of a particular street to be in order: what we know of streets militates against the general interpretation, which is what would be indicated for want of anything to determine it otherwise, but conditions for the particular interpretation are not fulfilled. Hence the need for a prefatory 'there is', or a word such as 'some': 'There is a wide street' or 'Some street is wide'.

It might be thought that the notion of presupposition has a part to play here. After all, if someone says, 'A street is wide', we might feel like protesting that this is the first we have heard of the street in question. However, it may also be 'the first we have heard' of the stone in question when someone says, 'A stone shattered my windscreen', yet this does not prompt the same reaction. It is more a matter of a requirement of specificity not being fulfilled that results in oddity, rather than a use of a form of words to make an affirmation about something when the existence of that thing has neither been explicitly stated as a preliminary nor is otherwise evident.

However, if elimination of the general reading is to leave us with an acceptable interpretation, specificity may have to be provided in more than one respect. Consider 'A man was clean-shaven'. This could have the more general reading, amounting to 'Men used to be clean-shaven', as in the context, 'In those days a man was clean-shaven', but both temporal and spatial specificity are otherwise called for. We have the latter in 'A man there was clean-shaven', but the predicate, which signifies a state, is less acceptable than would be an episodic term. This latter sentence is not, of course, totally unacceptable. It is less odd if the point of the utterance is, as it were, to give a value of x for which 'x was clean-shaven' is true, rather than to fill in a detail in a description of a given setting. However, if the latter is our aim, if a sentence occurs as part of a narrative, then it is required to relate to the relevant scene. An indication of place will clearly help in this respect, as will a tense inflection which makes it clear that it is a matter of something that happened during or at the time in question. Thus, we could say, 'An umbrella was broken', where an act of breaking is being reported—French *fut*—and we could say 'An umbrella there was broken', where 'was broken' signifies a state rather than an episode—French *était*—though again the latter makes greater demands on the linguistic context if it is not to sound unnatural. What would be far less likely to engage appropriately with the setting is 'An umbrella was broken', where the static reading is invoked. This discussion could, incidentally, be carried on in terms of unquantified plurals, or of mass nouns rather than count nouns. Whereas 'Dust was white' is relevantly incomplete, 'Dust was thick on the floor' passes muster.

As a related question, we might ask what is amiss with 'A procession will be at noon' and 'A reception was at the Grand Hotel'. Does the indefiniteness of the subject account for the awkwardness? Not entirely, certainly, since the same subject with a different verb may be acceptable: 'A procession will take place at noon', 'A reception was held at the Grand Hotel'. Does the fault then lie with the verb? Again, it cannot be just that, since the same verb may go quite happily with a different subject: 'The procession will be at noon' and 'That reception was at the Grand Hotel'. The sentence, 'A reception was at the Grand Hotel', is like 'A cry was loud' and calls for the same remedy—either an appropriately episodic verbal phrase or a more definite subject. In fact, the verb 'to be' can be of service here, but only when it signifies the kind of event which can befall movable things: we do not have 'A gap was between her teeth' or 'A dispute was at the works', but we do have 'A duke was at the Grand Hotel' and 'A fire-engine was at the corner of the street'. If the sense of the noun is not such as to allow it to combine with the verb in this use, then the required specificity will have to come from elsewhere, as, for instance, via a 'the' or a 'that' in the subject phrase. Combining 'to be' with 'there' is also a possibility, 'there' preventing 'to be' from having this rather special sense and giving rise to a phrase having a more suitably episodic reading denied the bare copula. So, 'There was a dispute at the works'.

As with much of what has preceded, this last discussion has involved deciding how various overall effects, various features of a sentence, are brought about, where the possible factors responsible are both numerous and difficult to assess. I shall now leave this uncertain area and conclude by surveying the more general theme which I have been elaborating and which, I hope, stands some chance of survival despite the errors that have no doubt found their way into the details of its variations.

It is quite generally recognized that understanding sentences calls for an understanding, not merely of individual words, but also of the structural relations which connect them. A variety of such relations may be identified: the modifications of nouns by adjectives and verbs by adverbs, the relations of verbal phrases to definite and indefinite noun phrases respectively, and so forth. It is these latter relations that I have fastened upon, but I regard them as instances of a more general type of structural relation, that, namely, in which one term can be said to determine the application of another. This relation, thought of as covering application in a variety of respects, certainly appears to be of a kind which should engage us, and this for at least two reasons. First, we have the immediate connection with truth, relations of this type playing an obvious role in any explanation of the truth conditions of a given declarative sentence. Here too we note how another semantic notion, that of reference, is very much to the fore, a particular realization of the notion of application being that of reference, whether explicit or covert. Second, the relations in question are very much relations to be found in actual language, not merely in some theoretical representation thereof. So, for instance, there is no appeal to a step-by-step construction of sentences which might risk rejection on the grounds that we do not in fact proceed in that way; or which, alternatively, might risk losing any clear meaning as a result of a dismissal of such a consideration as irrelevant. The kind of ordering involved is logical: in the sentence, 'Tim's parents have retired', we have a dependence of 'parents' on 'Tim's', in that the latter dictates the application of the former, and a like dependence of 'have retired' on the whole phrase, 'Tim's parents'. One such relation may presuppose another, in that it will be incomplete until the latter is specified, but no temporal order of construction is demanded.

This approach tends to be in contrast with that of logicians and even of linguists. The problems of analysis posed by such sentences as 'A straight beats a flush' and 'I dealt a flush' are likely to be met simply by having recourse to universal and existential quantification respectively, with perhaps in addition a claim that the interpretation of these noun phrases is indicative of certain deep-structure derivations. For instance, it is suggested in Perlmutter [1970] that it is because 'a' comes on the one hand from 'one' in the deep structure, on the other hand from 'any', that it has the different readings it supposedly has. I have no objection to representing 'A straight beats a flush' within current logic in the way proposed, but the overall agreement at the level of the sentence does not necessarily carry over to a mapping of individual terms onto one another in such a way that we could affirm an equivalence in meaning with respect to 'a' and 'any', an equivalence which would force us to acknowledge more than one sense for the article. Generality can be expressed in a number of ways, and to understand what is characteristic of 'a' we must appreciate how a certain absence of determination results in the phrases in which it occurs making just that contribution which they do make in this regard. This is important, not just for the sake of accuracy on the particular point, but for understanding how the language works with respect to, for instance, questions of scope. Furthermore, the explanation given leaves no room for rival accounts of meaning which postulate deep-structure origins in terms of, say, 'any': in failing to reflect the dependencies to be found in the actual pattern of usage, such an account bypasses precisely those factors which give a necessary and sufficient determination of meaning.

4

SUBJECTS AND EXISTENCE

It was suggested above that the sentence, 'A crocodile is a reptile', behaves analogously to a sentence with a name in subject place, in that a similar ordering is involved, the application of the predicate being restricted by that of the subject. If this ordering is taken as definitive, we might think of the subject–predicate pattern as extending to practically any sentence containing a grammatical subject, whether or not covert or identifying reference is involved. On the other hand, there is some point in reserving a special category for the referential cases, if only to separate them from the less straightforward constructions, such as those in 'A car was not provided', 'A bus should be along soon', and 'A cat may have killed the parrot'. If there is no question of a parallel with the use of a proper name, no 'saying of some cat that it may have killed the parrot', for instance, then we have a departure from the favoured pattern which may be seen as problematic. If we are not asserting P of S, what are we doing? How do the two parts of the sentence fit together?

It is true that the question, 'Of what is the grammatical predicate being affirmed or denied?', will not meet with a satisfactory answer in cases such as these, but with the shift in perspective brought by the preceding analysis, what we should be asking when reference is absent is how the application of the noun phrase is determined by the remainder of the sentence. So long as we can answer questions about the way in which a general term interacts with other elements in the sentence, we have a basic understanding of the way the sentence functions, even if there is no determination of a general term in such a way and at such a point as would make for the subject–predicate pattern, logically understood. And it is evident enough how negation, modal auxiliaries, and adverbs like 'supposedly' can result in a suspension of what the verb would otherwise imply with respect to the grammatical subject. It is not so much that the subject takes on a different use in such a sentence, where a different use might relate to, say, 'standing for' a different kind of object, as that its standard or positive use is simply suspended. Roughly speaking, when the grammatical subject is definite, a logical subject, it has a determining role *vis-à-vis* the predicate; when the subject is indefinite, the dependency reverses, this role shifting to the predicate, whose various possible qualifications can then have corresponding repercussions upon the subject.

If we are interested in systematization, we might seek a canonical representation of sentences of this class in which an operator such as 'It may be the case that' attaches to a sentence of the simpler form, a sentence which, without the qualification, would carry the existential implication. Thus, in saying 'It may be the case that a cat killed the parrot', we perhaps make it clearer that it is not a question of coupling a qualified predicate with a namelike use of 'a cat', but that the qualification affects the assertion of the whole sentence, or through qualifying the assertive force of the verb qualifies the applicability of the subject. Again, this formulation shows how such sentences can be rewritten to feature a constant factor, in the form of the embedded sentence, and a varying operator, a reflection of the fact that in many such cases we have forms of words to be invoked when we are at some distance from circumstances which would warrant the simple indicative.

The resources of the language generally provide us with a natural enough conversion to the canonical form, but a greater difficulty is presented by 'want' and related verbs. We can put the problem in the following terms. Our basic understanding of a noun such as 'saw' is shown in affirmations and denials, whether explicit, as in 'This is a useful saw', or implicit, as in 'The saw was blunt' or 'I dropped a saw'. Sentences containing auxiliaries such as 'must', 'may', and 'should' can then be understood as introducing a modification of this role; they may present complications, but complications within the basic framework. However, in such a sentence as 'I want a saw', or, to take another example, 'They fear a resumption of hostilities', it may not be clear how any such complication of the basic pattern is to be discerned. In what way might there be a qualified affirmation of the applicability of the noun phrase?

It is important to specify what the problem here is supposed to be, to make clear that it is not just a 'problem' to be resolved by opening one's eyes to the wide range of constructions showing the same relevant behaviour as the supposedly exceptional intentional verbs, or by abandoning an unsupportable preconception, such as the preconception that in using a noun phrase we must always be talking about something. But given that the problem is to be thought of as suggested, how is it best put to rest? There are various models which we might think to invoke. For instance, 'wanting' is close to 'lacking', and there is nothing puzzling in the fact that my lawnmower may lack a vital part without that part's existing; here it is the implicit negation, as in 'being without' or 'not having', that makes for the failure of the existential implication. Again, and of greater relevance, 'want' has a variant, less peremptory in tone, in 'would like', which suggests a comparison with sentences relating to the future. With the sentences, 'I shall plant another row of carrots' and 'I may plant another row of carrots', 'another row of carrots' falls under the restriction to intention or possibility that modifies the verb and we can say only that the applicability of this phrase is intended or anticipated, or is a possibility, by contrast with 'I planted another row of carrots', where the verb implies determinate existence. With wanting to have a saw it is likewise with respect to the larger unit that the qualification imposed by 'want' attaches in the first instance, but it is transmitted to the phrase occurring within as object: the future realization of the relevant possibility is desired, and therewith, in effect, the future applicability of the embedded noun phrase. This is the model for the simple 'I want a saw', the desire being not merely that there should be a saw, but that it should be mine, though the bare 'to be' may be in order with, say, 'want a miracle', as with 'fear (expect) a miracle', which can be analysed in the same way. Again, looking for is looking to find and hoping for is often hoping to have, and in either case we have to do with an infinitive which overlaps with the future tense in its use and for which a more or less uniform analysis is possible.

The above paraphrases are hardly revelatory and they do not put an end to all the pertinent questions. It is of some use to expand 'They fear a resumption of hostilities' in such a way that its dissimilarity to the paradigm, as 'They are frightened of a snake in the loft', is more apparent, and the consequent assimilation to this pattern with provision of an intentional object of fearing accordingly less tempting. The suggested form of analysis may achieve this, at the same time indicating more positively that the use which the verb implies for the noun is of a familiar kind and continuous with its basic use. However, we may now be confronted with a clause, 'that there will be a resumption of hostilities', which threatens to intrude a still more intractable object of fear.

This more substantial question will engage us at a later stage. For the rest of this chapter our concern will be with an aspect of the more straightforward preliminary: occurrences of logical subjects—actual or potential—where association with a verb conveying a 'propositional attitude' threatens to produce a context in which elementary principles of identity go by the board. Fortunately, it proves easy to ward off this threat, and therewith any need to make our usage conform to any complex set of principles governing the behaviour of logical subjects. The considerations which lead us to this conclusion are unsurprising—where they are not already familiar—and while the analysis of the relevant noun phrases may bring in unexpected elements, the overall impression is that any serious problems in this area are going to be hard to come by.

Something similar holds for statements of existence, another setting in which noun phrases are seen as troublesome and which will have our attention before we pass to intentional contexts. Certainly, discussion of such statements tend to be somewhat unreal, philosophers' eyes being so often closed to any factors not directly related to the restrictive framework in which existence is commonly formalized. Once more it is the obvious considerations that appear to emerge as the most fruitful.

18. Existence

Statements of existence are among the most notorious of those statements which are thought to take us outside the subject–predicate form: if someone says, 'A higher mountain

than Everest does not exist', he can hardly be alluding to a
certain mountain whose non-existence he then proclaims. It
is surely when, as here, existence is being denied, that a departure from that form is most apparent. There may be some
distortion involved in regarding 'A new civic centre exists' as
on a par with 'A new civic centre has been opened', but there
does not appear to be the same pressure against referring to
something when affirming its existence as there is when denying it. If this asymmetry could be sustained, it would look
very much as if 'not' rather than 'exists' were responsible for
any distinctions in reference which separate the two forms:
reference to a foolproof lock is not required of the sentence,
'A foolproof lock does not exist', but nor is it required with
'A foolproof lock has not been fitted to this door', and quite
generally when the negation can be relocated in a 'no' preceding the subject. Such negative sentences can be handled without the need to think in terms of a special referent, called
upon to furnish a subject for the attribution which cannot be
found among referents of the customary kind, and the doctrine that 'exists' is not a predicate simply gives way, in so far
as it is correct, to a mundane observation about negation. If
this were all there were to the doctrine, it would involve a
mislocation of record proportions.

As far as affirmative sentences are concerned, the plausibility of the doctrine varies from example to example. We
might well come across a sentence beginning with a sign of
intended reference, as in 'A certain volcano exists which . . .',
and we may well have in mind a particular shop when we say
'There is a grocer's shop down the road which is open on
Sundays', not to mention the obvious cases of reference and
qualified existence introduced earlier, as in 'The Pharos of
Alexandria no longer exists' and 'This library would not have
existed but for the generosity of our benefactor'. On the other
hand, the question, 'Which pulsar do you mean?', hardly
seems appropriate in response to the assertion, 'A pulsar
exists', and the corresponding query is even less in order in
response to 'Flying saucers really do exist'.

We have two main verbal phrases to investigate, 'there is'
and 'exists'. Let us begin with the former and let us ask what
light is shed on the function of the accompanying noun phrase

by the analysis of 'There is a pulsar' as 'Something is a pulsar'. With sentences of this latter type there is normally no predication involved. In asserting, 'Someone has left the door open', we should not usually be asserting *of* someone that he had left the door open; not usually, though 'Someone is not eating up his dinner' shows another use. We do of course imply that 'has left the door open' is predicable of someone, but we do not actually thus predicate it. Similarly, if there is no covertly referential use of 'a book' in 'A book is missing from this shelf', then predication too is absent. Such lapses of predication are common enough, and they are just a reflection of the absence of complementary reference, predicates (in the strict sense) needing subjects as much as subjects predicates.

We are entitled to include covert reference under reference in this connection, since the former as much as the latter threatens any natural interpretation of the claim that 'exists' is not a predicate. With respect to 'Something is a pulsar', then, it is likely that the predicate which occurs in actual predications, such as 'This is a pulsar', occurs here only potentially. This makes for a continuity between the two cases, however, which sets each apart from another construction, namely that in which an adverb of place is coupled with 'is a pulsar', as in 'Here is a pulsar'. In the latter we are certainly not predicating 'is a pulsar' of something named by 'here'; nor, on the other hand, is 'here' a stand-in for a more specific designation of an object; the sentence is like neither 'Something is a pulsar' nor 'This is a pulsar'.

What holds of 'here' holds also of 'there', where this is given its full value as an adverb of place, as when pointing one might say, 'There is a pulsar'. When, furthermore, the 'there' is weakened, so that its deictic element is lost and we have a statement of what there is rather than of what is there, it is still this use that is the model, not that to be found in 'Something is a pulsar'. Rather than with this we might see a comparison with 'Somewhere is a pulsar'. Whereas 'something' does duty for a more specific identification of something of which the following phrase, 'is a pulsar', might be affirmed, the role of 'somewhere' is quite different; it generalizes not with respect to logical subjects, such as 'this', but with respect to more definite spatial terms, such as 'here', 'there', and 'within our galaxy'. However, while there is no predication of 'is a pulsar' with respect to something named by 'here', this is not to say that 'a pulsar' is not being applied to something by one who says 'Here is a pulsar'. On the contrary, what I have described as the basic use of such a general term is as much a possibility in this context as when the speaker supplies a noun phrase indicating that to which the general term is to apply. It is a mistake to suppose that a predicative use is the only alternative to a referential use of a noun phrase—and hence to suppose that, since 'a pulsar' is not a logical subject in 'There is a pulsar', the logical form of this sentence can be made plain only in a formulation making use of a (potential) predicate. Those who speak of 'there is' as a 'second-order' predicate—through being ostensibly a predicate which attaches to a first-order predicate—are guilty of this kind of confusion. To repeat: when joined with an adverb of place, a descriptive phrase is not used as a predicate, so anything which completes it into a sentence while maintaining this use is not to be deemed a predicate of a predicate.

The analysis in terms of 'something', along with the general framework in which it has been located, has exerted a considerable attraction upon philosophers and logicians. It is felt that bedrock is reached with atomic sentences, sentences containing a proper name and associated predicate, and that existential sentences are to be thought of as somehow derived from these, whether in the form, 'Something is an F', where we replace the proper name by a pronoun, or in the equivalent 'There is an F'. We can grant a fundamental place to the ascription of characteristics to individuals, to things which might bear names, but that does not make for a recognition of any one linguistic form as in some way primitive, since there is more than one way in which this fundamental activity might translate into linguistic form. Thus, it could hardly be maintained that proper names are more basic elements of the language than are general terms, so that 'Fido snored' enjoyed priority over 'A dog snored', and the work done by demonstratives might be taken over by spatial and temporal adverbs of the appropriate kinds. With respect to existence there can be overall sameness despite differing ways in which particular and general receive expression; certainly, 'There is an F' need owe nothing to the existence of sentences exemplifying the favoured paradigm.

The comparison suggested with 'here' can be extended to sentences with other verbs as well as with other spatial terms. Consider the sentence, 'An old man sat in the rocking chair'. Here the action or state reported may be one among a succession of such within the person's known history, an action or state ascribed to someone identified prior to the time implied in the predication. If, however, we shift to an ordering in which the locational phrase precedes, as with 'In the rocking chair sat an old man', the implication that the person was identified prior to the sitting is contra-indicated; it is rather that the verb indicates how the man first came to our attention, or how he was when first we became aware of him. A similar absence of prior identification is likely with 'Near the gate stood a policeman'. The locational phrase directs us first to a place, at which there is someone describable in a certain way, whereas placing the noun first is appropriate to the case where identification precedes the action reported. There is, needless to say, no hard and fast distinction here, though if 'stood' is taken as a preterite, and not as signifying a state, we should have to say 'A policeman stood near the gate', rather than the version given.

The verb 'to be' is the most general of the verbs which, like 'stand', 'sit', 'lie', 'come', and 'arose', can be used here, and 'there' as an adverb of place gives us one of the most general locational terms. What of 'there is' in its existential use? Just as with 'Here is a comfortable spot' we purport to identify an area where 'a comfortable spot' is a fitting description, and similarly with a locative use of 'there', so we might suggest that the existential 'There is a comfortable spot' amounts to saying that somewhere the description is applicable, or, more generally, simply to affirming the applicability of the description. However, there is a further function with which we can credit 'there', which is notable for its retention even when a specific locational term occurs, as in 'There is a comfortable spot at the bottom of the garden'. I remarked earlier that we could say, 'A fire-engine was at the corner of the street', but, not so readily, 'A dispute was at the works', disputes not being the sort of thing which might move about from place to place.

Coupling 'there' with 'was' will exclude the inappropriate reading, giving us a form which can be invoked alongside a locational term, as with 'Here there was once a library', in preference to 'Here was once a library'. More generally, having lost any locational role, 'there' in this use serves to occupy a position which is not desired for the accompanying noun phrase, to act as a filler which releases the noun phrase for a more appropriate positioning in the sentence; 'there' enables us to dissociate the verb 'to be' from an immediate connection with the grammatical subject, and thus from the inapposite interpretation which that verb would then have.

It is the relatively formal, contentless use of 'to be' that we find in 'there is', not that use to be discerned in 'Has the post-man been yet?', or even that in 'The train is now at platform 6'; and, as I say, it is to prevent 'to be' from being taken in this other way that we combine it with 'there', its force in this combination being as with the copulative use, so merely to indicate the applicability or affirmability of the accompanying noun phrase. But not necessarily to affirm that phrase *of* anything, since it may be completely detached from any such use, as with 'There is a difference between an American and a Canadian accent', or 'There is still a possibility that he will change his mind'. Here we are not thinking in terms of something's being a difference or something's being a possi-bility—the kind of case for which the existential quantifier, 'For some x, x is a . . . and . . .', makes sense. I mentioned in chapter 2 that, in the absence of identification, nothing was lost in the transition from 'The height of the tower is 125 feet' to 'The tower is 125 feet high'. Similarly, 'There is a difference between an American and a Canadian accent' can be rephrased as 'An American accent differs from a Canadian one'. Saying there is a difference is saying they do differ, the affirmation given by 'there is' being re-expressible in the straight verbal form. We may also note that, if something of greater substance is involved, something with respect to which we may more readily speak of identification, 'exists' may be more in place. Compare 'There was an agreement between the ministers' with 'An agreement existed between the ministers'.

I say that the verb 'to be' has a purely formal use with 'there', being indicative of no more than affirmation. But now

I apparently find myself in a position similar to that in which Frege was placed by his analysis of existence, only for me it is expressions that have come to play the part of concepts. That is, I suggested that to construe a statement of existence as being about a concept was possible only if such a statement were replaced by a certain form of paraphrase, and even then it would not be 'exists' that attached to a designation of a concept, but only some such phrase as 'has an instance'. Similarly, while 'A black hole exists' may rephrase as something like '"a black hole" is applicable to something', the analysis is at the level of the sentence. 'Is applicable to something' is not a synonym of 'there is', but is clearly, unlike the latter, a predicate of words.

What has primarily to be acknowledged is that, if the noun phrase attached to 'there is' is not used with either covert or identifying reference, then 'there is' does not say anything about anything, so neither about words nor about concepts. This is not to say that it attaches to words only in the sense that it is followed by or juxtaposed to a noun phrase. It is related to that phrase in determining how it is to be taken, and what it determines in this respect is as I have stated, namely, the applicability or affirmability of the noun phrase, something which we have seen to be determinable by verbal phrases generally. In this respect we can continue to profit from the comparison with 'Here is a pulsar'. When this is asserted, 'here' will pick out a region of space and 'a pulsar' will be applied to something in that region, while 'is' will make explicit that the application is present and affirmative. This it can achieve without having in any sense to be about either word or concept.

There is a question that has intruded from time to time, the question of the alleged logical superfluity of the copula. Let us stop to look at this, by way perhaps of confirming what I have said about the role of the verb 'to be'. What does 'logically superfluous' mean here? Presumably that, as does happen in many languages, the same information could be conveyed in a version without the copula—as with 'Me Tarzan'. Could it be that the copula is superfluous in that it provides the most general or the most likely fill-in for the gap which would result from its deletion? That, clearly, is no sense of 'logically superfluous'. On this analysis, it is only if we suppose what is allegedly superfluous to be reinstated in, say, 'Their house a bungalow', that we can interpret the sentence, whereas genuine superfluity requires either that the copula make no contribution at all, or else that its function already be duplicated by some other part of the truncated sentence, that we have redundancy in the usual, full version.

And is there redundancy in 'Their house is a bungalow' or 'A crocodile is a reptile'? Does either 'Their house a bungalow' or 'A crocodile a reptile' in effect eliminate one occurrence of a duplicated or otherwise unnecessary term or function? The answer is 'No'. It would clearly be wrong to say that, as the language now works, the copula was otiose in the original sentences, when it makes all the difference between a sentence and a non-sentence. Juxtaposition of two noun phrases could be variously interpreted. An infant might naturally think in terms of a corresponding spatial juxtaposition—a relation covering *on, in,* and *by*—intending 'Lady bicycle', for instance, as meaning that a lady is on, not that she is, a bicycle. Adding the copula eliminates such a possibility and contributes a positive alternative. We could say it was superfluous only if the standard interpretation of a bare noun phrase in that position were the one which the copula made explicit. This is so for some languages, but English is not amongst them.

What is true is that, as I say, the basic use of a common noun—or adjective—is to be explained in terms of its affirmation of or application to things, a function which is variously imposed upon it by elements in the sentence, and which 'is' makes explicit. It is accordingly natural to have this as an automatic reading unless an interpretation to the contrary is explicitly signalled. The verb 'to be' is, of course, not superfluous as a sign of tense, and it can find room for the expression of differences in aspect, as in the difference between 'He was unreasonable' and 'He was being unreasonable'. There can also be an indication of mood, but beyond such general features the contribution of the verb is purely formal: in 'is a bungalow', the applicability of 'a bungalow' is affirmed or made explicit; there is no expression of anything that anything *does.* And this is true of 'to be' quite generally, aside from the special use noted. There is not a different use of 'is' in 'This is a pulsar' as against 'There is a pulsar', whether locative or existential; the same formal use is at stake throughout, any difference being traceable back to differences in 'this' or 'there'.

I have compared sentences of the form, 'There is an F', with sentences containing an initial locational phrase, such as 'In the rocking chair sat an old man', there being in neither case any concern to report an episode in the known history of an antecedently identified person or thing. With 'There is an F', any question of identification is likely to pertain to the question of what it is that is thus describable, in the sense that the direction of fit relates to the identity of the thing to which 'an F' is to be fitted, not to the identity of the F to which 'there is' is ascribed. With 'A fortune-teller is now at the fair', we have a possible contrast with the individual's whereabouts at other times, a contrast which is quite absent from 'There is now a fortune-teller at the fair'. Here we note that 'There has always been a fortune-teller at the fair' does not imply anything as to the identity of anyone, does not imply that the same fortune-teller has been there over the years.

I said above that reference is not invariably absent with respect to 'There is an F', a covertly referential use of the noun phrase being particularly likely when further locational information is provided, as with our example, 'There is a grocer's shop down the road which is open on Sundays'. However, this is not in the least surprising or troubling, for it is surely not right to describe the noun phrase as the *subject* of 'there is'. As has just been indicated, the sentence no more has a subject than does the form of words, 'There is a grocer's shop', with 'there' used locatively. In whichever way 'there' is taken, I can be said to have in mind a particular grocer's shop in speaking thus—it may after all be the case that there is a particular thing that I am describing—but the characterization given by the noun phrase is, as it were, the end of the business, not a necessary preliminary to delimiting a predicate in accordance with the ordering which we found to define the subject–predicate form. In this respect 'exists' may offer a contrast. We do have 'there exists', which falls in line with 'there is', but, especially when further qualified, 'exists' can join with a noun phrase in such a way that its application can be said to be dictated by that phrase, as with 'A wall has existed there for centuries', when we suppose there to be covert reference to a single wall. We notice too a similar range of contrasts which bring this into comparison with 'A fortune-teller is now at the fair', rather than with sentences with 'there is'.

What is it that distinguishes the members of G.E. Moore's well-known duo, 'Tame tigers growl' and 'Tame tigers exist'? One obvious, but none the less important difference, is that 'exist', unlike 'growl', is not something that tame tigers do, not something they go in for. In this instance we might well appeal to the form 'There exist tame tigers' to show how 'exist' has at best a dummy subject, with 'tame tigers' more in the nature of a complement. It is not only 'exists' and 'there is' that fail to signify an event or episode within the history of a creature or thing, something which it does or which befalls it, but the same observation can be made with respect to the verbs in such sentences as 'A dam was constructed', 'A portrait was painted', 'An explosion occurred', and 'A meeting was held'. Constructing a dam is not a matter of engaging in activities directed towards an already existing dam, but the relevant activities will have the dam as outcome. Again we note that the question, 'Which one do you mean?', makes sense with respect to these noun phrases.

But now some tension may be felt with respect to what was said of 'A wall has existed there for centuries'. This is not like 'An angler has been fishing there for years', where fishing is something that can be taken up intermittently and at a variety of locations. Existing is not in a comparable way something that the wall has been there engaged in without respite—not, as I say, something which a thing might be said to *do*. Granted, but it is the temporal condition that is the focus of possible contrasts, as indeed is better conveyed by 'A wall there existed for centuries', which does not suggest the wrong sort of contrast.

19. *Logical subjects and* oratio obliqua

So much for noun phrases as they occur in the company of 'there is' and 'exists'. Of existence generally we shall see more in the next chapter; for the present I shall continue with an examination of other contexts in which the behaviour of noun phrases has been a matter of dispute. I said earlier that while a qualification such as 'possibly' or 'probably' bears upon the predicate rather than the subject, it is conceivable that we should have the latter use. On one view, something like this latter use is more than a possibility; not so much that 'possibly', say, is not to be located in the predicate, but that, through qualifying the predicate, it results in a suspension of the standard identifying use of the subject. If true, this would be most unexpected. In saying 'Their garden is possibly larger than ours', or 'It could be that their garden is larger than ours', I incur the same commitments, and indeed make the same general use of the descriptive phrase, as if I state categorically, 'Their garden is larger than ours'. As the language now works, the modal qualification is not capable of taking the subject term in its scope, in the sense of making either the existence or the identification of something thus denominable no more than a possibility, but the logical subject stands firm against any qualification that the modal might impart to other terms in the sentence.

Consider qualifications with 'probable' or 'probably'. There are three relevant uses which an associated noun phrase might enjoy, depending on whether existence is or is not implied by it, and, if it is, on whether or not use of the phrase rests on knowledge of identity. None of these uses is *induced* by 'probably', but the operative factors are quite independent. I may assert, 'Virginia's friends would not recognize her now', with or without knowledge of the woman's friends, and nothing is altered in my use of the subject phrase if I weaken this to 'Virginia's friends would probably not recognize her now', or to the version with the adjective 'probable'; the modal qualification would not, for instance, extend to the question of the existence of the person's friends.

Furthermore, the truth of a probability judgement is in no way dependent on the form which the reference takes—to take another misconception which is as prevalent as that concerning scope. Suppose that most Belgians speak French but that the majority of Europeans do not. That is not a consideration which makes for a difference in the truth values of 'This Belgian probably speaks French' and 'This European probably speaks French', said of the same man. There is no presumption that relevant reasons must find their way into the form of identification used. If the speaker shows by his use of a particular description that he is aware of a factor which is relevant, then this is likely to be reflected in the assessment of probability which he offers, but if he should shift to a form that is less informative in this respect, there is still no call for him to revise his assessment to match the broader class. He is not stating a generalization about *any* Belgian or *any* European, and his failure to make explicit a relevant item of information need not mean that he has lost sight of it.

As far as reference is concerned, the situation is similar with the kinds of qualification to be found in such sentences as 'Reginald is suspected of being a hypochondriac', 'Our next-door neighbour is supposedly a medium', and 'Mr Clark thinks that this picture is lovely'. In any standard use of these sentences there will be straightforward reference on the part of the name 'Reginald' and the phrases 'our next-door neighbour' and 'this picture'. Again we seem to be dealing in trivialities, but since dissent from them is at least as common as agreement, we can hardly let the matter rest here.

We are, then, to investigate further the mode of occurrence of the proper name or other ostensible referring expressions in contexts typified by clauses governed by such verbs as 'believe', 'know', 'think', 'say', and 'suspect', along with related adverbial constructions. The question commonly and rightly to the fore in such investigations is that of the possible substitutability in such contexts of one expression by another having the same reference, since unrestricted substitution seems to be required if the ostensible referring expression is to stand its ground in the face of the qualification introduced by the verb, supposing its use to be as in contexts in which it is clearly functioning as a straightforward referring expression. Thus, while it appears far easier to allow than to deny reference with respect to the name 'Michael Innes' in 'Edward thinks that Michael Innes wrote *Appleby Plays Chicken*', we may have second thoughts when we consider whether the truth of this proposition guarantees that of the version with 'J.I.M. Stewart' in place of the *nom de plume*, 'Michael Innes'.

We have a principle of extensionality for referential terms which I shall designate as E and which states that if a and b are one and the same, then whatever is true of a is true of b. Accordingly, if substitution of 'b' for 'a' results in a change in truth value, we are obliged to conclude either that the reference of the names is different, or else that the names do not function referentially in the context under consideration. Thus, if we accept that Michael Innes and J.I.M. Stewart are one and the same person, and affirm 'Edward thinks that Michael Innes wrote *Appleby Plays Chicken*', but reject 'Edward thinks that J.I.M. Stewart wrote *Appleby Plays Chicken*', on the grounds that Edward is unaware of the author's true identity, then we shall have to deny referential occurrence to at least one of the names as they occur here, or else abandon the principle of extensionality.

We have already seen that, if the notion of a referential term is taken broadly enough, substitution is not invariably legitimate. Use of a definite description, and even of a name, may be backed by bare knowledge of or belief in existence, without the requisite knowledge of identity, in which case we are not always entitled to substitute for a term in the former use a term which, whilst applying to the same thing, presupposes knowledge of the latter kind. Hence the questionable status of the argument, 'He thinks the place where this wine comes from is east of Bordeaux; the place where this wine comes from is Cahors; therefore, he thinks that Cahors is east of Bordeaux'. If introducing the name in place of the description means implying a knowledge of identity which the person in question lacks, that substitution has resulted in a distortion of the original thought. To ensure that the principle of extensionality separates the good from the bad, a suitably restricted reading of the key phrase, 'true of', is called for, a sentence containing 'a' being reckoned true of a if and only if it really is *of a* that what is said is said; that is, if and only if it is supposed that identifying reference to a is made by the use of 'a'.

As we saw, it is not necessary that every valid inference involving the relevant terms should observe this restriction; other principles of inference may require less. On the other hand, it is not easy to see how this more cautious formulation could be faulted. However, apart from the version which we have implicitly rejected, there are others which are not beyond attack. Quine, for instance, has formulated the following principle of the *indiscernibility of identicals*, which I shall label E': 'given a true statement of identity, one of its two terms may be substituted for the other in any true statement and the result will be true' (Quine [1961], p. 139). That the two principles E and E' are discernibly non-identical is plain enough. Thus, the former is so basic, we find we can go little beyond repetition if we attempt to give it a justification: if a and b are one and the same then of course whatever is true of the one is true of the other, for there is then no 'other'. The argument is essentially just a variant of the law of identity—a thing is what it is—with the need for care in our reading of 'true of' providing the only complication. With E', by contrast, it is not so evident that exceptions cannot slip through: a and b may be the same thing, but it does not necessarily follow that whenever 'a' occurs you can substitute 'b', *salva veritate,* since the result may not qualify as saying something of the same object with merely a difference in the designation thereof. For this we must further require that 'a' and 'b' occur *as* designations. Indeed, E' is two stages removed from the correct form, E, since it does not even demand what might be termed reference in a weaker sense, where unique existence, without knowledge of identity, is all that is required.

The unreliability of E' is quickly shown. For instance, it may be known to me that the captain of the golf club is the same person as the treasurer of the tennis club, but while I may wish to be the treasurer of the tennis club, it does not follow that I wish to be the captain of the golf club. I could so intend the statement that my wish to hold a certain office was expressed without use of the definite description as a designation of a particular person, the person currently holding that office; *a fortiori*, there will be no question of replacing one designation of that person by an alternative designation. It is quite clear, however, that while the first formulation of the principle of extensionality remains intact, the second version is violated. And so much the worse for that version. As indicated, it is precisely at the point where we are unable to appeal to the trivial justification available for E that we find a divergence between the two, and there is nothing surprising in the possibility of a breakdown of E' once we see the kind of example which may have this consequence.

The example of the *nom de plume* is similar. Someone, Edward, who observes a book entitled *Appleby Plays Chicken*, with the author's name given as 'Michael Innes', may be said to believe that one Michael Innes wrote the book, but only in the sense that he believes that that is the author's name, or at least pseudonym. If this is the sum total of his knowledge of the author, the question of using an alternative designation of that author in 'Michael Innes wrote *Appleby Plays Chicken*' does not arise. On the other hand, to the extent that we consider that identifying reference has been made, reference to someone whose identity is known, to that extent, I shall argue, we can agree to a rephrasal in terms of the name 'J. I. M. Stewart'.

This suggests a hypothesis (cf. Cartwright [1971]). If we encounter occurrences of names which cannot be supplanted by other names with the same reference, then these names do not occur referentially. And similarly for other forms of referential term. That is, E can be held without exception, any seeming counter-example being in fact an exception to E', the relevant name either not being used referentially, or being mentioned rather than used. (The use/mention distinction is not an entirely happy one, but its shortcomings do not concern us here.) If this hypothesis proves correct, any sense of paradox will be dispelled, since E' furnishes a principle on which we can cheerfully yield without damage to our intuitions.

It is certainly true that the resolution of a seeming paradox often does proceed in accordance with this hypothesis. Consider the following familiar route to such paradox. We take a trivial premiss, one of the form 'a is a', and suppose that for any person N with his wits about him it should be correct to say 'N knows that a is a'. Thus, 'Norman knows that the capital of Australia is the capital of Australia'. In accordance with a true identity, in this instance, 'Canberra is the capital of Australia', we then infer a conclusion which is far from obvious, indeed possibly false: 'Norman knows that Canberra is the capital of Australia'. However, if this inference is to cast doubt upon E, we must be able to construe the description in the seemingly nugatory statement of knowledge as referential at the occurrence for which a substitution is made, and this is not something which can automatically be assumed. Norman will no doubt assent to the proposition, 'The capital of Australia is the capital of Australia', but quite possibly just as an instance of 'a is a', as a generality requiring no knowledge of identity, or even perhaps of existence: whatever is the capital of Australia, if such there is, is the capital of Australia. No threat to E is posed by an inference on this basis; only E' suffers.

Life is so simple for those philosophers who always know that the last bus is the last bus and the shortest way home the shortest way home, but for most of us this knowledge does not come easily. Once we tie the description down to a referential use at its first occurrence, and at its second to a non-referential use, the triviality of the statement of what is known comes up for questioning. Is it always obvious that a is a? Not at all. We can easily imagine ourselves saying, 'It was not obvious to those present that the Vicar *was* the Vicar, so effective was his disguise'. Similarly, I can on a dark night fail to realize that my own house is my own house without being prey to uncertainties about the law of identity. It is not even necessarily trivial to claim that a is a—it depends how you put it—and it might well be surprising that the fastest man over a mile is the fastest man over a mile, just as I may have no idea that a given word means what it means. There could be an occasion for saying, 'Norman does not know that the capital of Australia is the capital of Australia', namely, when we are using the first description as an alternative designation of Canberra, so might equally have said, 'Norman does not know that Canberra is the captial of Australia'. True, it may be needlessly mystifying of us to use a formulation which suggests that the ignorance is the ignorance of the mentally defective, but we are not worried about the infelicitousness of the phrase used, only whether its unsuitability is such as to yield a conclusion whose falsity would compromise E.

Similar considerations apply to the exploitation of other trivial truths, such as 'The oldest spy is a spy'. The universal assent with which this would be greeted does not imply that the oldest spy is known by us all to be a spy. Spying may be a hazardous career, but at least there is no *a priori* disclosure of one's role as soon as one qualifies for such a title as the oldest, the shrewdest, or the most incompetent spy.

Threatened violations of E can be fairly systematically evaded in this way, but there are further possiblities. First, let me formulate explicitly three general positions which have been adopted at one time or another on the use of names and other referential phrases in these troublesome contexts. (1) The names which occur in *oratio obliqua* and the like never occur referentially, so there is no violation of E. (2) Names may occur here referentially, but inferences in accordance with E never take us from true premisses to a false conclusion. (3) Names in these contexts are not purely referential, but the way reference is secured is relevant to the truth or falsity of the proposition in which they occur. It is with this last possibility that the phrase 'referentially opaque' is sometimes associated, with the meaning 'not purely referential'. However, it is sometimes taken as equivalent to 'not referential at all', a very different reading. I have yet to encounter an undoubted instance of an opaque context in the sense specified by (3), but there is no lack of contexts which the description fits in the second interpretation.

(3) is in one respect the most attractive alternative, in another respect the least. It is attractive, in that we may well feel that the exact choice of term is important to the accuracy of a report of a person's words or thoughts, that we must restrict alternative designations to those which the original speaker would have been in a position to adopt. June says, 'I am hoping that my cousin will come to tea', but if she is unaware that her cousin is her husband's mistress, we might think it incorrect to report her as 'hoping that her husband's mistress would come to tea'. On the other hand, the position is unattractive in a major respect. Since it concedes that

reference is being made, it invites application of the principle of extensionality, but since it allows that truth value can be a function of something other than accurate reference, it envisages the possible violation of that principle.

Both (1) and (2) endeavour, in totally opposed ways, to preserve *E*. With an important emendation, either might be associated with Frege: there is reference on the part of a proper name in *oratio obliqua,* but what the name stands for is its sense, not its customary referent. This is Frege's doctrine, not simply in respect of contexts of belief, knowledge, suspicion, and reported speech or thought generally, but also with adverbial final clauses beginning 'in order that', subordinate clauses introduced by other conjunctions, such as 'whether' and 'when', and clauses depending on verbs like 'command' and 'forbid' (Frege [1892a], p. 68). Thus, as well as the example just given we might add such a proposition as 'Robinson sold the portrait in order that his nephew might be financially independent'. Knowing more about the nephew in question, we might embellish the reference: 'Robinson sold the portrait in order that his ungrateful and scheming nephew might be financially independent'. But will this do as an accurate statement of the man's purpose in selling the portrait? 'Obviously', Frege says, 'the purpose is a thought' (op. cit., p. 68)—*offenbar ist der Zweck ein Gedanke*: thinking that his nephew would in consequence be financially independent, Robinson sold the portrait. Certainly, if the man had been in a position to accept the expanded description, he might well not have aimed at the realization of the thought as thus expressed. Whereas (3) allows that reference to someone is involved in this use of 'his nephew', however important the form it takes, Frege wishes to deny any reference whatsoever to the person in question. As before, we might wish to say that, if 'his nephew' stands for anything, it stands for the man's nephew, but Frege's claim is that it stands for something quite different, namely, its sense.

We shall consider shortly whether reports which deviate to this extent from the words featured in the original thought or utterance can be reckoned acceptable. First let us look at the specifically Fregean complication, the supplanting of the customary reference by the sense of the name used. The very notion of a name as having sense is one which we have found relevantly mistaken, but without resurrecting difficulties in this quarter we can point to uncertainties in the present approach. How is the use of the phrase 'stands for' (*bedeutet*) to be justified? Frege is thinking in terms of a parallel with contexts in which the name has its customary reference, contexts in which we may vary the name without affecting the truth value, so long as identity of reference is maintained. In indirect speech the customary referent is not being picked out by the name, but we can, without disturbing truth or falsity, replace a name by another having the same sense. The name must stand for something, and the necessity for a restriction to terms having a common sense indicates this sense as the constant referent of the name.

There is some analogy between the principles of extensionality appropriate to terms which have reference and meaningful terms which do not, but acknowledgement of the analogy does not require us to speak of a phrase such as 'his nephew' as *standing for* its sense, rather than simply as *having* a sense. If 'stands for' is to be used in a way which matches the use appropriate to proper names in direct speech, we should surely require that the referent be presented as a subject of predication, but the sense of a name or description is not something of which the remainder of the sentence might significantly be predicated, even supposing there were any question of the relevant predication in *oratio obliqua*—a supposition that might be encouraged by the misuse of the notion of predication exposed earlier. But is it fair to read such an implication into 'stands for'? Might I not be guilty of supposing that my use is the only one possible? If our concern is with the phrase as it applies to proper names as logical subjects, then my characterization is far from arbitrary, but in any case something like this reading is necessary if there is to be any point in insisting on *stands for* rather than the simple *has* a sense, so the objection is not so easily avoided.

Frege, clearly, is thinking in terms of *reporting* someone's belief, as presenting it for consideration without as reporter participating in any of its commitments. Would it help to construe the overworked 'stands for' in this sense? With respect to a thought, perhaps it would, but with respect to the sense

of a word or phrase, surely not. I can make no sense of 'reporting the sense of the phrase "his nephew"', nor of 'reporting
the sense of *P*', where *P* is a sentence—unless this means
'reporting that the sense is such-and-such'—and the briefest of
reflections on the grammar of the construction should indicate
that this is not simply the result of a weakness on my part.

What we are left with, it seems, is the claim that a potential
referring expression occurring after conjunctive 'that' has
sense but not reference; not that such an expression *stands
for* its sense, but perhaps that it *stands in for* any other expression having the same sense. This is to claim, in effect, that
oratio obliqua is subject to similar restrictions as those which
govern reports in *oratio recta*. Thus, when I report, 'Terence
said that Beth had been ill', there is allegedly no normal referential use of the name 'Beth' by me, but, in the emended
version that has emerged, it is in this respect as if I had uttered
the explicitly non-committal 'Terence said, "Beth has been
ill"'. Matters are not, of course, as simple as this, since for
Frege it is problematic whether, in saying 'Terence said that
Beth had been ill', I can claim to be giving an accurate report
of the person's thought. No appeal to an identical referential
use of the name 'Beth' is to the point, as far as the customary
reference is concerned, and since I can perhaps associate with
the name only what for me is its sense, I may well depart from
the original thought in this respect. Which simply shows that
the notion of sense has no part to play in an account of what
is understood or communicated in such a case. What counts is
identity of customary reference.

As far as reference is concerned, the conventions which
govern the form, 'Terence said, "Beth has been ill"', are surely
not extendible to the indirect version. Nor can it even be said
that the difference lies in a licence to vary the original referring phrase, provided only that sameness of sense is preserved.
If we consider what determines choice of such a phrase in
relating another's thought, we find that factors to do with
the reporter's current situation may loom large. If a neighbour,
Mr Clark, favours me with the judgement, 'I think the picture
in your hallway is lovely', I may, if the picture is now before
me, say 'Mr Clark thinks that this picture is lovely', or even
'Mr Clark thinks that this hideous picture is lovely'. Leaving

aside this extra qualification, it is clear that the pressure is towards an adjustment of the original designation to fit in with my present position. Similarly, when talking to the person who has been referred to, we should use the pronoun 'you' in preference to the original name or description. Someone says to me, 'That colleague of yours is not to be trusted', but conveying this sentiment back to the person in question I say, 'It has been said that you are not to be trusted'. I cannot take over the original designation as it stands. (A good account of the considerations determining mode of reference is given in Urmson [1968].)

Such familiar adjustments show plainly enough that occurrence in indirect speech is no bar to the appropriation of a name by a reporter for his own referential purposes. Clearly I, as the person reporting, bear some responsibility for the choice of referring expression; there is very often a presumption that I am using it to refer, as indicated by the way I vary it to meet changes in circumstances, and by the appositeness of the question, 'Whom do you mean by "*N*"?'. There is not invariably such a presumption, as we shall see, but if the noun phrase does not allow of a non-referential use in this connection—as with 'that'—or is an established name of something, there is no suspension of reference.

This commitment is particularly plain when continuity of reference is being maintained within and without reported speech. If I say, 'The nurse informed the doctor that she would be late', I purport to pick up the reference of the unproblematic 'the nurse' by the pronoun 'she' within the clause. Consonant with this is the awkwardness attaching to the use of a name which one is not in a position to employ referentially. If someone, Terence, says 'Beth has been ill', and I have no idea who this person Beth is, I may stay with a direct speech version, 'What Terence said was "Beth has been ill"', or I may eliminate the seemingly referential use of the name by speaking of 'someone Beth' or 'someone called "Beth"'. Lacking all relevant knowledge, I should not tend to use the straightforward indirect speech version.

It is also relevant that we must exercise some control over the choice of referring expression if what we say is going to be a correct statement of what someone believed. If a person is under the mistaken impression that 'Tutenkhamen' is the name of a contemporary pop star, his sincere avowal, 'Tutenkhamen is receiving a lot of publicity', is not reportable as 'He thought that Tutenkhamen was receiving a lot of publicity'. Not at least felicitously, though usage is not entirely uniform here, and we might say that the person was 'under the impression that Tutenkhamen is a pop star', meaning no more than that he thought that 'Tutenkhamen' was the name of some pop star, and not implying that he was under a misconception concerning a long-dead Egyptian monarch.

We have rules for the sequence of tenses in reported speech, rules which, in English (and in German), may require us to depart from the actual words uttered by the original speaker. So, if John's words were 'Beth has been ill', we report this as 'John said that Beth *had* been ill'. The change in tense does not lead us to say that the speaker's thought has been distorted. On the contrary, failure to adjust the original tense may result in an incorrect report. Why, then, should it be supposed that we cannot make similar alterations to referring expressions to match spatio-temporal shifts in perspective? Of course, we may not have the knowledge required to duplicate the speaker's reference, but then there is the direct citation, without intrusion of our own use, of the person's words. I am not intent on forcing anyone to pretend to knowledge which he lacks, but only saying that the construction under discussion is in general earmarked for use by those who have the relevant knowledge.

But if the general view advanced under (1) is extravagant, it would surely also be wide of the mark if we were to conclude that, provided only that the noun phrase succeeds in singling out the right object, no restriction is to be imposed upon possible substitutions. It is true that indexical expressions may have to be altered to accord with a change in surroundings, but there are other forms of referring expression, and other arguments to show that more than incongruity may result from unrestricted substitution. To take an example of a familiar type, a man could believe that Paignton was in Torbay, but think that the town he was in—Paignton, no less—was not in Torbay. Wanton substitution will surely leave us saying that he both does and does not believe that Paignton is in Torbay, a contradictory state of affairs.

Variations on this *reductio* are frequently trotted out, but unfortunately not in the company of a vital if elementary distinction concerning the application of negation to the verbs 'think' and 'believe', 'N does not think (believe) that x is F' is generally interchangeable with 'N thinks (believes) that x is not F'. 'He doesn't think you stand a chance' means 'He thinks you do not stand a chance', whereas 'He didn't mention that you were here' is not interchangeable with 'He mentioned that you were not here'. When so used, 'He doesn't think Paignton is in Torbay' has the force of 'He thinks Paignton is not in Torbay', and it is not absurd to hold that this may be a person's opinion, even though he also thinks that Paignton *is* in Torbay—though if we know this to be the person's opinion we may well hesitate to use the first version. *He*, of course, holds beliefs which cannot be reconciled, but imputing these beliefs to him does not involve *us* in contradiction, which is what is needed if the inference which we draw in accordance with E is to be to its disadvantage as a logical law. To take another example, why should a person not believe that a certain river begins in the north-west, yet at the same time think that it begins in the north-east? There is no necessity that he should correctly relate the different stretches of the river with which he is familiar, nor that his judgements as to origin should be unimpeachable. What we must not do in such cases is suppose that belief in the negative proposition automatically makes for disbelief in the affirmative proposition, a supposition which the common equivalence between 'He does not believe that x is F' and 'He believes that x is not F' understandably encourages.

Similarly, just as a person may believe that wine which he has tasted is claret, so he may also be of the opinion that the same wine is burgundy—not because it has dulled his feeling for the principles of logic, but because he has sampled the wine on different occasions. However, there are still cases where a damaging contradiction appears too close for comfort and where the pressure is relieved only by a more careful construal of the verb. Consider. A woman is prepared to say of a certain friend, 'Brian does not speak German', but on an occasion when she does not recognize this friend she overhears him speaking German and would be prepared to assent to, say, 'That man over there speaks German'. In such a case I think we should be happy to say, 'She took Brian to be speaking German', but less happy to say, 'She thinks Brian speaks German'. If the thought or impression is reported in episodic terms, then the sense of paradox is diminished. It is like the case where tasting the wine on one occasion leads us to give one verdict as to its type, whereas another taste at another time leads us to a conflicting verdict. Embarrassing for a connoisseur of wines, no doubt, but not the stuff of paradox. But now, once we move to the non-episodic 'thinks' or 'believes', we generate a certain tension with the other belief. We may well be unwilling to say, just on the strength of the woman's episodic impression, that she thinks that Brian speaks German, simply because the habitual 'thinks' clashes with those occasions when she is prepared to assert an opposing view. Usually we pass readily enough from the speaker's 'I think' to 'she thinks', but in such a case 'she thought' may be all that is strictly licensed: on this occasion she thought that Brian spoke German, though it is still accurate enough to say that she thinks he does not. In a similar way, conflict may be lessened by insisting on an episodic reading for the verb in the subordinate clause: she thought that Brian spoke German, it is true, but spoke German on that occasion rather than spoke the language more generally.

But is it even true to say that on the particular occasion she thought that *Brian* was speaking German? I should wish to say 'Yes', but I feel the force of the opposing inclination. However, I suspect that this inclination becomes a conviction only if we concentrate on one point of view, that of the person whose thought is being recorded—in effect taking 'think' as equivalent to 'think to oneself'—and adopting something like the vantage point of the novelist, with his 'inner eye' turned to the thoughts in the form they occur to the person. In thus giving prominence to the speaker's or thinker's way of formulating his or her thought we lose sight of other equally relevant considerations, considerations relating to a live use of words in situations in which the knowledge of our audience becomes a factor, situations where, because of the necessity for singling out the person referred to in terms which would be suitable for our audience, we unhesitatingly use identifying expressions which the person being reported was in no position to employ.

Moving to an example of another kind, we could say 'Oedipus intended to marry his mother', if we could say 'Oedipus intended to marry Jocasta'. The sense in which the former may be false when the latter is true is that in which Oedipus is stated to have had the intention to marry whoever should turn out to be his mother, and that is not the reading in which 'his mother' is referential. Again, even of the most fastidious person it might be true to say, 'He wanted to eat the contaminated sausage', but meaning no more than 'The sausage he wanted to eat was contaminated'. The qualification, 'under a description', is often invoked in these contexts. Perhaps to some purpose, if we are concerned to stay close to the words used in expressing a desire or intention and are not at the same time making referential use of them, but the notion is misapplied if it is thought that a man may want or intend to eat a particular sausage, say, 'under a description'. It has no place in apposition to a phrase like 'this sausage' used referentially. Equally mistaken is the belief that an event can be said to be determined only under a certain description.

Again, suppose I consider the Chancellor of the Exchequer to be extremely dangerous as far as the good of the nation is concerned, while regarding him as a thoroughly sincere and likable person. Suppose he suffers a stroke and is no longer able to carry on in office. I may be sorry that this has happened, in that he was a man who meant well, but glad that it did for the sake of the country. I can indicate the reasons for my differing inclinations in this way, but not by saying 'I am glad the misguided Chancellor of the Exchequer has suffered a stroke, though sorry that the likable minister has met with this fate'. Overall, am I glad or not? There is no way of avoiding this question by making use of the two different designations, as if that gave me two different individuals towards whom I might consistently adopt different attitudes. Once more, any help that 'under a description' might offer is more than likely to be illusory—though we shall shortly have some more constructive observations to offer on a kindred possibility.

I formulated the principle of extensionality, E, in such a way as to ensure that substitution should not result in an added implication of knowledge of identity. Inferences in accordance with this principle may be worthy of attention, to the extent that some have been loath to accept them, but of greater interest are inferences which, while seemingly of this form, in fact proceed on another basis, or which, while not strictly valid, are none the less reckoned generally acceptable. So, for instance, if Hiram plans to visit every capital city in Europe, does it necessarily follow that he plans to visit Tirana, of which he has never heard? If the anthropologist is anxious to meet the oldest man in the village, whoever that may be, can it be said that he is anxious to meet the witch-doctor, Oko, if that is who he is?

If someone expresses a wish to purchase the most valuable object in a sale, whatever that may be, and the object in question is a grandfather clock, we might say that there is someone who wants to purchase the grandfather clock, that the clock has a prospective buyer. Certainly, what the buyer wants is the grandfather clock, taking 'what the buyer wants' non-referentially, and we should not normally worry about a shift to the referential reading, or an equivalent form. Similarly, the man whom the anthropologist is anxious to meet is the witch-doctor, as it happens, so—in a sense—he can be said to be anxious to meet the witch-doctor, or Oko, if that is his name. In either case, we might say, that is what it amounts to in the circumstances; not only do we have the irreproachable 'The person he is anxious to meet is Oko', but we may let pass the more demanding 'He is anxious to meet Oko'. We assume that the person will abide by what he has said when he has the further knowledge, that he will not undergo a change of heart or mind on learning exactly who or what it is that he has expressed a desire or intention to meet, visit, purchase, or whatever. On the other hand, that we are in some cases relaxing a stricter condition can emerge when unwanted conclusions threaten, conclusions which actually conflict with what the person holds. As stated, a man's plans may involve him in visiting Tirana, but if we know that bringing this to his attention is more than likely to lead him to change these plans, we may hesitate to say that he plans to visit Tirana, preferring the more cautious statement: that is what his plans at present commit him to.

When, in chapter 2, I insisted on coupling reference with

identification, in a certain restricted sense, it may have seemed that I was imposing an unreasonable limitation on possible references to persons and things. The rationale behind that restriction becomes plainer when we consider possible conflicts of the kind just indicated. I may know a variety of individuating details about a person—that he was the last Mayor, the successful Liberal candidate, the person who opened the new swimming pool, the author of such-and-such a book, and so forth—in the sense of knowing such descriptions to apply to a single man. Suppose I add to these a further correct belief: this person is over sixty years old. But now suppose that the man in question is in fact known to me, though I am unaware that he is as just described and I take him to be much younger than he is. In such a case I think we should say that I thought him, Marshall, if that is his name, to be under sixty, that I did not know that he, Marshall, was over sixty years old. And, in general, if there is any competition between two such sets of beliefs, we shall give precedence to those expressible in a form that attributes to the believer the kind of identification which is consistent with a radical misconception as to the nature of the person or thing identified. We have no difficulty in making sense of statements like 'He thought that the shadow was someone's coat' and 'He mistook his slipper for a snake' which betray just such a misconception. Even if it means ascribing to someone a failure to appreciate the character of something as a physical object, we may have to accept such a characterization because there is no doubt what it is that the person misdescribes, his pointing or touching making his intention absolutely plain. Words are chosen for their supposed suitability in identifying to others something of which we already have knowledge, knowledge which in these cases is not dependent upon the appositeness of the words used. So, it may be quite clearly a shadow that is taken to be a coat, quite clearly this man that I think is not yet even middle-aged. But there is something which can give when my belief is merely that there is a person over sixty who was the last Mayor, and the rest. I do not strictly identify anyone as such, take this man to be so-and-so. It is of course possible, as I explained above, that one should take the same person to be F and not F on different occasions, but in the present case it is surely not a matter of being generally wrong about a man's age while sometimes appreciating just how old he is.

However, as I also have indicated, the strict usage is felt to be important only when there is otherwise a threat of conflict, or where we might be taken to be ascribing knowledge of identity when it is absent. Furthermore, as well as the tolerance which we show here, there is to be noted a more liberal use of certain terms, notably indexical expressions, which we might have thought tied to the stricter condition. The pronoun 'you' is an interesting example. If I am told that someone will call to repair the telephone and a woman presents herself, I might say, 'I expected you to be a man'. 'You', and other pronouns, may be considered in place however the question of identity works out; so, . . . you . . ., i.e. . . . the person sent, whoever it might be . . . Again, while being well aware that the castle before me is firmly placed in Kent, I might still state, 'I had thought this castle was in Yorkshire', my original observation having taken the form, 'Leeds Castle must be in Yorkshire', say, where this would have meant something like '"Leeds Castle" must be the name of some castle in Yorkshire'. We might, incidentally, use a name in reporting a person's belief about the existence of something. There is no problem with 'He does not suspect that this island exists', nor even with 'He does not suspect that Surtsey exists', where we name the island. The ignorance is with respect to there being an island at a certain place, and any island thus located has the identity implied by the name, so we do not distort the man's possible thought by referring to it in this way. Indeed, we might consider formulating the principle of extensionality in such a way that there is a presumption that any term can be replaced by a term applicable to the same thing, the possible exceptions being recognized only when they become critical. However, for those whose interest is in formulating a logical principle, the present procedure seems to be more in place.

20. *The possibility of opacity*

On entering into a subordinate clause, a name or other referential term does not automatically give up its referential rights and become subject to a new code of laws. This, perhaps the main point of the discussion to date, appears trivial, but its neglect is responsible for a number of philosophical aberrations of particular complexity. Most obviously we have Frege's theory, but there are others. For instance, H-N. Castañeda believes that an unanalysable third-person pronoun lurks in such a context as 'The Editor of *Soul* knows that he is a millionaire'. According to Castañeda [1966], this does not entail 'The Editor of *Soul* knows that the Editor of *Soul* is a millionaire', since the man may not know that he is editor, which means that the most natural explanation of the pronoun—that it goes proxy for 'the Editor of *Soul*'—is not available. However, use of the definite description here need not presume any such knowledge. Perhaps it can be so intended as to make this demand, but all we need, and what we definitely have, is a use in which it does not. Whether referential, as here, or not—as with 'The Editor of *Soul* must inform the publishers as soon as he is appointed', understood as a generalization—the analysis goes the same obvious way. Reject this and the task of giving an alternative analysis will inevitably appear hopeless and the ensuing complications equally inevitable.

What are we to say about the possibility just alluded to—that, in effect, terms in *oratio obliqua* may sometimes be understood as subject to restrictions more comparable with those which govern reports of the actual words used? It is sometimes thought sufficient explanation to say that verbs like 'think' impose an 'intentional', an 'opaque', or some other reading on a following noun phrase, but the point here presupposed—that such a reading is at least a possibility—together with the claim that the verb is endowed with such a capacity, can certainly be found wanting in some cases. Consider the sentence, 'The Inspector thinks the murderer is one of us'. This may feature 'the murderer' in either a referential or a non-referential role, so either as welcoming or as repelling substitutions. The verb 'thinks' certainly does not force one reading over the other—with, say, different senses appropriate to each—and we may also observe that if substitutions are not allowed, that is not because the Inspector can single out the person in question only under the given description, that he thinks of him only as 'the murderer'. If he does not know who the person is, he does not single him out, refer to him at all.

In this instance we can see room for two uses of the descriptive phrase, though it is not easy to see how one can make use of this form of words yet remain uncommitted on the question of the existence of a murderer. This poses a problem, in that it is often implied that such a phrase as 'the Inspector thinks' can cancel *any* use on the part of the reporter; not that we, as reporters, are obliged to select from the less demanding uses of a descriptive phrase, but that, as with direct quotation, so a qualification with 'thinks' can serve to dissociate the speaker from any commitments which following noun phrases might otherwise incur, requiring only that these phrases give an accurate rendering of what was said or thought.

This is not a possibility that appears easy to support. Phrases like 'the Inspector thinks' can qualify a following *verb*, in the sense of dissociating the reporter from its commitments, and that qualification will be transmitted to certain other noun phrases, as the implication of porcine existence, definite in 'Farmer Giles sold a pig', becomes conjectural in 'Farmer Giles is thought to have sold a pig'. However, not only does a phrase like 'this pig' remain untouched by such qualifications, but it is quite obscure what use it might enjoy if, as is frequently supposed, it could be said to be within the scope of the qualification introduced with 'thought'.

Things are looking black for those who claim to see opacity throughout such contexts as these, and we may wonder whether there is anything short of quotation as a device for detaching oneself from the commitments of referential phrases. First, we note that there are two questions here: (1) Is it possible to employ these various namelike expressions without purportedly referring to someone or something? (2) can we go so far as to cancel *any* implication of existence when using such an expression in a subordinate clause? (1) is the more straightforward. There may be little we can do with such a phrase as 'this pig', but definite descriptions, and even proper names, allow of non-referential occurrences, occurrences which set them outside the range of applicability of the principle of extensionality, E. (2) takes us back to Frege, who appeared to regard the shift from having their customary objects as referents to having their senses in this role as being for names what the shift from indicative to subjunctive is for verbs (Frege [1892a], p. 68), the subjunctive mood serving, in German, to detach the reporter from what he reports. This parallel may bring to mind the account of 'indicative' and 'subjunctive' descriptions put forward earlier. I suggested that these labels might be invoked in distinguishing the two readings possible for the definite description in the sentence, 'He wished he was the child's teacher', the former going with reference— or at least with the implication of existence—the latter with the merely hypothetical reading, where no identity is intended. I now suggest that the same uses are to be discerned in 'He thought that the child's teacher was going to call' and 'She thought her grandfather's ghost was haunting her'. To get a feeling for a subjunctive reading of the former is perhaps not easy, but it is a possiblity more easily discerned in the latter, where it is clearer that there need be no commitment to existence and *a fortiori* no impressing on us of an ostensible referential use. In applying the term 'subjunctive' I do not mean to imply that there has been any ellipsis of a verb allowing of a subjunctive interpretation, or any other form of 'derivation'; it is more a matter of the applicability of a description which, if couched in sufficiently general terms, will apply both to the verbal form and to other constructions for which it might constitute a close paraphrase.

We may attach the epithet 'subjunctive' to noun phrases which are non-committal with respect to existence, since it is such an implication that the subjunctive mood commonly cancels, but with the example of Spanish in mind we might thus designate the reading in which it is specifically reference that is suspended, since the subjunctive there may signal a lack of knowledge of a satisfying individual without affecting the implication of existence. See Rivero [1975], where it is also claimed that the indicative/subjunctive contrast with respect to the verb 'is' in the Spanish for 'He wants to marry a girl who is blonde and with freckles' goes with knowledge of identity or the lack thereof.

My 'subjunctive' account provides something of what is wanted by seekers of opacity, but without implying that phrases like 'he thinks' are responsible for the relevant behaviour of the noun phrases. I claimed earlier that 'probably' and similar adverbs do not induce an altered reading of an associated noun phrase of the type in question; unlike purely general terms, the use of definite descriptions and kindred forms is determined by considerations independent of the verb, so remains unaffected when the verb is qualified. This holds for adverbial qualifications quite generally, and is a point of some importance. It is widely held that terms like 'possibly' and 'he thinks' can have definite descriptions in their scope. If I am right, this reverses the correct ordering: we must first decide the use of the noun phrase and the correct construal of the modal or other qualification will then fall into place. Furthermore, it is because we can in this way bring about a different reading of the sentence overall—a difference which may affect truth—that we are entitled to distinguish uses of definite descriptions that differ semantically, and not merely psychologically.

That these various qualifications are powerless to neutralize existential commitments is particularly clear when individuating conditions are furnished by the context. There is no disowning such a commitment with 'He hopes that the man over there will help', and phrases like 'this mule' remain as stubbornly deictic as ever. Similarly, if someone asks, 'You are the man who was enquiring about train departures, are you not?', we have to report this as something like 'He thought I might be *a* man who had been enquiring about train departures', with indeed a subjunctive reading to 'had been enquiring', if we wish to detach ourselves from the implication that there was such a person. While, incidentally, we might say, 'Bertie thought that the largest number was composed solely of nines', without supposing there to be a largest number, much as an atheist might say, 'Veronica is confident that God will provide', I suggest we should prefer the less misleading 'Bertie thought there was a largest number composed solely of nines', and perhaps 'God' can be invoked without impunity because in the relevantly generous terms in which we judge of these matters it is felt that there is such a being in Christian tradition, or whatever, even if not in reality.

The statement, 'Phosphorous is larger than Hesperus', is not happily reported as 'He thought that Phosphorous was larger than Hesperus' by one who knows the names to be names of the same planet, and to get away from the referential use we may have to resort to quotation: 'He thought that "Phosphorous" was the name of some planet which was larger than Hesperus' would be one possibility. Could the original actually have such a reading, a reading which would amount to citing the words initially used? This suggestion covers more than one possibility. Thus, if it is proposed that, say, 'He said that the man who sold him the car was dishonest' can be regarded as interchangeable with 'He said, "The man who sold me the car was dishonest"', or some other synonymous form, then I think we should prefer the analysis already offered. Use of quotes enables us to dissociate ourselves from *any* commitment with respect to the words quoted, but the construction with 'that' is more restrictive, as we have just seen with 'He hopes that the man over there will help'. My conception of phrases like 'the man who sold him the car' as having a subjunctive reading is more appropriately selective: we cancel commitment in the desired respect, but we retain a referential use of the pronoun 'him' and we do not take the further step of using a device which requires greater fidelity to the original form of expression.

However, it does seem that we might think of quotes as in effect being used in a selective way, for all that may mean is that the relevant commitment is suspended—quotes, after all, have no reality in the spoken language. So, the statement, 'He wanted to know who Roger was', might just come to 'He wanted to know who "Roger" was the name of'—in the sense of 'whom the speaker meant by "Roger" on that occasion'. Similarly, perhaps, a sentence like 'He said that the disgraceful behaviour of the team could not be excused' might be understood as 'He said that "the disgraceful behaviour" of the team could not be excused'. Here we also note the familiar conflations of use and mention, as when an actual referential use of an expression is followed by such a phrase as 'if you will pardon the expression'. In such a case the noun phrase has to be taken twice over, once referentially, once not, with substitutivity possible only in the former case. This, incidentally, appears to be the closest we get to a context describable as 'referentially opaque', if by that is meant that we have reference but that the form it takes is relevant to truth value.

In 'He said that "the disgraceful behaviour" of the team could not be excused', the closeness of the description to an explicitly verbal phrase—'the team behaved disgracefully'—is apparent, and therewith the nature of the suspended commitment. Again, contrast 'The teacher said that the last child to finish would have to stay behind' with 'The teacher said that the child who finished last had had to stay behind'. The former makes no significant commitment with 'the last child to finish', no reference which the reporter might wish to disown, but the infinitive is appropriately non-committal; in the latter, 'the child who finished last' differs in the verb, so in what that means for implied existence. As names and demonstratives indicate, this simple division of cases is not universal, but even with terms of these kinds it will be appropriate to express in verbal form the matter of existence on which a reporter may wish to remain uncommitted, and in general it would appear that an extension of the approach proper to the explicitly verbal part of the sentence is called for; exchanging referents just does not seem to be a move that could have the desired effect.

Turning now to a different possibility, though one that again exploits the verb, suppose that I mistakenly identify someone opening the gate as an acquaintance by the name of 'Black'. There is a sense in which I do not take Black to be opening the gate—he, after all, is nowhere around—but I do take the person opening the gate—White, let us say—to be Black. Indeed, there appear to be two ways in which 'He thought Black was opening the gate' might be said of me: one in which we can substitute for 'Black' any designation applicable to the person opening the gate, the other in which we cannot. The latter may be paraphrased as 'He thought it was Black who was opening the gate', and this takes us back to the style of reading which I suggested we might have in an undeveloped form with the simple 'Andrew agreed', when this has the force of 'It was Andrew that agreed'. Such a reading would make the noun phrase accessible to the kind of qualification ordinarily confined in its scope to the predicate; introductory adverbs such as 'possibly' and 'probably' need not just pass over the name *en route* to the verb, but they could furnish a qualification at this initial point, and it is only to be expected that phrases like 'he thought' should be comparable with adverbs in this respect.

I mention this possible reading, since it could be that it expresses something of what is wanted by those who seek 'opaque' contexts. However, while it does provide contrasting construals of '*A* thought *B* was *F*', it does not appear that we are prohibited from varying our choice of '*B*'. It is true, as I say, that we cannot use designations applicable to the person or thing that is *F*, but we can make sense of alternative designations of what in fact '*B*' singles out. If you report me as thinking (mistakenly) that Black was opening the gate, you can substitute another designation of Black without doing violence to truth, even if your substitution may be found unsuitable to the circumstances. We have a difference in possible directions of fit with respect to the two construals, but in neither does the construction force a non-referential reading of '*B*' upon us. That possibility, in so far as it exists, will reside in the particular character of '*B*'. Perhaps, for instance, it is a description which is not backed by knowledge of identity. And, of course, whatever the possibilities, there is again no question of seeing in Fregean senses, intentional objects, individual concepts, or whatever, as substitute referents.

Let us now take a last look at the more perplexing of the contexts which have confronted us. Suppose that *A* finds himself at a dinner seated next to someone whom he seems to recall having been next to on the same occasion a year ago. In reporting *A*'s thought we may single out the person now next to him by any applicable designation: if he takes the man to be the same as the person he sat next to before, then he takes Walter, if that is his name, or the treasurer, if that is his title, to be that person. Indeed, it can even be said that he takes the man who sat next to him before to be the man who sat next to him before. Can we take the same liberties with the second term? In particular, can we say that *A* takes the person now sitting next to him to be the person now sitting next to him? The apparent silliness of this formulation can be lessened by building up to it in the way just indicated, thereby keeping to the fore the concern with the man's identity—it is a matter of A's thinking that the person is the person he is, which need be no sillier than a person's surprise that a certain word means what it means— but doubts may remain. Can we really say: it was only when he was onto the fish that A realized that the man he was sitting next to was the man he was sitting next to? It is certainly extraordinary to charge the given description with such an identifying role in this context, because of the difficulty of seeing beyond the condition reported to the matter of identity: A does not simply realize that he is sitting next to someone he is sitting next to, but he realizes that the man he is sitting next to is the man he is, and that is, of course, the man he is sitting next to. An utterly inept way of putting it, I agree, but not such as to take us from truth to falsity, and that is the main concern.

If this is not accepted, then we must either deny reference to the term for which we make substitution, or else deny that the original and the term substituted have a common reference. Reference is not easily denied. The case is not like that where wondering who Roger is is a matter of wondering whom the speaker means by 'Roger', rather than wondering about someone we thus identify, and the way we attempt to single out a person, using phrases which differ in sense, goes against Frege's solution—denying sameness of reference and casting the distinct senses in the roles of differing referents. The interpretation of 'referential opacity' which I can accept—where the description is taken twice over—does not appear applicable, and my other suggested construals have nothing to offer.

So what is left? If reference is not going to budge, it is identity of reference that must yield: if it really is the case that something holds of a but not of b, then a just is not strictly identical with b. I say not *strictly* identical, but a could be the same F as b, for some F, provided that F is merely an equivalence relation, implying identity only in *some* respects. And this is not absurd. The same batrachian can have distinct phases, as tadpole and frog, and we could similarly appeal to differences which come with time in specifying different 'person-phases': just as distinctness of frog and tadpole is consistent with their being the same batrachian, so being the same person is now an equivalence relation applicable to distinct person-phases. As such it does not force the identity of the phases which it relates, but we can consistently say that what holds of the one such need not hold of the other, just as the frog is tailless, the tadpole not.

Such a way of speaking is what I had in mind at the end of the discussion of names and sense, and I shall now make a more explicit connection with that topic. Let us suppose that a person has, as it were, two identities: the bespectacled weakling reporter, Clark Kent, and the airborne righter of wrongs, Superman. Someone, struck by the facial resemblance, begins to wonder whether Clark Kent might not be Superman. We could correctly say, knowing of the identity, that this person's wonderment is directed towards Superman, but to the extent that the names are tied to a person in his two different roles, we can make sense of a difference that qualifies as a difference in reference, allowing that not everything that can be said of the one can be said of the other: Kent wears a conventional suit, Superman does not—rather than: Kent only wears a suit in office hours, not as Superman. So we have a choice: wondering whether this man—Kent, Superman; it does not matter how we put it—is Superman; or, wondering only with respect to Kent: is he the same person as Superman? With the latter it is understood that 'Kent is Superman', construed as an identity, would be strictly false: the two alternate, they never coalesce.

Consider again the standard example of Phosphorous and Hesperus. If a referential use of the names means an interchangeable use, it may be wondered how anyone could ever have been unaware that Phosphorous was Hesperus, given the short step to this from the knowledge that Phosphorous is Phosphorous. But, as we have pointed out, this latter knowledge is not to be automatically assumed. We can fail to realize that the postman is only the postman, and not an intruder, and there have doubtless been many occasions when Phosphorous has not been recognized as such. Suppose it is insisted, however, that the names in 'They did not know that Phosphorous was Hesperus' simply *cannot* be varied, but are referential none the less. In that case the references draw apart: we do not forsake planets for the senses of the names, for ideas, concepts, or whatever, but 'Phosphorus' becomes restricted to Venus as it appears in the morning, and the identity becomes an equivalence relation between this and the evening phase. Compare the way we speak of 'the British sun' and 'the Spanish sun' as if they were different suns, rather than of 'the sun in Britain (Spain)'. It is with this kind of extreme case—where we can speak of a difference in reference—that I am inclined to speak of a different *understanding* of the names. Certainly, nothing short of this obliges us to speak thus, though again, this is not to deny a place to the notion of an individuating condition in an account of the use of the name.

Unpromising though it looks, this analysis reflects tolerably well certain aspects of our use of names in the troublesome cases, which means primarily those in which belief and the like are directed towards an identity. So, suppose A realizes that the man who has just come out of a shop is the man he saw go in ten minutes previously. If this man is Brown, does it follow that A realizes that the man who has just come out is Brown? On a first reading, this inference seems quite absurd, but then A does, we are supposing, realize that the man who has just come out is that man, the man who went in earlier, viz. Brown; not only does the conclusion appear to force itself inexorably upon us, but so long as we bear in mind that use of the name need imply no more than that a correct identification was made, it is a conclusion which we need not seek to avoid. But if we can convince ourselves that this is so, we can convince ourselves still more easily of the possible truth of A's likely avowal, 'I did not realize that the man who came out of the shop was Brown'. So how is this to be construed?

A, we may suppose, connects the name 'Brown' with someone who has had a certain history, some of which is known to him, outside the episode in question; indeed, knowing who it is that 'Brown' names is perforce knowing of at least one such identification beyond those given. As it might present itself to A, the question whether the man who has just come out of the shop is Brown is one of the truth of an equivalence relation—indeed, the grammar of our talk here, where we ask whether 'they are' the same person, reflects this perspective. On learning that the individual currently observed is a temporal continuation of Brown, A may stay with an affirmation of this in terms of an equivalence relation, though he is now also in a position to associate the name with the more recent identification, thus joining us in the use which, I in effect hypothesized, we were able to make of the name. In that use it could be said that he had realized that the man who came out of the shop was Brown—though again some reflection may be required to readjust to this possibility—and all I have been trying to do is offer a restatement that is closer to the use of the name that A was in a position to make. It will doubtless be noticed that what has emerged compares with a Fregean account in terms of the possible senses of a name, our varying identifications filling this role, but in so far as we envisage a departure from the known reference of the name, it is by supposing a restricted reference rather than an associated sense that might enter in that capacity.

There are other terms which might find a place in this general discussion, mass nouns being an obvious possibility. Confusions concerning reference and intentionality have also arisen with respect to the pronoun 'I' and with verbs of perception and sensation, but I know of nothing here that takes us beyond the analyses given. As a rather different kind of phenomenon, though related to the general topic, I might mention the following from Geach [1972], p. 93. Given

(1) The only man who ever stole a book from Snead (namely Robinson) made a lot of money by selling it,

we are not entitled to pass to

(2) Robinson made a lot of money by selling it.

This might be taken as proof that the phrase, 'the only man who ever stole a book from Snead', is not referential, but while it is true that descriptions containing 'only' are not usually chosen as forms of identification, we should not wish to rule out the possibility, here clearly suggested by the namely-rider. I suggest that this is just a case where a little imagination is needed to provide a context in which (2) might be uttered on the strength of (1) together with the identity. And this is not too difficult. I assert (1) and you say, in incredulous repetition, 'He made a lot of money by selling it?', or 'You mean Robinson made a lot of money by selling it?'. Hardly natural forms of words in this instance, but hardly an example to make us rethink our ideas about referential terms and substitutivity.

21. Modality and substitutivity

Then, of course, we have modal contexts. The number of planets being 9, a number necessarily greater than 7, it seems to follow that the number of planets is necessarily greater than 7. Indeed it does, provided that when we conclude thus we are using 'the number of planets' in a genuinely referential capacity. Such a usage may be unusual, a referential role being more likely to be associated with 'the number of *the* planets', but there is nothing in the least paradoxical in saying of that number which is, as it happens, the number of the planets, that it is necessarily greater than 7. Given merely that the number in question is 9, it is a number which of necessity exceeds 7, and that no matter how you refer to it. This is not to deny the possibility of another reading according to which 'The number of planets is necessarily greater than 7' is false, but in this, the more likely reading, where the sense is roughly that of 'There are necessarily more than 7 planets', there is no reference to 9 and no violation of the principle of extensionality, E (cf. Smullyan [1948]). As a parallel example where the terms deemed intersubstitutable diverge in their roles, consider 'The president of the society is always a student; Martin is the president of the society; therefore, Martin is always a student'. Again no violation of anything other than principle E' with such an argument.

This attempt to show the referential opacity of modal contexts is nothing more than a feeble play on words, and among the sporadic efforts at reviving it I know of none that avoids errors of the kind we have exposed, the most common being to represent as a designation of a natural number an expression having quite a different role. There is accordingly no need to question quantification into modal contexts of the appropriate kinds, an operation whose inadmissability would be paradoxical in the extreme. That the conclusion allows of an interpretation in which it can be validly drawn has come to be recognized by the originator of the argument, Quine, but since this interpretation commits one to essentialism, it finds no favour with him. That is, it apparently commits one to the view that some of the properties of a thing may be essential to it quite independently of the language in which the thing is referred to, a view which is thought to be quite unacceptable (Quine [1961]).

It should be emphasized just how extraordinary the failure of existential generalization would be in this instance. It is intolerable to regard 'the number of planets' as functioning referentially, as picking out some number, in 'The number of planets is necessarily greater than 7', and at the same time to deny the legitimacy of the inference to 'Some number is necessarily greater than 7'. If we really are speaking of some number, then surely we can say as much. The feared essentialism, by contrast, does not surpass human understanding. If I say of 9, 'This number could not have failed to be odd', the mode of designation does not provide a basis from which the oddness of the number can be inferred, but the modality is not on that account suspect. Being odd is necessary to being this number, the number this is, and that is no less intelligible because we have suppressed a specification of the known number. We shall return to this topic in chapter 5.

Quine has a further argument to show the impossibility of quantifying into modal contexts, an argument which avoids reference to singular terms, such as 'the number of planets'. In Quine [1961] it is claimed that while the condition on x given by '$x = \sqrt{x} + \sqrt{x} + \sqrt{x} \neq \sqrt{x}$' has '$x > 7$' as a necessary consequence, the condition given by 'There are exactly x planets' does not, and this is taken as giving independent confirmation that necessity enters only with a particular specification of x. However, the question is whether either specification has as a consequence that x is a number which cannot but be greater than 7, not whether it is a necessary consequence of either that x is greater than 7. Quine may have got away from singular terms, but not from the earlier confusion about what precisely it is that 'necessarily' qualifies.

And does 'There are exactly x planets' give a determination of a number having the desired property, a number which, of necessity, is greater than 7? It is not at all clear that, without the assistance of the unwanted '$x = 9$', or something like this, we can infer anything as to the number, the conclusion that x is greater than 7 being no less remote than that it is necessarily greater—which would, of course, in turn follow: if we can infer that 9, or some number, is greater than 7, we can infer the modal form, and if we cannot then we have not been given a relevant determination of the number.

I claimed earlier that names and namelike expressions generally stood outside the qualifications that came with 'possibly' and 'probably'. The position here is much as with clauses governed by such phrases as 'he thinks', but in either case it is the exception that has been considered by many to be standard. However, just as our appeal to a 'subjunctive' use of descriptions enables us at least to make sense of what is supposedly the rule in indirect speech, so we should expect that this reduced use of noun phrases will have to be invoked if we are to see such phrases as subject to modal qualifications. It is true that the sentence discussed—'Their garden is possibly larger than ours'—gave no support to this possibility, but with a more abstract noun phrase the dissociation from any form of reference is easier, and we can speak of a subjunctive as well as an indicative reading of 'the number of planets' in 'The number of planets is necessarily greater than 7'. In the latter case it is a matter of whatever actually is the number of (the) planets, and if that is 9 then the sentence proclaiming that that number is necessarily greater than 7 is of course true. In the former case it is a matter of whatever should happen to be the number of planets, and such a number is not necessarily greater than 7. When the description is indicative, 'necessarily' compares with quite untroublesome adverbs, such as 'considerably'. With this reading, style of reference is just as irrelevant to the truth of 'The number of planets is necessarily greater than 7' as it is to that of 'The number of planets is not much greater than 7'. Indeed, these are contexts where substitution is especially straightforward, not even requiring knowledge of identity. From 'The number of planets is greater than 7' and 'The number of planets is the same as the number of Muses', we can infer 'The number of Muses is greater than 7', without the benefit of any further knowledge as to what that number is, and adding 'necessarily'—unlike 'he thinks'—does not make the slightest difference.

The defence which I have offered for the inference to 'The number of planets is necessarily greater than 7' has been criticized on the grounds that it commits me to regarding all true statements of identity as necessarily true (see Thornton [1969]). However, this commitment is neither unintended nor unwelcome—if of no great moment either. If Scott and the author of *Waverley* are one and the same person, then it is necessarily true that Scott is the author of *Waverley*. This is how it must be, given that a referential use of terms is maintained throughout—as is required if the putative identity is to be genuinely such—for to suppose that Scott might not have been the author of *Waverley* is to suppose that Scott might not have been identical with a certain person, a person who in fact wrote *Waverley* and who, of course, is none other than Scott himself. Again there is a correct proposition which is being muddled with this: 'Scott might not have been the author of *Waverley*' is perfectly in order once the definite description has relinquished any referring role, for then we are simply saying that Scott might not have written *Waverley*; or, more accurately—in view of the subjunctive reading called for—that Scott might not have been the one to write *Waverley*.

While care in identifying and interpreting ostensible referential role is about all that is needed to steer clear of paradox in these modal contexts, there is a version of the planetary argument due to L. J. Cohen which appears to be aimed at reinstating the conclusion rejected—that substitution of co-designating expressions and quantification into modal contexts are illegitimate—but which bears only on the substitutivity of sentences, not of names (Cohen [1966], pp. 355-7). Cohen suggests that the above premises may be formulated:

For all x, necessarily, $x = 9$ only if $x > 7$,

and   For all x, there are x planets if and only if $x = 9$.

These are then said to yield by substitutivity the false conclusion:

For all x, necessarily, there are x planets only if $x > 7$.

However, the substitution is clearly—and avowedly—with respect to a sentence, or sentence form, not a name, and quite apart from any considerations to do with names we can see that the argument form is invalid. This is perhaps most easily shown by replacing '$x > 7$' by '$x = 9$':

> For all x, necessarily, $x = 9$ only if $x = 9$,
> For all x, there are x planets if and only if $x = 9$,

with conclusion now

> For all x, necessarily, there are x planets only if $x = 9$.

Since it is logically true, the first premiss can now be dropped, leaving us with a licence to proceed directly from the second premiss to a modalized version of one of the implications which it comprises. This is clearly wrong, and the full argument form is no more valid that its analogue in propositional logic, viz. if we have 'P if and only if Q' and 'necessarily Q only if R', we may infer 'necessarily P only if R'.

22. The Frege argument

The failure of substitutivity with respect to propositions of identical truth value poses a problem only if such failure makes for opacity, i.e. only if the failure of substitutivity can accordingly be extended to names occurring within the propositions. I do not think that this extension can be made, but there is an argument, dubbed 'the Frege argument', which is commonly thought to show that it can, given only that logically equivalent propositions may be substituted for one another.

Consider, for instance, a sentence of the form, 'P before Q'; so, 'The minister was an architect before he turned to politics', or 'Joan's father died before Joan was born'. We should be inclined to suppose that replacement of 'Joan was born' by a logically equivalent sentence would not lead to an alteration in truth value, but we should not be inclined to deny extensionality or transparency in this context: surely any other way of referring to the person Joan will preserve truth? However, if the Frege argument is correct, we are forced to deny extensionality if we wish, as we doubtless should, to deny truth-functionality. Thus, 'Joan was born' will have the same truth value as 'Joan's father was born', but we could not say 'Joan's father died before he was born'. The context is not truth-functional, but if we have extensionality we have in the Frege argument a device which enables us to effect the kinds of substitution that truth-functionality would legitimize. All that need be assumed is the intersubstitutability of logically equivalent sentences.

One way of presenting the argument is as follows. The proposition, 'Joan was born', is logically equivalent to '$\hat{x}(x = x$ & Joan was born$) = \hat{x}(x = x)$'—where '$\hat{x}(\ldots)$' is read as 'the xs such that . . . '—for if the former is true then the left-hand side of the latter collapses into the right-hand side, the result being a true identity, while if it is false this makes for a difference between the two sets and consequent falsity of the statement of their identity. However, we also have that '$\hat{x}(x = x$ & Joan was born$)$' specifies the same set as does, say, '$\hat{x}(x = x$ & Joan's father was born$)$', given that 'Joan was born' and 'Joan's father was born' agree in truth value. Since we are also supposing that our context allows of substitutions based on logical equivalences, we can replace 'Joan's father died before Joan was born' by 'Joan's father died before $\hat{x}(x = x$ & Joan was born$) = \hat{x}(x = x)$', and since we have by hypothesis an extensional context we can substitute our alternative designation of the same set, producing 'Joan's father died before $\hat{x}(x = x$ & Joan's father was born$) = \hat{x}(x = x)$'. But now a parallel logical equivalence allows us to simplify this to 'Joan's father died before he was born'. Since this is patently absurd, we must abandon the idea that the context in question is extensional.

One who accepts this reasoning shows a touch of intellectual heroism, not unlike a man who, finding himself unable to refute Zeno's argument to show that Achilles never catches the tortoise, settles for this as the correct conclusion. Such willingness to follow the argument wherever it leads is admirable in either case, but in either case our admiration may be tempered by the feeling that what seems plainly true on more familiar, well-established grounds, should carry greater weight in our overall reckoning. Of course, Zeno's argument is not met by proving that Achilles does catch the tortoise. That we all know. The challenge is to see where a seemingly impeccable piece of reasoning has in fact gone astray. Likewise with the present argument.

However, it might be suggested that, at least with sentences of the form 'P before Q', we have independent grounds for denying extensionality or transparency. After all, is it not possible that a referential phrase should embody a temporal element which is essential to the truth of the statement? Well, let us suppose that our designation embodies such an element, to the extent of incorporating a condition which holds only at or for a time, as 'his well-kept garden' in 'Jonathan was proud of his well-kept garden'. Can I replace this by 'Jonathan was proud of this overgrown garden', given that 'this overgrown garden' does in fact pick out the same garden? I do not see why not, so long as there is no implication that the description which holds now held earlier. Such an implication is lacking in this instance; nor do I imply that the overgrown character of the garden was the source of the man's pride, though it could be obscure why I should offer such a unhelpful description. Again, grandfather can say to granddaughter, 'Your mother used to keep us awake at nights', without implying that motherhood had been reached at a very tender age. To the extent that there is logical pressure against free interchange of such phrases as 'your mother' and 'our first baby', it is pressure to treat them in accordance with the pattern suggested with 'Clark Kent' and 'Superman', the apparent identities in which they unite being construable as merely equivalence relations with respect to *same person*. But relaxing strict identity in this way means that no challenge to extensionality is offered.

What then is wrong with the Frege argument in its present application? Should we query the equation of 'Joan was born' with '$\hat{x}(x = x$ & Joan was born$) = \hat{x}(x = x)$'? There is some lack of grammatical connection between that part of the formula read as 'the xs such that . . .' and the following 'Joan was born' which might lead us to argue that we had wellformedness only in accordance with the most liberal of conventions, but I shall not go along with that objection. Nor do I wish to object on the grounds that logical equivalence is to be denied because of different implications carried by the two sentences, in so far as one implies the existence of a certain set whereas the other does not. We might read '$\hat{x}(. . .)$' as those things, if any, which . . .', eliminating reference to a set but preserving reference of a kind. At all events, there can be some latitude in our understanding of 'logical equivalence', enough perhaps to allow that such an equivalence can coexist with such a difference.

Let us look more closely at the whole context, 'Joan's father died before $\hat{x}(x = x$ & Joan was born$) = \hat{x}(x = x)$'. How are we to read the equals sign which unites the two set expressions? I mean, what *tense* is to be introduced here? Not, surely, the timeless present. We do not wish to say 'Joan's father died before $\hat{x}(x = x$ & Joan was born$)$ *are* equal (or identical) to $\hat{x}(x = x)$'; if 'are' really is timeless, we can make no sense of the 'before'. Tense is clearly logically relevant to a sentence governed by a temporal conjunction such as 'before', 'when', 'while', or 'after', and alteration of that tense may well destroy any logical equivalence. But this is no great problem. We simply insist that Joan's father died before the two sets *were* identical, since there would have been a time when 'Joan was born' was not true. Of course, this can be replaced by some kind of timeless analogue—or so many would think—but then that will have repercussions for the use of 'before' quite independently of whether the resultant sentence is embedded in this controversial context or in the original version. But now, what are we to say of the identity of $\hat{x}(x = x$ & Joan was born$)$ with $\hat{x}(x = x$ & Joan's father was born$)$? These formulae, I wish to say, do not give designations of the same objects. We might say that eventually each set or totality came to be identical with $\hat{x}(x = x)$, and hence with one another, but the former came to be the same as $\hat{x}(x = x)$ at a time subsequent to that at which the latter underwent the same reduction. That is, since there was a time when 'Joan's father was born' was true but 'Joan was born' false—given a certain amount of explanation of the use of the proper name—'$x = x$ & Joan was born' defined a false condition at a time when '$x = x$ & Joan's father was born' defined a true condition, and hence reduced to '$x = x$'. The argument is accordingly blocked by the failure of the namelike expressions to be co-designating.

These considerations of tense, of sets coming to coincide, sound quite foreign to any set-theoretic considerations of a conventional kind, And that, of course, is the whole point. The required logical equivalence is established only by deeming logically irrelevant just that feature which, as far as the connective 'before' is concerned, is logically crucial. This is why it is unsatisfactory to fasten on the different implications with respect to the existence of $\hat{x}(x = x)$. Even allowing that a difference in this regard shows non-equivalence, it would have been puzzling in the extreme if preservation of the right tense had resulted in actual falsity—puzzlement which would not be lessened by incorporating the assumption of existence in a protasis on which the rest of the argument would be conditional. Provided that the suggested reading is adhered to, we continue to specify the same time when we move from 'Joan was born' to '$\hat{x}(x = x$ & Joan was born$) = \hat{x}(x = x)$', as indeed we should if we replaced 'Joan was born' by any other proposition which reported a simultaneous episode. That is, if Joan was born at the same time as was Jill, then 'Joan's father died before Joan was born' will not alter in truth value with a change to 'Joan's father died before Jill was born'. Conversely, if we vary the time reference, then, even if this is not relevant in other connections, we are varying what is logically relevant in this respect. It is as simple as that.

As is to be expected, the Frege argument is similarly unsatisfactory when directed towards such sentences as 'He used to have his most profound thoughts while lying in the bath' and 'Jenny stuttered badly when she was small'. But what of that other favoured context, sentences of the form 'P because Q'? Here espousal of extensionality would supposedly take us from, say, 'The car would not start because the battery was flat' to 'The car would not start because the tyres were new', given that the second half of each sentence is true. I shall not consider the argument in detail, but merely point out that logical equivalence may be no guarantee of substitutability in such contexts. A proposition P is logically equivalent to '(P & Q) or (P & not-Q)', for suitable Q, but it is far from clear that we can automatically pass from 'Roger was miserable because he was hungry' to 'Roger was miserable because he was hungry and married or hungry and unmarried'. More persuasively, conjoining the mathematical truth, 'There is no rational square root of 2', with any other proposition results in a conjunction which is, in the intended sense, logically equivalent to that proposition, but while 'I am telephoning because I wish to make an appointment' may be true, this virtue will hardly be transmissible to 'I am telephoning because I wish to make an appointment and there is no rational square root of 2'. Why? The clause, 'because I wish to make an appointment', gives the speaker's alleged reason for his telephoning, something being one's reason if it forms part of a pattern of reasoning which the speaker actually employed or which, at least, he would sincerely accept as accurately characterizing his train of thought. However, there is little scope for 'There is no rational square root of 2' among the considerations which might lead one to telephone for an appointment.

Even more dramatically, it might be argued that a single form of words may connect with different explanations depending on precisely what is to be explained. There may, for instance, be a difference in what is conveyed by 'Meg was upset because *Sue* married Peter' and 'Meg was upset because Sue married *Peter*'. Logical equivalence does not appear in doubt here, but nor does it seem the sole factor on which the appropriatness of the explanation depends. This case is argued in Dretske [1975], but it will not escape notice that this is once more an instance of the use of a name in which it is becoming possible to subject it to qualifications generally reserved for the predicate, which makes for the beginnings of distinct interpretations of the sentence depending on which names, if any, are thus subjected.

Are there perhaps independent grounds for urging that such contexts are none the less not extensional? Quine's argument concerning the number of planets has been hopefully, if hopelessly, extended to the case of causal necessity by Dagfinn Føllesdal, who claims that even if the man who drank from a given well is identical with the man born in place p at time t, we may not pass from 'It is causally necessary that the man who drank from that well got poisoned' to 'It is causally necessary that the man who was born in p at t got poisoned' (Føllesdal [1965]). The argument does not call for comment at this stage, but there are other cases, minus the modal muddle, which raise the same kind of issue, cases in which the description chosen gives some indication why 'because' was used. Thus, 'The Chinese ambassador refused to stay because the Russian ambassador was present', where it is because the man in question was the Russian ambassador, i.e. held that office, that the Chinese ambassador refused to stay. He would no doubt have refused whatever the identity of the Russian ambassador. However, the helpfulness of the description in giving an indication of the reason does not mean that truth is not preserved if we use another form of reference. We might still say, 'The Chinese ambassador refused to stay because Ivan was present'. As long as there was an identifying reference in the first sentence—which of couse there might not have been—this substitution of a co-designating term preserves truth, while if there was no reference, then we are not dealing with an example which puts the principle of extensionality to the test.

I have looked at applications of the Frege argument to sentences with 'before' and 'because'—and might equally have considered '. . . explains . . .', '. . . even though . . .', or '. . . despite the fact that . . .'—rather than to modal contexts, since nothing new arises in the latter case and it is in any event useful to confirm that our practice of varying the choice of referential term in these contexts has nothing to fear from this general form of argument. An unthinking, Pavlovian labelling of numerous contexts as 'referentially opaque' has been one of the more pervasive errors of much recent philosophy; this, coupled with the occasional introduction of bogus referents when the failure of substitutability is thought to show absence, not of all reference, but of the customary reference. With the exception of referential terms which must be taken twice over, the behaviour of such phrases is for the most part pleasingly simple: either there is reference of the normal variety, in which case the principle of extensionality, E, remains intact; or there is not, in which case suspension of reference is all we have—no violation of extensionality and no unaccustomed referent.

If there is a complication, it is in finding that use of referential terms supposed by some to be standard in *oratio obliqua*. Frege envisaged entry into this context as bringing with it two changes: referential terms come to designate their senses and verbs go into the subjunctive mood. The latter is generally true. I do not assert 'you had gone' when I assert the larger

'Henry thought you had gone', and a subjunctive reading provides a way in which I may detach myself from the commitments of the verb. There is, however, an asymmetry in this respect between verb and pronoun: I still purport to make referential use of 'you', as indeed I might of any other noun phrase that has such a use in *oratio recta*. In general it is difficult to retreat from such a use, but its avoidance requires us to exploit once more a suitably non-committal verbal form: so, 'Jane thought that John had a second wife who had left him' rather than 'Jane thought that John's second wife had left him'. If we can make use of the latter without implying the existence of a second wife for John, it will be because, I suggest, the noun phrase allows of a reading which is appropriately described as 'subjunctive', unfamiliar though this label may be in this connection.

A final point in defence of this characterization is worth noting. It is only if the context features an appropriate qualification with a verb such as 'thinks' or an adverb such as 'necessarily' that there is any semantic reality in a distinction between a use of a noun phrase in which substitution is allowable and a use in which it is not. This is in harmony with, and indeed explained by, the notion of a subjunctive use, the subjunctive being predominantly a dependent mood, and not to be found in a main clause. The qualifications which associate with the relevant subordination do not, in the present contexts, *induce* the subjunctive reading, but they appear none the less necessary for its occurrence.

5

EXISTENCE AND ABSTRACTIONS

Berkeley's observation that 'we have first raised a dust and then complain we cannot see' may well have come to mind at several points in the last chapter as we set about our vain search for something in the way of a serious problem to grapple with, and it applies even more emphatically when we turn, as we shall now do, to the topic of 'ontological commitment'. However, while it seems right to dismiss many of the ontic antics which result in the fleeting appearance of a problem in this area, a number of questions manage to survive as genuine. We shall go over some of the considerations which may help clarify the simpler amongst them, leaving their less tractable brethren for the next two chapters.

23. Ontological commitment

The contemporary preoccupation with reference may seem curious. If what is really pressing is the question whether certain things, Fs, exist, then why not ask straight out: Do Fs exist? The consideration that a particular form of words does not carry commitment to Fs would not appear to be of much significance if the answer to the direct question is in the affirmative. If Fs do indeed exist then this is a fact which is going to have to be reckoned with, even if there are occasions on which seeming reference to them proves to be illusory.

Of course, the question of the referential role of an expression continues to be of interest even if the direct account is more basic; in particular, the central role of reference in any account of the semantics of a language is sufficient to justify the current preoccupation. However, there may be another reason why, given a concern with existence, the indirect rather than the direct approach is preferred. The direct question, 'Do numbers exist?', is in place for anyone who thinks the question purely factual, allowing of a yes or no answer; but for one who, for one reason or another, does not share this assumption, it may be more natural to shift attention to the question of the commitments of one's words, and, most notably, the commitments of noun phrases involved in reference or seeming reference. This is very much in keeping with the approach which enquires after what is *needed*, ontologically, if what one says is going to stand a chance of being true. If we wish to accept certain propositions, and if the truth of these propositions calls for the existence of certain entities, then, in view of the importance of the theory for which these entities are required, we permit ourselves to postulate their existence.

This approach is, I contend, in error. It is certainly often in place to have reservations about a question which invites a yes–no answer, and the fittingness of such reservations is apt to increase in proportion to the philosophical character of the question. For instance, since by ordinary standards there quite clearly are numbers, we naturally expect, or suspect, a special interpretation for 'Are there any such things as numbers?'. Why otherwise put the question? However, if there is any doubt as to the meaning of the words used, any postulation is premature; what is needed is clarification, a more detailed indication of when the use of the words is in order.

This need is particularly pressing with respect to the key term, 'entity', a term which formulations of the relevant questions rely on heavily, but which is somehow not thought a proper subject of scrutiny and clarification; indeed, which even appears to be taken to invest the issues with a measure of clarity, and not, as would be more fitting, to be recognized as one of those terms whose misuse, or at least uncritical use, is a major source of the problem. Thus, much contemporary 'ontologizing' proceeds as if based on something like the following recipe: you subject ordinary language to gross distortions, reading your own confusions into its innocent idioms; you then dismiss these idioms because of what you claim to have found them to imply, and you replace them by a formulation in which deviant uses of the vernacular are coupled with the symbolism of formal logic, presenting the result as a significant technical advance over the incoherences of ordinary language. A good example here is the way in which events are sometimes dealt with. The question, 'Are there events?', odd though it may strike us, is surely to receive the same answer as 'Does anything ever happen?'—an emphatic 'Yes'. However, there is a shift to an interpretation along the lines of 'Are events entities?', or 'Are there such entities as events?', and not surprisingly the inappropriate term 'entity' presents us with an issue whose sense is no longer clear and leaves the way open for a semi-formal version which retains the obscurity, or, alternatively, for an explicit rejection of the ordinary notion of an event.

Again, one who says that he witnessed a curious event yesterday, or that there was a time when he could run a mile in five minutes, is not likely to impress us with his philosophical daring, but the situation seems to change when he is charged with thereby committing himself to an ontology of events and times, with positing these entities as well as material bodies. I said the issue seems to change; well, it *has* changed when in place of our familiar idioms we have the grandiose but ill-defined jargon of 'ontology' and 'entities'—ill-defined, but highly suggestive of more substantial items, items which one might think of as in the same logical space, as it were, if not in the same physical space as material bodies. And, of course, this is no accident. The issues just cannot get going unless our ordinary language is supplanted—unwittingly, perhaps, or with the aim of giving a paraphrase—by such philosophical verbiage. In similar fashion it is supposed that talk about the meaning of a word must be talk about some entity, and since the nature of that entity is deemed to be obscure, our normal use of 'meaning' is rejected or severely qualified. Here perhaps more than anywhere else the insensitivity to language and the accompanying primitiveness of the philosophical pronouncements are most in evidence.

It is not generally considered a great loss if ordinary language is thus crippled or ignored, since the philosopher's concern is with something far grander: a language for science. However, while a semblance of scientific exactitude may be conveyed by the use of symbolism, this is frequently a cover-up for confusion, poverty of thought, and a refusal to take the task of analysis seriously. Similarly, the appeal to scientific procedures, such as that of 'postulating entities' for the sake of a fruitful theory, is widely misconceived—as if postulation, rather than downright assertion, were sufficient acknowledgement of the unclarity infecting an existential proposition; when, clearly, we are not in a position to consider any such postulation until the terms in which it is couched are understood. If there is a suspicion that, say, talk of some kind of universal is incoherent, it is not to be allayed by speaking of what *may* rather than what *does* exist; 'may' is in general less demanding than 'does', but yields nothing to it on the requirement that its subject term be intelligible. There is a place in science for forging on in a pragmatic spirit, but while to treat in this way an inadequately defined philosophical proposition may give some satisfaction to the scientist manqué, it is to turn one's back on the philosophical task.

This is not to say that questions about what there is or exists are not important, or easily resolved, since the question of analysis may present considerable difficulties. The language contains many forms of words which to all appearances serve to designate something or other, but when we ask what exactly they introduce, satisfactory answers may be slow to suggest themselves. So, for instance, the more general question, 'What are we speaking of when we say that a child knows the meaning of w?', appears to survive rejection of the association of 'the meaning of w' with anything describable as an *entity*, but its answer is not entirely evident. More seriously, we have the uncertainties provoked by such units as clauses and participial constructions, along with the terminology relating to items which seem to hover uncertainly between the propositional and the worldly, as 'fact' and 'condition'. This is one area where there are problems worthy of some honest toil.

As I have indicated, there is in some quarters a reluctance to 'quantify over' times, events, or numbers, for instance, since this move is taken to bring with it adherence to an ontology of such things. But, of course, there are times, events, and numbers, if there are true statements which allow us to make such inferences as that there was a time when such-and-such an event took place and that there is a number which is so-and-so, and there patently are such true statements. These are not philosophical questions, any more than it is a philosophical question whether moas still exist, or whether there is a desk in my study. True, philosophers have been known to speak as if they were authorities on questions of the existence of furniture, but whether or not there is a desk in my study is not a matter to be decided by a philosopher *qua* philosopher. In order to show that, contrary to our impression, this room was devoid of such an object, a philosopher would, like anyone else, have to persuade us that a state of affairs obtained which our understanding of the assertion required us to recognize as falsifying what we said, but knowledge of such circumstances calls for no more and no less than knowledge of the practices and procedures which go with the ordinary, everyday understanding which we have of propositions of the type in question; it is not such as to bring into play any expertise which the man may have in his capacity as a philosopher. This is not to say that empirical matters fall outside his sphere of interest; on the contrary, that sphere can embrace anything and everything. It is just that he has no special authority to determine the truth on such matters. Nor do I wish to deny that, by considering what a proposition means, we could justifiably come to the conclusion that it could not be true. I maintain merely that this is a possibility that can be allowed only so long as there are no circumstances in which the proposition would be reckoned as true in accordance with its accepted interpretation; any interpretation which a philosopher might advance must be accommodated to the fact, if fact it is, that there are circumstances in which the given proposition is recognized as having this status. Meaning is not secondary to truth in the sense that a grasp of the former presupposes actual familiarity with circumstances in which one is entitled to assert the proposition, but if there are in fact such circumstances, then this is something with which any suggested interpretation of the proposition must be consistent.

One is reminded of Berkeley on this point. Generally speaking he is careful, indeed anxious, to make out that what he is saying is not in contradiction with what the ordinary man believes: he is just saying what such beliefs amount to in his eyes and repudiating what he takes to be a mistaken construal of them. However, on occasions he is led to say such things as that sugar is not really sweet; to deny, rather than to render in alternative language, what is commonly and correctly believed (cf. the first of the *Three Dialogues between Hylas and Philonous*). It may be that this is a slip, that he has made an unfortunate choice of words in opposing the view that sweetness is a property of sugar quite independently of any facts about human taste experience, but, as it stands, his way of formulating the position he wishes to defend is unacceptable.

The kind of move which I am supporting can be clarified by a comparison with an argument labelled by Quine the 'fallacy of subtraction' (Quine [1960], pp. 206-7). Against one who holds that 'if we can speak of a sentence as meaningful, or as having meaning, then there must be a meaning that it has', Quine would argue that 'we could as well justify the hypostasis of sakes and unicorns on the basis of the idioms "for the sake of" and "is hunting unicorns"'. Since we attach no meaning to 'There are sakes', there can be no question of deducing this from anything, but of course we can understand 'There are unicorns' and we can recognize that this is deducible from, say, 'Several unicorns are in this very room'. One who denied this would presumably be under a misapprehension about the contribution made by the predicate, 'are in this very room'. There is no question of always refusing such inferences, but only of sorting out the correct from the incorrect. Thus, in (charitable) support of what Quine says about meaning, we might point out that there is certainly in general no guarantee that we can pass from a use of N as a mass noun to its use as a count noun. This is most obvious when the latter use does not exist—we have 'arson' and 'bribery', but not 'an arson' or 'a bribery'—but even when that use is available, the inference is not automatic: we cannot pass from 'having time' to 'having a time', for instance, and if we can go from 'having meaning' to 'having a meaning', or to 'there is a meaning that it has', this will exploit more than the fact that the noun enjoys the two forms. I am out to defend only moves actually sanctioned by linguistic practice, and not to champion a general principle so formulable that it might be countered by examples such as those cited: the failure of 'There are sakes' and 'There are unicorns' as inferences from the given premises casts no doubt on the inference from, say, 'The meaning of w as v is recognized by my dictionary' to 'There is one meaning of w that is recognized by my dictionary'. The only question is the familiar one of precisely what it is that is responsible for the existential implication; the question, that is, of how function is to be assigned. The legitimacy of the inference does not require that we should have assigned a sense to anything comparable with 'There are sakes'.

To make a related point, if such a proposition as '6 is a perfect number' really does 'commit us to an ontology', then, provided this proposition can be shown to be true, this consequent ontology will hold no fears for us, since the initial safeguard of truth will persist through any generalizations based upon it, and we are assured that any mistaken inferences concerning kinds of thing or implications relating to what is involved in there being such things as numbers will be of our own making. And, indeed, reflection upon actual examples, such as this, readily confirms this observation. There is no problem in showing that 6 is perfect—i.e. is equal to the sum of its divisors, itself excluded—and nothing in this procedure to provoke fears of a commitment to entities of an unintelligible kind.

Similarly, we are familiar enough with occasions on which we might say that we witnessed an unusual event or happening, and at a loss to know how this could be challenged as a way of speaking. The kinds of mistake which we do make and which would lead us to retract an assertion of this kind are not such as to leave us wondering how this form of words could have application more generally, but the coherence of the words remains quite unimpugned by factual error in particular circumstances. Nor does the fact that the words license an inference to the proposition, 'There was an event which we witnessed', constitute any kind of hazardous plunge or commitment. An illuminating analysis of the notion of an event may be desirable, but it could hardly result in our questioning this implication; this is part of the linguistic data, a trivial move in the language game with which any analysis will have to be consistent, part of the given network of relationships which fix the place of the term 'event' in the language. And if it is wondered why an analysis *must* observe such constraints, the answer is simple: failure to do so will mean that, whatever one is giving an account of, it is not our ordinary notion of an event.

'But surely it is a perfectly reasonable policy to deny a place in our ontology to entities which are by common consensus problematic; surely the decision to postulate such entities should be taken only when simpler explanatory hypotheses have been found wanting'. This way of posing the objection is, I suggest, quite inappropriate to the kind of issue at which it is being directed. First, we note once more the unexplained intrusion of the term 'entity', a term which is patently not related to such a well-defined range of linguistic responses or intuitions as are 'there is', 'event', and the other expressions which figure in our original propositions. 'Entity' is largely a philosopher's term, possessed of a lack of clarity which enables disputes as to whether something is an admissible entity to thrive and flourish with all the appearance of questions of fact or of substance; as if we knew quite well what was at stake when we were considering whether events, numbers or times were entities; indeed, as if it were obvious that in speaking of a time when such-and-such an event took place we simply had to be prepared to make out a case for speaking of certain 'entities' as the referents of our words 'time' and 'event'. It is quite inappropriate to liken the issue to one which may arise in the sciences, when we are wondering just what things and in what numbers must be supposed to exist if we are to account for phenomena so far observed. In the context of ontological commitment, questions of what there is are of interest only when the questions of definition have been decided, for it is only when the wrong decision can be a source of actual error that there is point to a concern with not postulating entities beyond necessity: one says there are two things of a certain kind and there turns out to be, as a matter of fact, only one. If it is just a way of speaking that generates new entities, there is nothing to worry about, no matter of substance at stake, no day of reckoning on which our profligacy will be brought home to us.

This is not to say that there can be no distinction between reasonable and unreasonable decisions as to the usage of 'entity', which even without further clarification can, when the exact sense is unimportant, be of some use as a stylistic variant of related terms. The word is vague, but not so vague as to allow of application quite indiscriminately. It seems fairly clear, for instance, that it has no business to be associated with such terms as 'event', 'happening', 'movement', or 'change'. What is important is that its applicability should not come to be regarded as a 'test of reality', so that changes, say, should be considered something less than real if not thus categorizable. Nor should the behaviour of 'entity' be taken to match that of 'there is', so that doubt as to its applicability should bring with it doubt as to the applicability of the verbal phrase, thus leading us to the absurd position of querying whether there really are changes and events, decisions, accidents, wars, meetings, and so forth. And, of course, there can be no question of *eliminating* any such unwanted phenomena: you can eliminate reference to something, but you cannot talk it out of existence. Given the intelligibility and the truth of, say, a proposition to the effect that there was an event of a certain kind, elimination of reference to that event is simply a matter of closing one's eyes to what has occurred. It is not something to boast about, to claim as an achievement.

Should we in fact be threatened with mysterious entities, then so long as their specifications make sense, we shall have to reconcile ourselves to the possibility that accepting them should become inevitable. If I avoid having to acknowledge anything peculiar in the world of abstractions, among meanings, facts, numbers, and the like, this is because any monsters that threaten prove to be the offspring of grammatical confusion, and not because I am fortunate enough to be able to get by with an alternative hypothesis.

'But your argument supposes there to be a sharp distinction between questions of language and questions of fact, and this is not so'. It is true that a question of the existence of *F*s will remain indeterminate to the extent that it is not clear what counts as an *F*, but this is better expressed by saying that for the non-linguistic question to be decided the uncertainty in question must first be removed, rather than by saying that in such a case the distinction between the linguistic and the non-linguistic is not a clear one, any unclarity in the particular case surely being remediable, even if that means stipulating, as with a scientific redefinition, as to how *F* is to be understood. In any case, propositions about numbers, events and times—of the mundane sorts that may well be in question—

do not suffer from the relevant unclarity. By this I do not wish to imply that these terms, or related more specific expressions, are well defined, if by this is meant that anyone has actually provided us with a good definition, a comprehensive account of their usage, but they are well defined in the more important sense that their actual usage is clear. That is, there is by and large no hesitation in our responses over the question whether the use of such a term is correct on a given occasion, not only in terms of usage—is 'time' the precise word we should be using here?—but often also in terms of fact—is it the case that there really was a time when I could do such-and-such?

It is worth pointing out that the sense in which I say that the word 'entity' is vague is not the sense in which I might apply this to 'thing'. The word 'thing' is vague in the sense that it is highly unspecific, so contributes little information. There are comparatively few nouns in the language—though names of places and times are exceptions—which cannot be replaced by the all-purpose 'thing', but 'entity' is vague in that it pretends to be more specific, less general than 'thing', without its being clear what its differentiae are. For some the word appears to be suggestive of materiality—you can say 'A funny thing happened to me on the way to the lecture', but not 'a funny entity'—but in non-philosophical usage the idea of wholeness may be more important, as in 'a corporate entity'. In either case it is hard to be precise. The word simply lacks the firm roots in ordinary usage which would make it reasonable to suppose that with a bit of work one might formulate a clear account of its meaning.

This is, incidentally, the reason why ordinary language is so important philosophically. To be sensitive to its virtues it is not necessary to have an exalted opinion of the wisdom of its users, a distaste for technical jargon, or a belief that the distinctions it enshrines are essential for all purposes and can never be overlooked, but these virtues relate to the fact that, by and large, ordinary usage means an *established* usage, and that means, for the kind of proposition that concerns us here, established truth conditions or assertibility conditions. Such conditions determine what there is, and accordingly the 'ontology' which must be adopted if we are to do justice to the facts.

In this discussion I have consistently used the term 'there is' rather than 'exists'. This has been intentional, since the confusion involved in supposing that 'there is' and 'entity' go hand in hand is made even worse by bringing in another term which has its own points of difference with each. Thus, if the question raised were whether or not events existed, the answer could reasonably be 'No'. Events occur, take place, or perhaps happen, but for the most part we do not speak of them as existing. But, of course, that is not to say that there never are any events; that would mean that nothing ever happened. 'Exists' has something in common with 'entity', to the extent that it is not used of things which take time, occur, or take place, as in the above examples of sentences where 'entity', despite its vagueness, would be seen to be inappropriate. On the other hand, if 'entity' is suggestive of materiality, which appears to be why some wish to withhold it from, e.g., numbers, then it is certainly not a term that goes hand in hand with 'exists', for there is nothing amiss with saying that possibilities, needs, differences, or other patently non-material subjects exist.

I suggest that the answer to the question, 'Do events exist?', is a simple 'No', but those who are inclined to debate such questions are unlikely to accept a resolution of the matter that relies on consideration of what it would be correct to say, even if they are themselves prepared to say that events do not exist. What the denial of existence to events could mean, if not that 'exists' is not correctly used of them, is not clear; it is not the simple factual question, whether anything ever happens, since this is presumably not in dispute. The disputants would not, I suspect, be prepared to be pinned down to saying that it was either a linguistic or a non-linguistic question, seeing the two as inextricably tied, though given that this particular commitment is not liable to be challenged— and is not a philosophical matter if it is—it is hard to see why anyone should resist a sorting out along the lines indicated. Certainly, there must be some lack of clarity in the philosophical usage of the key terms if the fact that there are events does not settle the issue, and this being so it is premature to attempt to decide the matter by reference to such factors as simplicity and economy, let alone conditions which, like 'ontological purity', are even more obscure in sense than the propositions under discussion.

Nor does the existential quantifier hold out any prospect of great enlightenment. The introduction of this device is never, to my knowledge, associated with a satisfactory elucidation of the troublesome terms, terms such as 'entity', with which some would wish it to keep company, or with any account of principles on which one might consider various familiar forms of words as within or outside its scope—as, for instance, 'There is a surprise in store for him', 'There is much to be done', 'There is a chance of a frost', or 'There is no telling what might happen'. An appeal to the quantifier does not render clarification of such sentences unnecessary, though if anything, its intuitive sense, or its use in accordance with one plausible form of definition, would often seem to take it away from the company of 'entity'. Thus, if it is explained in terms of the passage from a sentence containing a proper name, as 'Paris is a city', to the open form obtained by deleting the name and substituting a variable, 'x is a city', whence we form the quantified version, '$\exists x(x$ is a city$)$', the weight of the explanation will fall on the notion of a *name*; the quantifier itself will tell us nothing about this. If, however, we do not set so much store by the occurrence of the *proper* name which the variable is supposed to supplant, we could form '$\exists x$(Paris is an x)' from the original sentence.

This latter construction conforms well enough to a general idea which we may find ourselves invoking when we explain the quantifier in the first case, viz. that it is sufficient, though perhaps not necessary, for the truth of '$\exists x(x$ is a city$)$', that there be some way of replacing the variable in 'x is a city' by a proper name so as to yield a true sentence. The explanation for '$\exists x$(Paris is an x)' goes exactly parallel, with just the substitution of 'common name' for 'proper name'. We may note too the possibility of a matching generalization with 'something' in either case: 'Paris is a city' yields not only 'Something is a city', but also 'Paris is something'; further evidence that the quantifier can be assigned the same role in either context, if we so wish. Nor need we stop at names: verbs too could be generalized upon, and perhaps even other parts of speech. But to say now that we are admitting into our ontology all manner of strange entities is to suppose that the quantifier makes sense only where it is allied to the notion of an entity, which is not only the retreat into obscurity yet again, but a retreat into the arbitrary as well.

Leaving aside generalizations in these directions, the reading 'For some x . . .' appears best suited to cases where we have to do with something identifiable in other terms, so not with 'There is a chance of frost' or 'There is a need for caution'. Such cases, along with the difficulty in taking in mass terms, as with 'There is room for compromise', show that the quantifier does not have a strong claim to match the range of 'there is', but its main service, from our point of view, is not to explain but perhaps to focus our attention on differences and extensions of possible interest. Roughly speaking, elucidation is demanded by rather than on offer from the 'objectual' reading of the quantifier, and while the 'substitutional' interpretation is more adaptable to the range of contexts in which 'there is' turns up, it does not even pretend to explain the roles of the diverse phrases which the variable of quantification may supplant.

Since the possibility of replacing a phrase by 'something' is sometimes triumphantly pointed to as evidence of some kind of significant commitment, it is worth emphasizing the triviality of this possibility, which tells us nothing about the character of the phrase supplanted. If I need a bath, then I need something; if a dragon doesn't exist, then something doesn't exist; if I marvel at your tact, then I marvel at something; something is certain, if it is certain that you will die, and there is something you don't know if you don't know where I live; if I didn't catch the drift of your remarks, then there was something I didn't catch, and if you insulted me you did something. For reasons of delicacy, or because I failed to hear all that was said, I might use the phrase 'that something something man' in reporting a person's words. There is nothing of any philosophical consequence in this convenient use of 'something', and it would be quite absurd to think of there being an issue here on which thinking men could reasonably divide, some 'countenancing' this move and its commitments, others having reservations about its legitimacy, yet when philosophers solemnly speak of the acceptability or otherwise of second-order quantification, they are often, beneath the technical jargon, talking of nothing more substantial than this.

24. Reductive analyses

When confronted with a troublesome form of words, it is natural to try to rephrase in a more perspicuous idiom, but the implications of the availability of an alternative are often misunderstood. So, for instance, it is sometimes suggested that instead of employing a noun we might in some cases make do with a more innocent adverb, as with the suggestion of 'I sense painfully' as an alternative to 'I have a pain', the advantage of the new way of speaking being that we are no longer able to formulate questions about the identity of pains. The procedure here may or may not be defensible. There is a case for the possibility of such a translation if it can be argued that, because questions of the identity of pains do not arise, a possible obstacle to an adverbial analysis is avoided. However, to admit that there is this loss of expressive power in passing to the adverbial version looks very much like admitting to a deficiency in it as a translation, given that it is not particularly difficult either to understand or to answer the question whether two people could experience the same pain: if the identity is not to be merely a matter of pains of the same kind, it will be a matter of pains having (in addition) a common location, as with the example of Siamese twins who suffer a sting in their shared flesh. In the kind of reductionist formulation which we flirted with earlier, it will be a matter of its hurting the one where it hurts the other. We have here a question which can be avoided, but avoided only in the sense of ignored. The assumption must be, then, that questions of identity with respect to pains are not merely perplexing, but in some sense incoherent, in which case a form of words which showed up this incoherence, or which could not even begin to express it, might have something to be said for it. This is not a possibility that is in fact realized, but looking at the question from this perspective is at least an advance on turning one's back on the question in the hope that it will go away.

A common difficulty with reductionist programmes is that translations work in either direction, leaving the reductionist in the uncomfortable position of having to agree that, if his proposed reduction can be carried out comprehensively, then we are just as much entitled to speak in the way to which he takes exception as in that which he prefers. Indeed, perhaps he has implicitly given us a licence to extend the former way of speaking by introducing new nouns of the appropriate kind to match any existing locutions of the favoured type, thereby— on his way of looking at it—proliferating the undesired entities still further. A similar failure to take one's reductions seriously is found when talk of postulation is persisted with even when a translation has been furnished. If the sense of 'He always has a sullen appearance' really is preserved in the move to 'He always appears sullen', then the reverse transition is not accompanied by the *postulation* of anything, in particular of suspect 'appearances', there being no respect in which the truth of the substantival version is open or uncertain, given the truth, happily conceded, of the version with the verb.

As I have indicated, what we should wish to say, if we see value in translations of this kind, is that their very possibility tells us something about the behaviour of the noun in the supposedly problematic version; it may be that, for instance, the noun, as a noun, is in some way idle, that its full substantival function, and hence the customary commitments of that part of speech, are not being exploited; or, more likely, that the noun is not the kind of noun that it at first sight appears to be.

The model here might be prepositional phrases, such as 'in charge of', 'in need of', 'in accordance with', 'in return for', and 'by dint of', or verbal phrases such as 'give way to', 'keep pace with', 'lose sight of', 'set fire to', and 'take note of'. Nouns in such combinations show varying degrees of substantival force. At one extreme there are locutions which, like 'in spite of' or 'in keeping with', involve nouns which do not occur in the same sense outside that, or a very similar context, and where an analysis of the phrase will have to proceed by taking it as a whole, and not treating the noun as a significantly isolable element. In intermediate cases there is scope for, say, modification by an adjective, as with 'in sole charge of' or 'in complete accordance with', and at the other extreme we have the full range of substantival function. Thus, we can form 'in the old cupboard by' and 'in the cupboards by' as well as the simple 'in the cupboard by', and we already have article determination, whereas with the 'true' prepositional phrases such modifications are not available to the same degree.

In many cases this merely shows that we have to do with a mass noun rather than a count noun, but, more important, is the analysis of such forms of words as 'in keeping with' or 'give way to' really more straightforward than the analysis of a noun which shows all the features appropriate to that status, and in particular which invites questions concerning existence and identity? There is, after all, the question of how precisely such phrases work, the way they connect with the circumstances of their use, whereas the behaviour of fully fledged nouns is in general easier to understand. Certainly, a problem of identity conditions would seem to arise only if it has an answer: if, in a given case, we can confidently say that a question of identity has a clear sense, we come close to contradicting ourselves if we then confess to having no idea how its answer is to be determined. Consider the two sentences, 'I have an allergy to pollen' and 'I am allergic to pollen'. Use of the noun phrase, 'an allergy', may suggest identity conditions of a certain form, but what suggests this is pretty much what answers it; certainly, we do not have to look far to find an answer: you may have the same allergy as me in that you too have an allergy to pollen.

But how can I be so confident that this example is typical? Well, what kinds of identity condition arise? Broadly speaking, conditions which are either locational or sortal. The latter must be taken to include a variety of conditions, such as sameness of degree—as in 'They showed the same enthusiasm'— or a further category added, but there is nothing mysterious about the categories required, nothing which should encourage the protest that we do not *need* allergies, or whatever, given the alternative idiom—as if, despite the reduction, there was a commitment which it was in some way desirable to avoid.

As a last example, consider the term 'knack', as this occurs in such contexts as 'He has a knack for mending things'. At the silly extreme we meet the concern about whether or not knacks should be denied admission to one's ontology. If, as usual, the ontology is an ontology of entities or objects, with the physical as the paradigm, then a knack can be turned away without further ado. If membership for *F*s follows on there merely being such a thing as an *F*—where, for a knack, that is settled affirmatively by the truth of some sentence of the form, 'He has a knack for . . .'—then again no question that is difficult to resolve. And no complication with identity: if you and I both have a knack for saying the wrong thing at the wrong time, then we have the same knack. The question of substance concerns neither existence nor identity, but only meaning: what is it to have a knack? As a rough approximation, we might say that to have a knack is to be able to bring off a certain kind of action, or whatever, with adroitness. It is not easy to pin down the precise sense of the phrase, but that is not because there is some mysterious entity which proves elusive, something which in the end we might just have to postulate. But why *a* knack? Where is the unity, the singularity, which makes for the appropriateness of a count noun? As with sameness, so here it is to the prepositional phrase that we look, what the knack is a knack *for*; that is what confers individuality, what makes it a matter of this knack rather than that.

It may seem extraordinary to suggest that most of what customarily passes for ontology is not a philosophical matter at all, that many of the propositions thought to be problematic are, if the familiar interpretations of the words are respected, straightforwardly decidable as true or false without need of prior analysis. If it does seem extraordinary, this just shows how prolonged exposure to a way of thinking can be as effective an influence as actual argument. But, of course, even if a large number of existential questions fall outside the philosopher's special competence—a competence which relates primarily to *reasoning*—the difficult questions of analysis still remain. In advance of any finer analyses we know of general kinds of thing which an adequate inventory of the world would have to include, but the analyses themselves may hold surprises. *A priori,* there would appear to be scope for drawing connections in an illuminating way, for assigning priority to certain notions, such as those of space and time, and for arriving at a more systematic and comprehensive view of whatever it is that our philosophy should be dreaming of.

25. Generic 'the'

There are many nouns which allow of interpretation at two levels of generality, being associated either with a spatio-temporal criterion of identity or with a criterion that is merely sortal. Ascent from the former to the latter may be thought of as an ascent from the concrete to the abstract, so if we wish to have some understanding of the nature of the 'commitment to abstract entities', it should be profitable to consider more closely the relation between these two levels.

Consider, for instance, noun phrases containing 'some' or 'all'. These are generally to be thought of as indicative of a certain number, or a totality of individuals, as in 'Some passengers were injured' or 'All seats are booked', but they may also be interpretable in terms of types. If asked to expand 'Some trees are deciduous' we might cite a plurality of types of tree rather than attempt to indicate individual members of these types, and 'All birds build nests' might likewise be thought of in terms of species, which we might conceivably enumerate, rather than individuals, which we could not. On the other hand, if it is true that in talking of some or all trees we may be said to be talking of kinds, species, or types, it is also true that our subject matter is essentially trees, thought of as elements of the lower level. I do not mean that there is a simple reduction such that we could say: for 'all birds', understood with respect to types, read 'all birds', understood with respect to individuals. 'All birds build nests' rephrases as 'Birds of all species build nests', and the unquantified 'birds' does not necessarily conceal an implicit 'all'. But at least there is a rephrasal along these lines.

A similar device is to be found in the use of phrases containing generic 'the'. Thus, in speaking of 'the eye', 'the backhand drive', or 'the ladybird', as in 'The eye is an extremely complex organ', 'Some find the backhand drive difficult to master', and 'The ladybird is not a kind of bird', we make use of a construction, available for most nouns, which to all appearances presents certain items as subjects of predications.

This appearance goes deep: there is not just the trivial possibility of substituting 'something', but there is surely a sense in which we are speaking about a particular stroke, a stroke with its own individuality, its own distinctive features and character, when we are discussing the backhand drive. It is for all the world like a single thing, the bearer of a certain well-defined range of attributes, and not a wit less real for its failure to be individuated as a stroke made at a particular time and by a particular person.

Again, consider the sentence, 'They were discussing the journey from London to New York'. Use of the definite article before 'journey' could rest on a restrictive condition such as 'which they had just taken', which would ensure reference to an item of the lower level, of the favoured type, but in the absence of an implied condition of this sort and with the neutrality of the verb in the relevant respect, it is open to us to read the sentence in the maximally general way, the occurrence of 'the' depending on no more than the condition stated, viz. 'from London to New York', which, through being detached from reference to a journey on a particular occasion, appears to introduce an item of a more abstract character.

On the other hand, there are considerations which, it might be thought, we must balance against this impression. We have come across a number of ways of expressing generality: 'Backhand drives are difficult', 'A backhand drive is difficult', 'Any backhand drive is difficult', 'All backhand drives are difficult', and now 'The backhand drive is difficult'. As is to be expected, there are differences in the uses of these forms, but the subject matter seems basically the same: items to which 'a backhand drive' is applicable, actual or hypothetical spatio-temporally individuated actions of a certain kind. Similarly with 'They were discussing the journey from London to New York'. The absence of further individuating conditions surely leaves the definite description with a highly *general* application, rather than application to a peculiar kind of individual. A failure to be tied down to a particular occasion is not to be construed as a positive attachment to an item of a different nature. Contrast 'We enjoyed the journey from London to New York' with 'The journey from London to New York is tiring'. In terms of specificity of reference, the demands of the past-tense 'enjoyed', supposing it to be a past definite, are greater than those of the habitual—better: unmarked—'is' (or 'enjoy'). The continuity of topic, however, is evident, the difference being just one in the degree of generality involved. It is true that, in the general case, we are still speaking of a single journey— indeed of a particular journey, in one use of the term—but the sense in which this is so cannot make for a rival to the interpretation in terms of an observation about repeated occasions. We gain nothing by interposing a further 'abstract object' to be the referent of 'the journey from London to New York', instead of clarifying the relation of this phrase to individual instances. Similarly, the abstractness of a mass noun, such as 'water', which comes with its dissociation from locational criteria of identity, is not to be thought of in terms of reference to something abstract.

Again, the interchangeability of 'the F' with 'an F' and 'Fs' is of course matched by the agreement in predicates, and the kind of predicate which attaches to 'the F' is one which surely determines its subject as concrete, if that is the character of an F. The cuckoo lays its eggs in other birds' nests, an activity of creatures of flesh, blood, and feathers, birds to be found in particular places at particular times, not an activity of a creature which is at some remove from the familiar spatial settings. This appears to be quite general. The predicates attachable to 'the cuckoo' may sometimes require the plural 'cuckoos', sometimes the singular 'a cuckoo', but, figurative uses aside, one or other is surely always in place. Which seems to confirm the original suggestion: generality can be introduced in a number of different ways involving verbs, determiners, adverbs, and other parts of speech. Generic 'the' is one such device, but it is in no way 'creative'. It gives us a deceptive variant on the other forms, but it does not mark ascent to a new range of entities.

This rejoinder is basically correct, but there is a risk of overstatement in what it denies. This risk concerns two issues, reference and existence. Given our rather restricted use of the term, we can deny that reference occurs to the extent that misidentification fails to be a possibility with phrases like 'the cuckoo' and 'the backhand drive', even if the determinate character of these phrases, together with satisfaction of the relevant existence condition, means that reference in accordance with a less demanding requirement is more clearly possible. It is on the matter of existence that a denial would be quite uncalled for: we can happily grant that phrases featuring the definite article in this use are superfluous, but we can hardly deny that there is such a bird as the cuckoo or such a stroke as the backhand drive. On the contrary, for there to be such a bird just is for there to be cuckoos; this is, it must be stressed, just the kind of equivalence that the analysis provides. It does not suggest renderings without the generic article for all cases other than that in which existence is asserted and then simply declare the existential form to be false, but a systematic rendering is available throughout, truths being mapped onto truths in every instance.

There being such a stroke as the backhand drive is a shade more complex, in that there are two renderings to choose from: it could be a matter of someone's having at some time made a stroke thus describable, or it could be merely a matter of the possibility of such a stroke. At all events, existence poses no problem, even if it is more naturally understood in a less concrete way than with the existence of a bird. In keeping with this we may also note a greater tendency for 'the backhand drive' to occur where it would also be possible to make a more restricted reference. I am thinking here of such sentences as 'He plays the backhand drive better than his partner'. Again, all that is involved is the playing of backhand drives, but if singularity of type rather than plurality of performance is what interests us, this use of the definite article is well suited to that emphasis. Compare 'He plays the violin execrably'. It is likely that no reference is intended to a particular violin, but we have a form of generality comparable with that to be found in such phrases as 'travel by car' and 'leave school'. Here we meet with a use of what are usually count nouns which is appropriate when we have no interest in or knowledge of the identity of any relevant car or school. Insert the indefinite article and the nouns now occur with a certain potential, to single out one car or one school among others. It is because, when associated with the narrower criterion of identity, a count noun can be used both in application to a single individual and to express generality in its plural form, that this use can be considered more fundamental than that with generic 'the': since the latter is suited only to the expression of generality, there is some justification for seeing the significance of a reduction in the possibility of passing from the latter use to the former, rather than in the opposite direction.

While practically any count noun can combine with generic 'the', the noun 'man' will not do so unless qualified, as in 'The prudent man does not invest in national savings', or in that celebrated paradigm of an abstraction, 'the average man'. It is worth remarking the affinity which this has with 'the eye', 'the internal combustion engine', and the rest, though it is also true that 'average' can introduce a complication that is not paradigmatic. For 'The average man has 2.3 children' we have the reading 'Men have on average 2.3 children', i.e. 'Men average 2.3 children apiece', but what of the existence of the average man? This makes sense in terms of the existence of representative or typical men, but 'Men on average exist' will not do, the effect of the qualification '(on) average' being to restrict the predicate to objects taken collectively, the plural subject comparing with that in 'Careful drivers are few and far between'.

It hardly needs mentioning at this stage, but the generality involved in generic 'the' is that of the simple plural rather than the plural with 'all'. Nor is it appropriate to think of 'the F' as selecting an arbitrary F, or necessary to incorporate 'the F' only into sentences that are intended as non-contingently true. All these common accounts break down with such sentences as 'The kiwi is found in both islands' and 'The rabbit was introduced into the country by the early settlers', though in particular cases it can happen that one or other of these analyses is adequate. There are, we might mention, phrases which we should naturally group along with those containing generic 'the' but whose nouns do not have the corresponding simple plural. We have 'the public' and 'the clergy', but talk in terms of these is not resolvable into talk in terms of 'publics' and 'clergies'. The blanket reference to individuals is, however, transparent enough.

I say we should not spoil a satisfactory analysis by turning around and denying the existence of the cuckoo, or whatever. The interesting cases are not those where the denial of existence is motivated by a general distrust or misunderstanding of the construction, but where particular necessary conditions are found lacking. Take the phrase 'the will of the British people', as it occurs in the sentence, 'The present policy is contrary to the will of the British people'. There need be nothing amiss with this way of speaking, no 'illegitimate reification', in so far as what we have is simply an alternative expression of generality. There is no call to protest that there is no such thing as the will of the British people, on the grounds that, say, there is no person signifed by 'the British people', but the protest is justified if the necessary unity in individual wills is lacking. If there is disagreement from person to person in what is willed, different people being of a different mind on the matter in question, then the use of the description, 'the will of the British people', which clearly purports to discern uniformity, is illegitimate. Similarly with 'desire' and 'need' when used in this way. Though the extent of the generality may not be well defined, such a use of 'the' requires some degree of generality to be established before we have singularity in the appropriate sense. Apart from errors of this kind, the most common cases of illegitimate reification or hypostatization generally involve some form or personification—think of romancings about the activities of Nature—though even here the same point may apply: if some single factor could be identified as contributing significantly to the states for which Nature in all her wisdom is thought responsible, we might be able to make sense of this isolation of a single agent; as it is, however, the factors in question tend to be too multifarious to furnish any useful abstraction.

26. Identity

Questions of identity have been to the fore in our discussion of troublesome noun phrases, and they remain there when we turn to consider the differences which divide nouns into their two principal classes, those of count and mass. First, however, identity itself calls for some individual attention. When discussing the principle of extensionality, E, I did not concede that anything might be out of order with that principle. If the behaviour of ostensibly referential terms in modal contexts or in *oratio obliqua* demanded that we rethink any principles, it was only the patently flawed E' that had to give way. E, together with its converse, go to make up what is sometimes described as 'Leibniz's Law': a and b are identical if and only if whatever is true of a is true of b. This law, along with the classical theory of identity which it embodies, have not only been thought threatened by the contexts so far considered, but a further challenge is presented by questions of identity over time. We speak of a child and an adult being the same person, even of a caterpillar and a butterfly being the same creature, but use of the correspondingly different designations is perhaps not as indifferent as the identities would appear to imply. What holds of the child—good health and small stature— may well fail to hold of the adult which he becomes. Is it enough simply to be more explicit with distinctions of tense? Make clear that any differences are temporally separated—the same person *was* healthy and *is now* decrepit—and any suggestion of inconsistency vanishes. However, that answers a question of reconciliation which does not now trouble anyone, the real difficulty coming with the apparent conflation of child and adult induced by the common application of the phrase 'same person'. Similarly, my son and I may have attended the same school, St. Horace's, but that school could have consisted of quite distinct buildings during our respective school days. So, an apparent identity of school with buildings at each time, but non-identity of the buildings at odds with identity of our schools. What is to give? We must deny any identity between school and buildings, at either time. A statement like 'This is St. Horace's' looks very much as if it makes just such a claim, but we simply cannot identify school and present school buildings if we wish, say, to date the beginnings of each differently. And the child is not to be considered identical with the person? The threat here is that transitivity of identity will have us equate child with adult, when what is true of the one is not always true of the other. We go some way towards this identity with statements like 'The child was in later life an avid philatelist', but the tendency is to refuse to allow 'child' and 'adult' to span both phases. If it none the less seems hard to accept non-identity of child and person, remember that the non-identity is not of the sort that might hold *at* a time, child and person existing side by side. It is *over* time that the difference in what 'the child' and 'the person' refer to emerges, but it is a real enough difference and one for which Leibniz's Law provides a sensitive enough litmus. In the case of the school buildings, the non-identity may be much more apparent: no gradual transformation of the one set into the other, but demonstrably distinct buildings coexisting.

But why not lay the blame for any tensions at Leibniz's Law itself? If we say that those buildings and these buildings are the same school, but that the former have been burned down and the latter are still standing, this can surely be taken as contradicting that law. Not at all. We have, after all, conceded a difference in the buildings, so there will of course be some respect in which they differ even if there is some other respect in which they agree. Still, does this not show identity to be relative, not the absolute notion which the classical theory requires? Not sameness or difference *tout court,* but sameness *qua F* coexisting with difference *qua G*? What it does show, perhaps unexpectedly, is that we may meet with an equivalence relation where we might have thought we had strict identity; it does not show that there is no place for such identity. There will be cases of sameness which do not allow for distinctness in any respect whatsoever, and it is just this kind of complete identity that Leibniz's Law isolates.

As advanced in Geach [1962], p. 157, and [1972], p. 238, the claim that identity is relative involves more than one thesis. Not only are statements of identity said to be incomplete so long as the respect in which identity is being considered is not specified, but it is also thought possible that different *F*s should be the same *G*. On the first point, it is true that sentences of the form '*x* is the same as *y*' may suffer from some indeterminacy, but they are not commonly understood as affirming the kind of identity that is at stake with Leibniz's Law. Thus, with 'The carpet you saw there last week is the same as this one', it may be uncertain how close a comparison is intended, but it would be clear that two distinct carpets were under discussion. On the other hand, if we say that *x* and *y* are one and the same, a form appropriate to 'numerical' identity, it is far from clear that we leave open any significantly different alternatives. The necessary incompleteness obtains only in so far as we can speak of a choice as to the way the sentence might be completed, but in many cases any such choice is illusory. However, this is of no great consequence. Perhaps the intended identity is sufficiently determined without addition of a clause like 'same F', but so long as it makes sense to say that two things can be the same F but different Gs, for suitable choice of terms, the crucial possibility is acknowledged. And, indeed, the language does allow us to say as much: two people may be the same nationality and the same colour, but not the same religion or profession.

It may seem unkind to illustrate the relativity thesis with such examples, given the way they immediately direct us to a contrast with what we might call a 'genuine' identity, as 'Molière and Jean-Baptiste Poquelin were the same person', an identity for which being the same F implies being an F. So, let us go back to our earlier style of example: we can say that the caterpillar and the butterfly are distinct, but the same organism. And, of course, we shall allow that there can be such equivalence relations, that they are not strict identities. The claim of substance comes when it is said that this is the pattern for every seeming identity, so that whenever we said that x and y were the same F, it could none the less make sense to say they were different, or different Gs for some G. But this is simply not so: the comprehensive identity involved in saying that Poquelin and Molière were the same person leaves no room for a difference.

Geach has performed a valuable service in making us more alert to the possibility that what looks like a strict identity may turn out to be only partial, with the important consequences that this has, but there is no question of completely eschewing strict identity, of claiming with any plausibility that we must *always* leave room for adding 'but different G' when we have 'same F'. Temporal complexities make for the possibilities mentioned, but a retreat to relative identity is quite unnecessary when we have to do with two interchangeable names of a single person, neither having unshared temporal or other relevant connections; and, empty though it may be, 'a is a' is a form of proposition which we should not

wish to renounce as perhaps only a half-truth. Geach holds
that strict identity, with its involvement with the notion of
all properties, lays us open to the semantic paradoxes. These
are not, I believe, paradoxes that should trouble us for long,
but in any case it is curious, even if it is common, to give this
involvement a prominent place in an account of identity.
When establishing an identity we do not have to grapple with
the impossible task of checking all properties of *a* and all those
of *b* to see if they tally, but what we look for is some condition which both *a* and *b* satisfy and which is satisfied by only
one thing. In this way we find that we are both talking about
the same concert, for instance, there having been only one
concert at the time and place in question. From this it follows
that, if the concert you are talking about began late, then the
concert I am talking about began late; that if the former
received good notices, then so did the latter; and so on. This
'and so on' does not conceal an infinity of conditions whose
completability is both necessary yet impossible, but we simply
have a pattern that may be repeated indefinitely. And that is
something we know through knowing the truth of the identity,
not something which has to be established *en route* to that truth.

To enquire after the contribution of 'same' is to enquire
after the associated condition or the condition which it supplants: the same ship, i.e. the one that was on that run at that
time. This brings 'same' close to words like 'that' which convey
such conditions, and suggests too that we regard 'same', and
'identical', as intensives: the same man, the very man, the
man himself. This latter step may arouse our suspicions concerning the notion of a *criterion* of identity. We could propose
a criterion for two bodies being the same in volume—that they
should displace the same amount of water—but what is the
criterion for my best friend's being identical with your worst
enemy? There is no question of a test for a certain relation's
holding between two persons, but when we try to ascertain
the import of 'identical with' we promptly pass to nothing
more than the original statement minus this phrase, a statement to which the phrase may appear to lend no more than
emphasis. In terms of one of our parallels, what would it
mean to speak of a criterion for 'very' in 'They got married
that very day'? Could it be that the adjectives 'same' and

'identical' have taken on an inflated role with their ascent to nounhood, at least when the nouns occur in philosophical discourse?

It is here that the notion of a condition which 'same' supplants, a condition which is satisfied by only one thing, gives an important supplementation to that of a bare intensive. We can allow that questions of the identity of a bird, let us say, will resolve into questions as to whether a given bird satisfies a certain condition, whether it is the bird which . . ., and that any number of different conditions may have this role from occasion to occasion, with, at least on the surface, none of the unity which we might have thought to accompany the notion of a criterion of identity. However, such conditions may realize some particular principle which specifies more generally how things characterized in the way in question are individuated. So, for instance, questions of identity with respect to birds, lakes and mountains are in general terms questions of location, and we can acknowledge the general connection of the noun 'bird' with locational criteria whilst recognizing that it is left to particular phrases—many, but not indefinitely various—to furnish specifications of that general criterion from time to time. And, clearly, there is a contrast with criteria appropriate to items of different kinds—to colours, shapes, prices, and virtues, for instance.

Again it is identity over time that offers us most to think about. The sparrow nesting in the eaves is the same sparrow as was there last winter. What would be involved in a criterion for such an identity? An inductive ground will not do, and in avoiding this we may easily find ourselves talking nonsense about the sparrow's continuing to be itself, for instance. What does Leibniz's Law prescribe? That everything true of the one should be true of the 'other'. That may not look helpful, but it may look even less: it may seem that in certain circumstances it cannot fail to yield an inappropriate affirmative decision. For, I can list predicates currently true of the sparrow at this time and conjoin them with those which held last winter, the tense differences guaranteeing consistency. So long as I respect the different times, it does not matter what I say about the earlier bird and what I say about the bird now; the worst that will happen is that I shall have to acknowledge a drastically changed bird. Of course, the histories developed from each end may result in inconsistency when they meet, precisely when there are two sparrows, not one, but suppose there is no temporal overlap between last year's and this year's bird. Then we have an alleged difficulty with the classical account of identity, for in the absence of overlapping existences no contradiction will emerge, but, as far as Leibniz's Law is concerned, we shall have all we need to affirm identity: nothing now stands in the way of our ascribing all those predicates to a single bird, a bird which was initially as our earlier description, subsequently as our later description would have it. And, it has been argued, we need not stop at that, there being nothing in this conception of identity that prevents us from saying that a man might become a balloon, provided that the existence of the man ceases before that of the balloon begins (cf. Griffin [1977], p. 5, and references therein). As long as we are scrupulous in our use of tenses, our balloon man can collect all the predicates which held or hold of either. The balloon man had a beard and voted Labour then landed on a rose bush and burst.

Clearly, we do not want the truth of an identity statement to be contingent upon the fortuitously early demise of one of the individuals involved. Should we then simply say that a is the same as b so long as this hypothesis harbours no inconsistency, either in the world as it is or in the world as it would have been had a (or b) continued in existence? This might at least explain the readiness with which we regard tadpole and frog, or pupa and butterfly, as the same creature, there being no risk of the simultaneous existence of both members of either pair. Perhaps now nothing does stand in the way of speaking of a single thing, but the threat of arbitrariness—the only link being provided by the label we confer upon the thing's two phases—appears almost as serious as the threat of contradiction. For, if the latter is avoided, could we not consistently treat a past object, of whatever kind, as the same F—for some contrived F—as some wildly differing object now in existence? Indeed, might there not be any number of past existents which could be regarded as enjoying a continuing history through some contemporary object, and does this not simply reduce the whole conception to the absurd?

We should like, naturally, to know the extent to which these fanciful possibilities are restricted by the new provision, the provision that the identity should not have been affected had the earlier item continued in existence. This would appear to rule out all but those identities involving continuing objects which we now recognize, and even if we required only that *a* should have in fact ceased to exist before *b* came about, we need not be faced with an absurdity, so long as we did not describe as identities what were in fact only equivalence relations. If we can tack a balloon's history onto that of a man, we can make a similar extension to something else, having a balloon man and a broom man, let us say. What this means is that the same man—that is, strictly the same man—will fall under distinct equivalence relations, relations whose application may have little point, but which will not lead us to identify a balloon with a broom. Indeed, specifying relations of this general kind is often important. We can add to our examples that of amoebae dividing, where sameness over generations is an equivalence relation, and imagined duplications of a body which are sometimes introduced in discussions of personal identity may be describable in terms of 'same person', when that represents an equivalence relation of a sufficiently undemanding kind. As far as Leibniz's Law is concerned, all that has been shown is its powerlessness when it comes to isolating spatio-temporal continuants. We reconfirm its status as a purely formal principle, and we leave it to more substantial principles to specify criteria of identity for items of particular kinds. Once more, then, we see how crucial is the role of a condition which is satisfied, or at least satisfiable, by at most one thing.

Locational criteria of identity do not come in just one form, and I shall now draw more explicit attention to one familiar complication which is useful in elucidating the question of essentialism. Something physical may be made up of parts which can be replaced without our having to regard the whole as a different thing of its kind. The molecules which go to make up a person's body are a case in point, where again we have, in the the relation between body and molecules, an equivalence relation rather than strict identity. Consider now the phrase 'this forest'. This may be used in such a way as to be independent of the actual identities of the trees which it comprises, so that we could say, 'This forest would have consisted of oaks rather than elms if the old man had had his way'. Here any forest would have counted as the forest in question provided, we may suppose, it had been located in the given area and, perhaps, planted at the time which saw the present growth initiated. Of course, we might not use 'this forest' in such a way as to make this a coherent observation, and with many phrases the comparable use is most unlikely. With 'this ring', for instance, the narrower criterion of identity is almost inevitable: we should be happy to say that a ring of another material would not have been *this* ring. Under the assumption that a ring cannot have its substance transmuted, we reject the supposition that this gold ring might (now) have been silver; there is no way in which something having the spatio-temporal history which this ring has or could have had might have been constituted by a different substance, but the supposition that a silver ring might have existed is always consistent with this gold ring's existing, side by side, so inconsistent with the possibility of an identity.

Consider now the essentialist conclusion which the allowable truth of 'The number of planets is necessarily greater than 7' appeared to support. What should be our attitude towards this conclusion? We may feel like saying that, if the inferences in question commit us to essentialism—well, then, they commit us to essentialism, something we must learn to live with, unwelcome though it may be. However, I think it is only an excessively narrow conception of relativity to language that would lead us to view such propositions as difficult exceptions. I can use 'this forest' in such a way that 'This forest might have contained oaks instead of elms' is true, and I can use it in such a way that the same form of words expresses something false. Here, as generally, logical possibility and necessity are surely to be explained in terms of considerations pertaining to language. With predications we may favour the pattern shown by 'This vixen is necessarily female', i.e. 'This vixen is, as the word implies, female', or the more explicit 'This female fox is necessarily female', i.e. 'This female fox is, *ex vi termini*, female', or 'This female fox is, I repeat, female'. Perhaps that pattern is not to be had in the present instance, but in relying on the implicit criterion of identity to support a necessary proposition we are exploiting a linguistic implication, a consideration relating to the particular usage enjoyed by the relevant term. With examples such as 'this ring' the point is obscured by the rarity of an alternative reading which might be appealed to for the contrast, but 'number' enters into a variety of phrases that are more flexible in this respect. Consider 'The number of unemployed fluctuates seasonally'. In a sense, a particular number is here at stake—the number of unemployed is to be distinguished from the number of those in receipt of supplementary benefits—but the criterion of identity is sufficiently broad to permit of a coupling with a predicate, 'fluctuates seasonally', which is rejected by the less general numerical specification, 'over 2,000,000'.

As a final point, I should like to stress the importance of distinguishing equivalence relations from identities when considering the modality of the latter. If something, a, is transformed into something, b, we may be able to say that a became b but that it might have become something other than b. We can put it this way if we suppose that a relates only to the earlier phase of that extended object whose later phase is named b. If, however, the names are not linked with the two phases in this way but are names of the same object, the object which embraces both phases, then we cannot say that a might have been other than b any more than we can say that a might not have been a. This distinction is overlooked in Chandler [1975], where the example of the ship of Theseus is taken to show the contingency of a true identity.

27. Mass and count nouns

I now take up the distinction between mass and count nouns. This distinction was introduced in purely formal terms: a count noun may combine with the indefinite article and form a plural, a mass noun may not. Modifiability by 'much' may be invoked to give a further characterization of mass terms, but even so we have an analysis which may not be found very revealing. One popular tactic that might be thought more fruitful is to appeal to the notion of a *part*: for a mass term, M, it is characteristic that any part of M is M. So, any part of water is water. This will not do, of course, for abstract nouns, like 'magic' and 'elation', but even with concrete terms it is not clear that it is satisfactory, for it is not clear that water, air, dust, grime, or whatever, can be said to have parts. To ensure that this applies we have to shift to talk in terms of a count noun which specifies an appropriate whole, as 'a pool of water' or 'a cloud of dust', otherwise it seems we must say something like: any (lesser) amount of water is water. This is quite trivial, and if we try to make it more substantial we meet with a further problem: will subdivision, for instance, always yield the original stuff? It all depends on the breakdown envisaged and what is broken down. Certainly, some mass terms do not relate to suitably homogeneous 'stuffs'. Can we cut up money, furniture, or footware and be sure that we are left with the same?

An alternative approach is given by Dummett's suggestion that the criterion of identity associated with a mass term is a criterion of identity over time only, whereas for a count noun, N, we shall also have a criterion for what constitutes one and the same N at any given time (Dummett [1973], pp. 573-4). So, if I can see the front end of a train and the rear end of a train, I may wonder whether I see the ends of a single train, whether it is all one and the same train that I see. Here the mass term 'water' provides a contrast. I can wonder whether the water on the floor is the same water as was in the glass—identity over time—but not whether the water here and the water over there are the same water, as if the water constituted a spatial unity, identifiable as such by 'that water'.

Of course, I can wonder whether this is the same *body* of water as that, pointing in different directions, but not whether this water is the same (water) as that in a sense which would amount to this. Terms such as 'body', 'pool', 'piece', 'serving', 'slice', 'item', and 'ray' can be used to impose a spatio-temporal criterion of identity, but that criterion is not to be read into the associated mass noun. In more traditional terms, we might say that it is not matter *tout court* that provides a principle of individuation, but matter differs in the relevant way only as distributed in parcels or portions, where 'parcel' and 'portion' are terms supposed associated with a spatio-temporal criterion of identity. Two identical pins are said to differ because they differ as to matter, and this is sometimes put forward as an alternative to the view that a different space-time location is the ground of the difference. However, if the pins are identical, then in one sense their matter certainly is the same; we have a material difference only in the sense that they are or consist of different bits or parcels of matter.

Phrases such as 'piece of . . .' can be used to impose a spatio-temporal criterion of identity—or of individuation: the application of these terms coincides in the use I make of them. This might be disputed on the grounds that 'piece' does not provide a term with which we may frame unambiguous answers to questions of number. A piece of coal can be arbitrarily divided into further pieces, so we are allegedly given no deter-minate instruction if asked to count pieces of coal. There can, it is true, be difficulties with pieces which threaten to break up once our counting is under way, but the mere possibility of arbitrary division is not disturbing. It is only *actual* divi-sion—an activity with a determinate outcome—that increases the number of pieces of coal. The piece of coal on the hearth can no doubt be fragmented in a variety of ways, but at the moment it is intact, a single piece of coal.

If there is a criterion of identity associated with a mass term, it is not, I say, the same as is associated with a phrase like 'pool of water' or 'piece of granite', where it is of course the count noun that dictates behaviour in this respect: talk of 'a pool' or 'a piece' may prompt the same queries as to identity as does the obscured train. Although Dummett's invocation of identity over time does not rely on such expansions for mass terms, he explicitly states that 'the criterion of identity associated with a mass term is always the criterion for the identity of a piece of *matter*' (op. cit., p. 574). Shift the italics from 'matter' to 'piece' and we seemingly emphasize an error. For present purposes, the term 'quantity', which he also uses, is preferable, since in terms of this we can raise the question of identity over time but not that of identity over space. We are speaking of a given quantity of water if we say we are now using the bath water to refresh the roses, but the oppos-ing extremities of a puddle or a lake are not happily identified as the same *quantity* of water. Even here, however, there is a danger of confusion. Our aim is to distinguish two classes of noun; it is accordingly not in place to move to the material mode, asking what questions of identity can be raised with respect to a quantity of water, say, since a quantity may be characterizable by phrases of either type, by 'pool of water' or simply by 'water'.

Dummett's approach to the distinction meets with a difficulty when we turn to count nouns which relate to temporally rather than to spatially extended phenomena. Think of 'a wedding ceremony' or 'a speech'. There is no occasion for singling out parts situated at different points of space and asking whether we have to do with the same speech, for instance, but we have only the temporal analogue, as when, after dozing off, I wake to enquire whether it is still the same speech that is droning on. But now we have lost the contrast which was apparently intended to distinguish mass nouns from count nouns: with either 'the same water' or 'the same speech' the meaningful question relates to identity over time only. There is, it is true, a crucial difference, in that with water what is the same over time is spatially circumscribed, not a phenomenon with a temporal unity. We can introduce the notion of a unity, whether spatial or temporal, in characterizing a count noun, and make use of the contrast in defining mass terms, but this is to go beyond the analysis proposed.

Other examples provide other difficulties. Dummett instances 'colour' as a countable which is characterizable in the way indicated: we have a criterion for the truth of 'This is the same colour as that', accompanied by pointing gestures in different directions. But we can also say, 'This is the same blood as that', pointing to two different pools of blood and meaning that the blood is in either case of the same group, and it is surely with this kind of comparison that the example of colour itself compares. The identity of the colour here and the colour there is sortal, a single shade of red being visible in either place, let us say. The model of an entity which is continuous across space, like a train or a man, is surely not of relevance here, even when we have to do with a continuous coloured surface. Again, 'patch of colour' or 'expanse of colour' may serve to impose the spatial criterion, but that is another matter.

The sentence, 'This is the same blood as that', raises the

question of an association of sortal criteria of identity with mass nouns. It also raises the problem of identifying mass nouns as such in certain contexts. So, 'That coffee smells good' might be used with respect to the kind—Moccha blend, say—or with respect to the coffee confined to the coffee-pot, and by 'that cheese' I might mean 'that type of cheese', as in 'That cheese is popular', or I might wish to single out a particular piece, as in 'That cheese has gone off'. We might invoke such examples to show the possible association of a mass term with the two types of criterion, sortal and locational, but it is not clear that we have to do with a mass term in the former case. With 'That cheese has gone off', use of 'cheese' as a mass term is clearly possible, but we note that 'That cheese is popular' rewrites as 'That is a popular cheese' more readily than as 'That is popular cheese'.

Still, the example with 'blood' is perhaps less questionable in this respect, so let us agree that, along with a criterion of identity over time, mass terms can be associated with a sortal criterion of identity. What does this tell us? First, it would seem to be just a reflection of the fact that a term like 'blood' can be joined both with phrases like 'on the carpet' and phrases like 'of group Rhesus-negative', such qualifications giving specific conditions for which 'the same' or 'that' may stand in. In fact, to say that the identity is 'over time' is not to give an accurate characterization of the non-sortal case. Dummett's claim is that 'same water' relates only to a circumscribed quantity of water identified at different times, but the question can arise as to whether two people are speaking of the same water even when the references are made at the same time. I should wish to unite the two cases under a common use of 'same water', to be elucidated in spatial as well as temporal terms, but whether this is agreed or not, the second possibility is one that calls for equal recognition. Still, this is not important. What is worth pointing out is that the sense of the mass term does not vary depending on what expansion of 'the same' is appropriate, but it is via 'the same' that any differences enter, in the ways indicated. Of itself a mass term is quite detached from any criterion of identity, whether locational or sortal, such criteria entering either with phrases like 'a drop of' or with conditions like 'on the carpet' and phrases parasitic on these, as 'the same'.

The very character of a mass noun—refusing the individuating apparatus of indefinite article and plural—is in keeping with this detachment, and the inessential character of any connection with a criterion of identity is shown by the possibility that we should have no use for 'same' in conjunction with a mass term. Certainly, you can know the meaning of 'blood' without knowing what is to count as the same blood, where this is a matter of blood of the same group, and if the noun is not even concrete then no question of a locational criterion arises. I regard 'anger' and 'jealousy' as of the same general type as 'sugar' and 'water' when it comes to the contrast with count nouns, so as far as this contrast is concerned considerations of identity over time cannot hope to be definitive.

It is characteristic of a term like 'soap' or 'water' that it is applied without regard to spatial or temporal structure, the kind of structure, of spatial or temporal boundedness, which nouns like 'cake', 'pool', 'game', or 'quarrel' import and with which we can associate possible subdivisions into parts or stages. Here we note a question of meaning which could be reckoned one of identity, as with 'Does "beard" cover a moustache?', whereas with a mass term the comparable question—'Does "water" apply to ice?', 'Does "jealousy" cover envy?'—makes no reference to what defines or comprises a certain whole or unity. Since we allow for recurrences of structure, we look to spatio-temporal considerations in differentiating Ns, 'N' a count noun, supposing sortal differences are not adequate to this task.

A further word is needed on aspects of this latter possibility, a possibility which can make for a fine distinction between certain mass and count nouns. It is clear that any rigid association of count nouns with a spatio-temporal criterion of identity is incorrect, since the formal criterion ranks 'wine', say, alongside 'doll' or 'wheel' with respect to its occurrence in such a context as 'I prefer a sweet wine'. In this use, 'wine' just is a count noun, but differences between wines, as dry and sweet or red and white, are made on a sortal basis, and not in terms of location. Still, we can discern the same pattern of identity in diversity, the former underlying the use of a common term, the latter underlying plurality and contrasting singularity. More interesting is the application of sortal criteria of identity to mass nouns. As I have indicated, this is not a possibility that is inevitably realized—we may have no occasion to speak of 'same anger' or 'same arson', for instance—but when it is exploited, why does it not leave us with a count noun? We have seen that count and mass status may not be easy to determine, and when the comparison is with 'cheese', say, as a mass term and 'a cheese', taken at a high level of generality, so to be connected with a proper name such as 'Camembert' rather than with a locational criterion of identity, the two are brought close together. Use of 'a' makes explicit the division into kinds and their separate character, making it possible for us to speak of 'counting cheeses', but the distinctions which underly the division are already recognized in the qualifications associated with the mass term. When the indefinite article reflects no more than a sortal unity, there may be little to choose between the phrase with and the phrase without the article, between 'A fine sand covered the surface' and 'Fine sand covered the surface', or between 'He showed an unusual efficiency' and 'He showed unusual efficiency'. True, there might be said to be a similar closeness when the article is indicative of a temporal unity, as in the distinction between saying that something calls for *an* investigation or *an* examination as against saying merely that something calls for investigation or examination. However, the gap appears at its narrowest in the sortal case, a case whose special character is also suggested by the incongruity of the bare noun plus article, without further qualification, as in 'a sand' or 'an efficiency', as though we had a term which was not fully a count noun, but lay somewhere between the two classes. Indeed, if, as with 'efficiency', we do not have a plural, then what we have is not, on my definition, a count noun.

I have indicated that certain count nouns may be associated with either a locational or a sortal criterion of identity. Such nouns, as 'word', 'record', 'bird', 'book', and 'weed', are numerous enough to merit a closer look. I am prepared to speak of the difference as one of meaning, but this may be resisted if it requires us to ascribe a double meaning to so many words in the language. Still, the double meaning is at least systematic, and there is a very good reason for saying that the noun itself is the source of the two readings. The reason is the inevitable one that we can eliminate a double sense from other terms with which the count noun occurs and the ambiguity may still remain. So, 'The bird of which she is most fond has a bright plumage' may be intended in two ways: as about an individual bird or as about a species of bird. A double meaning for 'bird' would make the two readings possible, and since the accompanying words have none of the required ambiguity, a double meaning for 'bird' it is.

What poses the real problem is the dual nature of the contexts in which such words often occur, part of the context seemingly requiring the broader interpretation, part seemingly requiring the narrower. Thus, 'The dish they are eating was a favourite with Matthew', 'The game being played here is also played in Scotland', 'The record you just heard is very popular', 'Our garden suffers from that weed too', and so on. In all these I wish to say that there is a specification of a type, and that incorporation of such a phrase as 'they are eating' does not serve to individuate in the narrower respect. One thing is certain: such phrases *cannot* associate the nouns with the narrower criterion of identity if the sentence as a whole is to be coherent. But if phrases such as 'they are eating' do not serve to individuate in this way, what is their contribution, and how can we make sense of their association with a phrase of the higher type?

To allow, as we must, that multitudes elsewhere may be enjoying the very same dish, we must recognize that the phrase 'they are eating' can have what we might call an 'identificatory' function, serving to identify a type; and it is quite possible that a phrase having this role should fail to impose the narrower criterion of identity, that a condition which might individuate for the noun in one sense should serve merely to identify the type in the other sense. The question we are left with is that of how the abstract character demanded for 'dish' can be reconciled with the temporally bounded activity of eating, an activity which would appear directed exclusively towards more 'concrete' objects. However, the combination is intelligible, for 'dish' here comes to 'type of dish', and a type of dish, i.e. a dish of a certain type, certainly can be what one eats. At worst we are forced to see a figure of speech, such as syllepsis, in some combinations: the sentence, 'He has just broken a record that is currently popular', appears to collapse the two readings of 'record' into its one occurrence, and not without some discomfort.

The argument so far has brought us to the unsurprising conclusion that count nouns are, in virtue of their sense, associated with a criterion of identity, whether locational or sortal, that they signify a spatial, temporal, or sortal unity. With mass terms, by contrast, there is no such association. A mass term can be variously determined in its application, but such determination is imposed upon it by other linguistic devices and is not dictated by its sense or senses, devices which may or may not apply in a given instance. As an intermediate case we have that of certain mass nouns turned count; here grounds for introduction of the indefinite article lie in recognition of singularity of type, but there is not the range of behaviour typical of a count noun.

It is easy to see how the use of 'an *N*' in association with a sortal criterion of identity simply provides a variant means of expressing generality with respect to the more restricted case. Thus, in 'A bird can become extinct without anyone knowing', we are said to be speaking of a species; here we do not meet with a use of 'a bird' as in 'A bird cannot survive a week without water', even though both are devices for the expression of generality. There is a different sense of the noun phrase, the former being paraphrasable in terms of 'birds of a given kind', taking now 'birds' in the other, more familiar sense. In short, we either use a term employing a criterion of identity which requires quantification or the equivalent to express generality, a sum of individual cases, or else we take a term which, through having no such associated criterion, requires no such device. A simple matter of alternative expressions of generality.

The use of mass nouns is in some degree comparable with the latter case. First, the difference between these and count nouns is not to be sought in a difference in their respective referents—both can have application to stuffs, for instance—but the difference is one in their grammar, in the kinds of modification that each will accept. It is sometimes thought that mass terms present an awkward combination of roles, being now like proper names of substances, now like general terms true of particular or arbitrary quantities. Such an analysis need not be mistaken, but it should not be thought that such a term as 'asbestos' changes radically in character as we move from 'Asbestos can be dangerous', for instance, to 'This is asbestos'. It is rather that in its interaction with other parts of the sentence, the noun is variously determined in its application. So, we can accept that 'asbestos', 'porridge', and 'seaweed' are names of stuffs, but this does not stand in the way of reading sentences beginning 'Seaweed is . . .' as variants on 'Whatever is seaweed is . . .', as with 'Seaweed is a source of food', or as variants on more restricted propositions about quantities, if, as with 'Seaweed was strewn over the rocks', the predicate—or some other term—makes this demand. Where mass terms come more into their own is in statements of amount or volume. Their detachment from particles like 'a' makes it possible to use them in abstraction from considerations of spatio-temporal boundedness or individuality and to combine them with partitives like 'much' which give a measure of amount rather than of number.

In regarding sentences such as 'Asbestos can be dangerous' and 'This is asbestos' as involving different operations upon a constant term, 'asbestos', we suggest a comparison with the way in which general terms were found to be dependent on the remainder of the sentence. The comparison is even closer if we allow ourselves to prise the indications of number off the count noun, viewing 'seat', say, not as a singular, but as a noun radical which might enter into association with numerical indices, as at present, and which might also occur without singular or plural but with quantitative terms such as 'much'. We should then have an element which had no essential connection with criteria of identity, but for which the notion of pure application would be central, application which might be variously determined in the ways proper to each class of noun. As the language now works, this breakdown is not in general possible, a mass use not being invariably guaranteed by a count use, or vice versa, but this is largely an accident, and the most useful picture remains that of a descriptive form to which may be attached determiners of various kinds—including, we might add, modifications appropriate to verbs. Given our earlier observations on noun and verb, even that degree of generality seems admissible.

Let us now follow up those uses of mass nouns in which they appear to provide variant expressions of generality. Thus, water is found only in discrete amounts in the form of pools, drops, glassfuls, and so forth, and these accordingly constitute the subject matter of an unrestricted statement about water. This is not, we may note, to think of water as a single individual with its parts scattered. Any amalgamation of quantities of water leaves us with just another quantity to which a statement about water will apply, and we shall never in this way assemble something of which 'water' is the proper name, so that its identity now comes to be defined in spatio-temporal terms. On the other hand, this is not to deny the admitted likeness between mass terms and proper names. In 'Water is wet', 'water' is the name of a single stuff, and our describing it thus does not require support from a dubious picture of a whole reconstitutable from its scattered parts. The singularity just is a matter of singularity of type, of a relevant sameness of individual quantities of which 'water' is true.

It is plausible to argue that if any stuff, such as water, exists, we could come across it, identify it as such, but we can come across something like water only in space and time, so we can expect it to take the form of a locatable amount. However, not all stuffs occur in a straightforward state. Think of oxygen and hydrogen as they occur in water, or even of the cream in coffee or the tannin in tea. If a substance occurs in a mixture, or in suspension, it will occur in discrete amounts—globules, grains, or the like—which can in principle be extracted. But, of course, it is a discovery that identifiable milk globules are to be found in coffee, and in some cases there is no such intermingling of substance with substance, the two having an identity recoverable by, e.g., separation in a centrifuge. Thus the oxygen and hydrogen in water. In what sense, then, *is* oxygen in water? In a different sense, clearly, from that in which there may be sand in water; we do not expect that, while leaving the water as water, we shall be able to detect in it a substance displaying then and there the defining characteristics of oxygen. Oxygen can, it is true, be in water through being dissolved in it, but that again serves only to make the contrast. However, if oxygen cannot be thus identified, what right have we to say that it is in any sense *in* water? Our justification for this derives from the consideration that water can be broken down into oxygen and hydrogen, and generated by combining these elements.

That there are two senses in which oxygen is or can be in water is evident, but it is thereby evident that only in one is there any guarantee of occurrence in spatio-temporal volumes, however diffuse. None the less, this does not make for an insuperable difficulty for the thesis which it appears to refute, since it at most obliges us to make room for hypothetical propositions about the occurrence of a stuff in the requisite form. To say that oxygen exists in a chemical compound is either to state its presence there as an identifiable stuff diffused through the compound, or to affirm its presence in the compound as an ingredient element, recoverable by a breakdown of the compound. In neither case is the reference to oxygen in this basic, uncompounded form eliminable. This deals with the sense of 'exists', but even less is required when we are concerned with propositions about a stuff, as when we say that oxygen assists combustion. In saying this I do not mean that water will, because of the oxygen in it, assist combustion, but only that the oxygen which you can get from water will do so. General statements about oxygen are not tested by dealing with the element as it exists in compound.

We repeat, then, the conclusion which we reached with regard to the more general of the two interpretations for count nouns. Just as abstractness here could be thought of in terms of generality with respect to the lower level, so with mass terms, likewise dissociated from spatio-temporal criteria of individuation, we have a similar interpretation, a sentence about oxygen, plaster, glue, string, straw, or whatever, being about arbitrary, or determinate, volumes or pieces of the substance. The behaviour of a concrete mass term is thus like that of a plural count noun, where the singular, if it existed, would apply to such spatially defined portions, or whatever exactly it is that exists at this lower level of generality. Sometimes a given noun allows of both uses, in which case we can choose either the plural count noun or the mass noun when stating generalizations. So, either 'War is terrible' or 'Wars are terrible', either 'Sound travels' or 'Sounds travel'. Ideally, such pairs as these would be the rule: either the noun is a mass noun, in which case it is suited to the expression of generality without the need for a plural termination—though with the assistance of, or at least lack of obstruction from, other elements in the sentence—or else it is associated with a criterion of identity, in which case plurality must somehow be marked.

Staying close to the first level, the level of spatio-temporally individuated items, whether individuals, events, activities, or whatever, has its attractions, in that it is here that the notion of the application of a noun is at its clearest, and therewith the notion of meaning as applied to such terms. Thus, our thoughts about space and time may be clearer if we remember that talk about space and time is talk about spaces and times: time passes if and only if times pass, and space is curved if and only if spaces, or particular regions of space, are curved. In some cases, an explanation may be required of the way in which the version with the less usual count noun is to be understood—if such a noun exists at all—and there can of course be figurative ways of speaking, as with 'Time waits for no man', the namelike form lending itself more readily than the plural to the personifications which may add to the perplexing character of abstract terms.

6

ABSTRACTIONS AND NOMINALIZATIONS

Concrete mass terms display their characters openly enough. Abstract mass terms are less forthcoming. They are joined in this by abstract count nouns, the two categories together being largely responsible for the cluster of issues which make up the problem of universals. I shall now combine some familiar and some less familiar tactics in a preliminary attack on this problem, beginning with points about identity and identification which make a connection with topics already discussed. After a brief look at propositions I then turn to an examination of number, taking as my text Frege's account of numerical propositions in *The Foundations of Arithmetic.* Dummett reports that the principle that the content of a statement of number is an assertion about a concept was all that, by the end of his life, Frege thought correct in his earlier writings on mathematics (Dummett [1973], p. xxiv). We shall find reason for thinking that even on this Frege was in error, and indeed that the despised formalists have as much to offer towards an account of number. Finally, I shall touch briefly on a question of existence which brings together the notions of possibility and infinity.

28. Sameness and difference with abstract nouns

Our starting-point is colour words occurring as nouns, as in 'Red means danger', 'Maroon is currently a popular colour', and 'Purple and gold look well together'. The behaviour here of 'red', 'maroon', 'purple', and 'gold' appears particularly congenial to the realist: the words can surely be said to function as a species of name, and what they name are equally surely universals, not spatio-temporally bounded individuals. The similarity between these and the mass terms already discussed is striking: in either case we have an independence of locational individuation which enables us to say that the same *stuff,* saffron, is encountered in many parts of the world and that the same *colour,* saffron, can be seen in equally many places. As an adjective, a term such as 'saffron' compares with a concrete mass noun in its dissociation from any criterion of identity; as a noun used of a colour, the comparison is so close, we might hope to simply transfer to it the analysis of mass terms which, in its essentials, would apply to the name of the stuff.

However, objections are possible. First, it may be queried whether words like 'purple' and 'gold' are really ever anything other than adjectives. True, 'black' looks like subject in 'Black is beautiful', but can this not be taken as elliptical for 'Anything black is beautiful'? As already indicated, establishing ellipsis is often no easy matter. It is most straightforward when the sense is incomplete without a further term being taken as understood, and when that term is uniquely recoverable. Here examples such as 'The fraud was exposed and the perpetrators brought to justice' come to mind. Other acceptable cases are those in which, while we cannot claim uniqueness of the term omitted, it is at least entailed by anything that the sense demands. This choice is acceptable since we are not taking the hypothesis of ellipsis as an historical hypothesis, but as a question of meaning. In the present instance we might well feel that 'Black is beautiful' can, for reasons of meaning, be thought of as an ellipsis, but with 'Maroon is currently a popular colour' there is not so much the impression of incompleteness, nor, it would seem, the possibility of adding a missing term.

A second objection is the familiar nominalist complaint that, say, the colour of the cup cannot be literally the same colour as that of the saucer, however alike they may be, and hence that my comparison with a single stuff dispersed in different places does not hold good. The colours of distinct objects can resemble each other as closely as can be, but the identity of each colour is, he insists, preserved. All that they have quite literally in common is a common description, the colour of each being as unique, as particular, as the objects themselves.

As far as our understanding of colour terminology goes, there is no room for this supposed distinctness. The two objects can have exactly the same colour. They may not, of course, but if there is a difference it will be a difference in precisely that: colour, or at least shade of colour. We simply do not count colours in accordance with the same principles as those which we apply to physical objects. The peas in a pod may be as alike as can be yet still remain distinct from one another, there being something which each has and which is not shared by any of the others, namely, its spatial co-ordinates, but it is not a ground for distinguishing the colour of one pea from that of any other that they are colours of different peas. What the nominalist has done is transfer to such qualities as colour the individuating criteria appropriate to material objects, whereas with colours the only such criteria are generic. To say merely that the colours exactly resemble one another still implies that the two are to be kept apart, that in some sense they remain distinct, when no basis for defining such distinctness has been provided. Again, a surface which is, as we should say, uniformly of the same colour, would on the nominalist's account consist of a number of distinct colours. How many? Where does one colour begin and another end? We can certainly speak of coloured areas—indeterminately, it is true, until their extent has been specified—but now it is areas, expanses, or surfaces *of* a certain colour—the same colour—that are distinguishable from one another.

Other examples make the same point even more clearly. If a shirt and a tie each cost £3·00, then the price of the one is exactly the same as the price of the other. There is no question of an inevitable difference which a closer examination can be expected to disclose, a difference which would force us to retreat to talk of resemblance; there is no difference whatsoever in the prices of the articles. Again, while there is a use of 'weight' in which it can be associated with a spatio-temporal criterion of identity—as in 'He dropped the weight on his toe', or in the phrase 'paper-weight'—a use in which we can say that no two distinct objects can be the same weight, this only serves to make the contrast with that use of the word in which two distinct things can be, quite literally, the same weight. And so on with height, length, strength, distance, volume, speed, density, shape, and other properties.

Is the realist correct if he says, against the nominalist, that one and the same colour, literally one and the same colour, can be in any number of places at the same time? Let us ask what sense we can make of the notion of location as applied to a colour. Where, for instance, is the colour of a cup? If anywhere, on its surface, but certainly not in the sense in which a three-dimensional substance, however finely spread, might be or rest on the surface. Normally we have no occasion to speak of the whereabouts of the colour, but only of the whereabouts of the thing that has the colour, or of the paint or pigment involved. Accordingly, we might suggest that the realist shares the nominalist's error, since he thinks of colours as a species of physical item, in the sense of allowing of location in space, but as distinguished from three-dimensional objects in allowing of location in many different places simultaneously—a characterization which applies to stuffs, such as sugar.

Once more the example of 'price' shows the error in sharp relief. We can speak of the price of butter in different countries, but the prices themselves are surely not locatable, hence neither locatable in many places, as the realist would have it, nor confined to a single place, as in the nominalist's less liberal scheme. At best we have the kind of relation mentioned in the last chapter, where it was held that a locational phrase in association with a word like 'weed' or 'dish' might serve only to identify a type, not to furnish a locational criterion of identity. Similarly, with 'the blue of her eyes' we have a phrase, 'the . . . of her eyes', which may be used to identify a particular shade of blue, so to imply a sortal differentia, but not to mark a locationally grounded distinction with the blue of something else.

We must be careful not to overstate the case against the nominalist. He is wrong in thinking that there can be no strict identity of the colours of distinct objects, which is for us the main point, but there is *a* use of 'colour' which does accord with his preconceptions. Someone may state that there is some colour in a certain painting, and we may ask to be shown where; it may be that the red has all been scratched out or that the blue has faded, that the green covers a larger area than the yellow. In many cases, what makes for the possibility of first-level individuation is the reliance upon paint or pigment, as bearers of the colours and from which this feature has been transferred, but even this does not seem to be essential. We can imagine colours in the atmosphere which were not associated with any form of pigmentation, but only with light, as in a rainbow. Whatever, then, the exact basis for the distinction, we could speak of differently located colours.

Such colours could, however, be identical in the more usual sense; there is nothing here to encourage the nominalist in his attack on this conception. What we have is simply a repetition of a feature noted with mass terms. The noun 'smoke', for instance, can combine with the definite article in a phrase which purports to apply to a given localized 'quantity' of smoke, as in 'The smoke filled their lungs' or 'The smoke from the burning ceiling was highly toxic', and it is in a similar fashion that we may speak of the red in a portrait as being unusually pure. However, as I say, this does not mean that colour terms invariably satisfy the identity conditions appropriate to physical objects which the nominalist favours. Indeed, colour terms are somewhat exceptional among words thought to signify universals. Incorporation of 'speed', 'density', or 'strength', for instance, into a definite descriptive phrase does not yield a phrase having a ready interpretation in line with that conceded for 'the colour'.

Even when such terms are introduced into a phrase of the form, 'the . . . of A', where 'A' singles out some physical object, there is no guarantee that the relevant identity conditions will match those of A. Let us consider this further in conjunction with the claim that, since they can be seen, colours must have location. I can certainly see the colour of the carpet, but this may be a matter of seeing what colour the carpet is. The implicit predicational tie here can stand in the way of such an inference as 'If I saw the colour of the carpet and the colour of the carpet was the same as that of the wall, then I saw the colour of the wall', and the same feature may make it doubtful whether an animal can be said to see the colour of the carpet—though in either case, of course, the definite description allows of more than one construal. The bearing of these points on the question of the nature of objects of vision is discussed in Rundle [1972], chapter 8; here let me simply observe that an appeal to perceptibility as a test of concreteness is of little use without an accompanying specification of the relevant grammatical context. What is established by such a locution as 'I heard how he had fared'? Does this show that 'how he had fared' specifies something concrete rather than something abstract? Think too of 'I saw what had to be done' as against 'I saw what had been done'.

Causal terminology is similarly in need of scrutiny if its applicability is thought of as giving a test of concreteness. Consider 'The weight of the bridge caused it to buckle'. It may be true that the weight of the bridge is the same as the weight of the church tower, but it does not follow that the weight of the church tower caused the bridge to buckle. Do we have in this consideration grounds for speaking of an individualized property or form, the weight of the bridge, which can be the subject of causal relations? The sameness involved here is not as in the realist's picture of the universal as being in many places at a single time: nor, on the other hand, is there any call to join with the nominalist in thinking of the weight of the bridge as somehow unique. The weight of the bridge is the same as that of the church tower just in so far as they weigh the same, and if the weight of the bridge caused it to buckle, then it is because the bridge weighed what it did that it buckled; again the implicit predicational tie shows the description to be of a kind for which substitution cannot be made. Given such a breakdown, do we really have a way of speaking which can be appropriately enlisted in attempting to give sense to the idea of the weight of the bridge as a concrete particular which can enter into causal relations?

But, to take another example, what are we to make of the fact that the colour of my shirt may change, or more generally have its own history, without anything else matching its changes, so without the colour of my tie changing, which was supposed to be identical? There can be no denying the possibility that the colour of my shirt should be identical with that of my tie, but the identity is not contradicted by the one changing without the other following suit: they simply were the same and are now different. Once more, it is only if the identity is thought of on the model of the physical that there is any appearance of a difficulty. If Tom's father is Tim's only uncle, then a change in Tom's father's routine will be a change in that of Tim's uncle, but Tom's routine may be the same as Tim's without a change in the former entailing a change in the latter. We have, clearly, different forms of identity here.

More useful to the nominalist might be a closer inspection of the phrase 'the same colour', not with an eye to discovering the narrower identity conditions in its typical behaviour, but with a view to showing the negligible character of its implications. We say that two objects can have exactly the same colour, but we can equally say that two objects can *be* exactly the same colour. 'Colour' is, of course, a noun, but as indicated earlier, it is often a stand-in for adjectival expressions, as in 'He is a colour she would like to be'. This is not a feature peculiar to 'colour'—cf. 'They are the same age'—but it is a feature of some note and one which perhaps reveals a divergence from the implications customarily carried by the use of a noun. The nominalist will presumably agree that two objects can both be blue, say, so if saying of two objects that they are the same colour is to be understood in such terms, there would appear to be nothing for him to fear from the use of the *noun*. Nominalists are, it is true, sometimes wary even of simple predications of the form 'x is blue', on the grounds that 'blue' might have a claim here to name a universal; realists, certainly, think that nothing less than possession of the universal justifies such a predication with respect to an object. Since the predication is just that, and not an impossible identity, the nominalist's fears are unfounded. The realist's search for justification will be looked at later.

The mass noun 'iron' names a single substance, but talk of iron is talk of the substance as it can or does occur, namely, in locatable, discrete quantities. The noun 'red' is a name of a single colour, but, if the suggested analogy holds, talk of red will be talk of . . .? Talk of what, exactly? Anything describable as 'red', would seem the obvious answer. True, we found reason for rejecting the suggestion that seemingly substantival occurrences of 'red' are elliptical uses, but the reductive thesis requires only *a* translation into predications featuring the colour word as an adjective. Success here need not turn on success in the special case in which the analysis is carried through by replacing an absent term. In some cases this will certainly be possible, but in others the analysis will be more roundabout. For instance, the popularity of maroon is not simply the popularity of maroon things, but popularity precisely in virtue of being maroon. The same pattern of analysis holds for comparisons between colours as being more or less attractive, striking, and so forth.

Quite generally, the terms with which we are concerned, terms which are taken to introduce a problem with 'abstract entities', appear to provide no more than stylistic variants for corresponding adjectival or verbal phrases: the depth of the pool is nine feet if and only if the pool is nine feet deep, the probability of a storm is high if and only if a storm is highly probable, and the child's happiness was exceptional if and only if the child was exceptionally happy. Given the etymology of these nouns the possibility of such rephrasals is hardly surprising. Indeed, we could think of them as sharing a uniform structure, typically being formed from an adjective to which some form of the verb 'to be' is attached—as terminations such as '-ity' suggest—in the sense that these are the elements that come to figure in a translation, except for those cases in which a simple verb provides the equivalent, as with 'love' or 'fear'.

There is, however, no completely uniform translation of sentences containing words of this kind and the form taken by the verb 'to be' may vary even with the same word. This is not surprising. Passage from verb to noun means the loss of certain characteristically verbal features, and since such features may differ among themselves, a single noun can come to represent a variety of verbal forms. Thus, the sentence, 'Its ductility is more important than its malleability' might be taken to cover the two clausal renderings, 'That it is ductile is more important than that it is malleable', where its being ductile and malleable is implied, and 'That it should be ductile is more important than that it should be malleable', where there is no such implication. Similarly, a phrase such as 'God's existence' might be expected to cover a variety of different ways in which 'exists' and 'God' are relatable—in a clause beginning 'that' or 'whether', and with the verb in the indicative or the subjunctive. Contrast 'The existence of God has now been established'—i.e. that God exists—with 'They were discussing the existence of God'—i.e. whether God exists. And there are other possibilities, the commonest breakdown perhaps being into phrases beginning 'how': 'Its viscosity depends on the temperature'—i.e. 'How viscous it is depends on the temperature', or 'How viscous it is depends on how hot it is'.

29. Identity and identifying reference

The way in which identity enters with our present abstractions is crucial in determining their character *vis-à-vis* less problematic, or allegedly less problematic terms. We have already had a glimpse of a possible divergence, and I should like now to present a fuller view of the relevant difference. I can say 'The volume of this cylinder is the same as the volume of this sphere', and I can give a faily full account of the kinds of measurements and calculations required to establish identity. Does this put volumes on a par with cylinders and spheres as 'objects'. No entity without identity, it is said, but is identity sufficient? There is an important, if neglected distinction to be drawn before we can answer this. We can say, 'The chair on the balcony is the same chair as the one you saw here last week', but we do not have 'The width of the chair is the same width as the width of the door', nor 'The volume of the sphere is the same volume as that of the cylinder'. The width of the chair may be the same as the width of the door, and chair and door may be the same width—the use mentioned above— but that is all. Again, the distance from London to Moscow is the same as the distance from New Zealand to Australia, but it is not the same *distance* as the latter. Finally, the time it takes to get from Oxford to London may be the same as the time it takes to get from Cambridge to London, but we say that the time at which the old man died was the same *time* as the time at which the grandson was born. Why these differences?

Consider the contrast made when both constructions are possible. The sentence, 'The chair on the balcony is the same as the chair in the hall', is appropriate to the case in which we have to do with two chairs, the same in kind, whereas 'The chair on the balcony is the same chair as the one you saw here last week' only implies the existence of a single chair. Now, to say that, e.g., the distance from London to Moscow is the same distance as that from New Zealand to Australia suggests the exclusion of a like possibility, when it is not one that makes sense in this instance. It suggests that we might have complete agreement in terms of distance, and yet that there could still be room for speaking of distinct distances; or better, that the two distances could agree in all respects but one, distinctness *qua* distances being preserved. This is very much reminiscent of the nominalist's attempt at warding off universals by treating occurrences of a property as distinct, each with its own individuality, however alike they might be.

If a coat is increased in price from £20·00 to £22·00, we can say that a single thing, the coat, at one time cost the lesser, at another time the greater amount. If, on the other hand, we say that the price has gone up from £20·00 to £22·00, it would seem that there is not a reference to something further, the price, which likewise persists through time and to which both figures can be ascribed. Again, a person may change in weight, and at the same time his weight will change, but his weight is surely not a subject of change in the same way, not a single thing which was now 12 stone, now only 10, and which had a continuing identity through either state. The absence of a single subject, other than the coat or the person, is strongly suggested by the predicational breakdown and those features of identity statements which we have just seen to be associated with a persisting subject: sameness of width, age, weight, price, or distance is just a matter of two or more things being just as wide, old, heavy, expensive or far away. Furthermore, we cannot say that the weight of this car is the same weight as the weight of that boulder, and the reason we cannot is, perhaps, because we are not strictly comparing two things, called 'weights', but the two things being compared are simply the car and the boulder.

However, it might be retorted that to make the contrast in this way is to fly in the face of a clear sense in which something *is* identical in the case of either width or weight, and a clear and legitimate sense in which we can be said to be comparing weights. It may just come to comparing things in respect of weight, but that does not contradict the formulation which makes out the weights as the subjects of comparison.

Similarly, the size of the stadium can be colossal without prejudice to its being the stadium that is colossal in size. We have the term, 'stadium', which collects predicates of various kinds—'is colossal', 'is expensive', 'is new', and so on. Some of these and other possible predicates we group together through their related meanings and refer to a new subject—the size of the stadium—thereby, from one point of view, generating something new, an increase in the things whereof one might speak, but an increase that has called for nothing more than a reorganization of existing resources.

If there is no identification of a certain item, the man's weight, when we say, 'His weight is 12 stone', this is perhaps because of the special form of this affirmation, a form that is not shared with 'The size of the stadium is colossal'. The distinction between stating and describing is relevant here. We commonly speak of stating our name, age, address, age, and nationality, and the words we use in doing so are not happily described as giving a 'description' of our name, and so forth. Nor does the pattern of reference plus predication appear to be present with such a stating. Take a sentence which allows of both readings, as 'What I wanted was a valuable antique'. It is possible that I am describing what I wanted, that is, the actual thing that I wanted, in which case the subject term will occur referentially, but it is more likely that I am stating what I wanted, in which case reference, and with it the predication, will lapse. Similarly, 'The result was a disaster' could be either a description—'The result was disastrous'—or a statement of a result—'A disaster was what resulted'. In saying that a person is 12 stone in weight and thirty years old I describe that person, but it is not in the same sense that I say that his weight is 12 stone or his age thirty. I state his weight and age, I do not describe them. *A fortiori*, 'his weight' and 'his age' do not name anything that I describe. Nor does such a sentence as 'Alec's age is thirty' present us with an identity, a pair of matching designations of a single item. We can say that Alec's age is thirty and that his age counts against him, but we cannot say that thirty counts against him.

With respect to examples of this latter kind, it might be suggested that what must be acknowledged is not lack of reference but referential opacity—in the sense that style of reference is relevant to truth. However, I see no way of elevating this suggestion to an argument. We have found general reasons for being sceptical of such a possibility, and in the present instance the peculiarities of the terms and of the construction into which they enter indicate that it is the assumption of reference that is at fault. It is dubious whether our use of such a phrase as 'Alec's age' can be said to constitute an identification of something as the person's age, and dubious whether 'Alec's age is thirty' can be reckoned an identity. Certainly, it is not 30 that counts against the man, even if that is his age, but *being 30*; the predicative character already seen in such phrases as 'his age' must be preserved in any particular substitutions. Similarly, if I measure the depth of the pool and the depth of the pool is the same as the width of the flower bed, it does not follow that I measure the width of the flower bed. The identity is not of the right kind for substitutivity to be a reasonable presumption. Again no call to speak of opacity, and again an implicit predication which the substitution would destroy: in measuring the depth of the pool I measure how deep the *pool* is, which has nothing to do with the dimensions of the flower bed.

To take another example, while it is true that in specifying a probability we give a fraction or a ratio, it does not follow that probabilities *are* ratios in any sense which would imply that once we had clarified the nature of the latter we should have done all we need to clarify the former. A ratio can provide a *measure* of the probability of an event, a specification of how probable that event is, but such a ratio can also be given in answer to many other questions in which probability is in no way involved. When I say that probabilities are not ratios, I do not mean to deny the truth of any such specification, any statement of the form 'The probability of e is n/m', but it is the construal as an *identity* that I reject, an identity which would license replacement of 'the probability of e' by the fraction correctly specifying that probability, and which would justify substitution of that fraction in such contexts as 'He is hoping to ascertain the probability of e'. We should not wish to pass from this to 'He is hoping to ascertain $\frac{1}{2}$', say, and the construal of 'the probability of e' as 'how probable e was', an expression of an obviously different type from the numeral, removes any mystery from the failure of the inference.

We continue to accumulate examples which disincline us to speak of reference, examples which appear to reveal the noun phrases as syntactically quite different from names. If talk of a man's age is talk of how old he is, talk of a naming function is surely misconceived. Here it is worth considering the kind of general term which can occur in apposition to particular abstract phrases. We do not say that the width of *x* is the same *width* as the width of *y*, nor do we speak in this way with respect to speed, density, specific gravity, and so on. However, while we do not repeat the noun after 'the same'— nor say that the width is the same *entity*—we can say that the width of *x* is the same property, dimension, feature or characteristic as the width of *y*. Or, a more realistic example, we might say, 'The weight of a body is not the same property as the mass of that body'. This is quite unlike the interpretation of 'The height of this cupboard is the same as its width', where no substantival completion is appropriate after 'same'. Words like 'property' are all too familiar in this role, but there are certain unexpected terms which may come to occur either in place of or in apposition to the more specific phrases. So, to consider or to ascertain the height of the tower is to consider or ascertain what, exactly? It is to consider or ascertain how high the tower is, of course, and the general term which seems best suited to the phrase in this expansion is the term 'question'. It is a question that we are considering, and the answer to a question that we are ascertaining. Similarly, to discuss the age of the universe or the immortality of the soul is to discuss certain questions, and to learn the value of money is, in effect, to learn the answer to a certain question.

This possibility is really not so outlandish. If we are right in looking to a predication as providing the key to an understanding of these noun phrases, then we should expect that the predication should occur in its variety of forms. We have already seen two—indicative and subjunctive—more than once, and declarative and interrogative gives us another possible choice. If such a term as 'question' or 'issue' is appropriate as a characterization of what we are discussing, considering, or whatever, when we are discussing or considering someone's age, weight, nationality, or profession, then we shall have, it would seem, not so much an object of extralinguistic reference as a citation of what it is that we are discussing, or at least a form of words that in some less direct way introduces a question—something linguistic—as whatever it is that collects the relevant predicates.

But, of course, 'question' is not always applicable: our abstract terms can harbour a predicational form of the kinds mentioned—indicative, subjunctive, declarative, or interrogative—and it is only in the latter case that we have this involvement. To consider the height of the tower may be to consider a certain question, but it may be to consider a certain fact—not *whether* the tower is so high, but *that* it is so high—an item which is as puzzling as any. Again, it is not a question that is at issue when we say, 'The height of the tower makes it dangerous', 'The bridge collapsed because of its weight', or 'The distance between the sun and Pluto is surprising'. If the distance between the sun and Pluto is surprising, it is not 3,666 million miles that is surprising, but the distance's being what it is, or (the fact of) its being 3,666 million miles, that is surprising; in terms of the cognate adjective, what is surprising is the sun's being so many miles distant from Pluto. Dissolution into a predicational form may be straightforward enough, but it does not make for a dissolution of all the problems in this area.

Let us pause and take stock. We began with the example of 'red' as a term ostensibly designating a universal. Tradition justifies such a choice, even if it is not necessarily typical of the terms which might qualify for this role. Its behaviour places it in the class of mass terms, which suggests that we invoke the kind of reduction of which we have seen these to allow, at least in the case of names of stuffs. So, talk of red is talk of red things. More complex and perhaps more typical is the abstract term 'redness', which in some of its uses we see as, in effect, involving the adjective 'red' plus some part of the verb 'to be', so as condensing various forms of predication. Thus, talk of redness may be talk of the degree to which something is red. It is this complex behaviour which makes us uncertain whether talk of reference is appropriate. If the union of noun and verb phrase is like that involved in an interrogative, we have a case that looks simple enough, but the declarative form is commonly thought to usher in such problematic items as propositions or facts.

The difference between the two kinds of case is important. I regard the clausal expansions of a term like 'redness' as attempts, however approximate, at capturing the meaning of the abstract noun, with the verbal and adjectival forms which we thereby invoke providing, as it happens, at least a partial reduction of a kind towards which a nominalist might be well disposed. However, when I say in the other cases that talk of red is talk of red things, I do not regard this as proven by the grammar, nor indeed do I set much store by its being proven by anything. In the relevant contexts, 'red' begins and ends as a noun. It is not an adjective in disguise, there is nothing deceptive in its likeness to a noun, in its seeming naming of a single colour. What is significant is not that it is, at the same time, an adjective, with a reduction to the latter use naturally suggesting itself, but that colours exist only as colours *of* various things. That is the consideration which underlies the reduction, much as with mass terms which, like 'zinc', are names of a single stuff, but a stuff which exists only in particular bounded quantities—though of course 'red' represents a further degree of abstraction, not being, as is 'zinc', a name of anything physical. In general, we shall just have to wait and see whether a reduction will be forthcoming: I suppose we can always find something appropriately describable as 'hot' whenever we have talk of 'heat', but the character of this noun is clear enough before that case is made out, and the fact that it is the dummy predications, 'it is hot' and 'its being hot', that we light upon when seeking paraphrases for the more complex grammatical contexts indicates that this search may sometimes be in vain.

If, on the other hand, I claim that we are merely talking about an inconsequential choice of idiom, as with the difference between 'Their poverty is appalling' and 'They are appallingly poor', I shall no doubt run foul of the realist, with his insistence that application of such a description as 'are poor' stands in need of justification by reference to the possession on the part of the individuals in question of just that state or character which 'their poverty' can single out. In failing to give this aspect of such phrases their due, I have no doubt shown myself as essentially of the same ilk as the nominalist who dismisses a general term as a mere *flatus vocis*.

This outstanding question is close to the other which we have set aside for the time being, namely, that of the behaviour of those noun phrases which have clauses as near relatives: with both we have to do justice to the belief that certain worldly correlates, such as facts or states, are what answer to and warrant the use of the relevant words. For the present, I merely wish to restate the point which was anticipated earlier and which appears to be responsible for the ease with which many of the suggested reductions go through; this is simply the point that terms for universals are dissociated from any spatio-temporal individuating character. This may seem trivial, an acknowledged starting-point from which nominalist and realist alike must proceed. However, much of the debate, particularly in ancient and medieval times, depends on thinking of universals as bound by the kinds of criteria appropriate to physical objects. Thus, the problem as to whether humanity could be completely possessed by a single individual, or whether the whole form of beauty could be present in each of many beautiful things. Being fully a man seems to call for complete possession of humanity, yet such possession appears to leave nothing for another individual to share in. What we have here is an argument which goes through various moves with an abstract term as if its behaviour had to follow that appropriate to terms with which we do associate a spatio-temporal criterion of identity. That debate may now have died, but the nominalist's difficulty in recognizing that the colour of one thing can be literally identical with the colour of another is of a piece with this more ancient nonsense. On the other hand, nominalistic reductions, though in error if they extend to denials of existence, reflect an awareness of, as it were, a lack of substantiality on the part of a universal, an acknowledgement of its reduced number of dimensions; and this is just another aspect of the relevant independence of space and time.

To see what point has been reached on the question of reference, let us first go back to the simpler cases. Reference in my favoured sense is lacking when there is no question of taking, or of having taken, something or someone to be the ostensible object of designation, as when, without identifying someone as anyone's mother, I say 'The child's mother must have abandoned it'. I take it that the child has or had a mother, but there is no one whom I take to be such. For that I require further knowledge, of a kind which would make it possible to say that I misidentified someone in calling her 'the child's mother'. It is only if we have such knowledge that the principle of extensionality is sure to apply to such phrases— one of the main reasons for tying reference to such knowledge— and, as other examples have shown, it is not sufficient for freedom of substitution merely that we know of some logically independent condition which the person or thing alone satisfies. Actual awareness of that person or thing, either at the time of speaking or before, is necessary (cf. Bell [1973]). If, on the other hand, identifying reference is not involved, an appropriately different form of words is often possible, as when 'He thought the girl's name was "Jean"' can be rewritten as 'He thought the girl was called "Jean"'.

As well as tying up with extensionality, this emphasis on the role of awareness makes for a connection with a more general point concerning meaning, giving us a further reason for regarding the favoured notion of reference as basic. A person's grasp of the meaning of a word can be shown by his ability to give a paraphrase, but ultimately we look to his use of words, whether original or paraphrase, in the right circumstances. Similarly, whom or what a speaker intends by his use of a designatory term is ultimately a matter of the extralinguistic connections he makes, of what he would single out, or would if he could, in a way that does not rely on the correctness of a description, but might indeed be at odds with any description he offers. Words are instruments of particular utility in the matter of singling out one thing from others, but knowledge of the relevant object can antedate the choice of words, possibly inapposite, that a speaker makes.

Where, incidentally, does fiction fit into this scheme? I am surely speaking of a well-known fictional character when I say that James Bond does not really exist, and I may say the same of Cinderella, Donald Duck, and the Pied Piper of Hamlyn. To deny reference here, it would seem, is not so much to display an appropriate sense of reality as to show a willingness to indulge in gratuitous legislation. And that is true, if the intention is to deny reference in any and every sense, but it is also true that identifying reference is less easily secured. There may be a perceptual basis which enables me to speak of identifying a character in a cartoon as Donald Duck, but if we have to do with no more than a narrative, there no longer appears to be the appropriate analogy with identifying a character of flesh and blood.

How does this conception of reference work out with abstract terms? To judge by substitutional behaviour, rather negatively: if Dick did not notice the colour of the car and the colour of the car was the same as that of the lampshade, it does not follow that Dick did not notice the colour of the lampshade. Again, if I believe, incorrectly, that a piece of wood is in the shape of a parallelogram, and accordingly consider it suitable for some purpose that I have, you could not report me as thinking that this trapezoidal shape—substituting a correct description—made the object suitable for my purpose. Awareness of an object's shape is awareness *that* an object is of a certain shape, and this, patently, is not the kind of knowledge that can remain secure despite a mistaken belief as to the character of the shape. For mis-identification to become a possibility in the relevant way, 'shape' has to occur in its other use, as with 'a ghostly shape'. Similarly, if we can say, 'She mistook his hostility for shyness', this will be because 'hostility' does not have here the relevant degree of abstractness, 'hostility' being hostile behaviour, a matter of hostile looks, statements, and actions generally, with the more specific criterion of identity possible for these. Once more nominalism goes astray if it insists on coupling nouns of the general class with spatio-temporal criteria of identity, but this is a use that some of them certainly can enjoy.

The implicitly predicational forms are conspicuous failures as far as identifying reference is concerned, but there are other possibilities. If Dick has never before seen the colour of the lampshade, that may mean that he has never before seen what colour the lampshade is, in which case substitution will destroy the crucial predicational tie. However, the phrase 'of the lampshade' could also be used to give an identification of a certain colour, where we might equally have said 'of the car'. Better perhaps, we could say that Dick has never seen the colour which this lampshade has, where it is not implied that seeing the lampshade in question is necessary to seeing this particular colour. With this use comes the possibility of *mis*identifying a colour: I say 'the colour of the lampshade', but the object is a hat, not a lampshade. This is hardly a way of being mistaken as to the character of a colour, but it is a possibility which, together with the way in which the identifying phrases may be varied, could be invoked in giving substance to the notion of reference.

If we can say there is such a dimension as length, a virtue such as generosity, or a trait such as nervousness, then we have surely specified possible objects of reference in some sense. *Anything* real can be referred to, and if reference is ruled out, that surely shows the language to be not as it seems rather than that something existent is not as it should be for reference to it to be possible. My notion of identifying reference involves two elements: omit the demand that something be identified and we are left with a suitable notion of reference to be understood in terms of a determinate condition coupled with a requirement of existence. However, considering just those among the present noun phrases which conform to the principle of extensionality, *E*, we may wonder whether it is proper to speak of reference even in this weaker form. Something which genuinely exists could still have existed if no one had ever introduced a means for speaking of it, but the dissolution of nouns like 'weight' and 'depth' into verbs like 'weigh' and adjectives like 'deep' may lead us to doubt whether there is the necessary independence of a way of speaking. Certainly, it may be felt that such reductions show that any 'entity' that the noun phrases might introduce is of a singularly exiguous character: a term which would pick out anything of substance must surely put up sterner resistance to these paraphrases.

Any actual denial of existence here would be excessive, if this implies that there are no colours, that things never have a weight, and so forth, but we can perhaps go along with the last point, the reduced character of the relevant items being, as I have indicated, a reflection of the absence of identity over time (and space). With a physical object we have something that can remain the same despite changes, as when the same plate is now hot, now cold. With colour, weight, speed, and so on, there is by contrast no persisting subject to be discerned: when the colour of the sky changes from blue to pink, there is nothing which unites uniformly with two differentiae so as to yield the two colours, but 'The colour of the sky was blue and is now pink' is more like 'The Prime Minister was Wilson and is now Callaghan'. Without the need to preserve reference to a continuing subject we are at liberty to reroute the notion of colour via a predicative expression, as 'The sky was blue (in colour) and is now pink'. Similarly, 'The weight of the suitcase was 50 lb. and is now only 44 lb.' becomes 'The suitcase weighed 50 lb. and now weighs only 44 lb.'. Finally, we may note that an absence of identifying reference has consequences for modality. We cannot say that 'The colour of my shirt is the same as the colour of my tie' is, if true, necessarily true, since that would entail 'My shirt and tie are necessarily the same colour'. Comparison and contrast with 'the number of (the) planets' is useful here.

30. Words and propositions

We move on now to consider at greater length two particular forms of universal. The class of terms comprising such linguistic or quasi-linguistic items as 'statement', 'proposition', 'explanation', 'story', 'excuse', and so forth, has been notorious for the extent of its contribution to disputes about abstract existence, with 'proposition' serving as one of the major paradigms, maligned or revered, of an abstract entity. I shall make a few observations on certain of these terms, again leaving the real problems until a later stage, and then proceed to an examination of number, that equally prominent and seemingly indispensable universal.

Our interest in words is such that the type tends very much to dominate over the token in our ways of speaking. In describing a word as 'archaic', 'a learned borrowing', 'cognate with "frail" ', 'a vulgarism', and so on, we should not be speaking of a word which knows no existence beyond its single printed or spoken occurrence. On the other hand, it seems clear that we are merely abstracting from anything particular to the word at the lower level, that our statements about words are to be referred back to these when their content is being considered.

Larger combinations, such as phrases and sentences, provide no larger problems in this respect. Again lack of interest in specific individuating conditions, and again ultimate priority of the level at which such conditions obtain. To find a more substantial issue we must consider either the possibilities which arise once synonymous forms of words are taken into account, or the problems which face us when, as with 'statement', a new dimension is introduced. Let me first explain this latter possibility. In describing a grammatically well-formed combination of words, e.g. 'The quick brown fox jumped over the lazy dog', as a *sentence*, there is no implication that what we have is a piece of actual speech. It will of course be so potentially, but only potentially if, for example, it occurs as an exercise in a typing handbook or with accompanying translation in a translation manual. It is presumably because it is in general so much easier to think of the written word in detachment from a use that we associate 'sentence' therewith, rather than with spoken utterances. At all events, it is only when used in the making of a statement, suggestion, protest, guess, complaint, admission, and so forth, that the words come to life. A statement is not just a certain grammatical combination of words, a certain species of sentence, but there is this other dimension imposed upon it, or at least envisaged as imposed upon it. However, although there is this addition dimension, this is no obstacle to our saying that it is *words*, thought of in association with a certain linguistic act, that are constitutive of a statement, as is apparent from the way in which cited words may occur in apposition to the term 'statement'. Thus, 'His first statement, "The company is bankrupt", was not strictly true'. Similarly, what goes to make up a warning, a suggestion, or a complaint, is a matter of words whose utterance is accompanied by the appropriate intention.

It might be thought that what actually occurs, or at least what can be described as the 'historic' item, is the stating, the statement being a matter of *what* is stated, and so of something explicable only in clausal terms, as in '. . .the statement that the company was bankrupt. . .'. It is perhaps the man's stating that can be interrupted, received in silence, ignored, or inaudible, and this stating is a 'historic' episode, but there is the equally plain consideration that certain things that can be said of statements, as historic items, cannot be said of statings: a man's statement may consist of twelve words, it may be ambiguous, incomplete, alliterative, clumsily phrased, and so forth, descriptions which, in varying degrees, suggest that 'stating' is not the term to provide a gloss on 'statement' in this sense.

The statement, as a historic item, has then two sides. In speaking of the 'stating' we draw attention to the speech act, to what the person was doing in uttering the words; what holds of this is not necessarily what holds of the statement as a certain sequence of words—uttered, of course, with the form and intention which makes for the specific differentia, 'statement'. Given that it has this second aspect, it is clear how we may apply such descriptions as 'unintelligible' and 'convoluted', how we can say of a statement that it was denied or misquoted. Given only the first side, the application of such descriptions becomes exceedingly obscure.

Certain of the inadequacies in the notion of a bare sentence are to be made good by bringing in the notion of a speech act—and therewith a live use of, e.g., referential terms, such as pronouns—rather than by moving to a level of abstraction where linguistic forms desert us. What of that abstraction involved in granting that when two people utter different words with the same meaning they may none the less be said to have made the same statement? There are two possibilities here, depending on whether it is sameness of general meaning that is preserved, or whether in addition we may allow the words to vary provided that sameness of person or thing meant is maintained. The first extension reckons as the same statement 'Time flies' and *Tempus fugit*—when these are or are envisaged as statements—and with the relevant conditions of reference satisfied, one who says, 'I am tired', may, on the second possibility, be said to have made the same statement as another who says 'You are tired'.

Traditionally, the question of identity in either case—though more especially the former—has been discussed in terms of 'proposition' rather than 'statement', with a clear movement away from anything as concrete as our statements have so far been. Thus, if an Englishman says, 'It is snowing', and a Frenchman says, at the same time and place, *Il neige*, then they are both saying the same thing, voicing the same proposition, a proposition which can be expressed in an indefinite number of other languages. As something which is in some sense common to the diverse linguistic forms in which it finds expression, a proposition can hardly be identified with any of these forms, but it is seen as standing apart from particular linguistic items, such items being thought of as bearing a relation to this one entity comparable to the relation between various names and their single bearer.

This argument has some force. If the proposition is to be identified with any one form of words, as the English version, then we can hardly deny the corresponding identity with any of the other sets of words, the French, German, and the rest. But to admit these identities is, because of the transitivity of the identity relation, to incur an impossible conflation of distinct linguistic items with one another. The identity must, then, be refused in each and every case. In this argument it is clear that the relevant sameness is supposed to hold in every respect. Does our understanding of 'same proposition' really make such a demand? To take an analogous case, suppose I were to say that the French *bonjour* was the same greeting as the English 'good day', that this same greeting could be expressed differently in yet other languages. It would be no objection to this to point to the different phonological and orthographical properties of the two, or of any of the other candidates, and to conclude from such differences that they could not actually *be* the same greeting. Their sameness as greetings can survive differences at this level, since these do not enter into the relevant notion of a greeting; it is, of course, sameness of use that is critical.

The familiar example of identical chessmen can also be

used to make the point. Two distinct pawns can be the same piece without either being identified with the other, without losing their individual identities as pawns. 'Are the same piece' is simply a stand-in for a phrase which, like 'are both pawns', is used predicatively. The analogy with propositions is clear. Once we associate sameness with an equivalence relation—sameness only in certain respects—rather than with strict identity, the way is open for saying that 'It is snowing' and *Il neige* can actually *be* the same proposition, or state- ment. Again, it is no objection that we have a marked phonetic difference between the two, since the sameness in question, a matter of sameness of meaning, is indifferent to divergences of this kind. We still have, of course, sameness of meaning to elucidate, a topic which will receive attention in due course. This matter aside, application of our treatment of words like 'dish', 'book', and 'weed' should finally tie up the point: phrases like 'the. . .which he just made' may serve merely to identify a type, and not to furnish a non-sortal criterion of identity.

31. Numbers

And now to numbers. We still have some unfinished business with Frege on this topic, and I shall consider further certain aspects of his account by way of introduction to the two principal uses to which numerical expressions may be put, and which must be sharply distinguished if we are to have any chance of giving a coherent account of the nature of number.

It will be recalled that Frege's view of numbers as self- subsistent objects was arrived at by eliminating the alternatives; most notably, by eliminating the possibility that numbers are properties of external things: 'The self-subsistence which I am claiming for number is not to be taken to mean that a number word signifies something when removed from the context of a proposition, but only to preclude the use of such words as predicates or attributes, which appreciably alters their meaning' (Frege [1884], § 60). But is it really true that numbers can *never* be ascribed to objects?

One point which Frege makes concerning the importance

of concepts in assignments of number might be granted immediately. One and the same collection of objects may fall under a variety of different concepts, and until one among the possible categorizations has been specified, the instruction to count the objects may be indeterminate. So, an army may comprise so many companies, so many platoons, so many men, and with each of these subdivisions goes a different interpretation of the order 'Count them', with a corresponding difference in the answer given, even though one and the same totality of men is involved in either case. I should have thought that the same point could be made with respect to the order, 'Weigh them', an instruction which Frege invokes to illustrate the contrast, but whether or not this is so we may agree to the necessity for specifying a concept in the context of counting.

Even on this point there is room for debate over exactly how much we should concede. The order 'Count them' may become determinate only on provision of a concept, and this is what I do concede, but is this order expandible by descriptions which, while applying to the same things, call for different answers? It is far from clear that the same things are being counted when we count different subdivisions of soldiers, and Frege's account patently does not apply to his example of finding the number of a pile of playing cards (op. cit., § 22): the choice between counting all the cards and counting just the honour cards at skat is a choice between the whole and only a part, not the same totality differently categorized. Frege might protest (cf. op. cit., § 48) that he is at this point only bringing out difficulties which arise with the assumption that it is objects that are bearers of number, an assumption that is eventually rejected; be that as it may, the necessity for specifying a concept has no tendency to show, as Frege would wish, that our ascription of number is to anything less than the men, the platoons, or whatever it is that we count. We naturally speak of finding the number of a group or collection of things, such as a pack of cards or the leaves on a tree, and Frege himself speaks of 'the numbered objects'—*die gezählten Gegenstände* (op. cit., § 40). Prima facie, what has a number is precisely what we count; it would be paradoxical in the extreme to say that what we count are the cards or the leaves, but that when we arrive at the figures 52 or 1,000 we do not thereby arrive at the number of those things which we counted, and the paradox is hardly diminished if it is conceded that we must classify objects in some way prior to counting *them*. Much of course depends on what the phrase 'those things' stands in for; it could be a simple plural, as 'leaves', but it could also be a more determinate phrase, such as 'the leaves'. The latter is the possibility on which my argument turns.

If the need to impose a prior classification takes us away from objects, thought of individually, it takes us only as far as groupings or subdivisions of objects—or to objects taken collectively; this last I find the more appropriate description: it is primarily and simply to the leaves, rather than to a collection of leaves, that number may be ascribed. However, Frege does have an argument which, if acceptable, would dispose of this claim: 'The green colour we ascribe to each single leaf, but not the number 1000. If we call all the leaves of a tree taken together its foliage, then the foliage too is green, but it is not 1000' (op. cit., § 22). It is true that although the leaves may number 1,000, 'being 1,000' or 'numbering 1,000' do not signify a property of any one leaf, and to this extent number is different from colour. But it is also true that if the leaves form a pattern, no one leaf can be said to have this property, though—to express it somewhat unhappily—the collection as a whole may, just as, taken together, the leaves may be heavy, though individually each is light.

It must be granted that when we introduce the mass term 'foliage' (*Laub*), as also perhaps 'collection of leaves', we have a subject that is ill suited to being linked with either 'is 1,000' or 'are 1,000', but then it is not surprising that a singular term is inappropriate when multiplicity is being ascribed. The term 'foliage' is out of place if we substitute it for 'leaves' in the order 'Count the leaves', but that is precisely what we conclude—that it is out of place here, not that you cannot speak of counting the leaves. Similarly, the legitimacy of saying 'The leaves are 1,000 in number' is in no way threatened by the impossibility of saying 'The foliage is 1,000 in number'. Frege's insertion of this step—replacing 'the leaves' by 'the foliage' to produce an incongruity—perhaps betrays an awareness that his argument is weak at this point. Indeed, he himself points out that in ordinary language we do attribute number to objects, as when we speak of 'the number of the bales', just as we speak of 'the weight of the bales', but he simply dismisses this usage as confusing—a defensible move only if his own position had already been made secure (see op. cit., § 52).

What *is* the property here being ascribed to the leaves? Simply that of being pairable off with the numbers from 1 to 1,000 inclusive; that, quite trivially, is what it is for given objects to number, or add up to, 1,000. A curious 'property', no doubt, but it is not this broad philosophical use of 'property'—German *Eigenschaft*—that Frege is querying, since his argument seems to require merely that we understand the notion in an abstract, formal way: numerical predicates are said not to signify properties of things in the sense that we cannot conjoin such a predicate with a term which is actually used to refer to any object or objects. The logical subject–predicate pattern is not to be located in assignments of number, but, as with certain ascriptions of existence, there is no more than an appearance of reference plus predication. This is the notion that is operative at the crucial points, though Frege is also concerned to point to differences which number shows *vis-à-vis* particular properties; so, for instance, the applicability of number over a much wider range makes for a difference with colour and solidity.

Frege frequently seeks to reinforce his general argument by pointing to the difficulties met with if we try to construe 0 and 1 as properties of objects. However, in the context of the present examples, where we are imagining counting objects and ascribing a number to what we have counted, 0 and 1 are genuinely exceptional. 0 plays no role in transitive counting and it will be superfluous to say of something that it is 1 in number, since the form of the noun and/or verb used will already testify to singularity. The special reasons which favour these numbers for Frege's purposes simply fail to apply as we proceed to larger numbers. Note too that it is no use dealing with the objection by supposing that we must be sceptical of 0 and 1 as numbers if we wish to distinguish them from the numbers that follow. We may have no doubts whatsoever in this regard, but still insist that their role in counting is significantly different from that of the larger numbers.

As already implied, the difference between Frege's position and mine on the allowable possibilities can be shown as follows: we can speak of counting bales and of counting *the* bales; ascribing a number to the bales is always a matter of ascribing a number to, simply, bales, and Frege in effect insists on this reduction, whereas I wish to hold that two distinct possibilities can still be maintained: if I say, 'The bales are fifteen in number', I am attributing something to the actual bales in question, while if I say, 'There are fifteen bales', the term 'bales' does not now feature as part of a phrase which is used referentially. Frege frequently shifts to a consideration of this existential form without realizing that the absence of the pattern of reference-cum-predication is due to the (particular) existential character of the assertion rather than to anything contributed by the numerical qualification. We should not expect that what holds of 'There are *n Fs*' should be automatically transferable to sentences in which phrases like 'the three bears' or 'the seven dwarfs' occur, phrases containing determiners which purport to tie down the general term to particular things.

But there is something peculiar about ascriptions of number. You cannot readily say, 'The bales are fifteen', but have to add 'in number', or substitute 'The bales number fifteen', and all I have shown is that, in so far as there are forms of words which, like these, could plausibly be thought of as constituting ascriptions of numbers to objects, this description still stands, despite Frege's objections. To try to get further under the surface of these ways of speaking, let us take up Frege's point that 'in language, numbers most commonly appear in adjectival form and attributive construction in the same sort of way as the words hard or heavy or red, which have for their meanings properties of external things' (op. cit., § 21). This is a curious way of classifying number words, their obvious affinities being with such terms as 'several', 'many', and so forth (cf. Benacerraf [1965]).

Like these, number words can occur attributively—'many tails', 'nine lives'—and, unlike the majority of adjectives, both are rarely used predicatively: 'many' may occur thus—'His faults are many'—but 'several' and 'most' are excluded. Note, incidentally, that it is number words rather than numerals that we are considering. Numerals are less often used attributively—'I have only one wish' rather than 'I have only 1 wish'—which does suggest a different role.

Also of interest is the way in which, like these less specific quantifiers, number words outrank adjectives: we speak of 'the six old houses' rather than 'the old six houses', just as we speak of 'several old houses' and not of 'old several houses'. In what way is this ordering significant? What does it tell us about number words? Such words, along with 'many', 'several', and others which, like 'same', 'certain', and 'other', connect with identity conditions, do not mark a contrast or a division within the species defined by the remainder of the noun phrase with which they are coupled, and in this they differ from most adjectives. In such a phrase as 'a popular national daily newspaper', we have an ordering of adjectives which in this instance reflects the way in which the class defined by the noun is progressively narrowed or contracted. The sense of a number word, however, like that of 'many' and 'several', is not such as to induce a like contraction of the initial genus. In 'twelve angry men', 'angry' marks a subdivision within men, but 'twelve' does not introduce a further differentia into the class of angry men.

It does no damage to Frege's position if we separate number words from adjectives—after all, he does not want them to compare with adjectives in their fundamental use—and the respect in which they differ shows one way in which number words do not signify properties: in 'frightening dreams' the adjective specifies a kind of dream, in 'four dreams' it does not; a numerical qualification does not provide a basis on which one thing may be distinguished from others of its kind, but, as indicated above, it is to be thought of as giving a measure of multiplicity of things of whatever kind. However, this reclassification does not take us to Frege's favoured substantival use, and there is still the question whether the latter is primary, whether 'The number of deadly sins is seven', so construed that 'seven' is namelike, should be our guide to understanding 'There are seven deadly sins'. It would be wrong, furthermore, to suppose that the only alternative to a namelike use is one in which the number word is used to ascribe a property to objects. What I call the 'attributive' use of a number word—indicating no more thereby than its position before the noun—can occur within both referential and non-referential phrases, in both 'Give me two pegs' and 'Give me the two pegs'.

On the question of priority, there is much that suggests an opposite conclusion to Frege's. Not only do we have this frequent use of number words in attributive position, but when they appear to function as nouns some talk of ellipsis is often possible. As a trivial example, in 'Two's company, three's a crowd', we are clearly talking about people, not about abstract entities, but even with a sum, such as 'Three and two make five', an analogous possibility arises. This may seem to feature the number words in the way Frege prefers, viz. as 'proper names', but it is extremely plausible to regard the sentence as representing, not an assertion about one entity named 'three', another named 'two', and a third named 'five', but as an abstraction from such particular sentences as 'Three apples and two apples make five apples', or more generally, 'Three things and two things make five things'. In either case the common noun 'apples' or 'things' might be said to 'cancel out', and can in the latter case be omitted altogether without loss to the sense. The plural, as in 'Ten sevens are seventy', is interesting here. It clearly supports a substantival interpretation, but in terms of a count noun, not a proper name. In the use in which it pluralizes, 'seven' means something like 'lots of seven' or 'lots of seven things'. So, 'Ten lots of seven are seventy', not 'Ten number sevens are seventy'.

This use aside, how many number sevens are there? We might say just one, but with + 7 and − 7 in mind, we might say two. Though we might also feel that there is something curious about such positive and negative numbers, familiar to us though they now are. Thus, the sense of the operations, plus and minus, suggests that the primary occurrence of + 7 and − 7 is in a context in which the terms of the operation are more fully specified, as in '0 + 7 = 7' or '9 − 7 = 2'. With such origins, the combinations ' + 7' and ' − 7' do not at all suggest a comparison with such designations as, say, '*h*' (for Planck's constant). ' − 7' is more like 'less seven' or 'reduced by seven', and ' + 7' has a similar role as an incomplete term; talk of possible increases and decreases by seven is talk of increases and decreases by the *same* number. It would seem quite extraordinary to conceive of ' + 7' and ' − 7' as *names,* let alone as names of different entities. The use of symbols also obscures a difference in such simple equations as '10 × 7 = 70'. We read this as 'Ten sevens are seventy' or 'Ten times seven is seventy', but the differing status of the number terms—singular or plural, qualifying or not qualifying 'times'—is in no way marked in the symbolic version. The importance of a satisfactory notation for the development of arithmetic is often stressed, but what is conducive to ease of calculation may obscure differences which are basic to our understanding of what is being symbolized.

The symbol '=' is another case in point. Equations such as '21 ÷ 7 = 3' or '$\frac{6}{4} = \frac{3}{2}$' are often thought of as identities, as involving the same notion as 'Jekyll is identical with Hyde', with the numerals providing names of a single entity. That Frege looked at the matter in this way is abundantly clear, as can be seen, for instance, from his 'Function and Concept'. The most generally applicable reading of '=' in arithmetic is, however, as 'equals', and the suggestions of this are quite different from those of 'is identical with': we talk of equality when it is a matter, not of two names of a single thing, but of two things which are assigned a common measure in a certain respect, so which satisfy a certain form of equivalence relation. What the subjects of the comparison are may not be evident from such formulae as '3 × 7 = 7 × 3', but the reading of this which reintroduces the suppressed reference to things counted provides suitable terms: three lots of seven things yields a totality which is equal in number to seven lots of three things. The shift from equality to identity encourages the view that we are speaking of relations between entities named by numerical expressions rather than comparisons between arbitrary collections. Once more the conflation of the two notions of identity and equality in the single sign '=' has the appearance of being just that kind of allowable simplification which makes formalization possible. Certainly, it does no harm within arithmetic, since calculations with figures in no way exploit it, but the risk that it will lead to a misunderstanding of either notion is realized in most philosophically oriented treatments of arithmetic.

The analysis of fractions goes much the same way as for whole numbers. A fifth, say, is a fifth *part*, three-fifths three such parts, the reference to parts being left behind when we abstract to the fraction, $\frac{3}{5}$. Here again the reasons for refusing to go alone with the naïve and superficially attractive view that number words are like proper names are very strong. Not only do our verbal renderings employ the numerical terms either as count nouns or in an 'adjectival' use, but we can attach little sense to the notion of the arithmetical operations as being operations on abstract entities in the sense intended, rather than on arbitrary, unspecified parts or fractions of things. I can readily understand the division of three fifth parts into seven eighth parts, but this ready understanding deserts me if I am required to interpret the operation of division as bearing upon just two objects, the abstract entity corresponding to $\frac{3}{5}$ and that corresponding to $\frac{7}{8}$. And what kind of operation could be involved when one entity is raised to the power of another?

An interesting context for 'number' is provided by such sentences as 'A number of people were invited' and 'I saw a large number of bees'. If I see a large number of bees I do not see a large number, where 'number' in this latter occurrence does duty for suitably' distant members of the series 0,1,2 . . . Again, if Alice purchases a number of presents, she does not emerge from the store brandishing the first perfect number, let us say. The phrase 'a number of', corresponds to an *attributive* use of a specific number word: 'A number of people—ten, to be precise—were invited'. There is no call to see 'a number of' as a generalization with respect to referential position in such sentences, and even replacing 'a' by 'the' need involve no essential change in this respect. I do not myself find that 'The number of planets is odd' rings quite true, and if 'the number of' is here a stand-in for a number word used attributively, so for 'Nine planets is odd' rather than simply 'Nine is odd', we have an explanation for the awkwardness. If we really wish to identify a number, 'the number of *the* planets' is the preferred form.

The general point is not confined to phrases with 'number', as we have already observed. You may, for instance, sit on a kind of sofa, but not on a kind. Like 'a number of', 'a kind of' stands in for an unspecified term used attributively; it does not channel an indefinite reference to something called 'a kind'. We noticed how the plural 'spanners' attracted the verb in 'The most useful kind of spanners are adjustable', despite the singular 'kind', and we see the same phenomenon with the singular 'number', as in 'A number of people were invited', with support for a comparable conclusion. Compare too the behaviour of the noun phrase in 'That colour dress does not suit her', 'It isn't the same size', 'I prefer the water this temperature', and 'This ladder is the length we want'. In this last we are not asserting an identity of a ladder with a length, but the phrase, 'the length we want', does duty for a phrase which, like 'fifteen feet', functions predicatively.

If the account given of the behaviour of number words in the expressions of sums and products is correct, it would appear that it is the use which 'three' shares with 'many' that is fundamental, Frege's account being accordingly like that of one who takes 'Many is more than a few' as his model, with the further extraordinary step of regarding 'many' as a name (cf. Benacerraf, op. cit., p. 61). However, there are uses of number terms that are more hospitable to Frege's analysis than this comparison might seem to allow; indeed, if the view of number terms as proper names is the 'easy' view, so the examples which I have chosen to show the other possibility are perhaps at some remove from the real difficulties. The connection between abstract operations with numbers, as expressed in numerical formulae, and the actual counting operations which we may perform with collection of things, is exactly as one would expect on the basis of a desire to abstract from unnecessary detail, but there are other statements which seem more clearly to be statements about numbers in their own right. Certainly, if I say that a given numerical expression cannot be construed as a designation of a number,

I do not say this on the grounds that the excluded possibility quite generally makes no sense, but there are indubitably forms of words, such as 'the least prime', or 'the highest common factor of 221 and 323', which can enjoy the use in question.

But what are we to say when the numerical expressions come straight from the system of notation, as '65' or '3.171'? Consider these sentences: '18 is even', '17 is a prime', 'What is the next number after 999?', '$3^7 \neq 7^3$', 'He can count up to 80' and '$\frac{15}{19} > \frac{2}{3}$'. In saying, 'He can count up to 80', are we saying something short for 'He can count up to 80 things'? Not necessarily. As an exercise in intransitive counting, counting up to 80 is just a matter of reciting the numbers from 1 to 80, and no counting of objects need be involved in this. On the other hand, it is fairly plain that the numbers which we list *en route* to 80, the numbers which we may write down, copy, and so forth, are combinations of digits known philosophically as 'numerals', and the only abstractness here involved is that required by the ascent from token to type. I say 'known philosophically', since I suspect there is a divergence from the ordinary use of 'numeral'. If I give you my telephone number I give you a series of digits, and if I take the number of a car I write down such a series, but we do not speak of a telephone *numeral* or the *numeral* of a car, whereas if the standard usage agreed with the philosophical—that employed in the nominalist's reduction of numbers to 'numerals'—it is hard to see why we should not. What in some respects comes closer to the sense of 'number' which I am considering is that given by the French *numéro*, as opposed to *nombre*. *Numéro* renders our all-purpose 'number' in the examples just given, or in 'draw a number in a lottery', examples where it is not a question of a number of things, or of the implicitly attributive use of a number word. A large number of things is *un bon nombre*, not *un bon numéro*. On the other hand, *numéro* is in place when it is a matter of a number of *a* thing—the number of a house rather than the number of houses—and more generally applicable, especially in the context of arithmetic, is the term *chiffre* ('figure').

At all events, numbers in the relevant sense are used in counting, transitively and intransitively, and can be written down, but they are associated with a broader criterion of identity than are numerals, as usually understood, a criterion sufficiently broad as to allow us to say that 80 and LXXX are the same number. As numerals, the two configurations of signs may be said to differ—indeed, it is often such differences that are to the fore when we have occasion to speak of 'numerals', as arabic or roman, for instance—but their typographical and phonetic differences do not stand in the way of their identity as numbers, given the level at which this identity is intended, the level, namely, at which our overriding concern is with sameness of meaning. That the phrase, 'are the same number', can consistently bear the requisite sense, a sense in which it does not imply an impossible identification of distinct things with one another, is amply clear from our recent discussion of 'are the same proposition'. When I say that 80 and LXXX are the same number, I do not mean the phrase 'the same number' to conceal an identification of some number, but merely to specify an equivalence relation. 80 and LXXX are the same number just in so far as they occupy the same place and fulfil the same role in their respective systems of notation.

Although we think of arithmetic as involving manipulations of these notational objects, an explanation of such operations as addition, multiplication, and division will take us back to contexts in which number words are assigned to collections of objects, to things counted, and so where such words are featured in their attributive use. Thus, 18's being even is a matter of eighteen's being an even number of things, so of eighteen things' being equal to twice some other number of things, and the truth of '$\frac{15}{19} > \frac{2}{3}$' ultimately involves a certain number of parts exceeding another number. Except when what we say is very narrowly concerned with the notation, we can say as much with the basic attributive form as with its more convenient symbolic replacement, despite the lingering reference to things counted in the former case. Thus while the representation of a sum as

six		6
nine	rather than as	9
two		2
seventeen		17

is apt to make us think of operations on what is numbered by 'six' and the rest, rather than of operations on 'six' which would parallel those on 6 in the numerical display, the end result is essentially the same.

When, as in the more usual representation of a sum, any attributive use is far in the background, I say that we are dealing with operations on numbers as notational objects. This, I find, strikes some as absurd: how can a numeral, an *expression*, for heaven's sake, be something that is added or multiplied? How can you take one linguistic sign away from another? There is a genuine question as to how an operation, such as taking away, which makes perfectly good sense when used of beads or matches, can be applied to the numbers themselves, and we ought surely to see this as a problem even before deciding on the character of numbers. A considerable shift of perspective is called for, but it is a shift that we do make. We happily talk of adding up a column of (badly written) figures and of taking one row of figures away from another, even if, when this is arithmetical subtraction, the taking away is not a matter of removing or erasing a digit, not identical with the corresponding operation of taking away a number of matches from a pile. Indeed, while they may be quite foreign to a formal system of arithmetic, it is precisely such rules as those relating to carrying numbers when adding and multiplying, that for actual arithmetic constitute, at a very basic level, the substance of the subject.

My suggestion is, then, that a numerical sign or expression has, explicitly or implicitly, an attributive use, or else the proposition or formula in question features the number itself as a logical subject, or at least as object of the relevant operations. The former use tends to go with number words—as 'ninety-nine'—the latter with numerals—as '99'. Only tends: '2 is company' and 'I lost 1' suggest absurd propositions about the numbers 2 and 1, but '2,857,901 is a lot of votes' does at least avoid a cumbrous form of expression. What I thus exclude is any appeal to the name/bearer model in explaining the use of numerals or their equivalents in words. In, for instance, 'We heard three knocks', the grammar does not allow the possibility that 'three' is endowed with a designatory role, and with such a sentence as '245 is a number which I have just chosen at random', or '245 divides by 49', I am actually presenting you with something to which the predicate attaches, not a *name* of such a thing. To refer to or designate a number, which is of course possible, we do not use terms like '245', but descriptions such as 'the number you got at the first count', or 'the number you last mentioned', and for names we may look to such letters as e, i, and π.

Any significant objections to my construal of the non-attributive use of number terms will seek to show that, at whatever level of generality we conceive of a series of digits, it cannot be the bearer of the properties which are ascribed to the number, but there is another objection which, although weak, is just worth a mention at this point, since it is relevant to other issues which we shall encounter.

It is commonly supposed that in speaking of a word, name, sentence, or other linguistic item, we must use not that item itself, but a name of it, this latter name being formed by enclosing the named expression in quotation marks. Why we 'must' condone such an abuse of the word 'name' has never been made clear. For the obvious reason. If I state, 'Her friend's name is "Sally"', then I simply give the person's name, not a name of it; similarly, if I correctly report that someone said or wrote, 'The end is nigh', then I cite rather than name the speaker's actual words. In any ordinary sense, the name or statement does not have a name, and to describe the quoted name or words as a name of the name or words is at best to adopt a convention about the use of 'name'—at worst, perhaps, to be taken in by the illogical vulgarism, 'What is her name called?'. It is in no sense to refute anyone who would wish to speak in the normal way and who retains some attachment to the idea that it is possible to state a person's name, rather than have to make do with merely giving a name of that ineffable item. Furthermore, the convention obscures an obvious difference between two ways of identifying a linguistic item. If, for instance, we write 'The first letter of the Greek alphabet is "α"'—or the same minus the quotes—we actually give the letter in question, whereas in writing 'The first letter of the Greek alphabet is alpha', we are only naming α.

The idea that you cannot have this direct/indirect contrast, that you cannot literally cite a person's words, is probably a reflection of nominalism of the crudest variety; as though 'word', along with other linguistic terms, could be legitimately used only in association with a spatio-temporal criterion of identity. This would be a particularly gross error with regard to 'word', since its most frequent occurrence is as a second-level term: words considered unrepeatable are seldom considered thus for logical reasons. The nearest we can get to the name relation is in the use of written words in giving a report of spoken words, or vice versa. The historical priority of the latter over the former may encourage this conception, but it is still not right. We can speak of the one as a *representation* of the other, but there is no naming, since what passes for the name may itself collect the relevant predicates of the item 'named', the two being different forms of the same thing. Again we glimpse something of the perils which face those who misconstrue phrases of the form 'is the same F as', seeing strict identity where there is nothing more than an equivalence relation to be found.

We may, then, happily continue to speak of the number as directly given rather than named in such contexts as '245 is the number I got at the first count'. And what is a number in this sense? As already stated, it is a measure of how many, of multiplicity. (This does not apply to fractions or to complex numbers, but this is intentional. I regard these as numbers in a different sense.) Collections of objects may agree or differ in respect of multiplicity; in the most general terms, this is to be explained by an appeal to the notion of pairing off the elements of the one collection with those of the other or others. A measure or characterization of multiplicity, taken at its most demanding—i.e. where a difference of one makes for a difference overall, so not as with, say, 'a few'—is given by the series of numbers, which we may think of as more sophisticated substitutes for the notches on a stick, for the tally which furnishes the concrete substitute for the collection counted. Collections of objects may be placed in groups, where a group contains only collections in one–one correspondence with each other; the number of such a group could be given by yet another such collection, as the notches on a stick might serve as an appropriate exemplar, or we can make use of the more convenient *figures*, as in our arabic notation.

This is not *so* far removed from the logicist characterization of a number as a class of all those classes similar to a given class, but the generality there introduced in terms of classes enters at a different point in our analysis.

Questions of the existence of numbers fall into two categories: if we are presented with a descriptive phrase, such as 'the highest common factor of 313 and 191', the problem will be one of determining whether this has application; if we are given an ostensible numerical sign, our task will be to determine whether a coherent interpretation of the appropriate form is prescribed or can be devised in the system—a question of sense rather than of reference. Realistic existential questions will generally be of the former kind, questions as to the possession of a certain property by some one of the known numbers. So, in asking 'Does an odd perfect number exist?', we are asking whether any of the natural numbers, supposed given, is both odd and perfect. The more radical query is less likely, since if the speaker as much as understands the numerical symbol, n, he is *ipso facto* likely to know the answer to the question, 'Is there such a number as n?'. However, someone might ask whether, for instance, there was such a number as $0/0$, a question, not of the existence of a bearer for this uncertain device, but of the meaningfulness, and of course more specific kind of use, of this concatenation of symbols.

The breakdown of the name/bearer model for numerals and numbers reveals the final absurdity of 'postulation'. What concerns us with a putative numerical sign is whether its use is clear and consistent; in the absence of these features, postulation is premature, and in their presence it is otiose. Perhaps we could make *some* kind of sense of postulation in connection with a hypothesis of meaningfulness, but there is certainly no independent question of the existence of a corresponding entity, as though, having given a coherent definition to, say, i—the square root of -1—a definition which fixed it in its relation to other numbers, we had accomplished only half our task, a genuine extension of the number system being recognizable only on discovery of an extralinguistic object which met the defining condition. Any comparison with the empirical case, where being well defined does not settle the question of existence, is surely quite misplaced.

Frege's early insistence that 'it is only in the context of a proposition that words have any meaning' (Frege [1884], § 62), was intended as a corrective to the demand to be *shown* the bearer of a name, but it might also be taken to forestall interpretation of certain expressions of the form 'an F of G'—'a number of eggs', 'a kind of bicycle'—'that F', and so forth, as units of the kind which they appear to be. We have mentioned that there is no passage from 'I saw a large number of bees' to 'I saw a large number', unless the latter is thought of as abbreviating something like the former, and we might instance 'function' as another important word with a similar logic: area is a function of length and breadth, there being an operation on the latter, length times breadth, which yields (a measure of) the area, but we cannot say 'area is a function' unless, again, as no more than an abbreviatory locution. Moreover, as we have already observed, the behaviour of certain noun phrases may be akin to that of a clause, but this may be apparent only from the occurrence of the phrase in context. Take 'the existence of God' away from its accompanying verb in 'He questioned the existence of God' and we are only too likely to overlook the correct parsing.

Members of the group of terms comprising 'number', 'kind', 'sort', 'type', 'brand', 'rank', 'sex', and so on, contrast in an important respect with another term which belongs in this discussion, namely 'set'. 'Class' may be like 'kind', as in 'that class of person', but 'set' will not do here; its affinities are more with 'group' or 'collection'—a set of knives and forks—it being understood that the members of the set relate to or match one another in some way, perhaps forming a totality that is in some respect complete. Some mathematical uses of 'set' may make sense on this model: '11 is a member of the set of divisors of 3,927' locates 11 among a totality or plurality of numbers. It is of interest to note that in general this reading poses no problem for membership of one set in another, since one plurality can easily subdivide into a number of pluralities, whereas the pattern of analysis exemplified by the reduction of '17 is a member of the set of primes' to '17 is a prime' meets with a difficulty when a set designation occurs to the left of the class membership sign. The problems which do arise arise with such basic sets as the null set and the unit set of a set or individual. The null set cannot be equated with its members, since it has none, and the unit set cannot be equated with its single element: one thing will be true of the set which is not true of that element, namely that it has the latter as a member. In such cases the set comes into its own as having an identity over and above that of its members, if any, and here the model of a *container*, something which can be empty though existent, seems to accord better with our understanding—such as it is—of the concept in mathematics. At all events, it is clear that on either reading—whether a simple plurality or a container is our model—the notion of *set* presents us with something more substantive than the notion of a *kind*, even though the commitments of the two are sometimes thought to be on a par.

32. Possibility and infinity

I maintain that, unless they reduce to the satisfiability of some condition by some number, questions of the existence of numbers are unreal if they are thought to require more than can be furnished by clear and coherent definitions, but this is not to say that what counts as an acceptable specification of a number is unproblematic, as attempts at introducing aleph-zero and the other denizens of Cantor's paradise so readily remind us: when infinity is being accommodated, we can be sure that difficulties relating to meaning and existence will be at their most acute, whether inside or outside mathematics.

Some of the difficulties here can usefully be linked to another source of existential anguish: the question of the status of possible individuals and possible worlds. Here if anywhere, matters of existence are not to be represented either as empirical or as pragmatic, as if in discussing the multitudes of possible worlds we were at last breaking though the confines of conventional geography, or as if we had only to decide whether acceptance of possible individuals served some purpose or other to justify invoking them—perhaps even supposing that the relevant formalizations were needed to explain the ways of speaking which suggested them. That a large measure of preliminary clarification is called for in this area should not be disputed: on the one hand, talk of possible individuals can

sometimes be given sense in terms of a transformation, extension, or simple acknowledgement of inoffensive locutions, as
when 'a possible F' turns out to mean no more than 'an actual
thing which could be an F'; a possible successor for a post or
a possible site for a new town make sense in these terms,
though 'a possible grasshopper' and 'a possible skyscraper'
present count nouns in a combination which lends itself less
readily to this style of interpretation, and while the interpretation may be adapted to them, it is far from clear that anything along these lines is what would commonly be intended
by those who wish to speak of 'possible grasshoppers' and
their ilk. An undifferentiated treatment of the two cases, the
tolerably clear and the largely obscure, may be a prelude either
to a mistaken repudiation of the whole conception, or to a
formalization whose interpretation may in consequence be
uncertain: for instance, with the clear cases, quantification
over possible Fs would amount to no more than quantification over things which could be Fs, so over no more than a
subset of actual things; with the unclear cases it may not mean
anything. In general, the problem is one of ensuring that
'possible' is taken seriously, that the qualification which it
introduces does not get misplaced and that we do not find
the merely possible F being subtly transformed into a species
of actual F. Some such move may, I suspect, have taken place
when it is argued that we can have an actual infinity, at least
with respect to abstract objects, and to this topic I shall now
briefly turn.

   Let us stipulate that two collections are *numerically equivalent* if and only if it is possible to put the elements of each
into a one–one correspondence, and let us say that a set is
denumerable if and only if it is numerically equivalent to the
set of positive integers. We now say that a denumerable set has
cardinal number $\aleph_0$. This approach amounts to an introduction of $\aleph_0$ as the answer to the question, 'How many positive
integers are there?', but in such a way as to ensure a numerically definite answer to that question. Or so it might seem.
The contrast here is with an answer which, like 'a lot', could
be given in reply to the question, but which obviously falls
short of providing a numerically definite measure: if there
are a lot of elements in each of two collections, it may none

the less be that the collections fail to be numerically equivalent, that they are not the same in number. No such possibility is risked by an appeal to $\aleph_0$, the specification given has seen to that.

However, this characterization of $\aleph_0$ simply passes over the point at which the possible indeterminacy enters, the indeterminacy which threatens its use as a well-defined numerical expression. For, in what sense can the positive integers *all* be put into one–one correspondence with the members of another set? An objector would no doubt say that we can do no more than make a start on putting into a correspondence the members of one infinite series with those of another; to say that they can all be paired off is to assimilate the series to a finite totality, as if we could run through each member in turn and perform the requisite operation upon it. If the operation is not completable, in what sense *can* it be done? An infinite series is an indefinitely extendible series, having an openness that is at odds with the assignment of a numerically definite measure. Infinite means unfinished, indefinite, or indefinitely prolongable, and it is only if we treat the infinite as having the basic feature of a finite totality, viz. being determinate as to number, that the question of introducing a numerical measure of the constituent elements arises. In an older idiom, the positive integers are integers 'without number', the qualification being all there is for $\aleph_0$ to symbolize.

This attack is not altogether satisfactory. It is at least a possibility that the notion of pairing the members of our series with those of another can be understood as making a lesser demand than the claim that we could in practice effect a pairing between the two series, where affecting a pairing involves some physical operation, an operation taking some finite time, however short. Provision of a functional expression enabling us to specify the image of an element in any arbitrary case is all that is required, and it would have to be argued that this committed us to regarding actual calculation through an infinity of cases as a possibility.

When we speak of the existence of a positive integer we are thinking primarily of the non-attributive case, so, according to our analysis, what is at stake is the existence of appropriate numerical expressions which, for the sake of simplicity, we can think of as taking the form of sequences of 1s. The number of such sequences actually in existence at any given time will be finite, surely, but we can still say that there are infinitely many positive integers, meaning that the number of possible sequences of 1s is infinite. But now, while we have been obliged to move into the realm of possibility to find our infinity, it would seem we have found it none the less. The number of actual sequences may be finite—as many as you wish, so we can speak of a potential infinity, but never more than finitely many at any given time; the number of possible sequences is, however, not thus restricted: here we meet with not merely a potential but an actual infinite.

However, this attempt to find an actual infinity is no better than any other attempt to show the satisfaction of a given condition by invoking a merely *possible* object as an appropriate value. We are committed to saying that the number of possible sequences of 1s is infinite, only in the sense that there is no limit to the number of sequences which one might actually have. From this it cannot be inferred that there in any sense actually are infinitely many sequences each of which one could have. That would be, in effect, to detach 'there exist infinitely many sequences' from 'possible' in such a way as to allow its extraction as an unqualified conclusion, 'possible' being reassigned a sense of something like 'could be realized' and predicated of this actual infinity.

There being no guarantee that the world contained limitless numbers of things of any kind, Russell felt obliged to postulate an axiom of infinity. This shows his approach to be wrong: mathematics is not constrained by contingent shortages of materials; it can be indifferent to what in fact exists. The crucial question is whether the absence of an actual infinity is contingent, or in general whether a proposed possibility really is such. I shall now briefly examine an aspect of this question in terms of one form of temporal infinity. Consider this proposition:

(i) The moon will continue to exist for ever

Does (i) express a genuine possibility? The word 'ever' comes at a point where we might have met with an unproblematic specification of a time—'a century', 'a million years'—but 'for ever' does not purport to delimit any such period. Yet what stretches of time are there other than those which are delimitable, finite, measurable, however long? An infinite period of time is not a period which could be realized; there could be no time at which we might say: the moon has, as predicted, gone on for ever.

We might say that something went on and on, and we can suppose it continuing indefinitely, in the sense that we might suppose it to continue without imaginining a termination, but that is not to imagine anything going on for ever, as if that signified a coverable stretch of time. The notion of a finite period contrasts with that of a period which, because it is continually being extended, is not one that can be given a definite measure, once and for all. When another contrast is sought it is as if 'for ever', from acting as an indication that the speaker could not or did not wish to specify the extent of a temporal period, came to be taken as specifying some actualizable period, but one which, since all the measurable periods were already allotted, had to be distinguished from these.

However, in rejecting (i), it may appear that we commit ourselves to

(ii) The moon will cease to exist after some finite time

Is that so? While we can make no sense of the suggestion that the moon might go on for ever, if this is thought of as signifying a definite, but non-finite, period of time, we can certainly grant that it might one day cease to exist. That is clearly a possibility, but the question is whether it is a necessity, given that (i) is to be rejected. Equivalently, is it not only the necessity of (ii) that prevents (i) from being a possibility? After all, if we refuse to allow that the moon should exist for ever, what alternative is there to saying that it will cease to exist at some time? Where a body is progressively disintegrating or decaying, we might be able to predict a time when it will have ceased to exist, but that is not the case we are considering. It is solely our rejection of (i) that is thought to make (ii) inescapable. Again, we might offer (ii) as a prediction, a prediction which could be considered from day to day, as fulfilled or not. That too would be different, so long as it was not thought assertible on the basis in question.

However, we might ask how assertibility on this basis is superior to the assertion of (ii) as an unsupported prediction. As a result of rejecting (i) we are supposedly in a position to assert the occurrence of a certain event at some unspecifiable time. Accordingly, however long a period we imagine elapsed, we can still insist that the event will take place. But one who accepts the 'proof' of (ii) based on rejection of (i) is in no better position than one who accepts it without grounds— there is nothing of which the former has greater assurance; both have the same expectations, both can say no more than the event may or may not take place on any given day or in any given year. The man who thinks he has a proof will no doubt claim to have certainty over the long run, but since that is not a time stretch endowed with any reality, his certainty is illusory.

We can hazard a guess as to what will have happened by some remote future date, but not as to what will have happened with respect to *all* future times. There is no such totality. We accordingly exclude the possibility that the moon should exist for all eternity as senseless. All we can consider is what we might know at some future date, and since at any such date it is conceivable that the moon should still be in existence, no necessity attaches to (ii). But it is not conceivable that the moon should be in existence at *all* future dates. That is quite right—or at least you might put it that way. The situation is unchanged if we reject (i), a rejection which amounts to no more than the claim that any time for which the moon might be said to exist is finite. That rejection falls short of putting us into a position to assert that the moon will in fact cease to exist after some finite time. Of course, if I am not prepared to assert P, it does not follow that I am prepared to assert the negation of P. That holds with some generality, but what is distinctive in the present case is the total absence of circumstances in which P could be deemed assertible, even that not being enough to push us to the assertion of not-P.

The argument has a parallel in the context of proofs of undecidability in mathematics. Consider a proposition to the effect that some natural number has a certain property, and suppose that this proposition is declared to be undecidable. It has been claimed that to establish undecidability is tantamount to establishing the falsity of the proposition in question—which would of course make nonsense of any proof of undecidability. After all, if the proposition is true, then it surely can be decided: the property in question being (by hypothesis) decidable—as opposed to the matter of existence— we can simply generate the sequence of natural numbers, knowing that at some time we shall encounter a number which verifies the proposition. To rule out decidability, then, we must rule out truth: there can be no number having the property in question. What has gone wrong here should be clear enough. It is illegitimately assumed that, having seemingly found an inconsistency in the supposition that the proposition is true, we can straight away move to an affirmation of its falsity. It is assumed, that is, that the proposition is one for which the law of excluded middle holds good, that it is indeed a decidable proposition.

7
NOMINALIZATIONS AND FACTS

The major topic of this chapter, sentence nominalizations, is one at which we arrive from a number of directions. First, at the conclusion of the discussion of intentionality, clausal constructions came to our attention as the focus of any residual problems in this area. To recapitulate, it had emerged that a verbal phrase might determine the application of an associated noun phrase, as in 'I can see a flag', and that there was reason to regard such contexts for indefinite noun phrases as basic. However, this made for a complementary difficulty with divergent uses. Sometimes, as with the modal qualification in 'A cat may have killed the parrot', we introduce no more than a minor complication into the basic pattern, but other sentences, notably those described as 'intentional', bear a less immediate relation to this pattern, and formulations aimed at showing continuity with the simpler cases may be at some remove from the original wording. Still, it does seem that in rephrasing 'They fear a resumption of hostilities' as 'They fear there will be a resumption of hostilities', we can indicate the involvement of the basic use in the former without having to invoke another realization of that use, one which is to be discerned in 'They are frightened of a snake in the loft', but which, if insisted upon in the present instance, would leave us with an object of fear when none as yet exists. However, it now seems we avoid one unwanted object only to have another step into its place, for it is surely an object of fear of some kind, if some exceedingly obscure kind, that is introduced by the version in which a clause comes to be governed by the verb 'fear'.

With our analysis of indirect speech we set out on another route to this topic. I claimed that noun phrases were not obliged to surrender their referential status on following such qualifications as 'he thought' and 'she hoped', but that the effect of these could be confined to the accompanying verbal phrase. They could have repercussions for a noun phrase if that phrase were non-referential, since if it is the verb that dictates the existential implications with respect to the noun phrase, a qualification of that verb, as in 'He thinks he caught a fish', will make for a qualification of those implications. If, however, there is no such dependence, if the noun phrase implies existence in its own right, as with 'He thinks he caught that fish', then it will remain untroubled by this qualification. As mentioned, we can sometimes allow for a departure from this pattern: whereas demonstratives remain resolutely thus, verbs allow of a weakening to a subjunctive reading, so if we can make out a case for something like such a reading with certain noun phrases, there is the possibility of both noun phrase and verb phrase having a parsing geared to the introductory qualification. If these possible relations of 'he thinks' to the following words are overlooked, this is in part, I suggest, because the dominating conception is that of 'thinks' as a transitive verb, with the following clause as direct object. If '(that) he caught a fish' is to be conceived of as a unitary object, a substantival term serving to name a thought or proposition, it is perhaps less easy to allow for the kind of interplay which we have found between the introductory verb and the terms within this unit. At all events, it would be useful to add to the earlier discussion an account of the way in which the introductory verb relates to its associated clause.

Finally, when discussing universals, we made some progress towards disentangling the peculiarities of terms like 'height' and 'redness' by drawing attention to their verbal expansions, as when we rewrite 'The height of the tower makes it dangerous' as 'The tower's being as high as it is makes it dangerous'. What this yields, however, is a predicational phrase which may seemingly be obliged by the surrounding context to have a reference, and this in a way that is at least as problematic as with a clause. A clause like 'that the tower is high' may present us with a troublesome propositional object, but 'the tower's being as high as it is' seems to force an equally intractable worldly item upon us.

33. Intransitivity and verbs characterizing speech acts

Let us begin with *that*-clauses, and let us concentrate on the occurrence of such a clause with a transitive verb, or what we should take to be such, this being one of the major constructions which appear to confer upon a clause a role that is difficult to fathom. The traditional example is that of belief. In 'David believes that he will succeed', the main verb has every appearance of being transitive, with object the following clause. It is not at all difficult to give substance to this impression: the clause occupies a position which can be filled by an undisputed noun phrase—'David believes my claim', 'David believes her story'—and the possibility of transposing the clause to subject position, as with 'That he will succeed is believed by David', surely means that it is a direct object of the verb.

However, if we can successfully challenge the superficial grammar, perhaps we may be able to stop short of introducing any problematic items as the objects of belief and the other propositional attitudes. Only perhaps, since to show intransitivity is not to show that what follows the verb must be non-referential. Absence of a passive for 'The teacher shook his head' and 'I mean you' can be taken as proof of intransitivity, but this does not debar 'his head' or 'you' from a referential role. In general, however, intransitivity would seem to make for a lessening of the pressure to introduce we know not what by way of objects for the propositional attitudes.

We can take a small step towards showing intransitivity if we can show that the relevant verbs are at least capable of occurring intransitively, and with some this much is immediate. Thus, in the context 'A Vd'—'A' subject, 'V' verb—we can insert any of the verbs 'protest', 'argue', 'telephone', 'object', 'confess', 'answer', and 'boast', to mention but a few, and the result does not require the addition of a noun phrase to complete it into a sentence. On the other hand, there are verbs which do not occur in isolation—'say', 'admit', 'declare', 'suggest', 'grant'—and with these the case for intransitivity is at first sight that much weaker. Of course, if V can occur intransitively, this does not prove that it is intransitive before a *that*-clause, and, on the other hand, if V cannot occur in isolation this does not prove that it is transitive either, since the sentence might be completable by something other than a noun phrase. The question then becomes one of the grammatical status of the clause—does it behave as a noun phrase?—but before tackling this I shall consider another way in which these words may be completed into a sentence, viz. by adding words in quotation, as in '"I have been cheated", he complained'.

Here 'complained' is surely intransitive, for the only possible candidate for object would appear to be the quoted words; but while you can complain *by* uttering words, the words themselves cannot be said to be complained. Nor is it just that 'words' is an inappropriate specification of the putative object in this connection; any other term, e.g. 'statement', 'proposition', 'utterance'—even 'complaint'—is equally out of place. Contrast this with 'He wrote "I have been cheated"', where it at least makes sense to construe the main verb transitively, with the following words or sentence as object. Other verbs which compare with 'complained' rather than with 'wrote' (so used) are the main verbs in

> 'It's not my fault', he protested
> 'You go first', he insisted
> 'She could be at home', he suggested
> 'I thought today was Tuesday', he explained

As they occur here, the verbs 'protested', 'insisted', 'suggested', and 'explained' are not transitive; indeed, we may wonder whether they are grammatically tied to the preceding quotations at all; they indicate what the speaker was doing in saying what he said, but perhaps the relation to his utterance is effected by mere juxtaposition and not by any further grammatical connection, or not by one that is customarily recognized.

In the report, '"It's gone", he exclaimed', the quotation does more than simply specify the words which the speaker uttered; it also refers us to his act of uttering these words, an act which is characterized by the phrase 'he exclaimed'. That is, enclosing words in quotes serves a double function: not only are the speaker's words reproduced, but the quotation represents a linguistic act or performance, and, moreover, an act or performance which does not require a transitive verb for its description. The role of the quoted words in presenting or mimicking an *act* is perhaps even more in evidence when we have inversion of the following subject. This survives in English in such phrases as 'said he', and in some languages it is the rule.

By contrast, with a such a sentence as 'He translated "I have lost the pen of my aunt"'—supposing it is not a matter of translating in these terms—the quotation merely specifies the words or sentence translated, it does not represent a linguistic act describable as one of translating. This is quite unlike '"I thought today was Tuesday", he explained', where the quoted words constitute an explanation, not what was explained; it is not like explaining (the statement) 'Space is non-Euclidean'. Again, a person might suggest (the sentence) 'She could be at home' as a paraphrase of another sentence, but this is to be distinguished from the report, '"She could be at home", he suggested'.

It is only verbs which can characterize speech acts of the kinds customarily associated with an intentional use of language, as in making an assertion, issuing a command, or asking a question, that can give rise to the indirect speech construction, not the kind of act that is reported by such words as 'copy', 'recite', and 'translate'. You can translate 'The cat sat on the mat', but you cannot be said to translate that the cat sat on the mat. If we say that a person whispered or stammered that he was coming, there has to have been an assertion on his part; not merely the production of words in a form which would make for the applicability of the descriptions 'whisper' or 'stammer'. Some verbs allow of both the transitive and the intransitive uses, but it is noticeable that when it is possible to pass from the direct to the indirect speech formulation, the direct speech version almost invariably features an intransitive use of the verb. To explain (the statement) P is not to explain that P, to suggest P (as a paraphrase) is not to suggest that P, and 'He wrote "P"' may not license 'He wrote that P'. (As with my use of quotation marks, my use of the variable 'P' here and elsewhere is not rigorous. It is to be supposed that the appropriate changes of tense and the rest accompany the transition from direct to indirect speech.)

These considerations give some support to the claim that the main verb in the indirect speech construction is not tran-

sitive. Of course, a person could still maintain that the verb
becomes transitive when it governs a *that*-clause, even though
it is intransitive when appended to a quotation, but it would
be surprising if such a drastic transformation were to be met
with. Moreover, there is the point that, leaving aside the disputed case of clauses, it may not be possible to complete
'A Vd ...' into an assertion by the addition of a direct object.
Consequently, if such clauses are direct objects, then in some
cases they are the only direct objects that the verb can govern,
which is anomalous, to say the least. You can complain about
something or object to something, but you can neither complain nor object something. So, although you can complain
or object that *P*, it would seem wrong to regard 'that *P*' as
filling the role of object. On the other hand, this point fails
for a large number of verbs, including 'believe', which undoubtedly do allow of a transitive use, and there are many
verbs, again including 'believe', which cannot occur appended
to quoted words; to these the above remarks have, as they
stand, no application.

34. Transitivity and the origins of the noun clause

If we accept intransitivity in the context of direct speech, it
might seem arbitrary to deny it, without further argument, in
the case of indirect speech. But there can be further argument,
with one powerful consideration coming from the history of
the noun clause construction, for which a commonly suggested
derivation seems to favour transitivity. Consider the following
reconstruction as proposed by *The Oxford English Dictionary*
(entry under 'that', vol. ix, p. 253):

(a) He once lived here: we all know *thát*
(b) *That* (now *this*) we all know: he once lived here
(c) We all know *that*: he once lived here
(d) We all know *thăt* he once lived here
(e) We all know he once lived here

We may grant that 'that' is no longer a demonstrative in line
(d), but this does not necessarily count against a continuation
of the apparent transitivity which the verb governing it has at
the earlier stages. However, there are several ways in which

the significance of the *OED* reconstruction can be challenged, as I shall now show.

1. Although the steps are set out in terms of 'know', it may be that this particular verb has been chosen more or less arbitrarily, the point being not so much that, historically, this development took place in this instance, but that the construction proceeded along these lines with respect to some verb(s) or other, and that, once it had been established, 'know that' was introduced by analogy. In particular, it may be that the construction developed with respect to some verb or verbs which were or could be unproblematically transitive, 'say' being the obvious choice here, and that the use with intransitive verbs became possible only when 'that' had ceased to be a demonstrative and had weakened to the conjunctive form which it has at stage (d).

2. I have cited this reconstruction as evidence for transitivity, but, as regards many verbs, it is doubtful that it lends any clear support to this hypothesis. When 'that' is coupled with 'believe', 'deny', or 'accept', it can be supplanted by a variety of more specific referential terms, such as 'what he said' and 'his claim', but similar substitutions in 'we all know that' result in unintended sense or nonsense. In line (a) 'that' must apparently refer to the preceding statement or sentence, *if* it refers to anything at all, but the rephrasal, 'He once lived here: we all know that statement', is highly dubious, and even if we can somehow understand 'know' as taking a propositional object, it seems to be impossible to make sense of this construction when we turn from 'know' to such verbs as 'suspect', 'fear', or 'expect'.

Could it be that 'we all know that' is to be understood as 'we all know that fact'? The sense of 'know' does not rule out such an expansion, which is of interest in providing an alternative to a propositional object, but once more this could not be the model for understanding more than a small number of the verbs that enter into the construction. Furthermore, even if some other completion were appropriate for the recalcitrant 'expect', 'fear', 'guess', 'explain', and so forth, there remain verbs which, like 'complain', do not combine with a demonstrative 'that', however expanded. It is true that with 'we all know (expect) that' it could be said that 'that' relates to the preceding words in the sense that we can meaningfully replace it by these words—'We all know (expect) he will come'—but it then goes proxy for these words not by referring to them, but by being simply a place-holder. Or, if you like, it will bear the same relation to 'we all know' as does the clause minus 'that', and whatever relation that is, it is not, in the case of 'expect', one of object to the verb, and very doubtful that it is this in the case of 'know'. Compare the use of 'that' as a place-holder in 'He is that', when echoing a remark like 'He is stupid' or 'He is a fool'. As with 'we all know that', use of the plural 'those' is not relevantly possible in this construction, the role of the pronoun being closer to that of a variable than a demonstrative.

3. It is not beyond dispute that the alleged final product, line (e), came about in the way suggested, but according to some grammarians the version without 'that' arose independently (cf. Jespersen [1927], Part III, p. 32). Once more, then, there is the possibility that analogy has been operative here, 'that' finding its way into contexts which originally lacked it, rather than having been dropped from contexts where it might at some stage have had demonstrative force. Lines (d) and (e) perhaps derive from a co-ordination of the two verbal phrases: 'We all know, he once lived here'; or, to take a different example, the derivation of 'He complained that he had been cheated' could be something like:

(a) He complained: 'I have been cheated'
(b) He complained he had been cheated
(c) He complained that he had been cheated

This version offers an extremely simple account of the transition from direct to indirect speech, and the priority of (b) over (c) goes well with the contention that 'complain' is intransitive, to be understood here in the same way as in '"I have been cheated", he complained'.

Not only does it seem implausible to base such sentence forms as 'He complained (objected) that P' on 'P: he complained (objected) that', but the sense of these sentences does not favour a derivation by ellipsis from, say, 'P: he complained of that', or 'P: he objected to that'. Such a derivation seems a possibility—supposing we do not have a later appearance of 'that' by analogy—with respect to some expressions which may govern clauses, as 'I am sure that *P*' or 'I am sorry that *P*', but in 'He complained (objected) that *P*', 'that' does not denote or introduce what was complained of or objected to, it simply prefaces a report of the terms in which the person complained or objected. As such, it has something of the force of 'to the effect that', and it is interesting to note that sense, if not idiom, is often retained if we replace 'that' by this phrase, or by 'thus': 'A complained (reasoned, guessed) thus: *P*'—a version which brings out the intransitive, act-describing role of the verb. Note too the occasional use of 'how' in place of 'what': 'How did he argue?', 'How did he answer?', both of which can be met with a reply of the form 'He argued (answered) that *P*'. To ask *how* here is to ask *in what terms* the person argued or answered.

An account of the use of 'that' which is continuous with the last suggestion, but more general, is to simply ascribe it the function of a punctuation mark, a comma—which in fact used to occur in this position—a dash or a colon: 'He complained: he had been cheated'; as such it serves as a marker separating the two parts of the sentence, not as a name-forming operator which would combine with the following words to yield an object for the verb, nor even as an anticipatory object for these words. It is not to be thought of as combining grammatically with either half of the complete sentence, but, as with (co-ordinating) conjunctions in general, it links two members of a complex without being an integral part of either. In this respect it is like the conjunction 'and', which may itself be not unlike a comma in its behaviour.

So long as we remain with sentences in which the main verb is in the active voice it is easy to play down the force of 'that'. In 'I know that he came', or 'They protested that she was innocent', the conjunction does not appear to induce any radical transformation of the following words, but, as just suggested, it is seemingly little more than a marker of sorts, and one which can be dropped to leave two sentences whose relation to one another is fairly unproblematic. However, the conjunction might be held to come into its own when the clause is in the position of subject, as in 'That we shall die is inevitable' and 'That they were still alive was not then known', for here it ostensibly does serve to convert the embedded sentence into a unit of a different kind. By itself a sentence cannot be conjoined with the predicates 'is inevitable' and 'was not then known', and by bringing it about that the sentence can be incorporated into a possible subject term, the conjunction 'that' has a use in which it is decidedly not dispensable. Furthermore, if we can form the passive with a clause as subject, that surely establishes beyond doubt the nounlike character of the clause and the transitivity of the verb. What more could be required for transitivity?

This separability of main verb and conjunctive 'that' makes for a difficulty with an analysis proposed by A.N. Prior. According to Prior [1963], the sentence, 'James says that man is mortal', is not to be parsed as 'James says/that man is mortal', 'that' joining with the following words to form a name, but we have an expression, '—says that—', which, while attaching to a name at one end—'James says that—'—takes at the other end not a name but a *sentence*: 'man is mortal'. This analysis enables Prior to compare '—says that—', '—believes that—', and so forth, with such unproblematic extensional connecting phrases as '—is a man and—', which can also be completed by filling the first blank with a name, the second with a sentence: 'James is a man and man is mortal'.

We may sympathize with Prior's desire to exclude clauses from the category of names, and we have seen that there is historical support for a division of the sentence after rather than before 'that', but however ill assorted an assemblage the combination of a former demonstrative with a sentence appears to be, it does show a unitary behaviour as subject in such sentences as 'That he did it will never be believed', thereby posing a problem for one who regards 'believes that' as an indissoluble connective.

The crucial cases are, then, those in which the clause figures as subject. If we cannot show that the superficial grammar of these is misleading, then our other observations aimed at possible clarification of 'that' make little impact. But might we not challenge subjecthood by challenging the supposed nominal status of clauses? The possibility is clearly one to explore, and here are three relevant considerations.

1. Although they can be combined with a predicative use of

an adjective, as in 'That someone has been here is clear', *that*-clauses do not allow of qualification by an adjective used attributively. We cannot say 'I know a clear that someone has been here'. Of course, it is also true that we cannot use either the indefinite or the definite article with a clause, though that does not of itself prove anything beyond divergence from a subclass of nouns. Proper names—which for present purposes are to be classed as nouns—are also (in English) generally resistant to the articles. But with clauses—and this is the real point of difference—we cannot have attributive adjectives with or without the article. (Clearly, you would not expect either article with a clause, given the overlap in function with 'that', at least in its original role.)

2. If we tried to insert 'clear' in 'I am aware that someone has been here', there would be pressure to introduce 'of': 'I am aware of a clear . . .' is the appropriate pattern for a following noun phrase. But this would mean a further divergence from present clausal behaviour, in that clauses cannot be governed by prepositions; 'except' is sometimes offered as an exception, but it is doubtful whether it can be classed as a preposition in this context. We can say 'He was unaware of the fact that P', but not 'He was unaware of that P'. Similarly, one cannot be said to be misled by that P, oblivious to or unconcerned by that P, but a genuine noun—though here we may sense something of an artefact—like 'fact', 'circumstance', or 'belief', has to be introduced to mediate between preposition and clause.

3. The behaviour of clauses in questions is interesting, and unlike that of ordinary nouns. We can say 'That he came surprised them', or 'That he came is regrettable', but we cannot so readily ask, 'Did that he came surprise them?' or 'Is that he came regrettable?'. We prefer instead 'Did it surprise them that he came?' and 'Is it regrettable that he came?'.

When an attempt is made to demonstrate that one phrase is less nounlike than another, there is a risk that the incongruity which results from putting the ostensibly less nounlike of the two in a sentence frame which can accommodate the other is attributable to the particular sense of the former rather than to its general syntactic function. Thus, we should not think highly of an attempt to differentiate 'his going' and 'his car' on the grounds that we can speak of 'touching his car' but not 'touching his going'. Similarly, it may be because of the particular sense of clauses that we have no call to form the genitive of a clause, even though this feature is otherwise characteristic of nouns. Here I am simply reiterating my main methodological observation, but it is one that bears repetition.

The first two of our three points appear to hold at a sufficiently high level of generality to escape this objection, but, especially with regard to the third point, it might still be argued that the feature in question is accidental. Could we not imagine that, with further developments in the language, clauses should come to be admitted to positions from which they are now excluded? We have 'That he can walk is clear' alongside 'It is clear that he can walk'; perhaps it is just a matter of time before we have the awkward 'Is that he can walk clear?' on a par with 'Is it clear that he can walk?'. As things are, it is less unnatural to say 'Was that he did it known to many?'. Similarly, we can perhaps think of interpretations of the other deviant combinations which would be reasonably realistic, not grossly out of step with existing usage, and even if we seem to have to put clauses to uses which are difficult to reconcile to one another, that is a situation not unknown to languages. Think how we vacillate between 'without his knowing' and 'without him knowing', pulled in different directions by considerations which are quite logical. Some degree of discord might have to be tolerated in the case of clauses, but that might be all.

35. Clauses as subjects

The real difficulty continues to be the clause as seeming subject, however restricted elsewhere its behaviour as a possible substantival expression, and to this problem I now turn. Take a verb which at least has a strong claim to intransitivity when used in the active before a clause; for instance, the verb 'understand' as it occurs in 'All those present understood that the chairman had resigned'. It is of course true that 'understand' may be transitive, and, in particular, that one can understand the proposition or statement that the chairman has resigned. But, equally clearly, understanding that P is not a matter of understanding the statement that P, any more than explaining

that you have been delayed is a matter of explaining the statement that you have been delayed. Further, while '*A* understood
(explained) that statement' can yield '*A* understood (explained)
it', the sentence, '*A* understood (explained) that *P*' does not
readily condense in similar fashion. These points confirm the
view that the clause is not nounlike, but our problem arises
with the sentences:

> (a) That the chairman had resigned was understood by
>   all those present

and (b) It was understood by all those present that the chair-
>   man had resigned

In (a) it looks very much as if the clause is playing the part
of a grammatical subject, and the verb to which it is attached
surely must, since it is in the passive, be used transitively.
Again, (b) seems to be just a variant of this, the subject clause
being heralded by an anticipatory 'it'.

But consider. The hypothesis is that the original sentence,
'All those present understood that the chairman had resigned'
features an intransitive use of the verb, being essentially equivalent to 'All those present understood: the chairman had
resigned', where, whatever the relation between the two
sentences, the second is not object to the verb of the first.
Taking now (b) we have a phrase, 'it was understood by all
those present', which is no more than a variant of 'all those
present understood', and the two connect with the following
clause in exactly the same way; the 'it' does not do duty for
this clause, but it is merely a structural 'it', introduced to
make possible the passive construction. If this is accepted,
then we have a way of dealing with (a) as well, since we can
regard it as simply an inversion of (b) with ellipsis of 'it':
'That the chairman had resigned (it) was understood by all
those present'. Similarly, inversion and ellipsis give the pattern
for interpreting

> That he is at least honest (it) must be granted
> That the funds were insufficient (it) was argued by Smith
> That he should be compensated (it) was agreed

In speaking of ellipsis I am not concerned—or not primarily—
with a historical hypothesis, but it is a question of the sense

requiring a dissociation of clause and following verbal phrase in the way this analysis exemplifies, and which keeps the versions with and those without 'it' on a par. There is, if I am right, no distortion of sense in inserting an 'it' as above.

I have suggested that when, as with 'It was understood by all those present that the chairman had resigned', we arrive at a version with the clause in subject position, it is not the use of the pronoun in an anticipatory capacity that is lost *en route*, but the 'it' in 'it was understood' is employed to avoid any reference to anyone, to give an expression at least as indeterminate as 'someone understood'. We are supposing too that in sentences with the clause in object position, as 'All those present understood that the chairman had resigned', the 'that' poses no problems, being eliminable without loss to anything but its punctuational contribution. The final step is to put the same interpretation upon the version with 'it'. With the possible role of anticipatory subject ruled out, this comes simply to 'The chairman had resigned, it was understood by all those present', with a clear likeness to the simpler direct speech construction. Or, for the most perspicuous representation we might recast this and the above examples as:

It was understood by all those present: the chairman had resigned
It must be granted: he is at least honest
It was argued by Smith: the funds were insufficient
It is agreed: he should be compensated

Questions concerning the phrases in these combinations remain, but there is a reassuring closeness to less troublesome constructions which make plainer that it is a matter of understanding thus, arguing to this effect, agreeing in these terms.

What of other relevant sentence types, as illustrated by 'That we shall die is inevitable' and 'The thought crossed his mind that he might have to admit defeat'? Once more, it would seem that the subject–predicate pattern is only superficially in evidence with the former, the version with 'it' being basic: 'It is inevitable that we shall die' rather than 'That we shall die is inevitable'. Given the way in which 'it' can almost be felt intruding into the latter—in order to dissociate the clause from a role which it is not thought to fill naturally—it seems reasonable to think of the sentence as having the sense which would go with inversion and ellipsis of the pronoun as before. In the second case there is no such tendency, or even possibility, to assign priority to a version with 'it', though in view of the close connection with 'The thought crossed his mind: I shall have to admit defeat', that does not make for a problem in this instance.

So far I have not attached much significance to the presence or absence of conjunctive 'that'. It perhaps has a greater frequency of occurrence with transitive verbs, in keeping with its demonstrative origins, and on the same basis we might expect an association with clauses specifying information already given. This case is argued in detail by Dwight Bolinger, who takes the 'that' in, e.g., 'I am amazed that many people objected', as reflecting the *given* character of the information communicated, information as it were there for the speaker to take an attitude towards (Bolinger [1972], chapter 7). It certainly is true that the conjunction can induce a difference, that its use is not arbitrary, but it is not clear just what has priority among its possible roles. Consider 'I thought you would change your mind' and 'I thought that you would change your mind'. With the latter, the question of the identity of what was thought is more in focus. *That* is what I thought, rather than something else, the conjunction giving unity, and therewith prominence, to the clause. With the first form, however, possible contrasts centre more, or at least as much, around 'thought': I did think so, that was my opinion, I did not simply hope or wish. Again, contrast 'I showed him I could swim' with 'I showed him that I could swim'. The latter rather than the former goes with the suggestion that I might have shown the person something else but that is what I in fact showed him, the 'that' serving to emphasize the exclusion of the other possibilities. Finally, compare 'I'm glad that the colour is right' with 'I'm glad the colour is right'. As a setting for the former we might have: 'I'm not so happy about the style, but I'm glad that the colour is right', for the latter: 'I'm glad the colour is right; she'd be disappointed if it didn't match'. I should think it more a matter of 'that' stressing the identity, against possible contrasts, of the following clause, with the givenness of the information being implied in consequence, so far as it is implied at all; indeed, perhaps it is simply through its function as a marker, rather than through its demonstrative character, that the conjunction serves to set off the clause in the way suggested. I do not dispute that the demonstrative origins of 'that' play a part in this feature of its present conjunctival behaviour, but I think that the notion of an anaphoric use may be overstretched in relation to examples such as these. However, I grant that the line between Bolinger's account and my own is a fine one, and what is perhaps of greater interest is the fact that there is a distinction here to be characterized at all.

We have now seen two ways in which 'that' may be of significance. It is obligatory if the clause is to occur in subject position, and it serves to confer identity on the clause. These points are not unrelated, subject position being one in which a phrase is given the kind of prominence which 'that' confers. Given that the passive can be dealt with as suggested, the general problem of analysis would appear to reduce to that of the further clarification of sentences in the active voice, as 'He admitted that he was in the wrong' and 'We hoped the crowds would have gone'. We must now perhaps allow that there is more of substance in the punctuational role of 'that' than was initially indicated, but it does appear that what the construction presents us with is at some distance from the model of verb plus object.

This, then, is our conclusion to date. Conjunctive 'that' has every appearance of acting as a name-forming operator, of converting a sentence into the kind of unit which, in allowing of both subject and object roles, compares most naturally with the referential terms which may also fill these positions. We can grant that the clause does indeed show a unitary character, but, if our account is correct, it is sentential rather than substantival behaviour that defines the relation borne by the clause to the remainder of the sentence.

36. Propositions and indirect speech

If there is no call to take seriously the claim that clauses are names of facts, thoughts, propositions, or anything else, there is still the possibility that a proposition may enter into the construction in another capacity: perhaps in apposition to 'that', as somehow constitutive of the clause, perhaps as something reported rather than named. Let us consider this possible involvement.

In some cases it is clearly possible to insert 'the proposition' before the clause without turning the sentence into nonsense. One may doubt, accept, or confirm that P, and one may doubt, accept, or confirm the proposition that P. This is not, of course, invariably true: the reading appropriate to 'I understand that he has gone abroad' is not such that we can introduce 'the proposition' without distorting the meaning of the original. Again, although each of 'I considered the proposition' and 'I considered that he had been negligent' implies 'I considered something', they appear so incommensurable that we should feel that the common implication had two meanings depending on its origin, the first being in no way a generalization upon the second. In the same vein, while we can warn that there will be trouble, we cannot say, 'That there would be trouble was warned'; this sounds incongruous, since it is only a person that can be said to be warned, the further use not having developed—though perhaps there are larger contexts in which this would not be impossible; compare the highly questionable 'That the economy would improve was hoped' with the passable 'That the economy would improve was hoped by many'. At all events, we do not detect a like incongruity in 'That there would be trouble was suspected', though 'was suspected' clearly bears a very different relation to the clause from that which it bears to the name in 'Carruthers was suspected'. The version, 'It was suspected that there would be trouble', a version for which we show a preference, is more congenial towards a correct understanding of the clause, less likely to make us suppose that 'suspect' takes two kinds of object and has, correspondingly, two very different meanings.

The statement, 'They believe that the defendant is innocent', is one in which we can find room for 'the proposition'. Does this show that what is believed in such a case is a proposition? We might feel that believing that the defendant is innocent is more a matter of believing in those terms, the genuinely transitive use being reserved for the cases in which 'believe' takes a designation of a person as direct object: believing that the defendant is innocent and believing the defendant do seem to be very different notions (cf. White [1972]). However, unlike 'suspect', 'believe' does appear to have a genuinely transitive use with respect to such objects as 'the report given in the paper', and it might be held that in the present case a proposition is extractible in a straightforward enough manner, the proposition, 'the defendant is innocent', being clearly displayed within the larger context. It could be agreed that this is not actually established by the mere occurrence of words which might have a propositional use—there is no occurrence of the proposition 'the defendant is innocent' in 'The man who was apprehended with the defendant is innocent'—but insertability of 'the proposition' would seem to guarantee occurrence of the words in the right interrelations, and it might appear that we are only going along with the obvious if we say that believing that the defendant is innocent is simply a matter of believing a certain proposition.

Given the basis on which this conclusion is being asserted, it is one which should hold no fears for us. None the less, the issue is worth further consideration. First, we notice that when 'proposition' and similar terms—'belief', 'claim', 'idea', 'suggestion'—occur naturally, their occurrence is often essential. In 'They debated the proposition that crime pays', we cannot omit 'the proposition', and a similar observation goes for 'I subscribe to the belief that heredity is more important than environment' and 'He contradicted the claim that the population was increasing'. Here too the proposition enjoys some independence of the debate in which it figures and which it antedates; similarly with the belief and my subscription to it, the claim and its contradiction.

On the other hand, in the construction without any such noun phrase, we typically have what we encountered with direct speech, namely, a verb which is descriptive of the speech act with which the words reported in the clause were uttered. This needs qualification to take in the class of verbs which, like 'hope' and 'fear', cannot be counted among the 'verbs of saying', but even without further clarification it should be clear how in either case we do not have to do with an act, whether linguistic or mental, directed towards a pre-existing object, whether in the world or in the mind. Boasting, arguing, and complaining that *P* are a matter of boasting, arguing, and complaining *thus*, in those terms, whereas debating, subscribing to, or contradicting a proposition are not necessarily, or even necessarily not, ways of asserting it. The *OED* account is seductive, especially if we limit our attention to a few verbs, such as 'say'—an approach which is as common as it is narrow—since 'saying that *P*' may seem to be obviously analysable in terms of an object 'that' with a clause in apposition, but it is only exceptionally that there is even a good case for this analysis.

There is, then, a risk that insertion of a term like 'proposition' brings with it a subtle distortion, taking us away from the conception of words uttered in a certain way to that of words which are the pre-existing object of an attitude. This is particularly clear when a change of sense is involved, as with 'I considered that he had been negligent' against 'I considered the proposition that he had been negligent', or 'I understand that he has gone abroad' against 'I understand the proposition that he has gone abroad'. However, granted that the act–object model, with propositions as the objects, for the most part breaks down, there remain cases where, as with 'believe' and 'deny', insertion of 'the proposition' makes neither for nonsense nor for radical change in sense, and it is not clear that the traditional analysis must be ruled out in such cases.

So we ask again: should we say that one who believes that the defendant is innocent believes a proposition?—or that one who denies that he is responsible denies a proposition? There are certainly uses which do not support this account, as with 'I believe we've met before', but at least the sense of 'believe' is not unfavourable towards the possibility in general, as we can see from a possible contrast with 'think'. If you ask me what the object in the corner is I may say, 'I believe it is a piece of sculpture', if I have heard someone say that it is, but if I am voicing just my own opinion I should say 'I think it is a piece of sculpture'. Whether as here, where it comes close to 'I gather . . .', or in its more solemn use, where 'I believe . . .'

affirms a commitment to a controversial view, as 'I believe that all men were created equal', there may be scope for talking in terms of acceptance of or adherence to a view or proposition which has, as it were, circulation outside the speaker's invocation of it. To this point we may add a consideration prompted by the passive construction. Clauses tend to make uncomfortable subjects, a formulation with the dummy 'it' often being preferred, but while the result of inserting 'it' in 'That he is at least honest must be granted' is acceptable, there is an incongruity in, e.g., 'That he was responsible it was denied by Smith', and it may be that the impropriety here of a structural 'it' is occasioned by the presence of a genuine subject. The verb 'deny' compares with 'believe' in suggesting an attitude towards a given proposition, and the grammar appears to bear this out.

All this reinforces what is in any event clear enough: it *makes sense* to speak here of believing or denying a proposition. To go beyond this, I suggest, we should have to argue that the meanings of the verbs—with perhaps the consideration concerning the passive—actually call for the existence of an independent item, the proposition, in the way indicated, and this, while it may be strongly suggested, falls short of being an actual implication. However, it is above all a matter of deciding what we are going to understand by the claim that a proposition is involved in various instances of the construction. We have indicated one interpretation, and we might also mention that a proposition could be said to occur as constituting the larger part of the utterance, or at least as being an entailment thereof, a possibility illustrated by 'There is, he admits, no other solution'. Here *proposition* comes to *assertion*; not, clearly, what is involved in general, but not an object when it does arise.

When there is no commitment on the part of the speaker, it may be possible to speak of the subordinate clause as constituting at least a report of a proposition—even if not a proposition which occurs as object—as with 'It was assumed they would come today'. Here our primary understanding of the words 'they would come today' is, I suggest, along these lines, so as rendering the spoken or written word with just those adjustments necessary to preserve the original meanings and references intended. The original will not be uniquely recoverable: it could have been or involved 'the children will go tomorrow', but any number of different referential terms may have been supplanted by those in the report, which may even be of words in another language. Still, it is surely in terms of such a transition that we are to give an account of the construction, and we should not be diverted from this approach by the objection that there will be occasions when nothing was actually said which might be thus reported. It may be sufficient that the person in question could be supposed prepared to speak in the relevant terms. Or, to change the example, in saying 'They promised they would come', we do not require that the persons in question should have actually said 'We shall come', or words thus translatable; in the relevant circumstances it may have been sufficient for them to have nodded. As long as what they did or said was, then and there, tantamount to an utterance of 'We shall come' as a promise, we can correctly report them as having thus promised. And likewise for the other verbs which may enter the construction.

37. Psychological verbs

The bulk of the outstanding questions, both on this last point and more generally, concern the so-called 'psychological' verbs, verbs such as 'imagine', 'hope', 'think', 'fear', and 'expect'. Verbs of saying are for the most part easy to handle, since their sense will tend to be such that actual speech is implied. With 'He complained that he had been cheated', for instance, the words following 'that' will surely purport to be a rendering of the terms in which the person complained, but the same formula is not applicable to 'He feared that he had been cheated'. Of course, fearing that P is not to be thought of on the act–object model, so there is no threat of a problem as to the nature of the object. No threat to us, that is; others have shown a hospitality towards objects for the various propositional attitudes which would no doubt extend to acceptance of an object even here. Thus Russell: 'It sounds natural to say one believes a proposition and unnatural to say one desires a proposition, but as a matter of fact that is only a prejudice.

What you believe and what you desire are of exactly the same nature' (Russell [1918], p. 218). Still, since 'He feared that *P*' cannot be thought of as a modification of '"*P*", he feared', a problem of analysis remains.

It is common to emphasize the differences at the expense of the likenesses between the direct and the indirect speech constructions. This may be misleading. Consider the pair:

> He complained: 'I have been cheated'
> He complained that he had been cheated

Each has a way of neutralizing the assertive force of forms of words whose use would more generally involve a claim on the part of the speaker, viz. 'I have been cheated' and 'he had been cheated', and we can regard the differences in the way this is achieved as secondary to what is accomplished by both. The two constructions draw even closer if we adopt the convention that the citation should profess to give no more than words equivalent to the original, and if, further, anything tantamount to utterance of those words is permitted, the differences between the two are quite minimal. This appears to give an adequate account of the semantics of the indirect speech construction, and the syntax too seems clearer: if we are to seek a subordinate role for the clause, it will not be as object, but as a sentence now denied its assertive force; that is, in place of a shift from sentence to name, we can view subordinate character in terms of a shift from declarative to subjunctive force, a movement which preserves the sentential character of the clause.

As indicated, however, this simple pattern may be complicated by the admission of psychological verbs, a class which we shall now investigate, though only to give a sketch of the kind of analysis which seems to me to be required. The most straightforward cases are presented by first-person sentences like 'I believe we've met before' and 'I hope we'll never meet again'. Here we may regard the words which follow the main verb as comprising a sentence co-ordinate with what precedes, as is shown by the possibility of relocating the latter at various points within the former. Addition of 'I believe', 'I hope', and so forth, indicates how the speaker intends the rest of what he says to be taken—a familiar enough notion (cf. Urmson

[1952]). Or, bearing in mind the similar role of such terms as 'supposedly', we might locate these phrases, at least in some of their uses, under the title of 'adverbials'.

But how are the second- and third-person reports to be construed? It might be suggested that, just as verbs of saying may attach to a specification of a person's words, so psychological verbs can be appended to a specification of a person's thoughts. We cannot offer '"He is at church", she suspected' as on a par with '"He is at church", she whispered', the person's spoken words being cited in either case, but can we regard the quotation in the former as applying to the person's thought? It is certainly the case that people's thoughts can be represented in the same form as their utterances, but even when recounting an interior monologue I do not think we should speak of suspecting in certain terms, as if 'suspected' signified a way of asserting or speaking. It is much more plausible to take 'she suspected' as part of the original thought or utterance, regarding 'She suspected he was at church' as based on 'I suspect he is at church', where these latter words, while expressing a thought, constitute direct speech utterances, and where the analysis given in the preceding paragraph applies. Similarly, with 'She expects there will be a strike', we look not to '"There will be a strike", she expects', where 'expects' has been assigned this impossible role outside the quoted words, but to 'There will be a strike, I expect' (she said), where it stays meaningfully within.

The common labelling of these verbs as 'psychological' may make it appear surprising that the spoken use is primary, but this surely is so: if we are in a position to say that someone suspected that such-and-such, the person referred to would usually have had to have uttered 'I suspect' or similar in addition to the remainder of the assertion reported. If the psychological verb expresses our own evaluation of the speaker's assertion, as in 'She fancied that he was at church', then there may be no such demand, but there are in English relatively few ways of expressing a suspicion or a hope other than by saying 'I suspect' or 'I hope'.

It is not just psychological verbs whose use in reported speech arises in this way: 'He bet that P' and 'He promised that P' typically come about as reports on 'I bet that P' and

'I promise that *P*'. Performatives and certain psychological verbs also compare in their role of indicating how their associated clauses are to be taken, and, as with J. L. Austin's comparison of 'know' with 'promise' (Austin [1946]), so we might look to the former class for an elucidation of the latter: in seemingly just indicating how its co-ordinate assertion is to be taken, 'I suspect' appears to share in the non-reportive character proper to 'I promise'. However, it is soon seen that the different relations to truth put paid to this comparison. If a person says 'I promise . . .', then, with only minor qualifications, it is true that he promises, and the claim, sometimes made, that a performative has a truth value, may come to no more than that. However, if it is suggested that it makes sense to say 'That's true' to someone's 'I promise', meaning more than this, a case will have to be made out for regarding the latter as constituting a confirmable report, a report recognizable as true without appeal to the occurrence of the utterance itself, yet as soon as 'I promise' takes on such a reportive role, its character as a performative is lost. The behaviour of 'I suspect', 'I expect', and the like, is quite different: there is falsehood if I say 'I suspect (expect) he's forgotten the date' and I have no such suspicion (expectation). What is significant here is that truth requires no more than truthfulness, a sincere expression of the person's state of mind. This, the possibility of lying, makes for a contrast not only with a performative, but also with a report which, like 'It's dark now', presents a claim for whose truth sincerity and understanding do not suffice. In saying 'I suspect', one does not thereby suspect, hence the crucial difference from a performative, but since understanding and meaning what one says together guarantee truth, the psychological verb joins the performative in being opposed to reports which, like 'It's dark now', are subject to contradiction from others.

The relevant categories are, then, three: understanding may suffice for truth, in which case we have a performative; understanding may have to be reinforced by sincerity to ensure truth, as with present-tense psychological verbs; and finally, while there is no further (non-trivial) condition guaranteeing truth, we can say that sincerity and understanding do not suffice—the most general case, where one individual's judgement enjoys no logical priority over another's. The scheme has been crudely stated and needs to be complicated to do justice to 'know' and certain other verbs, but it is a useful starting-point and for our purposes a starting-point is sufficient.

The assimilation of psychological verbs to performatives tends to go with an over-emphasis of their parenthetical role. Two sentences are interlocked in the indirect speech construction, either of which can link with other conditions, whereas if we insist on thinking of phrases like 'he suspected' as reports of parenthetical comments, there will be occasions when we cannot cope with the relevant dependencies. To clarify, with the sentence, 'If he had called, he would have known you could have come', there is no question of taking 'he would have known' as in any sense an eliminable comment, as it could be in 'If he had called, you could—he would have known— have come'. Clearly, it is 'he would have known' that is dependent on the initial condition, and is not to be bypassed by going straight to the subordinate clause in the apodosis. Similarly, it is the phrase with the psychological verb that relates to the temporal condition in 'Only then did he begin to suspect that all was not as it seemed'. Most obviously, we have negation. Such a sentence as 'He never for a moment suspected there would be trouble' cannot be traced back to a version in which 'I do not suspect' functions as a parenthetical comment parallel to 'I suspect' in 'There will, I suspect, be trouble'.

I suggested that phrases like 'I suspect' may sometimes be thought of as adverbial, but in the present contexts they must be restored to full co-ordinate status; perhaps, even, we could hold that the remainder of the sentence bears something like an adverbial relation to such a phrase, thus reversing the suggested subordination (cf. Kiteley [1964]). So, 'He never for a moment suspected: there will be trouble', and 'If he had called, he would have known: you could have come'. And just what is involved in these verbs thus used? We might try 'He was never for a moment prepared to say: "I suspect there will be trouble"', or 'He was never disposed to say "suspectingly": "There will be trouble"', with in either case some such addendum as 'or words to that effect' being understood. And for 'know' we might put forward something like 'If he had called, he would have been in a position to say: you could have come'. Whether or not we terminate in an analysis which presents us with the parenthetical form depends on the extent to which it is possible to indicate that what one is voicing is a suspicion, fear, suggestion, or whatever, without making use of such a comment.

Let me now draw together some of the main threads of the argument. The simplest among the relevant constructions are those in which, as with 'I agree, he has had a difficult time', we have a parenthetical comment in tandem with a clause which retains its status as a full assertion. This case is important with psychological verbs, but, especially when 'that' makes an appearance, it often seems necessary to acknowledge a subordinate status to the clause. Such status I understand in terms of a suspension of assertoric force. With 'I agree that he has had a difficult time', or 'That he has had a difficult time I agree', the clause, 'that he has had a difficult time', is called upon merely to present a possibility, the speaker's commitment to the corresponding assertion being conveyed by the phrase, 'I agree'. I thus see an identical clause in the context, 'I doubt that he has had a difficult time': the conjunction again serves to neturalize the assertoric force of the following words, but this time the introductory verbal phrase is not such as, in effect, to restore that force to these words. The clause so characterized is clearly describable as 'propositonal', meaning by this that a possibility is propounded rather than actually affirmed, but it is not implied that it is a matter of given information, of something that someone has already propounded, or of a pre-existing object of an attitude.

In so far as we have occasion to say such things as 'He hoped that P', when the person does not actually say anything which might be rendered as 'P', we can deal with the reports as before: our use of the indirect speech form is not so restricted as to require the use of actual words thus reportable unless the sense of the main verb of itself makes such a demand; a number of possible linguistic or non-linguistic acts may conceivably amount to hoping that P, and so suffice for the truth of a report to that effect. But what of the brutes? We can agree that thought and belief are very much tied up with possession of a language, but the likeness between an animal's behaviour and that of a language-user may lead us to speak of the animal in similar terms, to allow that certain things will count as, say, thinking that P in its case as well, the behaviour being as of one who would be prepared to assert or assent to P.

There is no new problem here as far as the present issue is concerned, given that a report of the relevant kind can be in order without language having been used, but it must be stressed that ascriptions of thoughts and the like to animals are to be treated with care, if not scepticism. To take an example which has come in for recent discussion, it is suggested that we might say 'The mouse fears that the cat will eat it'. There is no doubt that the mouse may be frightened of the cat, but why 'fears that the cat will eat it' rather, than say, 'fears that the cat will bite it', or '. . . pounce on it', or '. . . hurt it', and so on? The arbitrariness of using one description rather than another is a reflection of the very loose connection here between words and behaviour. One or other such form of words may be inviting, given what we should say in a comparable situation involving a man, but we should not overlook how important language is in giving content to a precise ascription of a fear, suspicion, and the like. Certainly, while we have some limited use for these anthropomorphisms, it would be ludicrous to allow such peripheral cases the power to threaten an account of the indirect speech construction which rested on tracing the words back to direct speech versions—supposing, that is, that the point had not already been covered by the open character of the preceding analysis.

As far as the combination of noun clause with noun phrase is concerned, the analysis follows obvious lines. For instance, in 'Her suggestion that they take the bus was ignored', we have, ostensibly, a report on a suggestion made in such terms as 'Let us take the bus'. Again, the only problem lies in defending this triviality against misplaced objections: the analysis is in no way threatened by our inability to retrieve the exact terms of the original, or even the right language, from the indirect speech version. Nor does it matter if on a particular occasion no suitable direct speech form is in the offing. This is not likely in the present case, but an account of the general construction which represents it as a report of a certain range of utterances is again not to be faulted in this way: if something else can be deemed to have the force of the spoken or written word, well and good; if, on the other hand, this is something which the notion in question cannot tolerate, again no problem, since in this event there will be nothing to report in the given terms.

Nothing new arises with the attachment to the clause of the noun, as opposed to the corresponding verbal phrase. In 'His suspicion was that there had been a cover-up', we have essentially the same relation between the words preceding the clause and the clause itself as we have with 'He suspected there had been a cover-up'. These can be represented as 'His suspicion was: there has been a cover-up' and 'He suspected: there has been a cover-up', either giving the terms in which the suspicion was, or could have been voiced, with the substantival version being no more than a stylistic variant of the verbal form. This equivalence between the two formulations sheds light on what is involved in the *existence* of suspicions, hopes, fears, and the like. There being a suspicion that P is a matter of someone (justifiably) suspecting that P, and if P is not to be thought of as a proposition which the person suspected, nor is it something of which 'is his suspicion' is true. There are forms of words which seemingly specify appropriate items for such an attachment, but a closer examination reveals (i) that the attachment makes no sense, and (ii) that the right sense for the construction is that made clear by the analysis in terms of the intransitive verb. This is, of course, without prejudice to the fact that two people can be said to have the same suspicions, which is no more difficult to grasp than the possibility that '. . . suspects that P' should be true of more than one person.

There is a considerable mass of detail which might be incorporated into a full discussion of noun clauses, but I hope that enough has been said to show the need for a radical departure from the act–object model. The thesis that desires, fears, wishes, and so forth, require intentional objects gave way to the observation that the relevant verbs have a qualifying force which blocks any inference to real existence, and the clausal formulations making this plainer are not to be accused of introducing their own troublesome objects. If we find difficulties in the view that a mental construct is designated by the clause when it is said that someone hopes, fears,

or wishes that *P*, this is not a sign that something more concrete, as an utterance or inscription, is to fill the bill. It is not
that, having failed to hit upon an entirely satisfactory characterization, we find it appropriate to hypothesize a variety of
objects in this role, but the role itself is a misconception
engendered by a faulty analysis of the verb and its relation to
the succeeding clause. If that clause is to be thought of as
subordinate to the main verb, this is because it enjoys a subjunctive (and possibly adverbial) role, not that of an object;
it is the broadly 'subjunctive' category—broad enough to cover
the infinitive in such a sentence as 'He hopes to find a suitable
site'—that deserves a place both in an account of the lack of
existential implications and in an account of the dependent
character of a noun clause, though in a tradition in which
a concern with the substantival has dominated, it is a category
that has been largely overlooked.

38. *Other nominal forms*

At this point we might look briefly at clauses of other kinds,
and at other types of construction related to clauses. How,
for instance, are we to handle the interrogative clauses in 'He
explained how the computer worked' and 'I can see how he
lost his job'? Intuitively, these clauses are less nounlike than
are *that*-clauses: given the role of 'that' in general, it is better
suited to suggesting substantival occurrence than are 'how',
'why', 'when', or 'where'. On the other hand, in terms of their
grammatical behaviour, interrogative clauses are if anything
more nounlike than noun clauses. Thus, an interrogative clause
can be governed by a prepositon, even if this is a usage which
many would frown upon, as in 'The problem of where to
house them arose', or 'As to why he did it, I am no better informed than you', and the behaviour of such clauses in questions is more on a par with that of ordinary nouns; perhaps
the grounds for the difference are of no great consequence,
but 'Is why he did it clear?' strikes me as a shade less unnatural
than 'Is that he did it clear?'. Note that such sentences as
'Was what he did sensible?' are not relevant here, since the
'what' is not an interrogative in such a case. Note too that the
basing of, e.g., 'That the pipe should be mended is clear' on
'It is clear that the pipe should be mended' is supported by

the analogous case of interrogative clauses, and the consideration that if the form of words in question is one for which
reference does make sense, then the construction with 'it' is
not possible. Thus, 'What he did is clear' has the equivalent
'It is clear what he did', but when the 'what' ceases to be an
interrogative we do not have quite the same transformation.
In 'What he did was wicked' we have a relative 'what', and a
very different construction in 'It was wicked, what he did',
where the 'it' is anticipatory for the 'what' in, it is said, the
sense of 'that which'.

I have been going along here with the received terminology,
but I might just remark that, strictly speaking, we do not have
to do with variant readings of 'what' at all, but that we have,
once more, a phrase—'what he did'—to which the distinction
between an 'indicative' and a 'subjunctive' reading is applicable.
Consider 'What he said is beside the point'. The meaning here
varies depending on whether the person's remarks are being
deemed irrelevant to the matter in hand, or whether it is beside
the point even to raise the question of what was said. Some
languages would use a subjunctive or conditional in this latter
case, the word for 'what' remaining as constant as in English,
and I suspect that our tendency to seek the difference in
'what' reveals Latin grammar, which marks the difference with
distinct pronominal forms, as a subtly distorting influence.
At all events, that there must be some difference in the verb
is very much indicated by the fact that *oratio obliqua* provides
the setting for the interrogative clause. So, 'Tell me what he
has done' as against 'What he has done is terrible'.

Asking when the next train is due contrasts with asking the
station master, just as warning that the ice is thin contrasts
with warning the skaters; objects enter only in the second
members of these pairs. Note that the contrast between 'that'
and the conjunctions which introduce indirect questions, as
'whether', 'when', 'how', and 'why', is a contrast which can
serve to characterize the former, conjunctive 'that' being
identifiable as a mark of the declarative, or at least the non-
interrogative form. The connection of the conjunction with
the demonstrative 'that' can mislead through making us overlook this feature; other uses of 'that'—as in, e.g., 'such that'—
should also be borne in mind.

Just as noun clauses raise a question about corresponding propositions, so interrogative clauses might be expected to prompt a query about a *question*. The involvement of a question in such sentences as 'He asked me when dinner would be served' and 'He asked him what to do' appears straightforward enough—note again the infinitive performing the role of a subjunctive in the latter—and while there is an increase in complexity with sentences like 'What he did is anybody's guess' or 'Why he did it is of no interest', a rephrasal in which a question figures is again forthcoming: 'What did he do? It is anybody's guess' and 'Why did he do it? It is of no interest'. Despite the nounlike behaviour of the clauses we are surely not to understand 'what he did' as a referential unit in 'What he did is anybody's guess', such a construal being in conflict with the sense of the conjoined phrase, 'is anybody's guess'. However, the analysis given does not imply that the description appropriate to the non-clausal version applies indifferently to either form. It does so only with whatever modifications are demanded by the transition from the version with an explicit question to that in which a clause is featured. This is parallel to the case of propositions.

Another construction which we might touch upon is the infinitive, since this too has both affinities to and divergences from standard nominals. In this instance the affinities are in fact somewhat limited, being restricted practically to the case of the infinitive as subject of a predicative adjective, as with 'To err is human', though we note occurrence in questions— 'Is to err human?'—even if 'Is it human to err?' rings more naturally. If, further, 'To err is human' is to be thought of as containing no more of a predication than does 'It is human to err', then there is little, if anything, left of nominal function in any troublesome form. At all events, the role of the infinitive in such sentences is easily grasped: it provides us with a way of expressing generality with respect to verb rather than noun. Thus, with 'To err is human' we abstract from the finite forms of the verb in association with particular subjects, but with the understanding that the truth of the sentence depends on truth in the particular cases. Similarly, because the infinitive is non-committal with respect to person, it may sometimes be employed when specificity in this regard would make for redundancy. So we have the accusative and infinitive—'She desired him to leave'—as an occasional alternative to the clausal form—'She desired that he should leave'.

The infinitive is sometimes said to occur as object of a verb or, in such a sentence as 'For him to go there is strange', as object of the preposition 'for'. I dispute the account of the latter, construing 'to go' only as part of a nounlike complex, and I do not think that occurrence as object of a verb is possible, since the passive is always excluded, not only when, given the verb in question we might expect this—as with 'I hope to come'—but even when, as with 'I want to go', there is not the obstacle of a generally intransitive use. Just as we sense a different relation in 'Is it necessary—to go?' and 'Is it necessary—your trip?', so 'I want to go' presents us with a different structure from 'I want your ticket'. But sometimes 'to V' is intersubstitutable with the verbal noun 'V-ing', so is not any parsing which decides that the former is never noun-like to be questioned? It is true that we can say 'I like walking' along with 'I like to walk', but there is a slight difference in sense, the '-ing' form being appropriate to the extended activity. Contrast 'I should hate to see you suffer' with 'I should hate seeing you suffer', or 'I should visit my aunt' with 'I should be visiting my aunt'. The use of 'to' often looks to the future—a temporal interpretation of a preposition indicative of spatial movement—particularly when it has the force of 'in order to', as in 'I am doing this to annoy him'. Again, contrast 'I hope to come' with 'I should enjoy coming', and 'He left the children to fend for themselves' with 'He left the children fending for themselves'.

When a word ending in '-ing' is to be described as a 'verbal noun', the justification for speaking of a *noun* is simple enough. As well as appearing with adjectives in predicative position, such terms can be coupled with an adjective used attributively, as in 'heavy drinking' and 'loud snoring'; they can be governed by a preposition—'He died from a beating'—form a plural—'rumblings'—take the articles and occur as direct object—'We heard the singing'. Indeed, they exhibit the full range of substantival behaviour, any limitations in particular cases being of the irrelevant kind attributable to specific meaning, not to syntactic incapabilities. As befits their verbal origins, their sense is generally such that they signify events, activities or their products—cf. the two senses of 'writing'—but their character as verbs has otherwise been lost.

This last point is easily demonstrated. With such nouns, the adjective rather than the adverb provides the appropriate modifier, they cannot be negated, and they can no longer govern a noun phrase as object. It is also true, however, that the features thus denied the noun can be instanced by the same form in another use. Consider 'I didn't count on his killing the cat'. In this the form 'killing' retains its verbal function, with 'the cat' as object: there is no necessity to insert 'of', as when 'killing' is a noun—'His killing of the cat was merciless'. Again, we have 'His opening of the tin was clumsy', but a different construction in 'His opening the tin was a surprise', with 'opening' holding on here to its verbal force, capable of governing a direct object. When we have to do with a noun we can form a negation of sorts by prefixing 'non'— 'the non-opening of the door'—an addition which leaves us with the same part of speech, a noun. When the transition to nounhood has not been made we can negate as with a standard verb: 'I didn't count on his not killing the cat', 'His not opening the tin surprised me'. Similarly, it is the adverb, not the adjective, that qualifies this form: 'I didn't insist on their talking quietly' or 'I didn't insist on them talking quietly'. With some verbs, we may observe, there is only the more verbal form. We do not have 'his resembling of his mother' or 'his having of a hat', but only the versions without the 'of'. 'His being F' and 'his having Vd' are significant cases in which we have only the verbal form, cases which provide a useful test for determining the character of the context in which they occur.

To what extent might the verbal form be at the same time nounlike? This possibility is of interest, since we shall find that the question of a possible referential use of the form becomes important, and it is also relevant to ascertaining how complexes containing the form behave as compared to clauses. Consider the sentence, 'I was surprised by his singing'. It would seem that 'his singing' can be treated as a referential phrase only when 'singing' is a noun, as when the speaker might go on with 'The singing could be heard from the bottom of the garden', or insert an adjective, as in 'I was surprised by his melodious singing'. If it is the verbal form, the so-called 'imperfect nominal', as would be evidenced by the expansion to 'I was surprised by his singing at all', or 'I was surprised by his singing loudly', then there appears to be no such reference, but once more we have a sentence nominalization, and one which might equally be represented by a clause. Thus, each of 'I was surprised by his singing loudly' and 'I was surprised that he sang loudly' presents a way of uniting the sentence 'He sang loudly' with 'I was surprised by that', and each way of accomplishing this results in a deceptive grammatical form. Less so with the clausal version in this instance, since a namelike expression is not so readily subordinated to the phrase 'I was surprised', but more so perhaps with the participial version, since we have then a form that is shared with the genuine noun, and government by two terms, 'by' and 'his', which would seem to reinforce such nominal status. We may note, however, that in the genuine nominal cases the possessive can be resolved into a phrase containing the article plus 'of': 'I was deafened by the dog's barking' becomes 'I was deafened by the barking of the dog'; no such transformation can be applied when the force is verbal, as with 'I was surprised by John's singing loudly', but we must convert to adjective plus noun, '. . . John's loud singing', with a possible change in sense. The use of 'by' is interesting, giving the participial version greater versatility than the clause in this respect. Sometimes the clause can also be invoked, as in the example given, or in 'I was unaware that he had left' as against the less likely 'I was unaware of his having left', but there are cases where the clause cannot be used without modification. If we wished to have a clausal rendering of 'I was misled by his not coming', we should have to resort to 'fact' or the like to link the preposition to the clause: 'I was misled by the fact that he did not come'. Conversely, there are many instances of noun clauses which cannot be represented by the participial construction. We can do little with 'He saw that he was outnumbered' or 'She found that the lock had jammed'.

The '-ing' construction often sounds clumsy, and the idiom is not yet in a settled state, competing as it does with the hybrid construction shown by 'I did it without him knowing' or 'I am responsible for you losing your job'. This alternative is sometimes thought ungrammatical or illogical, grounds for this residing in the consideration that the sentence curtailed after the disputed term is not extractible as a consequence. If 'I did it without him' and 'I am not responsible for you' are true when the respective larger sentences are true, this will only be by chance. What is important for us is that the preposition or the main verb does not govern the terms which do occur referentially, however illogical it may be to have them there at all. This is clear enough in the present examples, and in such a case as 'I don't like the child singing', it is likewise apparent that it is not a matter of not liking the child—nor, for that matter, of not liking the child's singing, where 'singing' is a verbal noun. That is, whether or not we maintain that grammar or logic has gone awry, the grounds mentioned for possibly thinking so at the same time relate to the feature of the construction that interests us.

39. Facts

It might be wondered why I have bothered with these rather infelicitous idioms. They can be awkward, it is true, and indeed they can be less straightforward than I have made out, but as well as providing some confirmation and complementation of what I have said with respect to clauses, they commonly figure at crucial points in certain philosophical issues of note. When, for instance, events and actions are under discussion, we often meet with considerable uncertainty in the handling of the participial construction. It may seem unexceptionable to say that 'John's singing' and 'John's singing loudly' can designate the same event, an event which may even be picked out by 'John's singing off key', despite the differences in the feature highlighted. Since, however, we cannot interchange these phrases in the context, 'John's being angry explains his singing loudly', we may have doubts: perhaps the context is non-extensional, presenting another setback to the principle of extensionality, or perhaps more than one event has to be acknowledged (cf. Beardsley [1975], p. 273). But it is the non-referential character of the participial construction that is the key to a proper understanding of the context, not reference to two distinct events, actions or whatever, or significantly different forms of reference to a single event or action. Similarly, although we can grant a possible difference in truth value between 'Jascha's playing the violin was intentional' and 'Jascha's playing the violin badly was intentional', this does not force us to recognize either non-extensionality or distinctness of actions (cf. Beardsley, op. cit., p. 274). Rephrase so that the intention to refer to an action or performance is not in doubt, and the allowability of substitutions becomes equally clear: if Jascha's violin playing was bad as well as intentional, then Jascha's bad violin playing was intentional—but only in that sense: that the performance had both these features, not that the badness was intended.

Events and actions can be joined by *facts* as notoriously opaque items whose understanding is very much bound up with grammar, and in particular with the grammar of sentence nominalizations. If we have a term which has been the subject of totally opposed views, none of which has emerged as generally acceptable, we might conjecture that a relevant misconception is shared by the various factions. With 'fact' this possibility is dramatically realized, as we shall find on probing beneath the superficial grammar.

With such a sentence as 'That smoking causes cancer is a fact', we tend to suppose that the clause names something of which 'is a fact' is predicated. Given this reading, a further distortion then suggests itself: construe 'is a fact' as specifying the category into which what is named by 'that smoking causes cancer' falls; that smoking causes cancer is a fact—that's the sort of thing it is; not an event, say, but a *fact*. This approach, with its further question, 'Are facts things in the world?', rests on a construal of the clause as subject in 'That smoking causes cancer is a fact'. Against this, I suggest that the sentence is to be compared not with 'That he was guilty was denied by Smith', where a case of sorts can be made out for logical subject–predicate form, but with a sentence in which the terms are related in the way proposed for 'That the chairman had resigned was understood by all those present'. The connections implicit in 'That smoking causes cancer is a fact' are better displayed by the form which can be made to yield this sentence by inversion and ellipsis of 'it', namely, 'It is a fact that smoking causes cancer', which in turn comes to 'It is a fact: smoking causes cancer', with again no question of the pronoun 'it' functioning as an anticipatory subject. As before, this is neither a generative nor an historical hypothesis, though support from the history of the word's usage would not be unwelcome. In giving these parsings the aim is to provide a deductive equivalent which shows more perspicuously the implications of the original.

But now, how *does* the 'it' function here? The consequences of 'is a fact' failing to attach to a logical subject will be grasped immediately, but there is a problem as to what exactly the pronoun is doing if it does not stand in for some more specific term to which 'is a fact' is relatable. We can readily accept that there is no reference on the part of the pronoun in, let us say, 'It is alleged that he was with her on the night of the murder', but this does duty for a personal construction, such as 'Someone has alleged that he was with her on the night of the murder', whereas with 'it is a fact' there is no similar un-problematic version to which we might have recourse in giving a paraphrase. Other comparable sentences are 'It is a pity that smoking causes cancer' and 'It is clear that smoking causes cancer', with their less innocent-looking transforms, 'That smoking causes cancer is a pity' and 'That smoking causes cancer is clear'.

Whenever 'it'—and 'that'—are used we naturally take it that they are intended to pick out something of which something is then asserted or predicated, supposing at least that the superficial grammar will bear this interpretation. There is a familiar exception in such idioms as 'It is raining' and 'It is unsafe in the city at night', but if someone says 'It is F' or 'That is F', then, by and large, we can ask 'What is F?' and expect to be given a more specific designation in reply. And in contexts of the kind which, broadly speaking, we are con-sidering, there are times when we can. Someone says some-thing and another comments, 'That is libellous'. Here we meet with no difficulty in explaining the reference of the demon-strative: it is to nothing more than the statement made, a suitable object of reference and a suitable subject of the given predicate.

But suppose the comment is 'That is a pity' or 'That is most unfortunate' or 'That is impossible'. To what does the 'that' refer? If the statement in question was 'Mabel has been ill again', then the comment is, of course, addressed to that statement, or, in a sense, made with reference to it, but not in such a sense that we shall have described the statement as 'a pity', and so forth. We can say, 'What you say is a pity', and 'that' may be thought of as behaving like 'what you say', but the latter, which is not the same as 'your statement', stands in for a clause—'that Mabel has been ill again'—rather than for the original 'Mabel has been ill again'. There is room for 'that' as a place-holder, and for a conception of reference adjusted to that, but nothing further appears to be either possible or necessary—we might, after all, respond with the simple 'Pity' or 'What a pity!'.

As another example, imagine a person saying, 'That's funny, I'd swear I left my keys on the table'. What, we ask, is funny here? And he replies: 'My keys aren't on the table where I left them'. Here again 'that' appears to be without a reference—except in so far as it provides a gap where a clause might go—but to be none the worse off for it. We might equally have said the simple 'Funny' and not lost the kind of connection which appears to be involved: i.e. '(That's) funny' is an observation we may make on being puzzled at learning that such-and-such is the case when we expected it not to be. Nothing more specific is required to which the comment might be tied by way of ascribing something to it. It may be a response evoked or induced by a statement, and its appropriateness is recognized by having regard to the sense of the statement, taken in conjunction with the speaker's expectations, but it need not in addition be *about* this statement, or anything which the statement introduces.

We have seen, too, that the participial construction adds nothing to the argument. To bring this out further, let us switch to an example that is more versatile for our purposes: 'That's funny, Tim is eating vegetables he won't usually touch'. That the child is or should be eating such vegetables can be said to be funny, and we can also say, if with considerable awkwardness, 'Tim's eating vegetables is funny', but in neither case does there appear to be any reference. The infant's eating could be funny—a comical sight—but to have any such reference we must change to the verbal *noun*, giving us 'Tim's eating (of the vegetables) is funny', and nothing like this will surely be intended by the original. One can find Tim's eating such vegetables funny without even witnessing his eating, in the relevant sense. Of course, it is the *fact* that the child is eating these vegetables, rather than his eating of the vegetables, that we may find funny, but all the addition of 'fact' does is introduce a note of finality, emphasizing that the child *is* eating the vegetables. More on this anon. Again, consider 'I am surprised that the glass broke'. The glass's breaking can, as an event, surprise me, just as it can frighten or deafen me, but I can be surprised that the glass broke, surprised at its breaking, without witnessing such an event. Yet I do know what surprises me; there is not the possibility of error that is attendant upon the assignment of a cause. The surprise is not induced by the event reported, but it arises on my learning that the event has occurred.

It is clear that the senses of the terms on which we have concentrated—'pity' and 'funny'—and the senses of any others in a natural extension of this list—'strange', 'odd', 'interesting', 'remarkable', 'amazing', 'a shame', 'a disgrace'—fit in well with the account offered, but terms indicative of such responses do not exhaust the relevant possibilities. Such adjectives as 'certain', 'probable', 'possible', and 'apparent' call for further consideration. We have, furthermore, to bring 'it' back into the discussion. Does this pronoun stand a better chance of being construable as referential in these contexts? Given the more emphatic demonstrative role of 'that' we should hardly expect so; 'it' enters into many more constructions in which its value as a pronoun is not exploited, and it comes as less of a surprise to find that it may be assigned a role as a dummy term in conjunction with adjectives or nouns only seemingly used predicatively. In the present connection we may note that 'that' is generally used with reference to a preceding statement in either of the senses possible, but that in the absence of any preceding statement 'it' is more likely, and has only a minimal appearance of referring to anything. Thus, in response to a remark of yours I may say 'That is impossible', but if you had asked a question, such as 'Is John at home?', I could reply with 'It is possible', 'It is likely', 'It would seem so', and so forth.

I say that with 'It is raining' and 'It is unsafe in the city at night' no reference is intended. Similarly with: it is dark, cold, crowded in there, comfortable here, stuffy in their room. It might be suggested that the pronoun did have a reference to the weather, the atmosphere, or some other sufficiently un-specific object, but while this may make some kind of sense in some cases, it hardly works for 'It is raining'. *What* can be said to be raining? This is one case where not even 'something' is substitutable. More important, even if we can think up a possible subject—'the rain'?—what is the evidence that this is to be understood, given that it is probably never made explicit? Could we not have the same idiom irrespective of the presence or absence of such a term in the language? We can say both 'It is stuffy in this room' and 'The atmosphere in this room is stuffy', but does the former owe anything to the latter?

However, is it the same with the 'it' in 'it is certain'? I do not mean that the two constructions should in general com-pare very closely, but do they agree on this negative point, the absence of reference, or do we, as some grammarians would have it, meet with an anticipatory subject in such sentences as 'It is certain that he will be on the next plane'? Here we note at once that it makes sense to speak of a proposition as 'certain', which makes for a disanalogy with 'It is raining', but there is also the question whether this is the correct way of construing the sentence. Perhaps it is just chance that we have here a term which is predicable of a proposition, that this is really an instance of a construction for which the possibility does not in general hold. So, it cannot be a proposition that is subject in 'It is a wonder they survived', 'It is a disgrace that he was dismissed', 'It is only natural that Jill should wish to play with children her own age', 'It is important that he should come', or 'It seems that we have lost'. With this last, indeed, replacing the 'it' by the clause is not even possible: we do not have 'That we have lost seems'. With 'It is raining' and 'It is dusk' we ask of 'rain' and 'dusk' only that they be subject to the two poles of affirmation and denial; 'rain' is not assigned to anything as the agent, and 'dusk' is not assigned to anything whose character it describes. This is not to say that we could not find something of which we might predicate 'is dusk', as 'is stuffy' might be true of the atmosphere; it is just that, when we ask 'Is it dusk?', we are concerned *simply* with the question whether it is or is not dusk, and not with whether something which we have identified is thus describable, with the implication that we have knowledge of something which may or may not turn out to be dusk. The uses of 'certain', 'a disgrace', and so forth, appear similarly limited in these clausal contexts. I do not mean merely that these are not attached to propositions as subjects, but that *any* specification of a subject is uncalled for. Some examples make this particularly clear: with 'It is impossible that he should come' we are saying that the person's coming is impossible, but 'His coming is impossible' cannot involve both reference to an event, say, and a dismissal of it as impossible; that would be like referring to something and at the same time denying that there was or ever had been such a thing. The comparison with 'It is raining' does, then, seem apt, and it is interesting to note that in topic-prominent languages, where the notion of subject has only a secondary role, there is no need for 'dummy' subjects, whether in sentences like 'It is raining' or in those like 'It is possible that you have been misunderstood' (cf. Li and Thompson [1976], p. 467).

If there were reference to a proposition in any of these contexts it would be only as problematic as the notion of a proposition, so not problematic at all. It is the absence of any such subject that makes for a difficulty. It was easy to explain how a phrase like 'he suggested' could combine with a clause without the latter becoming its object: in 'He suggested we wait for the bus' we simply have a report of the terms in which the person suggested, rather than terms which he suggested. In describing as 'structural' the pronoun in 'It is certain that he will be on the next plane', we deny any subject–predicate tie between the clause and 'it is certain', but the juxtaposition of 'it is certain' and 'he will be on the next plane' cannot be clarified by invoking the direct speech model of utterance and associated speech act. More helpful is the example of phrases containing psychological verbs, phrases which, in qualifying the assertion, could be considered to have an adverbial role. In the present case we can think of 'it is certain' as a variant on 'certainly'; the latter is in no way referential, and appears to make a contribution equal to that of the former. Sometimes an appropriate adverbial form may not exist, and there will be complexities with negative phrases—as we saw with psychological verbs—but at least we have a plausible alternative to a subject–predicate analysis.

The adjective 'true' is of interest here. The comment, 'That is true', can be uttered in response to a person's statement, and we can also expand this to 'That statement is true', as well as speak of 'a true statement', uses which are less readily available for 'possible' and 'probable' and which indicate that 'true' at least makes sense as a predicate of linguistic items, a genuine and not a subjectless predicate. However, it is also the case that in such a sentence form as 'It is true, P', a parsing which would relate the 'it' to the following statement as an anticipatory subject of the latter is once more far from obligatory. We can treat 'It is true, P' as equivalent to 'True, P', and make perfectly good sense of this without having to suppose an implicit predication. Indeed, the use of the response 'true' without any of its pronominal attachments is very familiar, and the form of words '"P" is true' most unfamiliar, which strongly suggests that, while it may be possible to take 'true' as a genuine predicate, it also allows of this non-predicative use, any added noun phrase making clear just which assertion it is being affirmed with reference to, but not which assertion has the property of being true.

It is important to keep both of these alternatives in view. So, there should be no question of querying the propriety of ascribing 'true' to a statement, in the sense in which this latter term may characterize a form of words like 'The secret got out', used or envisaged as used in the appropriate way. It is occasionally thought that when we speak of what was stated as being true or false, *what was stated* can be expanded only by a clause—'that the secret got out' rather than the original 'The secret got out'. Thus, when I claim that a person who utters the latter has said something true, what I pronounce true, it is said, is the same as what I should have judged to be so if the words had been *Le secret se fit jour*; the clause, 'that the secret got out', gives a suitably abstract specification of the truth-bearer, the words actually used do not. It may even be argued that, since a noun clause, as 'that the secret got out', names nothing, there is *a fortiori* nothing nameable of which 'is true' is predicable. Something like this reasoning, at least on the last point, appears to be at work in Strawson [1950b].

The misconceptions issuing in the exclusion of our familiar statements as truth-bearers have already been exposed: the possibility that speakers of different languages may none the less make the same statement is surely not to be secured by appeal to the possibility of giving an identical *oratio obliqua* rendering of their words; what is prior is the possibility of discounting the inconsequential differences between the respective statements and discerning the identity which warrants us in using the same form of words in a report of either.

On the other hand, while 'true' cannot be refused genuine predicative standing with respect to statements, those who make this refusal have perhaps perceived something of the difference which may separate terms with which 'true' will join. So, for instance, as already indicated, it would be a mistake to suppose a general match between the phrases 'his statement' and 'what he stated' on the basis of their interchangeability in 'His statement was true'. The phrase 'what he stated' will stand in for a clause quite generally, thereby numbering among the expressions with which it will combine such subjectless 'predications' as 'is likely', 'is a fact', and 'is possible', predications which cannot, or cannot without strain, attach to 'his statement'. We can say, 'What he stated is a fact', but not 'His statement is a fact'—at least not with the same meaning—'his statement' being a genuine subject. This is the explanation for these apparently inexplicable divergences—noted, but not adequately accounted for, in Austin [1954]. Conversely, there are predicates which attach to 'his statement' but not to clauses, and these will not always join with 'what he stated': 'His statement was careful', but not 'What he stated was careful'.

For many of the phrases which combine with clauses, phrases such as 'I see . . .', 'It is understood . . .', '. . . is a fact', 'It is likely . . .', and so forth, I have offered a pattern of analysis that is at first hard to accept. The seemingly real attachments of predicates to logical subjects and transitive verbs to their objects are rejected: clauses are held not to behave referentially, nor to embed an object of reference, and the sentences which they nominalize are found to enter into combination with sentences which are, logically, subjectless. How generally applicable is this approach? A survey of the kinds of expression which may attach to such nominalizations suggests that by far the greater majority of such complex sentences must be understood in these terms, that the satisfaction of the superficial grammar is what is exceptional. With sentences like 'It is raining' we can appreciate soon enough that the pronoun is just an artifice to save appearances, to bring about a token conformity to the subject–predicate pattern which the language demands. Clauses appear more plausible claimants to genuine subjecthood, but again it is form rather than function that is satisfied by their appearance in subject position.

Our main application of the preceding analysis will be in connection with truth and the further analysis of 'fact', but I might mention some of the other issues to which it is relevant. Most generally, perhaps, it helps in understanding the behaviour of nouns which seemingly enter into referential descriptions, but which do not happily apply either to anything linguistic or to anything non-linguistic. There *are* suspicions and fears that people have, but what such matters of existence come to may not be quite as expected. Similar observations hold for philosophically important terms such as 'condition', 'feature', and 'evidence'; much may hang on what exactly these attach to—in discussions of truth, say, or in the problem of universals—but to the extent that they act as stand-ins for non-designating clauses or participial complexes, any attempts at singling out appropriate items for them to describe are doomed to failure. Here too we recall some of the nouns which prompted this enquiry, abstract terms like 'height' and 'length' which fit into sentence frames more typical of clauses than of conventional nouns.

Particular verbs which govern clauses can also hope to have their senses clarified, psychological verbs being an obvious case in point. Thus, discussions about what is observable may involve consideration of the construction with 'see that', as when it is said that one can see that a person is in pain, or that one can see that a moving magnet is inducing an electric current in a coil, discussions which threaten to run up against intractable objects of perception and consequent obscuring of the issue. More generally, our analysis provides the beginnings of a corrective to a mentalistic interpretation of psychological verbs and their supposed objects. Again, we have important relations which may take clauses or the like as one of their terms, as when we say 'Its being made of platinum is what makes it expensive', relations which loom large in discussions of logical and causal relations, and, once more, of truth and universals. Or, there is the question of the nature of the physicalist identity as expressed in the form, 'Being in pain is the same as being in a certain physiological state'. The same event, it is supposed, but our analysis suggests other possibilities.

Most of these issues will receive further attention, but I shall now conclude with mention of a somewhat different application, one which, while able to profit from these ideas, lies outside our main concerns. This is the topic of conjunctions and their analysis. Consider the sentences: 'The ship sailed before we arrived', 'A burglar broke in while they slept', 'He went upstairs because he felt ill', and 'She is tired, although she has done nothing all day'. In English we are not made to feel a continuity with the problems generated by noun clauses, since the use of 'that' is not standard after conjunctions. We do have 'now that', but no 'that' with 'before', 'while', and so forth. Clearly, though, the pull which the logical subject exerts may lead us to think along the lines of the model of preposition plus noun when considering the conjunction with its following sentence, so that we might think we discern in, say, 'The ship sailed before we arrived', a pattern comparable to that in 'The ship sailed before midnight'. After all, if 'before' does not govern a nounlike expression, something which singles out what, in this instance, the ship sailed before, then how do the two connect? Once more, however, an explanation of the sense of the conjunction makes no demand that we conceive of the subordinate sentence in any such role: 'P before Q' is true if and only if P is true at a time before that at which Q is true, but this does not mean that Q need itself be a referential unit. There is *a* notion of reference applicable to the tense inflections in P and Q, but no namelike unit that 'before' might govern. Again, with 'He went upstairs because he felt ill', our task is to further explain the sense in which the second sentence may be said to provide a reason for the person doing what he is said to have done in the first, but in clarifying this there is neither necessity nor advantage in thinking of the latter as a designation. Finally, to assert 'P, although Q', is to assert each of P and Q, but with the implication that you would not expect P to be true given Q. Again, citation rather than designation is all we require.

8

FACTS AND TRUTH

We have already glanced at 'true' and looked more closely at the grammar of 'fact'. With an eye to the traditional problems in which these are entwined, I shall now examine each in further detail, beginning with 'fact'. Philosophers in search of the true nature of facts have turned for help to such diverse phenomena as events, states of affairs, situations, propositions, and thoughts. All to no avail, if my analysis is correct, an analysis which also contributes to the downfall of the correspondence theory of truth and related views concerning universals. After tying up our earlier discussion of this latter topic we move on to the thesis that 'true' is assertively redundant, a thesis sometimes thought to offer the only alternative to the correspondence theory. This is not so, though the elaborations of the redundancy theory needed to make it plausible bring us to an account that is not far from the truth, even if what we have can hardly be said to qualify as a redundancy theory. Once more we confirm the importance of being scrupulous in matters of assigning function.

40. Facts, states of affairs, and propositions

I claim that the following sentence forms are successively more illuminating:

> That smoking causes cancer is a fact
> It is a fact that smoking causes cancer
> It is a fact: smoking causes cancer
> Smoking in fact causes cancer

The grammatical differences between first and last are considerable, but there is no more of an attachment of 'fact' to anything designated in the first than there is in the last; for what could it be of which 'fact' were affirmed or denied?

This question is not generally taken as rhetorical, but the

possibilities commonly defended divide between true statements, propositions, or thoughts on the one hand, and on the
other hand, states of affairs, conditions, situations, or other
items hoped to be 'things in the world'. Let us explore this
latter category. I mentioned above a possible consequence of
construing the clause as referential in 'That smoking causes
cancer is a fact': we take ourselves to be categorizing whatever
it is that is thus designated, 'is a fact' being for these purposes
in the same class as 'is an event' or 'is a physical object'. An
example of this false turn is to be found in Austin's reading
of 'The condition of the cat is a fact' (Austin [1954], pp.
156-8). Here *the condition of the cat* is presented as the sort
of thing to which both the predicates 'is a fact' and 'is something in the world' may be applied. However, to say 'The condition of the cat is a fact' is not to set the condition of the
cat in its appropriate category, whence the status of facts as
worldly items might be inferred, but to make this assertion
is to say that the cat is, in fact, in the condition in question.
The appropriate reading comes out better with the fuller
version, 'The mangy condition of the cat is a fact', which surely
represents not a categorization of the sort alleged, but an
affirmation that the cat definitely does have mange. Again we
note that it is not a matter of identifying something to which
'is a fact' is attached, but of *stating* a fact.

It is easy enough to get a feeling for the right as opposed
to the wrong interpretation of 'The condition of the cat is a
fact', and rather surprising that the difference was not seized
upon by Austin; it is the kind of point to which he was usually
sensitive. Noun phrases like 'the condition of the cat' or 'the
death of Caesar' may encourage such a misreading, but the
clausal versions—'That the cat has mange is a fact', 'That Caesar
died is a fact'—will hardly lend themselves to the view that
reference to something extralinguistic is involved. Something
propositional, conceivably—though we shall not in fact find
favour with this—but hardly something in the world.

To show more directly that facts do not have the status
with which they were credited by Austin, we must show that
the characterizations which this would call for are not forthcoming, or, if the linguistic evidence is superficially favourable,
we must show that the grammar has to be understood as not

giving rise to the implications which might be expected. To bring facts down into the world, some minimal spatio-temporal location would appear to be required. Not necessarily occupancy of a place, but position somewhere at some time. However, the fact that the moon is devoid of life cannot be said to be spatially locatable, nor to occur at or for a time. The very awkwardness of this denial shows the reluctance of 'the fact that P' to enter into the required predication, let alone to express a truth when combined with 'is locatable'. Nor can this or any other fact be seen, heard, touched, or detected by any scientific device. And, of course, it is lack of sense, not of scientific progress, that stands in the way of any such detection.

When a proposition is true, it would in general seem that we have the makings of a possible reference, a reference which comes about by nominalizing the verbal part of the proposition and appealing to its truth as a guarantee that the relevant condition of existence is satisfied. So, from 'He fell' comes 'his fall', from 'She was dismissed' comes 'her dismissal', from 'It was dawn' comes 'the dawn', and so forth—very much a matter of the same event or state being captured in two different grammatical forms. Again, a more general noun phrase may be abstracted, as in 'He learned to play the harp, an accomplishment which stood him in good stead', or 'When the water level rose, the change was recorded by a gauge'. Could we not see facts as the most general of the worldly items thus introducible? We could not. This approach does nothing to meet the objections already raised: if 'He fell' is true then we have a fall to refer to, in additon to the person designated, but to say that the fall is a fact is to take us back to the verbal form—it is a fact that he fell—not to say what sort of event it was; again we note that while the fall may occur on the stairs before breakfast and because the man was in a hurry, we cannot say such things of the fact. Still more difficult are general statements and conditionals, as 'It is a well-known fact that eggs contain albumen' and 'It is a fact that you will get fewer colds if you take vitamin C'. What in the world are facts such as these?

Austin hoped to secure a worldly home for facts via a connection with events, which can be ascribed predicates of the right range: 'The collapse of the Germans is an event and is a fact—was an event and was a fact' (op. cit., p. 156). However,

this has rightly been considered to reveal an erroneous conception of the grammar, as a few embellishments of the sentence make plain: we can say 'The collapse of the Germans
was an event which occurred at an opportune time', but not
'a fact which occurred at an opportune time'. 'The collapse
of the Germans' can be taken at its face value when it signifies
an event, in the sense that the obvious grammatical moves go
through without our having to suppose it to behave in an
exceptional fashion, but the same phrase has a different function when coupled with '. . . is a fact', as has already been
pointed out with respect to the condition of the cat and a
person's fall. Here too a clause would have the same value:
'That the Germans collapsed is a fact'.

Could it be that 'fact' comes close in meaning to 'state of
affairs'? The two expressions do share a number of predicates:
we speak of either as unusual, distressing, surprising, or unexpected; we can ignore or adjust to either, ascertain, take into
account or overlook the one as much as the other. However,
this agreement coexists with a radical difference in role. We
may say that such-and-such a state of affairs is a fact, but this
is to be understood in a way parallel to the correct understanding of 'The condition of the cat is a fact': what is a fact is that
the state of affairs is as claimed, say; the assertion is not interpretable in such a way as to give any support to the idea that
'Facts are states of affairs' is true.

There is *some* rapprochement if 'actual' is added—'That is
a fact', 'That is an actual state of affairs'—but there is still too
great a disagreement with particular predicates for the two to
converge. You can speak of a resultant or earlier state of affairs,
but not of a resultant or earlier fact; a government can be responsible for the present sorry state of affairs, but not for the
present sorry facts; a state of affairs can begin and end, it can
continue for a time, but not a fact; a state of affairs can be an
improvement, may not be tolerated, must be changed—not so
a fact. Conversely, facts can be stated, established, or disputed,
but not states of affairs. We speak of the fact that such-and-such
and know facts about so-and-so; we do not speak of the state
of affairs that such-and-such or know state of affairs about
so-and-so.

The crucial difference is brought out by the consideration

that while we can state, dispute, or establish a fact, we can only state, dispute, or establish *that* a state of affairs is so-and-so. The phrase, 'is a fact', attaches to forms of words which, like clauses or participial complexes, involve a predication—hence the temptation to equate 'fact' with 'true proposition'—whereas 'state of affairs' at best overlaps with this role. On the other hand, we might also point out that *state of affairs* is a notion with its own peculiarities. It does not always do duty for expressions which are straightforwardly namelike, as we might at first expect, nor, on the other hand, do we need to give a complete assertion in specifying a state of affairs, but in giving such a specification we often make use of a rather curious construction: 'Father drunk at breakfast—what a sorry state of affairs!'; that is, to indicate a state of affairs we may juxtapose a name and a description, giving us something between a name and an assertion, or at least something that is not to be equated with either. The appropriateness of this formula is evident enough: a state of affairs is like a state of things—historically the earlier expression—which means: things in a certain state, and 'state' naturally relates to the predicative part of the sentence: 'He entered the room in a frightful state—covered with dirt, bleeding, and smelling of sewage'.

So much for attempts to show facts to be worldly items. Taking now the other set of candidates, it is fairly evident that no equivalence with 'true proposition' or 'true statement' is possible. First, though, it is useful to distinguish contexts in which the word 'proposition', and similarly 'statement', may occur. We can say 'The proposition that every event has a cause is undecidable', 'That every event has a cause is an undecidable proposition', and 'The proposition, every event has a cause, is undecidable'. We cannot say 'The proposition that every event has a cause is a fact'—though we may insert 'true' here—nor can we say 'The proposition, every event has a cause, is a fact', but the best we can do is replace 'an undecidable proposition' either by 'a fact' or by 'a true proposition' in 'That every event has a cause is an undecidable proposition'. It is surely significant that incorporation of either 'fact' or 'proposition' makes for the impossibility of the other. Similarly, we can say 'One fact about Roger is that he can be trusted', and also 'One true proposition about Roger is (the proposition) that he can be trusted', but not 'One fact about Roger is the true proposition that he can be trusted'.

These examples strongly suggest that the agreement which we do find between 'fact' and 'true proposition' proves nothing, the identity being only superficial. And, indeed, I claim that an underlying difference does reside, not so much in the nature of the clause in either case, but in the manner of the connection between the clause and its accompanying phrases. We can have a genuine predication in '"Every event has a cause" is a true proposition', but in 'It is a fact: every event has a cause' we have no such link. Furthermore, while a true proposition can be intelligible or detailed, a fact cannot be thus described. In short, we have differences in the application of 'fact' and 'true proposition', and differences in what may be said with respect to either.

Of course, the senses of 'fact' and 'true proposition' are close, and the view being considered is perhaps nearer the truth than the alternative rejected above: both facts and true propositions can, after all, be stated, which at least ensures that facts are not in the world. However, the peculiarity of 'fact'—that it will not attach to a logical subject—makes for a gap between the two which cannot be closed, and which defines the special character of 'fact'. To see this further, consider other replacements of 'fact' by 'true proposition':

The true proposition that he came counts in his favour
The true proposition that he came should not be overlooked
The true proposition that he came makes no difference
The true proposition that he came had not escaped me

The effect of substituting 'true proposition' for 'fact' is to provide the sentence with a logical subject having the clause 'that he came' in apposition, but the given predicates do not readily combine with such a subject, and the sense of the sentence is in consequence distorted. Introduction of 'true proposition' forces the grammatical predicate to attach to this as to a logical subject, when in fact the predicates share the peculiarity of 'is a fact', being likewise 'subjectless': it is not a *proposition* that escapes one, in the relevant sense, but the sentence, 'That he came had not escaped me', can be represented as 'He came. It had not escaped me', 'it' here being purely structural, not a pronoun doing duty for something more explicit, whether expressed or unexpressed. When the structure is displayed in such a form we can see that there is nothing against adding a further subjectless phrase, notably 'it is a fact'.

This is, of course, just a continuation of the theme of the last chapter. Phrases like 'he suggested', 'I understand', and 'is unfortunate' do not combine with a clause in the role of object or subject. Insert a qualification like 'the proposition', however, and we oblige the clause to give up its co-ordinate or adverbial status and become part of a complex which can be admitted to the sentence only in one or other of these roles. As we saw with 'I understand (the proposition) that he has gone abroad', the sense may not accept the new attachments which arise thereby, and 'it is a fact' just happens to be a phrase which shows this with some clarity.

The different forms of clausal connection, or lack of connection, can explain differences in the behaviour of terms which in general appear very similar. We saw one example with 'his statement' as against 'what he stated', and another concerns the objects of knowledge and belief. People can be said to know or to be aware of various facts, but not so readily to believe facts. Belief can be directed towards propositions, so towards what someone has said, but where 'what he said' does duty for a genuine object or subject, so not as in 'What he said was a fact', where 'what he said' abbreviates a clause, not a proposition or statement. 'Know' before a clause, however, is not a matter of 'know' before a propositional object, so in 'She did not know that fact', 'that fact' supplants a phrase of the right type, as 'that gentlemen prefer blondes'. Of course, 'believe' does have a use in which it keeps in step with 'know', but then a proposition is excluded as object. So, 'What she believed was a fact' is far more acceptable than 'She believed a fact'. The former can be taken simply as affirming the truth of the person's belief, not as characterizing the object of belief, whereas the latter threatens to force a 'a fact' into an inappropriate mould, one in which this rejected reading would be quite in order.

The question of the nature of objects of knowledge might arise with the claim that genuine knowledge must be *caused* by what is known. And what is known? Facts, it will be said. And in a sense rightly. If A knows that P then it is a fact that P. But there is no real object, nothing which might enter into a causal relation with anything. The apparent necessity here for a causal relation stems from the requirement that beliefs which are only accidentally correct should not qualify as knowledge. I may be right in saying that it is midnight, but the clock I am looking at may have stopped, with its hands pointing to the right time only by chance. My belief is correct, and it may be not unreasonable for me to assume that the clock is going, but we may well wish to say that, strictly speaking, I do not know that it is midnight. To exclude chance agreement of belief with fact, it is suggested that the latter must somehow determine the former, that one's justification for believing the proposition in question must relate to what makes that proposition true, so to the relevant fact. As the paradigm of a real relation, causality is then naturally regarded as the only serious contender for the relation required. Its actual unseriousness has now been established, but in any case a few words in expansion of 'know' soon indicate a different approach, which I shall now briefly sketch.

To know that P is to be in a position to assert or at least to tell that P. Roughly speaking, this takes two forms: I can argue myself into a position to assert that P, arriving at this conclusion by piecing together given evidence and general knowledge, or, more fundamentally, I may be in a position to assert that P as a result of being well placed, literally, to make the judgement, to tell how things are. I am able to say what is in the cupboard since the door is open, the light on, and the contents plainly in view before me. The two cases shade into one another, but it seems right to assign priority to those in which the invocation of general knowledge and reasoning is at a minimum, the judgements which manifest the knowledge being natural, unreasoned responses to the scene before one.

And what is it to be in a position to assert that P? This is a matter of being in a situation where such an assertion is warranted, where one's judgements on matters of the kind in

question have proved dependable, where error is either unknown or at least very unfamiliar. So, being an eye-witness
with an unobstructed view places one in a better position than
if one has to rely on the testimony of someone who was at
some distance from the event in question, and one's dependa-
bility is most in doubt when a mistaken assumption or faulty
reasoning is being relied upon. It is in this way that, as with
the example of the time, claims to know may be vitiated even
though a correct belief is in fact being entertained, and what
causal relations hold is a matter to be investigated against
a background of knowledge recognized as such by considerations of this non-causal kind.

41. 'Fact' and adverbial qualifications

One who wishes to dispense with facts can only hope to
dispense with the word 'fact'. What might he then have to seek
to express in other terms? What, that is, does 'fact' mean? It
would seem that the original sense, as in the Latin *factum*,
'thing done', still makes itself felt in present usage. To say
that something is a fact is to say: it is done, settled, decided;
there is nothing more you can do about it. That is how things
are; the time for taking steps to bring about a different state
of affairs has passed. So, men have been to the moon; that is
a fact. Not just a matter of opinion or speculation; not a
hypothesis which I am prepared to yield on, leave open to
question or in the air. This conveys something of the flavour
of 'fact', but it is perhaps too close to the ways of speaking
which I am holding to be deceptive. In giving an account
which is true to the subjectless character of 'it is a fact', there
is no requirement that we refrain from citing the proposition
with which the phrase is envisaged as associated, the proposition which appears to provide the explicit subject for '... is
a fact', but we do not want to offer an explanation which
fails to make clear that 'fact' does not function predicatively.
So, to speak more cautiously in this respect, we might say
something along these lines: in adding 'it is a fact (that)' to
an assertion, we are saying that we take ourselves to be fully
warranted in speaking in the terms that follow, that we are
not speaking merely conjecturally. It compares, if you wish,
with the assertion sign.

The focus of expressions indicative of possibility, probability, and certainty is semantically the verbal part of the sentence, the term which carries explicit verbal force and which may be modified to tone down or to emphasize such force, to qualify the attachment of the predicate to what is named by the subject. This is most straightforwardly done with an adverb, such as 'probably', and if the adjective is used its grammatical status prevents it from attaching at the point where it belongs. We *may* be able to attach it to the larger unit, so speaking of a probable proposition, but there is no need for any such attachment. Similarly with 'fact'. The adverbial 'in fact', though it can differ slightly in its contrasts from '. . . is a fact', best indicates the semantic function, with none of the misleading suggestions which surround the seemingly predicative uses. There being negative facts, for instance, means no more than the truth of such statements as 'The moon is not in fact made of green cheese'.

It is, I suggest, when incorporated *within* a proposition that an expression of possibility or actuality, probability or certainty is seen to function most straightforwardly, and we might argue that talk of propositions themselves as being possible, and so forth, is derivative. Certainly, the common distinction between *de re* and *de dicto* modality suggests a mistaken point of contrast. What is generally at stake here is not so much a contrast between a modality which bears now upon an individual, now upon a form of words. In either case the modality can be incorporated within the proposition, but in the one case a given term is used referentially, in the other it is not. Suppose that no reference is intended by someone who asserts 'It is possible that the next Prime Minister will be a woman'. There is no need to think of the phrase 'it is possible' as then being *about* the remainder of the assertion rather than as giving exactly the same qualification as is contributed by the adverb in 'The next Prime Minister will possibly be a woman'. What has been imagined is that 'possible' must be true of something or someone, and if not of a person, then at least of a proposition; what is actually decisive is the way in which the definite description is intended.

When discussing the construction with 'it', both as in 'it is dusk' and in 'it is certain', I excluded a referential role on the part of the pronoun: with 'it is dusk' there is no intention to further characterize something of which we have independent knowledge, knowledge which could survive the failure of this item to be thus describable, and the same holds of 'it is certain' when a clause follows. With 'it is a fact', similarly, the pronoun does not take the place of a more definite identification of some known item which we assert to have this character. However, I did allow that the case for reference was stronger with 'that' than with 'it', and indeed acknowledged a way in which we might speak of reference with the former, when 'that is a pity', 'that is certain', and so on, are used with reference to something someone has said. The behaviour of 'that is a fact' is again comparable, this being a comment we may make with reference to one statement rather than another, even though a statement cannot be described as 'a fact'. Similarly, in so far as we might wish to speak of *identifying* a fact, it will be a matter of one proposition among others intended as factual. So, 'That fact—I mean the fact that imports are rising—is cause for concern'.

The analysis of 'is a fact', and so forth, in terms of the adverbial 'in fact' appears less *ad hoc* in the light of the comparison with 'certainly', 'possibly', and the rest, and I have also tried to make the analysis appear less contrived by drawing on a likeness with the noun 'pity'. However, while 'That smoking causes cancer is a fact' and 'That smoking causes cancer is a pity' can be usefully compared, there are divergences between the two nouns. We do not meet with the isolated 'a fact', as we do with 'a pity', for instance. Still, perhaps this difference in behaviour can be explained in the following way. It could be, I suggest, that while the present use of 'fact' is as I have indicated, its grammar remains tied to its original usage, when it signified a thing done, so 'something in the world', as in the phrase, 'accessory after the fact'. Its grammar has not, as it were, kept pace with its shift in sense, so we do not encounter '(a) fact' as a comment that can be appended to an assertion in a way that is possible for '(a) pity', the latter never having had to adjust to a different usage. Similarly, unlike 'pity', 'fact' will readily unite with a preceding demonstrative, and functions as a count noun—just the features, evidently, which make the traditional styles of analysis so tempting. The connection of 'fact' with *deed* may also explain what reluctance we have to use the former with respect to propositions of logic and mathematics, though since our reluctance tends to be slight, there is perhaps little here to be explained.

Although finding that something is a fact does not involve identifying anything as an appropriate bearer for the title of 'fact', this does not mean that there is anything amiss with our familiar utterances in which we state that such-and-such is a fact, or that there is a fact, as with 'There is one fact that your theory cannot explain'; whether we take this latter as 'Something is a fact which your theory cannot explain', or appeal to 'There is something which is in fact so and which your theory cannot explain', it can hardly be said that use of the term 'fact' involves a commitment which we should do well to avoid. Supposing, that is, that the relevant sentences break down as I suggest. Contexts in which no accompanying proposition is cited, as with 'He has been informed of the facts', do not appear to introduce any significantly new complications, but there remains a possibly troublesome case which I touched upon when I remarked that 'fact' is often used to provide a term which mediates between a preposition and a following clause, the clause not being felt capable of direct connection to the preposition. I mentioned the examples of being unaware of, oblivious to, misled or unconcerned by the fact that *P*. There are many others.

The point of 'fact' here is to enable us to govern a clause by a part of speech which could not otherwise do so, but if it really only gives the appearance of effecting such a dissociation by interpolating something between the reluctant partners in the combination, if, as it would seem, the clause is simply in apposition to 'the fact', then it becomes difficult to see how the parts of the sentence fit together. We reject as ill formed 'He was annoyed by that people took the play seriously', offering instead the expansion with 'the fact', but how does this addition succeed in rendering the final form coherent? After all, 'the fact' just seems to qualify the clause in an inessential way, not to convert it into a new type of term altogether. Contrast 'I accept the fact that he has worked well', in which 'the fact' can be regarded as a grammatically dispensable filler.

However, I think that the difference here is of no great

consequence, the problem of fitting a clause into a context which retains the preposition being one of satisfying a purely formal demand. Clauses are not sufficiently nounlike to be admitted as they stand, so we add a noun which, like 'fact', does not alter the sense but does accept the preposition. We could omit 'the fact' if we could omit the preposition, which is often a possiblity. So, as well as 'He was annoyed by the fact that people took the play seriously' and 'She was surprised by the fact that the film was a success', we have 'He was annoyed that people took the play seriously' and 'She was surprised the film was a success'. The question of meaning is essentially the same for either form: the clause, 'people took the play seriously', gives the grounds for the person's annoyance, whether expressed as 'he was annoyed by that fact', 'he was annoyed by that' or simply as 'he was annoyed'. Similarly with the example of surprise. And in either case, if we want the emphasis that 'fact' may bring we can re-site it: 'He was annoyed that people in fact took the play seriously'. Even if a version without the preposition is not possible, it does not appear that 'fact' is the focus of any problem. Thus, we cannot omit 'by the fact' from 'He was misled by the fact that the men were wearing uniforms', but what we have to analyse is essentially the relation between the two sentences, 'the men were wearing uniforms' and 'he was misled (by that)', a relation which is one, not now of grounds, but of consequence.

I think that the analysis in which a clause can be introduced is nearly always applicable when we have something of the form 'x is a fact', but it must be allowed that 'fact' has more than one use, and in some people's speech is used readily enough of individual things or events, as in 'The corpse is a fact' or 'High prices are a fact'—though even here the clausal force may be felt, in that a paraphrase as 'That prices are high is a fact' or 'It is a fact: prices are high' still seems appropriate. If it is possible to say 'The corpse is a fact', it is still not possible to go on, except jocosely, with 'The detective tripped over the blood-stained fact'.

The matter is further complicated by the abundance of metaphors which surround 'fact': we speak of 'hard' facts, of 'getting to grips with' or 'facing' facts, of the facts as 'speaking for themselves', and so forth. Some of these combinations may have arisen when 'fact' bore a different sense, a sense closer to that of 'deed'; here we may think of an 'accomplished fact', a translation from the French, where *fait* still translates both as 'deed' and as 'fact'. However, there is no demand that we should be able to give a systematic account of the metaphorical uses—that is unlikely to accord with metaphorical status—and in general I do not think that there is anything in these various locutions to cast doubt on my treatment of what can reasonably be considered the central cases, even though we must allow that the term may move further away from these cases and gradually acquire a different role, as has already happened in its history.

Indeed, if a common conception of causality is to be accepted, 'fact' must already have undergone a dramatic change in the mouths of some speakers, since it is thought to be possible to say such things as 'The fact that there was a storm caused damage over a wide area'. I acknowledge that 'fact' is sometimes predicated of individuals or events, as in the examples just cited, but given that it is here associated with a clause, it is difficult to offer this charitable interpretation, or indeed to suppose that this is anything better than ungrammatical English. A similar specimen of dubious usage in the same area is provided by 'The cause of the glass's breaking is that it was dropped'. That the glass was dropped can be said to be the *reason* why it broke, but for 'cause' you would have to have something like 'Dropping the glass caused it to break'.

There are two main patterns to consider with respect to the relations which might, under a generous interpretation, be termed 'causal'. First, we may specify a cause by specifying an agent: 'Niacin can cause palpitations'. However, an agent is not generally a cause just by *being*, but by *doing*, and a fuller specification will often recognize this—'The beaver, gnawing away at the tree, caused it to topple', 'Water, leaking through the roof, caused patches of damp to form'—though the nature of the phenomenon sometimes makes any elaboration unnecessary, as with 'The fire caused the girders to buckle' and the corrected 'A storm caused damage over a wide area'. Again, we can focus on the action, as with 'Dropping the glass caused it to break'.

There are other cases which can be introduced here, but we reach a contrast when we turn to relations in which the terms are sentences or their nominalizations. So, 'He has decided to come, as he does not want to miss seeing his old friends'. When the larger units are involved, we generally speak of reasons rather than causes, substitution of the latter term for the former being fairly certain to result in nonsense, as is readily illustrated by modifying such sentences as 'You must have a better reason than that', 'The reason was that he was ill', and 'That is the only reason why he was invited'. To say that P gives the reason why Q is to say, roughly, that P occurs in a pattern of reasoning which accounts for Q. Or, to ask for someone's reason is, in effect, to ask how he reasoned. Here, as generally with nouns which attach to clauses—nouns such as 'suggestion', 'complaint', and 'explanation'—it is more illuminating to start with the cognate verb. Thus, suppose you ask me why I got up and I reply, meaning and understanding what I say, 'To answer the telephone'. How can I be so sure that I have correctly identified my reason for getting up?— a very real problem if it were a matter of assigning a cause. The request amounts to a request for information about the way I reasoned, and my knowledge in this regard is just a par- ticular case of the kind of knowledge which I have about the course which my recent thoughts have taken.

Sometimes, however, reason and cause move closer together. We may make no distinction between 'What was your reason for hesitating?' and 'What caused you to hesitate?'. Indeed, we have a number of alternatives here: 'Why did you hesitate?', 'What made you hesitate?', and 'What gave you cause to hesi- tate?'. These questions are similar to 'Why do you think your roses will not be a success this year?'. The reply, 'Because there is so much greenfly about', gives one's ostensible reason for thinking thus; the sense of the sentence does not connect with generation—how one comes to have the thought—but it is a sense in which by saying 'because P' we invite possible criticism on the grounds that P does not license any inference to Q, does not render Q probable. While we do not have 'The fact that there was a storm caused damage over a wide area', we do have 'The fact that there was a storm caused the farmers some concern', so it is not impossible to combine 'cause' and clause. Here the appropriate assimilation is in the direction of 'caused' to 'gave reason for' or 'gave cause for', rather than in the direction of worldly agents as referents for the clause. It gives no support to a reduction of reasons to causes as this is customarily intended, and we can continue to regard facts as excluded from the class of worldly items which may stand in causal relations to one another.

The association of 'fact' with clauses suggests that it has a linguistic rather than an extralinguistic referent, but if I am right it has neither. If, ignoring the presupposition in each of these rejected alternatives, the presupposition that there must be *something* to which 'a fact' may be applied, *something* thus describable, we then find that each leads to difficulties, we shall then perhaps be led to view the question in a different light: we cannot choose decisively between facts as true propositions, say, and facts as states of affairs, but since either has points for and against, we must base our choice on pragmatic considerations, as indeed we must treat the choice whether to tolerate facts at all. As with numbers, however, there is an appearance of a choice only for someone who has not troubled to follow up the implications of the language involved. Whether we choose to regard facts as in the world or as linguistic items, we shall end up by being forced to defend absurdities; there is no question of extending or refusing charity to mysterious entities, but acceptance or rejection of facts can only amount to acceptance or rejection of an innocent, if sometimes overworked and clumsy idiom, an idiom which we might avoid on stylistic grounds, but which there is otherwise no more point or credit in avoiding than there is in eschewing such commonplace words as 'fish' and 'chips'.

42. Truth and correspondence

I turn now to our other, related topic, that of truth. The use of 'true' in which it can be predicated of statements and other comparable subjects gives some support to one of the most venerable accounts of truth, namely, the correspondence theory, if only to show the satisfaction of a necessary condition for the acceptability of that account. If you cannot ascribe 'true' to a statement, then you cannot understand the term as signifying a correspondence between the statement and anything else. The subjectless, non-predicative use, on the other hand, as in the simple response, 'True', or as in 'He is clever, it is true' and 'True, he is clever', gives some support to the opponents of this theory. If you can give an account of 'true' here without having to relate it to a statement or proposition as subject, then, in a large number of central cases, you can apparently avoid any locution which would allow of rephrasal in such a way as to make clear that some form of correspondence is being affirmed.

Let us now consider in detail the two accounts of truth which are likely to go with each of these ways of speaking, the correspondence and the redundancy theory. The correspondence theory has enormous initial appeal. It seemingly derives support from familiar ways of speaking, as when we say that a proposition does or does not agree with the facts, and it is difficult to see how we can avoid saying that a true proposition must answer to *something*, that there is *something* which makes a true proposition true; there must, we feel, be some way of giving clear expression to these thoughts, and whatever it turns out to be, the correspondence theorist can surely claim it as his own. At this level, it may even be doubted whether there is anything in the slightest controversial about the theory; there *has to be* a duality of words and world; it can only be by reference to something other than a man's words that we can in general determine whether he has spoken truly, so if there is a problem it can concern no more than the details of the analysis.

However, the theory notoriously meets with difficulties which relate to more than the details; in particular, difficulties concerning the satisfactory specification of the second term of the supposed relation of correspondence, whether it be 'facts', 'reality', 'situation', 'state of affairs', or whatever. This is not to say that the first term—'statement', 'proposition', 'thought', 'belief'—can count on a ready acceptance of its role, but if the duality of, roughly, words and world is questioned, it is likely to be at least the second term of the relation that is deemed to be not as the theory requires. We need not query the intelligibility of the idioms which are apparently favourable to the theory, but this does not mean that the use to which these idioms are put is wholly innocent or even wholly relevant.

So, for instance, the general notion of a proposition's corresponding or agreeing with the facts is not at all unfamiliar, but it is at some remove from the idea of a corresponding fact paired off with each true proposition. It is, in the former case, a matter of a more diffuse relation, more a question of a general agreement or consistency, a 'squaring' between propositions and what has been established; conversely, a proposition fails to correspond when it does not fit or tally with what is known, when we should not expect it to be true given how things are, though in listing the facts in question we should not be likely to cite a direct negation of the proposition in question. However, the correspondence theory sees the relation as holding between a given proposition, P, and its unique correlate, commonly the fact that P. So, the proposition, 'There is life on Mars', is true if and only if it corresponds to the fact that there is life on Mars.

In considering this formula it is natural to focus attention on the notion of correspondence—e.g. is it correspondence *to* or *with*, and what is involved in either?—but there is an objection which makes this examination superfluous. If I assert '"There is life on Mars" is true if and only if it corresponds to the fact there is life on Mars', there is the risk, in speaking of *the* fact, of an unwanted implication that it *is* a fact that there is life on Mars. What is wanted is a version which is clearly non-committal in this respect, such as '"There is life on Mars" is true if and only if it is a fact that there is life on Mars and the proposition corresponds to this fact'. But now it is obvious that in this clearer statement the conjunct, 'the proposition corresponds to this fact', contributes nothing to the truth of the biconditional and can be omitted without loss, leaving us with the simple '"There is life on Mars" is true if and only if it is a fact that there is life on Mars'. Since this by itself is sufficient, it is surely an illusion to suppose that a further relation of correspondence is required. More accurately, there is no more of a correspondence than is implicit in this shortened version, no more than is involved in saying that P is true if and only if it is a fact that P, or—final ignominy— if and only if, in fact, P.

Of course, the formula which the theory prescribes proves to be *correct,* so the objection is not one of outright falsity, and we can allow that there should be a correspondence of a kind between 'true' and 'fact'. But the intention of the theory is not simply to have us accept some correspondence or other, but to have us accept that truth consists in a correspondence between linguistic and extralinguistic reality, or at least between thought and reality, when so far all we have is a thesis about the matching of contexts in which 'true' occurs with contexts in which we have 'fact'—the kind of thesis which would be trivially guaranteed if we simply had a synonym for 'true'. The theory could allow that correspondence should degenerate into some rather vacuous form of correlation, yet still be a theory worth consideration, if it implied that, except for the special case when we are talking about language, the terms of this relation were describable as linguistic and non-linguistic respectively. However, although we have established a necessary condition for the acceptability of such a theory, in that we have shown that 'is a fact' does not belong on the linguistic side of the divide, that it is not, unlike 'true', a possible predicate of propositions, we also know that we are not going to be able to enlist its help as a characterization of any worldly correlate. As we saw, the choice is not between postulating facts as metaphysical, though highly useful constructs, and affirming their reality as perfectly ordinary correlates of true statements which a robust common sense must recognize. Both views share the error of supposing that 'is a fact' can be taken as attaching to a name of something; whether it be said to be physical or metaphysical, we have no more than a minor frill tacked onto this misconception.

In parentheses, as a related variety of nonsense which our analysis can help expose, consider controversies as to whether we have to acknowledge a common extralinguistic reality, a domain of neutral facts which are as they are independently of our conception of them, facts awaiting transcription or encoding in language, a transcription which may, however, result in their distortion. Once more the debate can get going only if facts are thought to define an order of extralinguistic items, items which it makes sense to describe as 'neutral', which language can confront and by which it is measured.

My rejection of the correspondence theory does not depend on asserting an identity of meaning between 'fact' and 'true proposition' or 'true statement', and then concluding that the theory is trivial; that is an identity which I have been very much concerned to deny. Nor do I claim that the sense of 'fact' is too close to that of 'true proposition' for there to be any significant illumination from the theory. The correspondence theorist will insist that the two terms *must* be close in some sense, for it is their very closeness that is to make what he says plausible; if, despite their closeness, what kept them apart was the attachment of 'true' to propositions or statements and 'fact' to terms designating things in the world, the essentials of his position would be as he wishes; but he is right only with the former attachment, and even then what he says does not invariably hold.

But perhaps all this shows is that 'fact' is not the right choice as second term for the correspondence relation. After all, the feeling that truth must consist in some kind of agreement between words and world is likely to survive the elimination of one of the possible characterizations of the second term. There are others, e.g. 'situation' and 'state of affairs', to choose from. What is needed, if the correspondence theorist is to be finally refuted, is a demonstration that *nothing* could qualify as the second term of his favoured relation. Is such a proof possible? As far as showing the emptiness of any relation of correspondence is concerned, we already have the beginnings of a general argument. Our expansion of '"There is life on Mars" is true if and only if corresponds to the fact that there is life on Mars' will follow similar lines, with a similar revelation of redundancy, if we turn from 'fact' to 'situation' or 'state of affairs'. In general, we shall find ourselves with something like '"P" is true if and only if there is a Q such that P and the proposition corresponds to that Q', where no significant addition is made by the clause, 'and the proposition corresponds to that Q'—provided, that is, that the defining condition is indeed sufficient. Moreover, this argument goes through without requiring that 'Q' be like 'fact' in not signifying a worldly item.

Another relevant observation is the following (cf. Ratner

[1935]). In order to make a comparison between words and world, we must know how the world is, how things are in the relevant respect, but it is doubtful whether we can have such knowledge independently of knowing the truth value of the proposition which we were then to compare with reality. Awareness of an object, such as the carpet on the floor, is possible for one who has nothing more than sensitive feet, but awareness that the carpet is on the floor involves fitting concepts together in a way that is difficult to make sense of with respect to a being lacking in language. Accordingly, if what is required to provide a match for the true proposition is what one is here aware of, we have to assume that the person already has just that knowledge which the comparison was supposed to yield—to say nothing of the objection that the 'object' of awareness is not, in any case, anything in the world.

It is really this latter style of objection—that sentence nominalizations are in no sense names—that is fundamental, but again we may continue to feel that the correspondence theory must be essentially correct. We may not wish to place much weight on the notion of correspondence, with its suggestion of a structural similarity, but it surely must be allowed that there is something in the world in virtue of which a true proposition is true. Well, what *does* make a true proposition true? We know that 'the fact that P' does not provide a satisfactory answer from the perspective of the theory under consideration, and we have seen a general argument against the need to invoke any kind of relation of correspondence, so what remains?

There is some room for speaking of an agent as making a statement true in a causal sense; this is a description which we might conceivably use when something can be said to be or become the case as a result of a man's efforts. However, such an agent will figure only by accident, if at all, in the state of affairs or whatever that is to answer to the true proposition. So, if my activities somehow lead to rain, making it possible to speak of me as responsible for the truth of the prediction, 'It will rain'—admittedly a curious way of looking at it—I am none the less not a constituent of the state of affairs, the raining, which is surely what is intended as that in virtue of which the proposition is true.

I make this bizarre observation only for the sake of the contrast which it offers. 'What makes P true' is to be understood 'logically' rather than causally, as 'that whereby P is, or can be accounted true'. Compare 'What makes this house a good bargain?'. This is not to be read as 'What causes this house to be a good bargain?', as we might ask 'What makes this house so damp?', but we are enquiring after the features in virtue of which the house can be described as a good bargain. Other similar sentences are 'She is your mother's sister's child, which makes her your cousin' and 'He was born within the sound of Bow Bells. That makes him a cockney'. There is nothing suspect in this use of 'makes', either in such sentences or in 'makes true'; the question is whether it is a subjectless use, or whether the associated pronoun might designate something in the world.

Russell thought that 'Desdemona's love for Cassio' signified the 'complex unity' which made 'Desdemona loves Cassio' true (see chapter 12 of *The Problems of Philosophy*). Is this thought completely misguided? We do not mind whether the expression can be said to name a state of affairs, a situation, or what, so long as it designates something in the world and something which makes the corresponding statement true. 'Desdemona's love for Cassio' or 'Desdemona's loving of Cassio' qualify in one respect: they can function in a referential manner, as designations of worldly items; Desdemona's love or loving is a disposition, or in a broad sense an activity, which occurs at or lasts for a certain time. On the other hand, there is the obvious risk that, the more such a phrase is successful in naming something in the world, the more the sense of 'making true' would have to be inappropriately causal: neither love, loving, nor indeed lover can make the statement true in the relevant sense.

What would make it true that Desdemona loves Cassio is Desdemona's loving Cassio, not Desdemona's loving or love *of* Cassio, since what is required is not that we should pick on a single term within the proposition and demand of its reference that it make the proposition true, but it is to be a complex designated by the whole proposition that is to have this task. In 'Desdemona's loving of Cassio' the term 'loving' occurs as a fairly straightforward noun, no longer able to take a direct

object; in 'Desdemona's loving Cassio' there is no such development with respect to the single 'loving', but it is the phrase as
a whole that is analogous to a noun in its function, with 'loving' retaining its full character as a verb, capable of being
negated and qualified by an adverb. The possibility of being
negated is clearly important, since we shall wish to handle
negative as well as affirmative propositions, and we can readily
enough say that 'Desdemona does not love Cassio' is true in
virtue of Desdemona's not loving Cassio.

I say that 'Desdemona's loving Cassio' is as a whole analogous to a noun in its function. Does this likeness extend to
the possibility of referential function? This is, of course, the
crucial question, and the chances of its receiving an affirmative answer are, in the light of the contrast with the verbal
noun, very slim. To reinforce this consideration we might
appeal to negative sentences: what is to make 'Desdemona
does not love Cassio' true is Desdemona's not loving Cassio,
but it is difficult to know what the reference of 'Desdemona's
not loving Cassio' could be. However, this may suggest that
when 'loving' occurs unnegated there is not the same problem,
and that would be unfortunate: if the earlier arguments are
correct, the reference is equally absent in either case; it is not
a question of a special difficulty presented by the 'non-existence of negative facts', but the example of negative sentences
simply brings out more sharply the fact that the '-ing' form
retains the verbal status. Still, it does show that, and therewith
the lack of reference, in a decisive enough way.

To repeat, but with a change of example, the claim is not
that 'The barometer is falling' is not made true by the barometer's falling. We may not feel comfortable with the phrases
'make true' and 'true in virtue of', nor with the contexts in
which they occur, but I think that such ways of speaking,
which we have seen to have harmless analogues, are perfectly
in order. Indeed, the slightly clumsy versions with the '-ing'
forms are no more than variations upon versions formulated
in terms of sentences rather than sentence nominalizations,
with no commitments beyond those of the former. As well
as 'His being born within the sound of Bow Bells makes him
a cockney', we have the construction first given, 'He was born
within the sound of Bow Bells. That makes him a cockney'.

The reasons for preferring the one to the other concern nothing more than style. Similarly, as well as the participial form we have 'The barometer is falling. That makes "The barometer is falling" true', or 'Since the barometer is falling, "The barometer is falling" is true', and so on. I am dismissing none of these for lack of sense, but my claim is simply that in none of the versions given, nor in that with 'the fact that the barometer is falling', do we meet with any reference beyond that involved in the singular term, 'the barometer', within the whole complex. It is true that, superficially, there may be some appearance of reference as regards the larger unit, but the further possible expansions of the sentence—e.g. 'The barometer's not falling rapidly makes "The barometer is not falling rapidly" true'—indicate that we are dealing with the imperfect nominal, and hence with an expression which involves reference to no greater degree than does the un-nominalized predication, 'The barometer is falling'. What is involved again comes out most clearly with the adverbial forms, as 'The barometer is falling. "The barometer is falling" is accordingly (or: therefore, thus, hence) true'.

If I am right in denying a referential role to the gerundial construction, it is hard to see what relevant phrase could fare better in this respect, since that construction has a strong claim to provide the most general specification of what makes a true proposition true. With 'Desdemona's loving Cassio makes it true that Desdemona loves Cassio' we retain in 'Desdemona's loving Cassio' just those elements which recur in the proposition, not relying on the provision of any further term, such as 'fact' or 'state of affairs', which might be supposed, perhaps mistakenly, to give an appropriate expansion, as in 'the fact of Desdemona's loving Cassio'. The point is of some consequence, since a more general specification of the supposedly worldly correlate of a truth may not invite the earlier argument aimed at revealing the emptiness of the correspondence relation. Thus, the trivialization of '"P" is true if and only if it is a fact that P and the proposition corresponds to that fact' does not extend to '"P" is true if and only if there is a fact (situation, state of affairs) to which it corresponds', but if these non-referential gerundials are to be charged with specifying the correlate of the proposition, the dismissal of the correspondence theory has been no more than deferred.

While it is natural to regard 'what makes P true' as applying to something for which the description, 'in the world', would make sense, the inclination should weaken when we see how 'makes true' fits in with the many terms indicative of merely propositional connection, as 'thus', 'therefore', 'since', and 'so'. When clausal constructions are in evidence, some form of linguistic relation is often to be expected, not the causal relations which sentence nominalizations, along with '*makes* true', may suggest, but relations of ground and consequence, of justification and explanation. 'Makes true' is not a relation that bridges two very different orders, world and words, but it affirms no more than a deductive connection between one proposition and another, an affirmation which amounts to the feeblest of claims. The fact that the barometer is falling makes it true that the barometer is falling. Of course. But this says no more than: since the barometer is in fact falling, it is true that the barometer is falling—just the triviality into which we have already seen the correspondence theory collapse.

43. Further cases of 'making true'

Much the same issue may be presented by the problem of universals, as approached through the kinds of term, such as 'colour', 'length', and 'speed', which we looked at earlier. I maintained that these nouns provided us with variants of phrases featuring a related adjective or verb: to find out a man's age is to find out how old he is, to forget the location of a street is to forget where it is located, to despair of happiness is to despair of being happy, and so forth. There is a feeling that if reference to a universal gives way to some such predicational form, that is, despite any avowals to the contrary, to eliminate the universal; it is no longer spoken about, no longer named, but an adjective, say, is simply affirmed of some object. Surely the universal must allow of occurrence in a mode that is not thus reducible, for surely it has an existence as an entity which somehow answers to the predicate, a nameable feature in virtue of which the description applies, the use of the adjective is justified? If Evans and Jones are

both Welsh, this is a matter that goes beyond there being a
single description true of each. There is the answering universal, the common .nationality, which justifies application of
that description. How can it be true that both are Welsh but
that the predicate does not stand for something which people
can either be or not be? Again, even in connection with a word
like 'in', the basic idea, for those who are insistent on the
reality of universals, is often that there must be something
whose presence in or absence from the world can make for the
difference between truth and falsity with respect to a sentence
in which the word occurs. No one, surely, would deny that
the truth of what is said depends on how the world is.

We can certainly allow that, for instance, it is in virtue of
his being rich that Rockefeller can be described as 'rich'.
Slightly more informatively, though without changing the
issue, we can say that having a lot of money makes you rich;
that is, if you have a lot of money then you are rich, or thus
describable. But repetitions rather than explanations are all
that these ways of speaking will produce; or, if explanations,
explanations only of the meanings of words. There is no naming of a 'concrete universal', an 'individualized form', with
such phrases as 'being rich', or their more explicit nominal
equivalents, but as with 'what makes P true', so here we meet
with the verbal rather than the substantival '-ing' forms. Having
a lot of money makes you rich, it is true, but that is not—in
the sense intended—to be compared with: eating a lot of food
makes you fat. A better comparison is with 'Eating a lot of
food makes you a glutton', where this is not thought of as
a causal consequence of an activity, but where 'makes you a
glutton' comes to 'means that you are a glutton'. The illusion
that we have in x's being F, or x's F-ness, a substantive explanation of the truth of 'x is F' is one that is no doubt fostered
by the likeness to causal language.

If the conviction remains that there must, none the less, be
something worldly which justifies a correct predication, since
there must be a real difference in the world if P is true rather
than false, then it may help to recall the genuine events, activities, individuals, and so forth, whose occurrence or existence
truth implies. There is no shortage of these, but it is only
bogus referents, thrust upon us by a simplistic account of the

language, that I am denouncing. Nor are phrases which genuinely do specify universals being dealt with unfairly, but to
the extent that a description like 'the shape of this arch' picks
out a universal, as in 'The shape of this arch is one that the
Greeks found aesthetically pleasing', to that extent it functions in such a way that it can at best signify the subject of
a *causal* relation. Not a likely role with 'the shape of this arch',
but as far as the grammar goes it is a possibility, in contrast
to such phrases as 'the arch's being curved'. Similarly, the
noun 'red' remains as the name of a colour. There is no doubt
about the reality of what it names; indeed, it is just the reality
thereof that prevents use of 'red' as an appropriate subject
for '. . . makes P true', something of the form 'x's being red'—
or, in this sense, 'x's redness'—being required to complete this
sentence frame.

The realist's demand that we acknowledge the existence of
universals is reasonable, but its reasonableness may be obscured
through its association with the mistaken view that these essentially verbal phrases, or indeed explicit predicates, stand for
or name universals. There are two ways in which the predicative part of a sentence may be the source of a noun phrase or
seeming noun phrase: (i) we form a noun from part of the
predicate, from an adjective or verb therein: (ii) we form a
participial unit from the whole of the predicate. Take (i). In
'That blade is sharp', 'sharp' does not name a property. This
I intend merely as a grammatical point: 'sharp' just does not
enjoy the requisite naming role. With a noun in predicative
position we may be able to speak of naming, as one could be
said to name a tree with 'This tree is a laburnum', but what is
named is what is presented by the subject—an individual tree,
not a concept or a universal. However, while it is a mistake to
regard either adjective or noun as naming a universal, it is a
short step from recognition of the predicative use to recognition of a universal which one *could* name. As it happens, we
do not use 'sharp' in the required way—as a name associated
only with a sortal criterion of identity—and 'sharpness' tends to
behave clausally, but we might use either in a way that matched
'red' as a noun. To this extent, then, the realist is right: we
do not just stop at the idea of a predicate's being true of something, but we may acknowledge a corresponding universal.

(ii) is the more troublesome, especially when the subject term is retained in a possessive form. Expressions of this type appear to be referential, but so long as the verbal features are retained, this is only appearance. Here we can make out something of the incompleteness which Frege ascribed to concepts: the precise behaviour of 'the blade's being sharp' depends on the character of the further terms with which it associates, so in this respect it can be considered incomplete; nor, of course, does it stand for an object. It is (ii) and not (i) that provides a grammatical subject for 'makes P true', and this points up a confusion in the realist's denunciation of the nominalist for refusing to acknowledge the existence of a universal which would justify us in the application that we make of a general term: there is no designation of a universal with such a sentence as 'The blade's being sharp makes it true that the blade is sharp', but once more we have just a non-explanatory triviality.

The heart of the problem, and my answer, can be summarized as follows. A property, such as colour or shape, can be literally identical in distinct individuals; at the same time, what makes an individual the colour or shape it is, is surely something unshared, something peculiar to that individual. Clearly, a contradiction threatens. I claim, however, that in phrases like 'the shape of A', the qualification 'of A' does not provide a non-sortal individuating condition, does not exclude the truth of an identity, 'The shape of A is the same as the shape of B', for distinct A and B. I allow that the shape of A is what makes A square, or whatever, but 'the shape of A' is in this context to be compared with 'being the shape it is'; it names nothing, whether universal or particular. The seeming contradiction is the result of the two different uses to which these phrases are put. Or again, from 'I could never jump that height' and 'That height is the height at which you were last successful', we can infer 'I could never jump the height at which you were last successful'. Here there is a genuine specification of a universal, and a contrast with the implicit predication given by 'the height of the tower' in the invalid inference: I had forgotten the height of the tower; the height of the tower is the same as the height of the bridge; therefore, I had forgotten the height of the bridge. When we have genuine specification of a universal via a noun N there may be room for that use of 'the same N' which is appropriate to an N with its own identity. The height of the tower is not said to be the same height as that of the bridge, but the colour I like most and the colour you like least may be said to be the same colour, which confirms the more typical substantival character of 'colour' in this context.

A further case of 'making true' to consider is presented by subjunctive conditionals. Thus, Dummett imagines a dispute over the validity of 'Either Jones was brave or he was not', said of a man who never encountered danger in his life (Dummett [1959b]). Both parties to the dispute accept that this amounts to a disjunction of the two conditionals, 'If Jones had encountered danger, he would have acted bravely' and 'If Jones had encountered danger, he would not have acted bravely', but one party will not accept that at least one of these must be true, since it may be that however many facts we knew of the kind which we should normally regard as grounds for asserting such counterfactual conditionals, we should still know nothing which would be a ground for asserting either. In this event it is absurd to insist that either 'Jones was brave' or 'Jones was not brave' is true, since this is to commit oneself to holding that a statement may be true even though there is nothing which makes it true, nothing such that, if we knew of it, we should count it as evidence or as a ground for the truth of the statement.

Before considering this development, however, we might wonder whether both parties *should* agree to the analysis offered for 'Either Jones was brave or he was not'. The most natural interpretation of 'Jones was brave' is along the lines of 'Jones acted bravely'; that is, 'was brave' is taken to signify an actual manifestation of bravery—French *fut*. If the sense is more general, 'was brave' meaning something more like 'was a brave man'—French *était*—there is still a requirement that at some time or other Jones should have manifested bravery in order to be thus describable. If on no occasion did Jones show bravery, then an explicit conditional, 'Jones would have been brave if . . .', seems called for, rather than 'Jones was a brave man'. In either case, then, the sense of 'was brave' appears to decide the issue without our having to take sides on the further question. Still, while a conditionalization using 'would' makes for a replacement rather than a translation of the original, that does not matter for present purposes, since we can just suppose that the conditional itself is the object of our interest, and not to be examined because it supposedly provides an appropriate representation of the original categorical.

I have not denied that, if a proposition is true, there is something that makes it true, but only that anything having this role is to be found in the world. In general, specification of what makes *P* true is a trivial matter, as when we say that John's having a pet snake, or the fact that John has a pet snake, makes it true that John has a pet snake. The only question of substance is whether or not the putative fact is a fact, and, in the case of conditionals, the prior question of meaning that this may pose: the fact that, if Jones had encountered danger, he would have acted bravely—if fact it is— can be said to make the relevant proposition true, but it is not clear when we are entitled to say that this *is* a fact, that the proposition *is* true.

There are two possibilities here. First, we might transfer to subjunctive conditionals a use of 'true' which has its most straightforward application to indicative conditionals, where we can say that the truth value of '*Q*, if *P*' is the same as the truth value of *Q*, if *P*. This is the basic case. The conditional, 'If you whistle, Rover will come', may be quite lacking in any support yet still prove true, truth here being essentially a matter of the truth of the main clause, under the condition supposed, and not a matter of the reasonableness of the conditional in advance of the fulfilment of the antecedent. It is generally supposed that with a subjunctive conditional the possible truth of the indicative proposition corresponding to the antecedent is ruled out, but since the falsity of that proposition is not actually entailed by the conditional, it is possible even here to see truth in the terms suggested. So, if it turns out, contrary to expectation, that Jones did encounter a dangerous situation and was not found wanting in bravery, we might say that 'If Jones had encountered danger, he would have acted bravely' had been verified. This is especially natural when the tense is future, even though the mood is subjunctive, as with 'If Jones were to encounter danger, he would act bravely'. In either case, what makes for the truth of the conditional is essentially what makes for the truth of the consequent, the conditional form bringing no additional problems in this respect (cf. Rundle [1972], chapter 2, [1969], pp.79-84).

As well as pronouncing a conditional true on such a basis, we may also appeal to the possibility of inferring the consequent under the supposition of the antecedent, together with various auxiliary truths. We are often happy to judge 'If P, then Q' true before the truth value of P has been decided, much as we may use 'true' with respect to an unconditional but well-supported prediction, though in either case the more direct form of verification is primary: however strong the support for 'If P, then Q', so however reasonable its appraisal as true, the judgement is overturned by the joint fulfilment of P and not-Q.

If verification of the more direct kind is supposed ruled out, then the inferential connection seems to be all that remains for possible appraisal, and with subjunctive conditionals this is often quite clearly our only concern. Consider 'He did not come, but if he had we should have seen him', which stands no chance of being reckoned true on any other basis. And how do things stand with the pair, 'If Jones had encountered danger, he would have acted bravely' and 'If Jones had encountered danger, he would not have acted bravely'? It would seem that on neither use of 'true' need acceptance of the truth of the one or the other be compelling, that there need be nothing which makes either true. If the indicative corresponding to the shared antecedent goes unfulfilled, we have on the first use no truth value—unless it is then considered to reduce to the second—and there is no guarantee that we should actually have good grounds, or that there are any to be discovered, for either implication. This seems clear, and it also seems that essentially the same conclusion emerges whether or not we think of what makes P true as being in the world. The relevant considerations do not rely on a worldly status for facts, but it is necessary only that we should have the use of terms like 'fact', not that we should have one rather than another conception of their use on this point.

This last is the main consideration, but there is a complication that is worth a mention. Consider the two conditionals:

(a) If Jones had encountered danger, he would have acted bravely or he would not have,

(b) If Jones had encountered danger he would have acted bravely, or if Jones had encountered danger he would not have acted bravely.

A first impression on comparing the two is that (a) is valid whilst (b) is not, but the distance between them seemingly decreases if we rewrite (b) as 'Either Jones would have acted bravely—if he had encountered danger—or he would not have acted bravely—if he had encountered danger', which has something of the inescapable character of (a), rather than merely presenting us with two implications, neither of which need be compelling.

I shall discuss the acceptability of (a) shortly, but if it is not to be rejected, and if (b) does count as an equivalent, we might hope to make this more palatable by arguing against the necessity of supposing that at least one of the alternatives presented by (b) should be true. It may seem a flat contradiction to say that a disjunction could be true without that virtue passing to at least one of its disjuncts, but consider again an unconditional proposition in the future tense, as 'She will not outlive her mother'. If this is offered as a speculation, rather than as a reasonably assured prediction, we should not equate it with 'It is true that she will not outlive her mother'. Similarly, disjunctions provide a context where a propositional form of words may occur in a way that contrasts with use as a confirmable assertion, and where the endorsement provided by 'true' may accordingly not be in place.

Although there may be no grounds for saying that either conditional in (b) is true, one or other of the possibilities would have had to be realized. That is, if Jones had encountered danger he certainly would have acted bravely or not bravely. The acceptability of (a) thus appears assured, but it is useful to look more closely at negation to see why.

Consider a sentence containing a sign of negation, as 'He is not ill'. It is clear that this is not something we are entitled to assert just through *not* being entitled to assert 'He is ill'.

How might we come to assert the former? The pattern here is in general different from that which typifies affirmative statements, there being in the negative case a higher ratio of inference to observation than with the corresponding affirmation. This negative sentence, for example, would naturally arise as a conclusion of an argument such as the following: 'If he were ill, then he would have a temperature, or there would be some other observable symptoms; however, there are no symptoms; therefore, he is not ill'. Clearly, there would be a threat of an unending series of such arguments if every negation were to find its way in only as a result of such a pattern of reasoning, since the argument features a negation in addition to that of the conclusion—in this instance, 'There are no symptoms'. Very well, let us repeat the pattern, but in the hope that we are led a stage nearer a point at which the negation is asserted on a different basis, the point at which I am aiming being that where the inability to assert P is tantamount to the ability to assert not-P. So, I say 'There are no symptoms', and again I argue: 'If there were any then I should be able to detect them; I cannot detect any, so there cannot be any'. With this pattern of *modus tollens* we must again have a negation, and here the relevant one is, of course, 'I cannot detect any'. Do we now repeat the pattern or does this premiss have the desired character? That is, is it because I am *unable* to assert 'I can detect some' that I am *able* to assert 'I cannot detect any'? Provided that I have at least tried, that I have put myself in a position to tell, the answer is surely 'Yes'. So here we rest. The original assertion can, it emerges, be traced back to, or is founded on, an instance of negation which originates in the desired, and seemingly basic way.

Back now to our conditional, 'If Jones had encountered danger, then he either would or would not have acted bravely'. This, we might suppose, is easily justified: whatever the man might have done in such circumstances, it would have been describable as 'brave', or, failing that, as 'not brave'—allowance made for uncertain cases. Or, to bring out its conformity to the proposed pattern: if we had been unable to say that the man acted bravely, we should have been able to say that he did not act bravely. But, of course, this supposes the situation to have been one of the kind which reduces to the basic negation case; it takes as eliminated a possibility which only the supposed circumstances of the case, and not logic, can eliminate, namely, that we should fail to determine that Jones was brave yet not thereby find ourselves in a position to declare him not brave, or at least not be able to anticipate with any certainty finding ourselves in that position. It is important to note that the seemingly trivial disjunctive consequent, 'he either would or would not have acted bravely', is what poses the problem, without regard to the question whether, given the antecedent, we can reason to one or other of these alternatives. Perhaps we cannot, but the conditional as a whole is none the less assertible so long as we do have a reduction to the basic case.

As a contrast, consider the proposition: if the cat had fallen asleep, then either it would have dreamed or it would not have. In this instance there is a difficulty with each alternative, in that we are not at all sure how we could recognize when it was appropriate to speak of a cat as dreaming, when not. We should not reject 'If P, then Q or not-Q' on the grounds that we are warranted in asserting neither 'If P then Q' nor 'If P then not-Q', but it may be possible to reject it on the grounds that, even if P had been fulfilled, there might have been nothing which justified us in asserting Q and nothing which justified us in asserting its negation either. And, moreover, not merely no such telling indication at the time in question; we do not really know how, given our uncertainty as to what is involved, we could be in a position to pronounce authoritatively on either possibility. Again, consider 'Either Christ is mortal or Christ is immortal'. If I am not in a position to say that Christ is mortal, does that mean that, eventually, I shall be able to say that Christ is immortal? Not at all. There is doubt about this application of the law of excluded middle, precisely because there is no guarantee that the necessary reduction can be carried through.

In passing, we note that what makes a disjunction true is not usually the truth of one of its disjuncts, but the *exhaustiveness* of the alternatives presented—supposing them decidable. So, we query 'Either Labour or the Conservatives will win' on the grounds that the possibility of a Liberal victory has been overlooked. It is when, as with disjunctions, we have an assertion based on reasoning, that we may find some place for a non-trivial application of 'what makes P true', though the absence here of any worldly reference is particularly plain. Propositions of mathematics provide further illustrations of both these points.

While it is not intended as applying quite generally, the account given of negation in those cases where we reason indirectly appears to be an advance on accounts in terms of falsity, and accounts which presuppose an understanding of a near-synonym in terms of which 'not' might be defined. For certain basic cases the claim is that we are in a position to assert not-P when and only when we are not in a position to assert P; or, we learn to regard not-P as assertible in circumstances in which P is not assertible, where P and the circumstances are such that if P were assertible then we should know it to be so. This form of explanation appears satisfactory, in that it makes clear the recognizability of the circumstances in which the use of the negative form would be warranted. Indeed, we might draw a stronger conclusion. Suppose we found people making use of an operator which seemed to behave as our 'not', at least to the extent that speakers were not prepared to assert P so long as they were prepared to assert P qualified by this operator. Unless reductions of the kind indicated were generally possible, we should not be in a position to interpret the combination as the negation of the given sentence: nothing in these people's linguistic behaviour would impose this interpretation in the absence of such a possibility, but it would be consistent with their practice that the use of this operator applied to a declarative sentence P signified that they were not in a position to assert P. Indeed, if their serious use, the use in which they considered themselves justified in saying what they said, did accord with this interpretation, then this is all that they would in fact mean; a difference which is not imposed by or reflected in actual use is not a difference in meaning.

44. Truth and redundancy

Let us return to the sentence, 'Since the barometer is falling, "The barometer is falling" is true'. This has a less trivial analogue in 'Since the barometer is falling, *Le baromètre baisse* is true', and it would seem not to be as trivial as 'Since the barometer is falling, the barometer is falling'. However, on one view of the way in which 'true' is to be analysed—the redundancy theory of truth—'"The barometer is falling" is true' means no more than the simple 'The barometer is falling', so that we really do have no more than a simple repetition. A similar issue would arise with respect to the pair 'It struck him that the barometer had fallen' and 'It struck him that "The barometer has fallen" was true', or with respect to 'If the barometer is falling, the barometer is falling' and 'If the barometer is falling, "The barometer is falling" is true', and in these and other like cases I imagine we should be inclined to say that something distinct from the reductionist's version was at stake. How, without falling back on the correspondence theory—which does have a ready account of the difference—are we to explain why such sentences are resistant to these simplifications?

The form of words, '"The barometer is falling" is true', is highly unreal, but there is no shortage of larger contexts which raise the same issue, and which cast doubt on the alleged eliminability of 'true'. Consider:

> 'Casual shoes don't have laces' is true in virtue of the meaning of 'casual shoes'
> 'I am alive' is true whenever uttered
> One and the same statement, e.g. 'Parliament is in recess', can be now true, now false
> Since 'It is only seventy-six days to Christmas' can be true, at least one sentence not of subject–predicate form can be true

The issue of the eliminability of 'true' is customarily pursued without regard to an important division of cases, those in which 'true' is related to an explicit statement, as in these examples, and those in which it is not, as in 'It is quite true that he is competent'. In the former, what we must first consider is whether the direct reference to the statement can be eliminated without loss; only then, in general, can we address ourselves to the eliminability of 'true'. For instance, it is not just that '"I am alive" is true whenever uttered' fails to collapse

to 'I am alive whenever uttered', but it equally cannot be replaced by 'It is true that I am alive whenever uttered'. Reference to or incorporation of the statement counts as something
more than the occurrence of 'true' in such cases: retain 'true'
but switch to the clause and you still have nonsense, there
being now nothing to which 'whenever uttered' can attach.
This of course is not to say that some more roundabout form
of reduction might not be possible.

We can claim as a general feature of 'true' an implicit reference to the actual or envisaged making of a statement—note
the impossibility of, say, 'His being competent is quite true',
which appears to have moved too far from the statement-like
form—but over and above this there is the distinction between
the case in which the statement is actually cited and the case
in which it is not, with the possibility that a direct reduction
is thwarted not so much because of a feature of 'true', but
because the sense demands that the direct speech presentation
of the statement be maintained. However, whether our concern is with direct or with indirect speech, the notion of an
allusion to a statement is one of the more noteworthy and
generally recognized features of 'true', and I shall now stop
to consider the case where such reference is not so trivially
satisfied.

In announcing the arrival of the milkman I should not say
'It is true that the milkman has come', but simply 'The milkman has come'. When I have made my announcement, someone may ask, 'Is that true?', but now, of course, the statement
has been made, so a condition for the appropriateness of 'true'
has been satisfied. The same implication will be present in
a question, as with 'Is it true that the milkman has come?'.
If, similarly, I were to say 'I suppose it must be true that
carrots are good for the eyes' or 'If it is true that the Wilsons
have separated I shall be most surprised', I should give you
to understand that it has been said that carrots were good for
the eyes or that the Wilsons had separated—or at least should
be anticipating or forestalling a possible statement to this
effect (cf. Strawson [1950b], p. 191). Again, only if we wish
to preserve this allusion should we say 'If it is true that the
Wilsons have separated then Mr Wilson will wish to sell the
house', rather than the simple 'If the Wilsons have separated

then Mr Wilson will wish to sell the house', since the added implication of the first antecedent is not relevant to the drawing of the consequence.

The connection of 'true' with statements and assertions is fairly tight: guesses, answers, thoughts, suspicions, beliefs, suggestions, hunches, conjectures—these are not nearly so readily describable as true. Is it possible that the *only* difference between '*P* is true' or 'It is true that *P*' and the simple *P* lies in the citation of, or allusion to a statement which is involved in the versions with 'true' but absent from the simple, and seemingly more fundamental assertion? If the only difference resides in this, or in consequences which can be traced back to it, if the versions with 'true' are otherwise equivalent to the simple assertion, then we are surely not departing significantly from the redundancy theory.

It may sound paradoxical to suggest that we are not departing significantly from this theory when we also maintain that reference to another's statement is a standard feature of 'true', but so long as the difference over and above the simple assertion lies only in this, the two are clearly very close on the important points of comparison, notably the nature of their opposition to the correspondence theory. However, the redundancy theorist might wish to part company with this Strawsonian suggestion on another score, namely, the possibility which I allow that 'true' may be a predicate of a statement or a proposition. I made clear use of this possibility earlier when I said that 'The King of France is bald' simply is not true—not taking this as a way of talking about the King of France—but if, on the redundancy theory, saying 'It is true that *P*' amounts essentially to asserting (or reasserting) *P*, then there is nothing that 'is true' can say *of* the proposition: asserting or reasserting a proposition is not saying something *about* it. 'It is true that the hydrangeas are wilting' is not to be represented as an assertion about an assertion: 'it is true' can say nothing *about* the assertion incorporated in the whole, viz. 'the hydrangeas are wilting', for all it could say would be equivalent to 'the hydrangeas are wilting', and it is clear that the original does not reduce to the pleonastic 'The hydrangeas are wilting and the hydrangeas are wilting' (cf. Jones [1968]).

However, this objection can be met. With 'The hydrangeas are wilting, it is true', the assertoric status of the main clause ensures a subjectless reading for 'it is true', and even with 'It is true that the hydrangeas are wilting', where the force of 'are wilting' is merely propositional, this use of 'it is true' can be maintained. On the other hand when 'is true' is predicated of a form of words, as it may well be if we actually cite the words, then the latter do not figure as an *assertion,* so there is no question of asserting the same thing twice over. When I say, 'Your assertion, "The hydrangeas are wilting", is true', I am of course talking about an assertion, but the words whereby I identify that assertion are not used assertively by me. Of course, and this is what perhaps obscures the issue, the force of the whole utterance is such that we are committed to the assertion, 'The hydrangeas are wilting', but this is because the effect of 'true' here just is to convert a proposition into an assertion—taking 'proposition' as meaning 'unasserted form of words'. Quite generally, I cannot attach 'is *F*' to an assertion without denying it this status, without cancelling its assertive force as it enters into the predication. Similarly, on one reading of 'actual', there is no actual command when I say '"Scram!" is an impolite command', and no actual question when I say '"How old are you?" is a rather personal question'.

We might, then, offer the following account of 'true'. When the word occurs without a subject, as with the simple comment 'true' offered in response to something someone has said, it can be described as an 'assertion variable', a term which does duty for an assertion identifiable from the context, but which says nothing *about* that assertion. Compare the use of 'yes' in English, where other languages may tend to repeat the utterance with which agreement is being expressed. When used as a predicate, on the other hand, 'true' serves to convert a proposition into an assertion.

This account has a certain elegance, and it avoids objections which some forms of the redundancy theory may incur. For instance, if it is suggested that 'true' is interchangeable with 'I confirm that', we are threatened with an unwanted personal element in the pronoun 'I', whereas if 'true' just is an assertion variable at its relevant occurrence, we can appreciate that it is no less impersonal than the assertion it supplants. This is in keeping with a view which, for good reasons, has gained ground in recent times, namely, the view that it is more appropriate to seek an analysis of the meaning of a word which would enable one to predict or explain its functions in various rather specific speech acts—notably those of confirming, acknowledging, and endorsing, in the case of 'true'—than to take such functions as somehow definitive of the meaning of the word. In passing, I might mention that a feature already noted for conjunctive 'that', rather than the sense of 'true', may be what accounts for the concessive force which commonly attaches to 'It is true that P'. Compare 'It is true: the lock has been forced' with 'It is true that the lock has been forced'. While the former would be appropriate on making a discovery which confirms what someone has said, the latter is more likely to introduce a countervailing assertion—'It is true that the lock has been forced, but there are no other signs of damage'—and my suggestion is that by setting off the clause as a contrastive unit, the 'that' is better suited to a concessive use of 'It is true that P'. However, such a use is by no means inevitable when 'that' occurs. There can be other contrasts.

In applying his analysis to the variety of contexts into which 'true' may enter, the redundancy theorist is naturally drawn towards a 'general propositional form', introduced either by a variable supposed restricted to those sentences which may be pronounced true or false, viz. assertions or propositions, or by a characterization at a general level of such sentences (cf. Strawson [1967], p. 14). Thus, 'Whatever she says is likely to be true' goes over into 'If she says P, then it is likely that P', or, less artificially, into 'It is likely that things will be as she says'. In invoking this latter formula, it may seem that the redundancy theorist has moved too far in the direction of the correspondence theory. To say that P is true if and only if things are as P states is to come ominously close to maintaining that P is true if and only if it represents things as they are. However, the redundancy theorist has little to worry about on this score, at least from one point of view: if in such locutions as 'things are as P states' or 'P states how things are', 'things' is thought to do duty for the various subject terms which might figure in an appropriate sentence form, then the implied reference is clearly not to an elusive complex supposed to answer to the whole proposition, but only to what is ostensibly designated by a term within the proposition. The possibility of such reference is universally agreed, but it falls far short of what the correspondence theorist is seeking. If, on the other hand, 'things' is not thus confined, we have merely a rather loose form of words which is negligible in its commitments. I mean, it may be that 'It is dusk' can be taken as 'stating how things are', even though no 'thing' in the widest sense is having anything predicated of it. It is in this broad sense, rather than as featuring 'things' as a subject variable, that the redundancy theorist will wish to construe the phrase, but he can reasonably regard it as neutral in the relevant respect: once 'things' has ceased to be a variable in the way indicated it has ceased to be a variable altogether, being now an almost inert constituent of an idiom which has sense as a whole. If it is none the less insisted that there is rather indeterminate reference to a state of affairs, or whatever it is that is denominated 'what makes the statement true', we can simply repeat the earlier objections. No rescue operation has been mounted for the correspondence theory, just a misguided attempt to read special significance into this idiom with the all-purpose 'things'. Nor, we may note, does the conjunction 'as' introduce a comparison of the right kind, since it fails to join with words which designate.

It seems plausible to hold that to say of P that it is true is usually tantamount to asserting P, and to know that P is true is usually a matter of knowing that P. However, there are exceptions. If I have it on good authority that a sentence P in an unknown language is true, then I know as much, but there is not the further move to knowledge that P on my part. What I know is that things are as P states, whatever that may in fact be. Again, the form 'P is true' reduces to P only in virtue of some general condition's being realized in the particular case, and it is the character of this condition that we should like to see clarified by an illuminating paraphrase of 'is true', a paraphrase which would also make clear just what two propositions are being said to have in common when we state that they both are true: simply asserting the two sentences may conceivably *show* what they have in common, but we should like to know what that is; it is not simply that they *are* asserted, for instance. If I can say that two propositions are both true in that things are as each states, then I at least make some attempt at extracting a common feature.

Any satisfactory account of truth must recognize that 'is true' can function as a genuine predicate. Furthermore, just as we should not expect making assertions to do the work of 'is an assertion', or asking questions to make redundant 'is a question', so there would appear to be no expectation that 'is true' can invariably be eliminated in favour of a bare assertion. Whether the need to introduce something more into a rephrasal of a context with 'true' makes for a falsification of the redundancy theory, or merely for an allowable extension, will depend on the precise form that the expansion takes. So far I have really only defended the redundancy theorist against the charge that he has, in invoking the general form of proposition, succumbed to the view of his major rival. For the present that is where I shall leave the argument, while I consider certain of the terms close in sense to 'true' in an effort to bring out something of its special character.

45. Near-synonyms of 'true'

If someone says something with which I am in agreement, I am in many cases more likely to respond with 'That is right' than with 'That is true'. So, if you say, 'The telephone number of the zoo is 56789', I should signify my concurrence in the former, neutral way, saying the latter only, in general, if it were a matter of conceding or acknowledging something. 'Right', I suggest, goes with 'the right answer', one from among various possibilities, so with an actual or an implied question. The situation is essentially one in which one person is asking a question, or asserting something in a questioning way, of or to another person from whom he ostensibly hopes to extract the answer. Or, at least, we treat what the person says as if it were in answer to a question. Thus, the statement, 'You are single, I see', might expect a reply, might be a way of seeking confirmation, with 'That is right' as accordingly an appropriate affirmative response. Again, if I say, 'Guess what Sally did today', and you reply, 'She insulted the teacher again', I can say 'That's right' but not 'That's true'. Why not the latter? These words can of course be used in a context where the former would apply, but in response to the request to guess they are likely to have a questioning tone—'She insulted the teacher again?'. Even if this is not evident from the intonation, the reply, as a guess, will not count as a full assertion. If asked, 'Did you really mean it when you said she insulted the teacher again?', I might reply that I didn't really *say* she did, I was only guessing.

Other phrases close in meaning to 'true' include 'correct', '. . . is so' and '. . . is the case'. 'Correct' is very like 'right', particularly as in 'got right', with what this implies as to such procedures as calculation. It suggests precision, accuracy, and perhaps that error has been eliminated—as would agree with its status as an erstwhile past participle. Again we note the absence of any need to be related to an assertion: it would be odd to say 'My first thoughts on the matter were true' or 'Her hunch was true', but perfectly in order to describe my thoughts or her hunch as right or correct. 'That is so' is narrower than 'true', in that it has no analogue to 'It is true that *P*'. Here we have a very clear case of a phrase being used in reference to *P*, but not in such a way that *P* is subject—what you say may be so, but we cannot direcly relate 'is so' to an assertion: not '"Taxes are high" is so', or even 'That assertion is so'. On the other hand, it is in another way more general, being less likely to be associated with an intention to acknowledge something in the way that locutions with 'true' do.

The allusion to another's statement carried by 'true' opens up the possibility of particular forms of breakdown which attend people's statements and which 'true' excludes. Thus, in the question 'Is it true that the Wilsons have separated?', there is the suggestion, 'that is what people are saying', and consequent scope for taking the question as querying the truthfulness of the people concerned. This latter implication is by no means necessary; we could be wondering whether people might not have got things wrong, rather than been lying, but it is clear that such possibilities are raised by the allusion to what is being said but quite absent from the simple query, 'Have the Wilsons separated?'. Think too of the possible oddity of countering 'The Wilsons have not separated' with 'It is true that the Wilsons have separated' rather than with

'They have', an oddity occasioned by the absence of an appropriate statement to be endorsed.

Phrases with 'so' make a similar contrast with 'true'. You say 'He has won this race more times than anyone else'. If I query this with 'Is that true?', or 'Is that really true?', I am raising the kind of query which may be prompted by a statement—it may be a lie, an exaggeration, or not well founded—but if I ask 'Is that so?', I am addressing my query more directly to the subject matter of the statement. I might equally have said, 'Has he really?'. Similar in this respect is 'That is the case', which is often used in affirming something which a person has put forward only as a possibility, at any rate without committing himself fully to it. Someone says, 'If the present crisis continues, they will soon be laying off men at the works', to which it might be replied, 'That is already the case'. Much less likely is 'That is already true'. As its etymology suggests, saying 'That is the case' is like saying 'That is how things have fallen out': 'Since it is the case that . . .', i.e. 'Since it has happened that . . .'; 'It is seldom the case that . . .', i.e. 'It seldom happens that . . .', where 'happens' is not especially suggestive of chance, but is close to 'eventuates' or 'comes about'.

We instanced above a number of sentences which appear to involve an essential reference to a statement, and therewith an ineliminable use of 'true', as with 'One and the same statement, e.g. "Parliament is in recess", can be now true, now false'. Let us run again over what is perhaps the chief consideration in showing truth to be a genuine property of statements. In saying that an assertion is true we exclude certain defects to which assertions are prone. If someone says 'Henry will be returning by the last train', we should be less likely to query this with 'Is that true?', rather than with 'Is that so?', or simply 'Is he?'. The latter are in place if our query concerns no more than the matter in hand: is he or is he not returning by the last train? The former is appropriate precisely when the statement is the subject of our query: does it involve any distortion, exaggeration or deception? The connection of 'true' with its uses in other areas of the language is perhaps not irrelevant: think of a true copy, true love, the true rate of interest, and one's true feelings. The idea of something in which you can place your trust can be discerned here, perhaps making itself felt with respect to statements too, as well as, with 'a true copy', the idea of being faithful to something. At all events, when our concern is less with the virtues of the statement, more with what is under discussion, we are likely to talk in terms of 'being so' rather than 'being true', or to express our query in the terms given by the original statement. In saying 'That is so', we are thinking not so much of the statement as coming up to scratch, but of things being that way. That is so—i.e. that is how things are.

But how can there be room for such a distinction? The question whether 'He has a sense of humour' gives a fitting description, a description applicable to a certain person, and the question whether that person does or does not have a sense of humour—these are surely the same? In substance, yes, but there can be this essential equivalence without prejudice to the genuinely predicative character of 'true'. The status of 'true' as a predicate of propositions or assertions is no obstacle to the reduction, in so far as it can be made. It was suggested above that this predicative status could be accepted by the redundancy theorist, the role of 'true' being to convert a proposition into an assertion. However, it will be because it has the meaning it has that 'true' is enabled to do this, and not every interpretation of 'true' that was adequate in this respect could be accepted by the advocate of redundancy, the reading as 'corresponds to the facts' being an obvious case in point. Since we say 'That is true' in response to something someone says, it might seem that the role of 'true' in a genuine predication was not open to doubt, but we also say 'That is so' in the same circumstances, and the case for regarding 'is so' as a predicate of the assertion is far less convincing—indeed, we do not even have the construction with a clause, 'It is so that *P*'. It is, I suggest, 'That is so' that has the role which has been mistakenly assigned to 'That is true' by those who think 'true' redundant: 'That is so' simply reaffirms what has been stated against conflicting possibilities; it merely repeats or endorses the statement, but without saying anything about it. The effect of 'That is true' is, of course, the same, but is achieved in a way that differs on just this point, the point concerning reference to the statement. 'That is true' belongs with other comments appropriate to the statement, rather than to what the statement is about. Contrast 'That is true, if a trifle exaggerated' with the unhappy mixture in 'That is so, if a trifle exaggerated'. Again, suppose I am told that of the two statements, 'Sursilyan is a Romance dialect' and 'The Cretaceous Period followed the Tertiary Period', one is true the other false. I should then prefer to say 'If "Sursilyan is a Romance dialect" is true, then "The Cretaceous Period follows the Tertiary Period" is false', rather than 'If Sursilyan is a Romance dialect then the Cretaceous Period did not follow the Tertiary Period'. The latter is possible, but it does suggest an inappropriate ground for the inference. And, of course, I can wonder whether the first statement is true without even understanding it, so without wondering whether Sursilyan is a Romance dialect.

It is possible that I have overstated the difference which separates 'That is true' from 'That is so', that we must get closer to an actual repetition of the assertion in question if we are to find the right form to contrast with 'That is true'. But at least there is this contrast, and it does go against the idea that 'true', or the whole phrase 'That is true', can be described as an 'assertion variable', a notion which appears to be at the heart of the redundancy theory—compare the invocation of 'Ditto' in Strawson [1949], p. 268. But if it is clear enough that 'is true' can be a genuine predicate of propositions, so should be analysable in a way that preserves its status as such a unit, it is not clear exactly what it can affirm of a proposition.

46. The analysis of 'true'

Let us, then, look at the problem of defining 'true'. In claiming that the semantic function which 'true' endorses is that of assertion, or that it is primarily assertions or propositions that are spoken of as 'true', we fasten on the sentential or propositional unit as what 'true' may attach to. However, its attachments to the various components of the sentence are unequal, the particular point at which the assertive force is communicated being favoured. In 'Wendy was unlucky', the name does not present an affirmation which 'true' might endorse, but for that to be so an explicit or implicit association with a verbal phrase, as in 'It was Wendy that was unlucky', would be necessary. It is where we can negate that we have the possibility of contrasting alternatives, in such a sense that one may be selected and endorsed by 'true'. Again, the statement, 'The cautious child remained on the pavement', is not so readily described as 'not true' if the child in question is believed not to be cautious, supposing the statement otherwise in order. The matter of the child's cautiousness is not presented to us in such a way that we can express disagreement in this simple way. Again, contrast 'This heirloom is valuable' with 'This is a valuable heirloom', the latter being more appropriate to the case where the object's being an heirloom is a matter of new, and possibly questionable information.

But, of course, while the predicate is the natural focus of 'true', it is also the case that what happens elsewhere in the sentence can be relevant to truth, that there is a sense in which the statement, 'The cautious child remained on the pavement', is not true if the child is not cautious. It is not true precisely because something fails to hold here of 'cautious' which fails to hold with respect to the explicit affirmation, 'He is cautious': the adjective does not apply to the child in question. It would be misleading to respond to the larger statement with 'That is not true', just on the grounds that the child was not cautious, but to the extent that we can, with appropriate explanation, hold the statement not to be true on such grounds, we make appeal to a form of words, such as 'The child is not cautious', to which 'true' will be supposed to apply in the straightforward way.

Conjunctions present an interesting case. In 'He accepted the post because he needed the money', it appears to be 'because' that gives the focal point of assent or dissent, and so what 'true' might endorse, despite its unpromising conjunctival, so non-verbal form. Since it can be negated, we have these two necessary poles. Thus, 'It was not because he needed the money that he accepted the post', or, in the same sense, 'He did not accept the post because he needed the money'. However, without denying this, I should wish to say that what is being negated is a qualified verbal phrase, not simply the verb 'accepted', but 'accepted because . . .'. Comparison and contrast with such cases is of importance when the negation of conditionals is being considered.

Given this attachment to that part of the sentence which is the focus of assertion, we see how 'true' compares with qualifiers such as 'possible' and 'probable', and we also see how nothing may have been said if there is in fact no predicate or other appropriate term with which it can connect. So, for instance, failing indication of a further form of words featuring a more specific predicate, 'This statement is true' does not itself constitute a statement which can be described as 'true'. We may hesitate to speak of it as 'meaningless', given that we have a combination of perfectly meaningful words which can in more auspicious circumstances be said to express a truth or a falsehood, but there is certainly a sense in which the statement—if we can allow that description to stand—is not true, does not express a truth. However, switching now to the still more notorious 'This statement is not true', in speaking of this as 'not true' we do not license the inference that it is accordingly not true that the statement is, as it states, not true—and hence that it is accordingly true. This use of 'not true' does not presume that anything at all has been said, that we have a form of words which, in these conditions, makes any sense at all—and in this it is liable to diverge from 'false'. Given the way in which the threatened contradiction is scotched, before indeed the argument is even under way, it would be fanciful in the extreme to conclude that a definition of the English word 'true' must, if it is couched in English, lead to inconsistency—though theories of truth and meaning have been built on such flights of fancy.

The way in which 'true' endorses an assertion might suggest a definition of 'true' as 'assertible', or 'can be said'. If correct, such a definition would explain much. So, asking whether it can be said that P perhaps presumes to about the right degree that it *has* been said that P, and the impersonal 'it can be said' seems to capture all that is strictly implied in this latter respect by 'it is true'. We can explain how adding 'is true' to the citation of a proposition, P, is tantamount to asserting P: to say 'P is true' is, on this account, to say 'P is assertible', which clearly does have the required implication—as well as being equally odd as a piece of English. The account can also cope with such contexts as 'what he said was true', contexts where the total disappearance of 'true', as required by the redundancy theorist, becomes an embarrassment. And what is it that true statements have in common? They are all, of course, assertible. The awkwardness of combining 'true' with guesses or thoughts now receives some explanation, and the aptitude of 'true' for incorporation into certain speech acts—typically that of acknowledging—is now seen as a consequence of the meaning of the word.

However, the fit is far from perfect. There does appear to be sufficient distance between 'That can be said' and 'That is true' for the latter to be offered as a ground for the former—or at least we might appeal to the latter in specifying the relevant interpretation of the more general form of words with 'can'. More important, we have a simple divergence of qualifications appropriate to the one but not the other. Assertibility can be assertibility by someone, but not truth, and differences between such pairs as 'That can be said without fear of contradiction' and 'That is true without fear of contradiction' underline what is in any event obvious enough, namely, that there is nothing as explicit as a verb like 'say' or 'assert' buried in 'true'. The speaker is not to the fore, but it is more a matter of his words *holding* or *applying*. Here we note that 'can be said' must be a matter of 'can be said on the basis of the applicability of the words' rather than 'on the basis of being in a position to say'. However, it remains true that 'it can be said' sometimes gives the neatest paraphrase of 'it is true', especially with respect to subjectless uses of the phrase, as in 'It is true that there are other possibilities', or 'There are, it is true, other possibilities'.

My objection to the correspondence theory related to the requirement that the second term of the relation be 'in the world', an objection based on a consideration of the behaviour of, chiefly, 'fact', along with that of associated clausal and participial constructions. But are we now perhaps moving towards some point-by-point correspondence between a true proposition and various non-linguistic correlates? The role of the phrase which 'true' endorses can be described as that of *holding* or *holding of, applying* or *applying to,* or indeed of *fitting,* to take a term with echoes of correspondence, but in 'The cautious child remained on the pavement', the intended fit will simply be of the predicate, 'remained on the pavement', to what is picked out by the subject, 'the cautious child', not a fit of predicate to property in parallel to the relation of subject term to individual, as the suggestion might imply, nor of the sentence to a fact. If we can speak of correspondence, it will be in such a way that we are not required to convert nonnames to names, whether with respect to parts of the sentence or to the sentence as a whole.

Where does the redundancy theory now stand? With such a sentence as 'If it is Tuesday, then it is true that the office is closed', it is held that omission of 'it is true that' makes for no significant difference in what is asserted, though since the two forms are not completely interchangeable in their use, it is allowed that 'true' makes a contribution to be explained in terms of stylistic or other incidental nuances. This leads to a concern with the allusion to another's statement, an allusion which underlies such acts as those of endorsing and acknowledging which may be thought to give point to the incorporation of 'true'.

The involvement of another's statement can certainly be put down to the presence of 'true' rather than to any more general feature of the clausal construction: in saying 'It is clear that we have been badly advised' or 'It is possible that we have been badly advised', there is not the same presumption as with 'It is true that we have been badly advised', not the presumption that someone has alleged that we have been badly advised, or might at least be thought likely to do so. But what more precisely is the source of this presumption? Its absence with 'it is clear' and 'it is possible' is understandable, in that there is point to adding these phrases even if no one else's statement is being contemplated, but it is less easy to see what end is served by adding 'it is true' unless the statement in question is envisaged as made on another occasion. If it is now being put forward for the first time, and not so as to anticipate another's statement, 'it is true' does seem to be just a superfluous addition.

In fact it is possible to imagine other considerations which give point to this addition, but even when it is in place only if something more than the speaker's own assertion is involved, the suggestion of a statement to be endorsed is not a factor deserving of a significant part in an account of the meaning of 'true'. The sense of 'true' is to be explained in terms of what it says with respect to a statement or proposition, whereas an adequate explanation of how the relevant suggestion is generated can be given along the lines just indicated. I have allowed that the effect of adding 'is true' can be to convert a proposition into an assertion, but in passing from 'P is true' to P some appeal is made to the meaning of 'true', to what it implies for the associated proposition, and observations concerning the contribution of 'true' in the dimension we have been considering are powerless to provide a justification for this transition. Again, we may grant that '"F" is true of A' and 'A is F' are logical equivalents, but 'true' is not eliminable through being, as it were, a superfluous term which may simply be erased. With 'false' the point is even plainer: it is because we understand 'false' as we do that we can appreciate that the passage from 'It is false that the dealer reneged' to 'The dealer did not renege' is legitimate; indeed, the passage from the former to the latter surely involves an argument, however minor.

How much damage does this argument do to the redundancy theory? It does not destroy the claim that P and 'It is true that P' are essentially equivalent, but it does highlight the theory's failure to clarify the meaning of 'true'. Furthermore, there is no question of denying that 'is true' may affirm something of a proposition, any more than we might deny the possibility of a genuine predication with respect to 'That description is correct' or 'The earlier report was false'. As we saw, the attempt to avoid a predicational role for 'true' takes the theory in the direction of an analysis more appropriate to 'is so' than to 'is true': one who utters 'That is so' in response to an assertion endorses any reference-cum-predication in that assertion, but, despite the use of 'that', perhaps does not add a further reference-cum-predication with the assertion as subject. Sometimes 'true' furnishes no more than an abbreviatory device, a stand-in for assertions which is dispensable at the cost of nothing more than unwanted repetition, but it enjoys a clear predicational use as well.

Does the redundancy theorist's appeal to the general form of proposition enable him to give some sort of account of the meaning of 'true'? This will be hard to claim so long as we are presented with piecemeal analyses of individual sentences, with no indication of a general formula to be applied in new cases, yet if we do have such a formula it is not clear that the redundancy theory is still with us. It will certainly have come a long way if it is, and while we may allow that a phrase like 'things are as . . . states' can furnish an account of the sense of '. . . is true' which will explain much of what is left untouched by a mere declaration of redundancy, in offering such an elucidation the redundancy theorist is surely staying close to a more conventional scheme of definition: what he presents us with is a paraphrase to be considered on its merits like any other, not a defense of anything as radical as the *eliminability* of 'true'; indeed, it appears to be precisely because 'true' proves resistant to its own removal that such a paraphrase is called for. It is not 'true' that has been eliminated in any significant sense—just anything distinctive of a redundancy theory.

Though I do not wish to press the objection strongly, the behaviour of performatives can also be cited against the redundancy theory. To add to earlier remarks, we note that phrases to which this label is attached may be of two kinds. As well as what we might call 'strict' performatives, where to say 'I *V*' is thereby to *V*, as with 'I apologize' and 'I concede', we have phrases which serve to make explicit the speech act involved in the utterance of accompanying words, as with 'I shall not, I promise, let you down'; here 'I promise' compares closely with verbal phrases which may be appended to an *oratio recta* rendering of a person's words. When discussing psychological verbs I indicated that the application of truth in connection with such performatives as 'I apologize' was only after the event, and not in such a way that the speaker had to consider whether he had misrepresented anything in using the performative, supposing him to understand what he says. Phrases in the second category, here illustrated by 'I promise', may be comparable in this respect, but to the extent that truth and falsity have a direct application to them—as direct as with 'I repeat' in 'I shall not, I repeat, let you down'— to that extent we might well not wish to regard them as strictly performatives. However, this still leaves a number of verbal phrases to which the notions of assertion and reassertion apply readily enough, but without a complementary role for 'true', and this does seem to point to a deficiency in the redundancy theory.

In so far as it holds, the equivalence between 'It is true that *P*' and *P* provides a *test* for any proposed interpretation of 'true', and indeed suggests the beginnings of an analysis: 'it is true' surely must convey in more general terms what is made specific in the particular statement. And here the suggestion of 'things are as . . . states', or even '. . . represents things as they are', seems near the mark. We can reasonably set our sights only on a deductive equivalent, rather than a strict synonym, and in these terms what we have is both plausible and, it would seem, at a safe enough distance from anything that might qualify as a correspondence theory in any objectionable sense. I say that 'represents things as they are' is harmless; indeed, it has the advantage of focusing on the *aim* of assertions, of making clearer the kind of success that 'true' acknowledges. When I assert *P* I purport to represent things as they are, and when I say *P* is true I say that *P* does represent things as they are.

However, if we wish to keep as close as possible to the sense of 'true', then we should perhaps stay with paraphrases in terms of *holding* or *applying,* understood in a sufficiently broad way as to cover such subjectless sentences as 'It is dark'. To take this a stage further, we may say that the kind of correctness involved in truth is that in which a word or phrase is said to be a word or phrase *for* the activity, state, or whatever, in question. And what does that involve? If we say that it is simply a matter of how people speak with respect to such things, in such circumstances, it will be objected that the qualification, 'when they speak the truth', is called for. This objection is one to resist. Very roughly, a word becomes the word for something, *s*, so long as it is a dependable sign for *s*, and frequency or regularity of occurrence can be a sufficient guarantee of this status.

Needless to say, this is very crude, but I hope to have indicated a starting-point that takes us away from both correspondence and redundancy, and I am confident that the notion of expectations induced by regularities of usage is central to both meaning and truth. The next chapter may help bear this out.

9

TRUTH AND MEANING

Meaning is a notion that has been with us from the outset, intruding itself directly or indirectly into all the issues discussed, and it is now time to make it the subject of a more explicit investigation. It is a notion which, despite its ubiquity and indispensability, is not assured of a warm welcome from some philosophers, yet any attempt at disowning it could only be a resolution to forgo use of the *word*; distinctions of meaning, for instance, would have to continue to be acknowledged in any rational discourse, even if we refrained from labelling them as such. None the less, an explicit invocation of the term is for some a matter for apology, if not outright avoidance, this being in large part the result of an uncritical application of primitive models to the word, models which have led philosophers to take for granted that the word brings in train entities of a thoroughly undesirable character.

This area of debate constitutes the rather silly side of the subject, a side which the earlier elucidation of the behaviour of abstract terms and psychological verbs allows us to deal with fairly promptly. The more challenging questions, though not entirely unrelated, concern the connection with truth, a connection that is quick to emerge when we take up the notions of use and tone, and which we shall begin to explore after some of the misgivings concerning meaning have been despatched.

47. Meanings and entities

Given that the question, 'What is the meaning of *w*?', is so readily interchanged with the simple 'What does *w* mean?', it is surprising that doubts have seemingly not troubled those who perceive so clearly and distinctly that talk of the meaning of a word is perforce talk of some entity. We might at least expect that such equivalences, there on the surface of the language, would encourage the view that any commitment which the noun might carry can be of no great consequence, but their neglect suggests a determination to find fault with the notion at all costs. Among the words so far discussed, the affinities of 'meaning' are fairly obviously with 'height', 'age', 'price', 'weight', and the like: it follows similar verbs—'know', 'learn', 'determine'—and in such contexts it may give way to a clause in the way just indicated: to know the meaning of 'procryptic' is to know what 'procryptic' means—not to have made the acquaintance of some entity; to use the received terminology, the 'what' here is an interrogative, not a relative pronoun. Compare the paraphrase of 'knowing the weight of the boulder' as 'knowing what the boulder weighs', and other like paraphrases of nouns which answer to middle verbs—verbs, that is, with complements which, while necessary, cannot be made subject of a passive (cf. Stampe [1968], a rare instance of a thorough and perceptive examination of the peculiarities of 'meaning').

The common breakdown of 'meaning' into an interrogative clause makes for the appropriateness of *question* as the term which anyone in search of the kind of 'entity' associated with 'meaning' should light upon. If, for instance, you and I are discussing the meaning of 'true', then we are both discussing the same *question*. This question could be specified as the question of what the meaning of 'true' is, with the possibility that within such a specification we have a designation of some entity on the part of the noun 'meaning', but given the further reduction without loss to 'what "true" means', it would seem that 'question' is the nearest thing to an entitative term that is in any way involved here. However, this is not to say that every use of 'meaning' dissolves into a combination of the verb with interrogative 'what'. To say that a word has two meanings, for instance, is not to say anything thus analysable. It is true that the noun consistently paraphrases as 'means' plus other terms—so 'has two meanings' as 'means two different things'—which is enough to keep 'meaning' in the company of phrases which take their origins and consequent behaviour from verbal or adjectival forms—or can at least be thus treated—but we must look to other features of the word's behaviour if we are to confirm its non-referential role.

If our paraphrase leaves us with 'means something', or 'means two different things', we have of course these noun phrases to consider as possible points at which a referent or referents could make an entry. To meet that threat, we might hope to show that 'means' is not here truly transitive, any more than 'costs', 'weighs', and other middle verbs; however, we have already pointed out that intransitivity is not a sure guide to the role of a following noun phrase. We do not pass from 'The car turned the corner' to 'The corner was turned by the car', but that does not mean that 'the corner' does not function referentially. Generally speaking, the passive is not favoured if the person or thing signified by the subject cannot be said to have acted upon the relevant object—cf. our earlier example of 'The teacher shook his head' and contrast with 'The teacher shook the frightened boy'. Similarly, while we should not naturally rewrite 'I mean the one on the table' as 'The one on the table is meant by me', this does not prevent us from construing 'the one on the table' referentially. We must consider directly whether, in such a phrase as 'means two different things', we have a variable for referential terms— and if so, whether this is of any consequence. In the most common cases, as with '"just" means both "fair" and "only"', the answer appears to be negative: there is neither reference on the part of the quoted words, nor indeed are the words themselves what 'just' means. We shall take this further shortly.

With sentences like 'The meaning of "olid" is "fetid"', we do not have an identity of the right form for an application of the principle of extensionality—to forget the one is not to forget the other, for instance. Of course, we know already that the second term of this apparent identity does not have the required role, so we must again show directly that 'the meaning of "olid"' is not a referential unit. And it is clear enough that the role of this phrase is not to identify something in the way that I require for reference, that it is a matter of *stating* the meaning of a word, and not of further specifying something initially identified as the meaning of 'olid'. Here the rephrasal as '"olid" means "fetid"' shows plainly enough the evaporation of any seeming reference.

If we are to find a referential occurrence of 'the meaning of w', it will be in a context in which the apparent identity does not turn out to be merely a 'stating', but where it is combined with a term of the same type, as in 'The meaning of "tiro" is the same as the meaning of "novice"'. But here again the wrong behaviour is in evidence: it does not follow that if a man knows the meaning of 'tiro' then he knows the meaning of 'novice', or that a change in the one makes for a change in the other. The meaning of 'tiro' is not the same *meaning* as the meaning of 'novice'; the words simply mean the same. If any noun is to join with 'same' in the identity it will be 'question', though at the cost of making the identity false, the meaning of 'tiro' not being the same question as the meaning of 'novice'. Any identity in these terms relates not to items designated by 'the meaning of . . .', but to items specified in the gap therein, the appropriate truths being such as 'The meaning of the definite article in English is the same (question) as the meaning of "the"'.

If 'something' in 'means something' does duty for a word in quotes, it is not a variable for a referential term. However, this is not the only construction possible. Consider 'By "metallurgy" is meant the science of metals'. It would be more natural to suspend any referential use of 'the science of metals' and to enclose it in quotes, but there is nothing incoherent about this referential use. Even less natural, but not unintelligible, is 'The meaning of "metallurgy" is the science of metals'. This is like a sentence in Austin's translation of Frege's *The Foundations of Arithmetic,* where he speaks of 'the words hard or heavy or red, which have for their meanings properties of external things' (Frege [1884], § 21). So, then, a meaning can be something as unexpected as a science? Or, we now know that some meanings are properties? The meaning of 'metallurgy' indeed *is* a science, in the sense that a certain science is what is meant by the word, but 'the meaning of "metallurgy"' does not designate something which can be further classified as 'the science of metals'. Sciences are not describable as 'meanings', so that one might reason: 'This science has proved fruitful, therefore at least one meaning has proved fruitful'. The various things meant include sciences, gases, diseases, properties, games, activities, etc., but we do not identify the meanings of the relevant words with such things. Roughly speaking, there is no problem of the 'nature of meanings', since over and above things meant, which can be as many and various as you wish, there are no such things.

As a parallel to a statement of meaning we might take a statement of an aim, as 'His aim is a victory over the opposition'. In specifying the person's aim we are specifying what he is aiming at, his objective; we are not describing as 'a victory over the opposition' something which 'his aim' selects as a subject of this and other predicates. Likewise, talk of desires, ambitions, and needs is frequently talk of what is signified by the object of the correlative verb, though without quite the same scope for confusion as with 'meaning', since we commonly specify desires and the like by saying that they are *to* or *for* something, as 'His one wish was for a house in the country'. We can say 'His one desire was a house in the country', but no one is going to interpret this as asserting an impossible identity between the affective and the physical. However, there is the possibility of some such confusion when it is asked whether a desire can be the cause of one's action, given that the relevant desire cannot, it is supposed, be independently identified, i.e. cannot be identified except as the kind of desire that causes that type of action. There is a risk of confusion here in that, since identification of a desire is most readily understood in terms of a specification of what is desired—not a feeling, but something which often does not even exist—we are at a great remove from identification of a possible cause. If causes are to be found here, it is as *desirings*.

The analogy between 'meaning' and 'fact' is also worth mentioning. All sorts of things can be said to be facts—conditions of cats, states of affairs, declines of empires—but not in such a sense that we could say: those are the species of entities into which facts divide, some facts being, like some meanings, states of affairs, other facts being, like other meanings, features of things. And, just as it would be quite absurd to deny that there were any facts—in the sense in which such a denial would ordinarily be understood—so too it would be quite absurd to 'reject meanings', on the grounds that we could formulate more economical hypotheses, or that meanings were entities serving no genuine need. Any talk which involves 'meanings as entities' in any unacceptable sense is to be rejected, but it is not our ordinary everyday talk; that is not to be rejected, and in particular not to be rejected on the grounds that it has shortcomings when considered as embodying an explanatory hypothesis. As misconstrued by philosophers, so that meanings appear to be in the offing as entities (of some single general kind), the relevant language does not get as far as presenting any sort of hypothesis, extravagant or economical. As with number, so here talk of 'postulation', 'hypotheses', and the rest of the misplaced jargon, points up a fundamental failure to grasp what is involved in the notion of meaning.

The examples of meaning just discussed were a shade unnatural. We customarily use the noun only when we have two synonymous expressions, as in 'The meaning of "serendipity" is "the faculty of making happy and unexpected discoveries by accident"', where we also place quotes around the definiens, or make use of some similar device, as italics, or a colon after 'is', in order to abstract from any particular use of the definiens, to give a statement of meaning in a suitably general form. However, while such abstraction may often be appropriate, it is not obligatory with everything which might be called a statement of meaning. With the noun 'meaning' there is a preference for an associated expression which is detached from any referential use by the introduction of quotes or some such device, but 'means', as we have seen, is more widely used. As further examples, consider 'By "chlorophyll" is meant the colouring matter of leaves'—which does not necessarily imply that the meaning of 'chlorophyll' is 'the colouring matter of leaves'—or 'By "the magic years" is meant the years from 4 to 11'. Again, we can often indicate what is meant by a word by drawing attention to something which can in some sense be described as its referent, as in 'By "slicing" I mean striking the ball like this'. Here there need be no significant loss of generality, since the criterion of identity for movements is commonly such that if I can say that by 'slicing' I mean this movement, demonstrating as I speak, I can truly say that the selfsame movement is what another would mean by the word. The criterion of identity for 'this movement' is, or can be, such that another person can make the same movement; accordingly, I can offer such a performance as a rough indication of the meaning of the word without having to resolve a problem about unwanted reference to a particular instance. In general, the need for quotes or any similar device becomes less pressing as we move away from count nouns, which generally have a use only in conjunction with a further determination, such as an article, and on to words which, like mass terms, are suitably indifferent to the particular, as in 'By "industrial action" is meant industrial *in*action'.

The closer 'means' comes to 'refers to', the easier, perhaps, its role is to grasp. With 'By "glucose" is meant grape-sugar' or 'A "ceceril" means a letter *c* with a cedilla under it' we go some way to relating words with their corresponding worldly items. By contrast, such a sentence as '*neidig* means "envious"' seems to keep us entirely within language, generating the feeling that the meaning of the word is somehow elusive, ineffable: the best we can do is offer a word with the same meaning, but this meaning is never more directly indicated. We shall take this question up again shortly.

48. Meaning and use

To know what is meant by w, how w is understood, it would seem appropriate to enquire after the kind of *use* to which w is put. However, because of their differing grammars, any simple equation of meaning and use is to be ruled out, as substitution of 'use' for 'meaning' in such a context as 'He thought that the meaning of *coup de grâce* was "lawnmower"' soon reveals. The incongruity here is reminiscent of that which afflicts that other celebrated slogan, 'The meaning of a statement is its method of verification'. This makes little sense as it stands, but has to be considered as elliptical for something like 'The meaning of a statement is determined by its method of verification'. We could similarly speak of use as determining meaning, but if we seek an identity we must move to something like the clause, 'how w is used'. So, it could be claimed, to know the meaning of w is to know how w is used.

The appeal of *use* has been in large part due to the lesser degree to which it encourages a conception of meanings as entities, and it is still in place to mention this merit, since ways of thinking which are wedded to the wrong view are still encountered. To take one current example, consider how it is that one description, such as 'nun', may be inconsistent with another, such as 'abbot'. Realizing that the conflict has, of course, to do with the incompatible meanings of the two words, some have suggested that a 'componential' analysis will explain this, an analysis in which the meanings of the words are represented as combinations of different features, such as *animate, concrete,* and so forth. In this instance the contradiction would be traced to the inconsistency between the features +*male* and −*male*. There is a danger here of an excessively rigid account of meaning, but what is said is respectable enough, in so far as it isolates the source of the conflict. However, it is sometimes associated with a mistaken picture concerning what has been done—as if meanings were entities compounded of different features, some of which, like incongruent segments of a spatial object, could not be fitted to one another. Replacing this by an appeal to use, where this is not seen as something determined by or reflecting independently given meanings, 'semantic objects', puts the matter in a saner perspective. Since, too, differences in use are differences of which we may become apprised, any threatened occult or incommunicable conception of meaning—'mental semantic objects'—is discouraged. Furthermore, the notion of use appears to open up more fruitful possibilities for explanations of meaning. As already mentioned, the formula, 'The meaning of w is v', seems to keep us within the confines of language, but a specific statement of how a word is used perhaps offers some hope of an analysis of its meaning which does not presuppose an understanding of some synonymous expression.

The disadvantages of an appeal to use emerge most sharply at the point where differences in use threaten not to be matched by differences in meaning. Wittgenstein appears to have employed a conception of meaning in which it is highly sensitive to any variation in use, so that practically any change in the latter was reflected by a change in the former. However, our ordinary understanding of the notions leaves room for a constancy on the side of meaning despite certain fluctuations or variations in use. Thus, one common respect in which we can speak of a difference in the latter is with regard to a difference on the part of the users, as when we have two words identical in meaning, but one is characteristically employed

by one group of people, the other by another group: older
people may speak of a 'gramophone needle' where the young
speak of a 'stylus'; doctors speak of 'cardiac arrest' where
the layman speaks of a 'heart attack', and Americans use 'side-
walk' where the English say 'pavement' and New Zealanders
'footpath', differences which do count as differences in use
but which are not necessarily associated with any differences
in meaning. Again, think of the differences between standard,
colloquial, poetic, and other specialized uses. What separates
'broke and boozed' from 'penniless and drunk' is not a difference in meaning, but we can say that the former represents
a more colloquial use than the latter. Similarly with rhyming
slang, as 'Aristotle' and 'pride and joy' for 'bottle' and 'boy'
respectively, and with 'over' and 'before' as against their more
literary equivalents, 'o'er' and 'ere', or the standard 'I think'
and 'dog' as against the archaic 'methinks' and the baby-talk
'bow-wow'. There are many other examples which make the
point.

   In some of these cases we may hesitate to speak of sameness
of meaning, given that for one reason or another we do not
treat the two words as completely interchangeable, but for
nouns what appears to be the dominant factor is identity of
application. That is, we look for constancy on the side of the
things of which the word is used, not requiring so urgently, if
at all, any constancies on the side of the users or the contexts
of use: 'garbologist' may be a more high-sounding term than
'dustman', but they really mean the same thing.

   In narrowing down the relevant aspect of use in this way
we to some extent detract from the significance of the
notion in an account of meaning. What is important is not so
much the notion of how w is used, but the narrower notion
of what w is used of, a formula which brings us back to the
kind of semantic notion, not so far removed from that of
reference, which an invocation of use may well be intended
to supplant. What this suggests is that it will be the specific
qualifications that embody anything of substance in an analysis in terms of use, the appropriateness of this notion reflecting no more than the fact that words are among those items
which can be said to have a role, to connect with intentions,
a consideration which, given the variety of terms for which

this is true, is hardly pitched at the most useful level of gene-rality. To take an example of a different kind, 'A nod means assent' can be rendered as 'A nod is used to indicate assent', but to say this rather than 'A nod indicates assent' simply emphasizes the subjection of nods to human agency and pur-pose; it is surely 'indicate' as much as 'is used' that conveys the specific sense here of 'means', which is as we should expect in view of the continuity between the use of 'means' in connection with human agency and its use with respect to inanimate phenomena, as with 'Those clouds mean rain'.

As I have intimated, different overtones affecting putative synonyms may make us reluctant to speak of exact identity of meaning—a reluctance which is felt in proportion to the extent that we can associate different intentions as standard accompaniments to the use of the words. And, even if we have identity of application, two terms may contrast in the dif-ferent exploitable possibilities which their component parts offer. To make a point which we shall expand later, 'garbolo-gist' and 'dustman' each have, because of their structures, affinities with different groups of words, affinities which may make more natural an extension of usage of the one in a certain direction than of the other. The notion of sameness of mean-ing will perhaps tolerate some divergence in factors which do not make for a difference in range of application, but if there is a marked difference in tone, for instance, we may be unhappy to speak of strict synonymy: a translation which rendered any indelicate language by forms of words which would be totally acceptable to maiden aunts and church dignitaries would not be considered entirely accurate.

Even here, however, it might simply be said that accuracy requires more than synonymy, a good translation being true to nuances of tone, and so forth. At all events, while there are evidently still more compelling reasons for regarding it as in need of supplementation, what appears to be to the fore at this preliminary stage is the notion of identity of application. In many cases, though not all, this is equivalent to taking sub-stitutability *salva veritate* as a test of synonymy, either ap-proach looking to a constancy on the side of things of which a word is used, with a possible disregard for differences in other dimensions. However, such differences are worth considering further before we deal with the problems posed by the more central notion, and, as I have indicated, there is no shortage of forms of language which might be examined in this connection—colloquialisms, obscenities, neologisms, children's talk, officialese, slang, technical jargon, and so on. So, I may be diffident about using an obscene phrase, but not on the grounds that it misrepresented or misdescribed, not because truth is at risk; I may feel compelled to agree that the phrase fits, even if it is not one that I should volunteer, and even if I disagree I may still be reluctant to voice my disagreement in the terms in question. In very many cases where we find such a contrast with a standard word or phrase we have, as I say, differences on the part of the users side by side with constancies on the part of the things of which words of the two kinds are used, the non-standard word being associated with a group of people characterized by, for instance, a certain set of attitudes. Use of 'fab' or 'spiffing', say, threatens to brand a speaker as one of a certain social class, while the phrase 'like, man' places its speaker in a class of a rather different kind, and it is this general association that accounts for the overtones of the words rather than, necessarily, any attitude specific to the use of either. Again, compare 'the fuzz' with 'the police'. It is no doubt because a person does not wish to be grouped along with the relevant class—those who have a certain set of beliefs and attitudes, including a failure to be impressed by the police force—that he will use the neutral 'police' rather than 'fuzz'. The word is locatable in a sublanguage, and it is through this more general connection that it acquires the particular character it has, though in this instance we have the further complication of humorous overtones contributed by other senses of the word.

Transferred or metaphorical uses of words are both frequent and important. Consider the use to which combinations with 'rub' are put in the sentences 'Be careful not to rub him up the wrong way', 'I should like some of his expertise to rub off on me' and 'I admit I was foolish—don't rub it in'. An account of the meaning here of 'rub it in' might connect 'rub', not with any bodily action, but with the notion of dwelling or enlarging upon one of a person's less fortunate deeds or attributes. However, the word has this other setting, and the transferred use may bring the physical action to mind. That association may be said to define something of the 'tone' of an expression: it is not a condition whose fulfilment the speaker standardly intends to convey, but the association confers a certain character on the word, often humorous.

The above observations have some significance in explaining how the notion of *expressing an attitude* may be realized—taking 'attitude' in the broadest of senses. This is a notion that is commonly invoked in accounts of the tone of certain words, especially value terms, yet it is not always clear just how the attitude connects with the word. My suggestion is that in some cases we should look to an association between a word and the attitudes in general of its users, rather than—as with a word like 'nigger'—make the connection between the word and an attitude specific to it, or attempt to incorporate the attitude in a statement of the truth conditions of judgements in which the word occurs. Possession of the relevant attitude is not a condition for the correct application of the word, though if I lack the attitude in question it may be a mystery why I use the word; after all, if the association with the typical users and their attitudes is one of which I am aware and of which others will suppose me to be aware, why do I speak in this way when the attitude is one I should wish to disown? If I use such a word to deceive, I succeed in this through leading my hearers to infer that I have the attitude that goes with the normal use of the word, much as I might give a misleading impression of medical expertise by appropriating a technical term normally only heard in the mouths of those who genuinely do have the knowledge.

If it is said that a word is used to express an attitude or to commend or to guide choices, it is appropriate to ask *how* it succeeds in doing or is equipped to do such things, how the word works. Words do not fulfil their roles by magic, but there will be some explanation of how a given word comes to have the powers it has, an explanation which will generally involve connecting the word with something else, rather than appealing to those of its properties which, like its phonetic characteristics, are intrinsic to it. With words of moral appraisal, one obvious possibility is that a word is able to do what it does—guide choices or commend, let us say—simply in virtue of describing a trait or form of behaviour which, like honesty, kindness, or consideration, is generally valued by people. In such cases a full picture of the word is built up by supplementing an account of its meaning by an indication of the place that what it describes occupies among objects of human concern. Considerations of this latter kind need not, however, enter into an account of the word's meaning, let alone define a subspecies of meaning, 'prescriptive' meaning, or whatever.

A difference in use which is not one in meaning is likely to be a difference on the side of the users, but, as the example with 'rub' suggests, this is not inevitable. A more general division is that between what a word is a sign *for* and what it is a sign *of*. There may be much that we can infer from the use of a word, much that it is a reliable sign *of*, but this may have little if anything to do with the condition which defines the word's meaning, with what it is a sign *for*. The distinction is one of some importance in questions concerning the implications of what is said. Thus, if a person utters words that are declarative in form, as 'There has been an accident near the bridge', we shall normally suppose that he understands what he says, that he means it, and that he takes himself to be warranted in speaking in these terms. However, while we have, in his giving voice to these words, good inductive evidence for these conclusions, they are no part of what the words state or imply; there is no actual contradiction if he couples the utterance with a relevant expression of disbelief, nor any question of paraphrasing his words by 'I am in a position to assert that there has been an accident near the bridge'. The intuitionists are the most notable offenders on this point. Similarly, if I say 'It is probable that *P*', I do not as much as say: 'I am not in a position to assert *P*', but I give people to understand, by my use of the qualification 'probable', that I find myself in this lesser position. Again we have a condition that is commonly and mistakenly read into the content of the assertion.

49. Meaning and tone

Sameness of meaning, I have suggested, relates centrally to sameness on the part of the things of which two words are used, to which they are applied, but this supposes that we can speak in terms of using a word *of* something, and that is far from being invariably true. Furthermore, are we to say that a word which lacks any application is thereby meaningless? that two such words have (vacuously) the same meaning? Can it be true in any sense that identity of application makes for sameness of meaning? What of the notorious 'creature with heart' and 'creature with kidneys'?

With the bulk of nouns, adjectives, and verbs, we can speak in terms of *being used of, holding of,* or *being true of,* and so at least the possibility arises of considering sameness of meaning in terms of sameness of application. The problem becomes most acute with other parts of speech, such as prepositions and conjunctions. Here the natural strategy is to turn to a larger unit within which the troublesome expression can be incorporated and which as a whole can, in some sense, be said to have application. For prepositions, the sense in question will be that in which a phrase containing the term is truly affirmable of something. Thus, there are recognizable circumstances in which the egg is in the cup or the car in the garage, and we could accordingly say that a preposition had the same sense as 'in' if replacement of 'in' by that expression in such phrases as 'in the cup' or 'in the garage' resulted in phrases with the same application. Other prepositions, 'of', 'to', 'from', and so forth, could be treated similarly, and with conjunctions the hope might be that a truth-functional interpretation could be successfully pursued.

Leaving aside the more difficult parts of speech, what we have so far in our account of meaning is a combination of Wittgenstein and Frege. Knowing the meaning of a word is a matter of knowing its use, but in the sense, often, of knowing what it is used of; a matter of knowing its application, and, consequently, it would seem, of knowing when it is used or usable in assertions and denials, the framework within which the specific, differential character of a word is determined. In eliminating the unwanted aspects of use and considering only those which relate to sameness and difference on the side of the things of which a word is used, we fasten on bare truth as the determinative factor.

That is, sameness of meaning looks to be essentially a matter of preservation of truth value, and the meaning of a word a matter of the contribution which it makes to the truth or falsity of a sentence.

Classical predicate logic gives expression to a certain uniform conception of the way words work: sentence connectives aside, it is appropriate to terms having the form of predicates and which at any occurrence are either truly or falsely affirmable. The difference between one such term and another will reside in the different distributions of truth values which can be associated with either, which means: in the different contributions made to the truth values of sentences within which they occur. A purely truth-functional construal takes care of sentence connectives, and Russell's theory of descriptions is an attempt to bring descriptive phrases into this scheme, breaking such a phrase down into components which have true and false poles, components which can become, unlike proper names, explicit foci of negation. Although the system does find a place for names, some have wished to eliminate them in favour of predicates, predicates also being called upon to take over the role of adverbs, as when a suitable rephrasal enables 'effortlessly' to give way to 'effortless', or 'well' to 'good'.

If a word occurs as the focus of an assertion or a denial in various utterances on various occasions, we can come to see what it covers and what it excludes, to appreciate its 'differential sign value', as we might put it. The appeal to truth in explanations of meaning just is an appeal to such occurrence within declarative sentences, rather than in imperatives or interrogatives. Certain words, however, do not enter into a sentence in such a way that they are truly or falsely affirmable, even in the way suggested for prepositions. Examples of such recalcitrant expressions are, in certain of their meanings, 'which', 'why', 'well', 'yes', 'still', and 'however'. That such words force us to make some dissociation between having meaning and contributing to truth conditions is obvious enough; what is critical is our decision as to how in consequence they are to be handled.

Consider 'however', as we find it in 'The Financial Times index dropped six points. However, the pound had a good day'. Presence or absence of 'however' does not affect the truth value of the sentence in which it occurs, so the word appears to fall outside Frege's category of *sense*—asking, perhaps, to be put in the category of *tone* or *colouring*. This, I suggest, would be a mistake, a mistake which comes about through concentrating on the notion of truth, appropriate to the larger, propositional unit, when a broader notion of *appropriateness* is called for. Even though the former connection is lacking with 'however', we can still indicate when precisely the word is in place, when it is correctly or incorrectly used, and this gives us essentially the same type of explanation—in terms of the two contrasting poles—of its meaning. Thus, we can say that use of 'however' is appropriate or not, correct or incorrect, depending on whether or not what follows it constitutes a countervailing consideration to what preceded. In this way we bring the word into a pattern which I regard as basic to having a meaning, the pattern of a word in association with a condition which those who understand the word will thereby understand it to convey or communicate.

I say that 'however' is appropriately or correctly used when the condition mentioned obtains, but what is this more general notion of appropriateness that somehow avoids being truth? That is all. Use of the word is appropriate just in so far as the associated condition does in fact obtain: *S* can be a sign that a certain condition obtains, or is believed to obtain, without constituting an assertion to that effect; what is important, if the given condition is to define the meaning or *S*, is that *S* should be a sign *for* rather than merely a sign *of* that condition. It is true that for such a word we cannot test for synonymy by considering whether a putative synonym has an identical effect on truth value, but what must be considered is whether or not we have an association with the same condition.

As I have hinted, I take a different turning at this point from what might be expected from Frege. I say this on the basis of his treatment of the contrast between 'and' and 'but', a contrast which I believe confirms my own approach and which shows the appeal to tone to be misplaced. We do not use these terms interchangeably, of course, but when 'and' connects two clauses, as in 'Summer came and the days lengthened', we can replace it by 'but' and the appeal to variation in truth value is not sufficiently discriminating to bring out the difference in meaning induced. And, needless to say, a difference in meaning it is, even if on Frege's characterization of sense we have sameness, and are led to invoke tone or colouring in seeking to characterize the difference. In his discussion of sense and tone, Michael Dummett sets to one side Frege's inappropriate explanation of tone in terms of the propensity of the word to call up certain mental images, and fastens instead on the supposed distinction between asserting something and merely suggesting it: if what is merely suggested by a statement—as in the contrast suggested by 'but'—does not hold, the statement will not be false, but only inappropriate. Dummett observes that it is difficult *a priori* to find a place for such a distinction, for there being two different ways in which a statement might be factually incorrect, and he dismisses the attempt to give substance to the distinction in terms of examples such as that of 'but' (Dummett [1973], p. 86).

Frege characterizes the tone peculiar to 'but' by saying that the word hints at the existence of a contrast between what the second half of the sentence asserts and what you would expect, knowing the first half to be true. Dummett objects, on the grounds that this is too specific: the word 'but' does indeed hint that there is some contrast, relevant to the context, between the two halves of the sentence, but nothing more can, in general, be said about the kind of contrast hinted at. It is this indefiniteness of the contrast and the vagueness of the notion of relevance that stand in the way of proclaiming that the sentence is straightforwardly true or false and which lead us to suppose that a different notion, that of appropriateness, is required.

Part of the problem is still threatened in the use of the word 'hint' here, but in any event it would seem that the question of indefiniteness is not crucial. We might, after all, fasten on an expression which is more definite in the required respect, as 'although' or 'even though', and the problem would still be with us. Thus, if I say, 'He is coming to the dinner, but he is not very good at after-dinner speeches', there is indeed no necessity that the contrast should relate to the two clauses in the way Frege contends. I am not suggesting that there is anything unexpected in his unsuitability for this role, given that he is coming. However, if we shift to 'He is coming to the dinner, even though he is not very good at after-dinner speeches', the area of contrast is then drawn sufficiently narrowly; here the characterization which Frege offers for 'but' applies, the familiar demonstrative root 'th-' in 'though' and 'although' no doubt explaining the more specific involvement of the preceeding clause. The relevant indefiniteness is not with us in this case, but it is still in order to contrast the use of 'even though' with the corresponding explicit assertion: we do not as much as say that there is a contrast of the relevant kind, but one who understands 'even though' will correctly infer that we take there to be such, if we mean what we say.

The parallel here with definite descriptions and merely presupposed existence is particularly clear, and for a conjunction which provides a contrast in this respect we might turn to 'because'. The sentence, 'They fell because they were pushed', presents us with a straightforward falsehood if the second clause does not stand to the first in the right, reason-giving, relation; we have, correspondingly, an occurrence of the conjunction in which it is negatable: 'It was not because they were pushed that they fell'.

Many of the terms which we connect with correctness or appropriateness rather than truth have near relations in phrases which make the latter connection. So, 'however' appears to be a relic of a larger clause, 'please' is what now remains of 'If it please you', and adverbs like 'fortunately' and 'possibly' have corresponding adjectival phrases. When the adverbs are used we cannot express disagreement by means of a simple negation, but must use a more roundabout phrasing, possibly shifting to the adjectival form. So, to object in the relevant way to 'Perhaps he is at work', we may say 'There is no perhaps about it', and 'Fortunately, there is still time for them to get here' can be contradicted by 'There is nothing fortunate about that'.

Modal terms, such as 'possibly' and 'probably', are of interest here because of their possibly uncertain status—whether they make a contribution to truth conditions, or whether their use is to be appraised only as correct or appropriate. Consider the example of probability, where one of the main difficulties concerns verification. Are judgements of probability to be verified as we should verify a prediction? If not, what becomes of their seemingly empirical character, and where is their verification to be sought? According to Stephen Toulmin, to say 'I shall probably come' is to expressly avoid unreservedly committing myself; it is to make a guarded assertion (Toulmin [1958], chapter II). This account attracts the usual objections to a speech-act analysis—we are told what someone is up to in calling P probable, but of what it is for P to be thus describable we learn nothing. However, so long as Toulmin confines his analysis to the adverb, 'probably', he can perhaps turn aside such objections. For one thing, the non-assertive contexts thought to provide an obstacle to this style of analysis are not so readily invoked, the adverb sounding distinctly awkward in such a context as 'If you will probably be defeated, you would be advised to withdraw your wager'. Second, truth and falsity are often assigned to 'Probably P' as they would be to the simple P. Suppose someone is cutting an ordinary pack of playing cards and three succesive cuts have yielded three red cards, which have all been returned to the pack. If I say, 'It is probable that a black card will turn up on the next cut'— meaning: more probable than not—I am in error. Under the given assumptions, the chances of a black card are no greater than those of a red. With the construction, 'It is probable that P', what we are primarily concerned with is, of course, whether it *is* probable that P, and what happens as far as the *truth* of P goes is not decisive in this respect. To confirm or disconfirm the probability judgement we look to the reasoning on which it was based, not to the outcome of our operation with the cards. With 'probably', however, the focus shifts: if you say, 'The next card will probably be black', and it is, we may well say, 'You were right'. Here the dominant concern is with the truth of 'The next card will be black', notwithstanding the qualification which 'probably' introduces.

I do not say that there is a hard and fast division of cases along these lines, but we do at least have two possible usages, one of which better suits the adjective, the other the adverb. It is when the adverb fails to contribute to truth conditions that its role becomes difficult to explain and the kind of account offered by Toulmin becomes tempting, but I do not think that we can rest content with that account. It fails to differentiate 'probably' from such phrases as 'I should be inclined to say', and the more precise condition expressed explicitly by 'it is probable' can surely be expected to be identical with the condition which obtains if the use of the adverb is appropriate, just as with other such pairs, as 'fortunately' and 'fortunate'. The difference between 'probable' and 'probably' is just a difference in their grammar, with, most notably, a potentiality for affirmation and denial offered more directly by the adjective, and a qualification of force provided by the adverb.

With terms like 'probably' and 'although' there may be felt to be some uncertainty as to how the associated condition is best defined. Are we to say that 'although' is appropriately used if and only if the relevant contrast holds, or should we require only the *belief* that it holds? Here I wish to distinguish between appropriateness and correctness, notions which I have so far not kept apart. With some, but only some arbitrariness, I stipulate that appropriateness requires that the condition in question should actually obtain, whereas correctness is to call for no more than the relevant belief or intention. So, one who says, 'The preacher believes in hell, even though he is a fundamentalist', is likely to be under a misapprehension concerning the relation between belief in hell and fundamentalism, so that we may characterize his use of 'even though' as *inappropriate*, but so long as his intention is to mark a contrast of the relevant kind, we could say that he is using the phrase *correctly*. He would be using 'even though' incorrectly if he were mistaken as to its meaning, taking it to have the sense of, for instance, 'provided that'.

The inappropriateness which I have suggested might afflict 'even though', or 'but', is not the same as arises when a word has a tone which makes its use inappropriate in a given context. Consider the pair 'thank you' and 'ta', phrases which are almost interchangeable in meaning, but markedly different in tone. So long as it is used in expressing thanks, use of 'ta' is not incorrect, as I understand it, though on an occasion of some formality—when receiving a Nobel Prize, let us say—it would be thought distinctly out of place. How are we to characterize the two forms of inappropriateness— that in which it is, and that in which it is not an approximation to falsity?

With this question we are back to the distinction between a word as a sign *for* and as a sign *of* something, the former going with what is standardly communicated by a use of the word, as we might connect an intention to thank with both 'thank you' and 'ta', the latter relating to other factors with which the word is associated in other ways. A typical occurrence of 'ta' will be in highly informal, familiar, perhaps childish discourse, and it is because the context of use fails to be of this kind that we have inappropriateness, but an inappropriateness that does not negate the principal function of the word.

It is the more specific, overriding intention that defines the meaning of the word, even if it is also possible to make intentional use of the associations common to the broader class of words of which this is a member. So, if a person uses a locution particular to a certain sublanguage, as the language of hippies, Royal Air Force slang, or Australian colloquial speech, he may lead people to think that something is true of him, namely, that he belongs to the group in question. Again, christian names can be said to have a different tone from surnames, use of the former commonly being a sign of greater intimacy with the bearer of the name. When a word of phrase has a particular tone, the intention of the speaker may in fact be to induce in his audience a belief that he falls in the relevant category, but this would define the meaning of the word only if there were a generally recognized intention to this effect which a given speaker might exploit, something that can hardly be the case so long as that intention is subordinated to the standard communicative role of the word. Tone is like accent. By adopting a certain accent we can lead people to think that we come

from a certain country or region, but the association between
accent and origin is an all-pervasive feature of speech which
is excluded from the extralinguistic connections that are
definitive of meaning, of the 'message' that is conveyed.

But is it not possible that some general condition relating
to a whole range of words should deserve a place in an
account of the meanings of those words? Think of languages
which, like Japanese, make use of an extensive differentiation
of plain and polite forms—even for verbs and adjectives. The
use of the latter forms in expressing deference or respect is
surely a function of their meaning, yet if we admit this, what
grounds can we have for excluding other associations, as
those of a regional or social nature, from the same dimension
of meaning? If words are to be a recognized means of
communication with respect to a given condition, there must
be a regular association between those words and a desire to
convey to others that the condition obtains. If I dismiss
certain conditions as not involved in meaning, it is because I
am supposing the necessary constancies to be lacking, no
general pattern of usage revealing speakers to use the form
in question when and only when they wish their audience
to understand that the condition in question obtains. Lack
of this pattern will be particularly clear when, as with regional
features of languages, speakers will effectively have no choice
as to whether or not to speak in a way that presents that
feature, but in the case just introduced, where a choice is
possible, the intention to indicate respect could be a factor
which an account of the meanings of the relevant words
would have to encompass.

In discussing 'and' and 'but' I sided with Frege against
Dummett as far as the distinction between asserting and
suggesting is concerned. However, as I have implied, I do not
see the difference between these words as a difference
in *tone*, if this is to rank it alongside that between such
words as 'horse' and 'steed', or 'perspiration' and 'sweat'.
'Horse' and 'steed' might be said to agree in meaning but to
differ in tone, if the difference is merely in the poetic or
archaic associations of 'steed'; similarly, the less genteel
character of 'sweat' need not prevent identity of meaning

with 'perspiration'. If tone is explained with reference to
such terms, it is to be regarded as an accompaniment to
meaning—the tone *with which* something is said—or at least
as requiring a meaning that is not exhausted by tone. Even
words like 'alas', 'please' and 'well'—as in 'Well, we shall
have to see about that'—have a communicative role which
the secondary character of tone is not suited to embracing.
If there is any special tone to be associated with 'alas', it
relates to its slightly archaic character, not to its role in
expressing sorrow or concern. Certainly, there is no meaning
of 'meaning' in which 'and' and 'but' can be said to have the
same meaning, though to differ in some other way, no sense
in which a man's thought may be indifferently reported by
use of 'and' or 'but'; and I see no need to think of 'but' as
equivalent to 'and' plus something else, any more than there
is with respect to 'although', 'because' or 'despite the fact';
mere juxtaposition of clauses is sufficient to account for
any conjoining that might be thought a common element in
these terms. We explain the meaning of 'but' just as we
explain the meaning of any other word: by indicating what it
is a sign for, what condition is conventionally communicated
by a use of the word, and the difference in meaning between
'but' and 'and' is a matter of the different conditions
associated with either. Again I emphasize that the dissociation
from a connection with truth only means dissociation from a
certain assertive form, something that is immaterial as far as
conformity to the basic pattern of sign and thing signified
is concerned.

More insidious than mistakes concerning 'but' are the
widespread misconceptions concerning 'and'. With truth
seen as central in explaining meaning, it is natural to keep
it in view when giving an account of words which join
sentences as well as words which occur within them, and so
to give that explanation of 'and' which has now become an
accepted part of logical theory. Thus, we explain 'and' by
characterizing its behaviour as a truth-functional operator:
'P and Q' is true when and only when each of P and Q is
true. There are, of course, intuitionistic objections to such
an 'explanation', and the repetition of 'and' in the definiens
certainly reveals a failure to give an account of the conjunc-

tion which would be of use to one who did not already understand the term being defined. However, the intuitionist shares with the classical logician a belief that it is the conjunction of declarative sentences that provides the context for 'and' in its basic occurrence.

This common assumption is in error. There is no call to give a central place to conjunctions of sentences capable of being true or false, but the connection with truth, if any, comes through the character of the sentences connected, not through the connective, 'and' having the same sense in 'Hail and farewell', 'Twist and shout' and 'He sank and she swam'. So, how do we explain 'and'? In some languages—Otomí, for instance—speakers get on quite well without linking sentences by such a conjunction, the joint assertion of the two sentences being enough to indicate their joint assertion. As a sentence connective, 'and' does not enter into the content of what is said in any significant way, but it makes explicit that more is to come, it serves to indicate that the speaker wishes to add to what he has said. What he has said may be declarative, interrogative, imperative, or a mixture of these. If it is just declarative, then as far as truth is concerned, we say what would have been said had there been no 'and' at all, the conjunction being of only negative relevance in failing to qualify the assertions it connects.

Further qualifications are of course required to cope with 'and' as it occurs at other points in a sentence, but is what I have just said really adequate to the use in joining sentences? Since it is not now open to us to take the truth-functional account as central, relegating to a secondary role any other aspects of the use of 'and', we might wonder whether what on that approach would be excluded from an account of the word's meaning might not now be reinstated. This suggestion does not look plausible with respect to the question of the ordering of conjuncts discussed earlier, where the same explanation continues to hold, but it may appear that 'and' implies a unity of topic, a continuation of a theme. So, when the conjuncts are as far apart as those in 'In 1914 Aunt Agatha died and war was declared', we may think the use of 'and' appropriate only to the extent that the clauses can be related in some way to one another. In this case we have at least the common description, 'events which occurred in 1914', but failing any such connection we might well prefer to split the sentence up.

We might introduce such a consideration into an account of the meaning of 'and', or we might explain the need for this connection in other terms. The latter would certainly be my choice, but either way it would appear that there is practically nothing in common between the correct account of 'and' and its standard truth-functional account—a claim we can make with some confidence even if we do not as yet have a full account of the word. And yet, it might be argued, the underlying idea is akin to that which guided Frege in his characterization of sense, emerging via correctness or appropriateness, when we try to specify the circumstances of the correct or appropriate use of the word. Truth is too narrow to have an essential place in the explanation of 'and', but in giving an explanation of its meaning in the way indicated we at least stay closer to sense than to tone, closer to the mapping of words onto non-words which underlies the connection of sense with truth. This we may grant. At the same time, it does nothing to lessen the fatuousness of the truth-functional 'explanations' of 'and' which consistently disfigure texts on logic in an area where problems of correctly assigning meaning and function tend to go quite unnoticed.

We have now accumulated a number of contrasts which can usefully be surveyed together. The first concerns the different involvements of existence with respect to definite descriptions. On one account, the statement, 'The King of France is wise', is said only to presuppose the existence of a unique King of France, not to directly imply it in the way that would be true of, say, 'The King of France is alive and living in Blackbird Leys'. I see a difference, but I see it in terms of a distinction between what is and what is not explicitly affirmed, where explicitness is understood in terms of negatability, or, more generally, of qualifiability by an adverb. As far as the implication of existence goes, the two sentences are on a par, with no relevant difference which a new relation of presupposition need be called upon to explain.

Second, we have words which may be used to signify that

a certain condition obtains or is believed to obtain, but
which do not have a meaning that can be thought of in terms
of a contribution to truth value or truth conditions. Clear
instances are 'but' and 'however', a more complex case the
imperative 'Go!': this functions as a sign that the speaker
wants the person addressed to go, but in saying this are we
stating a condition that can be said to give the meaning of
the imperative?

Third, we have conditions which, however intimately
bound up with a form of words, certainly cannot be regarded
as involved in their meaning. So, the intuitionists are wrong
in saying that 'There is a convex polyhedron that is not
Eulerian' *means* 'I have found (constructed) a convex polyhedron that is not Eulerian', The notions of finding or
constructing simply do not enter thus explicitly into the
former, even though the truth of the latter may be inferable
with some reliability from that of the former.

Fourth, we have *tone*, as this is explained in terms of such
contrasts as that between 'horse' and 'steed' or 'prison' and
'nick'. Here we appeal to conditions of which utterance of the
word is a sign, conditions relating to the user or the setting, for
instance, but which are not such that a person using the word
in its accepted meaning will perforce intend to convey them.

The third and fourth categories can obviously combine,
but there is a question as to whether 'the', and comparable
words, should be taken over by the second category. We may
think not, on the grounds that varying 'the' might be expected
to result in a change of truth value with respect to its
containing sentence, but we also note that definite descriptions may stand in for a wide range of conditions, so that a
sentence of the form 'The F is G' can be made to be true if,
say, 'My F is G' or 'That F is G' is true, and our earlier
remarks on 'this' also suggest a different approach: both
'this' and 'the' apply not so much because appropriately
characterizable objects answer to them, but because they
can pick out something in accordance with the intention of
the speaker or some condition imposed by him. At all events,
the article can for present purposes join with words like 'but',
words which contrast with the third class. They contrast
with this class in that the conditions associated with them in

the way indicated are conditions which define their meaning, what is standardly intended, what the words are actually signs *for* and not merely signs *of.* This is where the crucial line is to be drawn, a line that we are liable to ignore so long as we look to sense and tone to provide suitable divisions.

50. *Meaning and intentions*

The analysis to date appears to hold out some hope for a uniform account of word meaning, but the uniformity which comes with the opposition to the cases where a word is merely a sign *of* something may be deceptive. Certainly, we need to look more closely at the intentional element variously involved in language, and the notion of *force,* as when we speak of an utterance as having assertoric or imperatival force, must also be investigated. We shall work around to these topics by considering the kind of appeal to intention that is to the fore in H.P. Grice's treatment of meaning (cf. Grice [1957] and [1968]]).

In saying 'When his outer door is shut it means that he is busy', we are speaking of a sign or indication that a person is busy, but not necessarily one brought about in order that anyone should come to this conclusion. On the other hand, although this is not what is said, the man may in fact wish to signify that he is busy, and this in two ways. First, he may bring about the sign with this express purpose, but not because he wants others to know that he wishes them to interpret the closed door in this way; he knows they will infer that he is busy, even if they do not infer his intention to communicate that; it is the drawing of this inference, and acting upon it, not any hypothesis about his intentions that they may form, that is important to him. Second, there is the possibility that he does wish them to discern his intention to indicate to them that he is busy: he wants them to conclude thus from what they find, and he wants them to know that that is what he is thereby trying to communicate. Conditions pertaining to recognition of intentions are important when it is question of meaning to communicate something, of transferring a wish or a belief, not merely bringing a wish or belief about. The person wants us to grasp two things: what he means by keeping his door closed, and that he is trying to communicate an intention to us.

How does this approach work out with language? Imagine we come across a primitive tribe of men, not known to possess a language. Suppose that a man from this tribe is regularly observed to utter a certain sound when, and only when, confronted with a dangerous situation, a sound transcribable as 'perygl', let us say. Could we say that this vocable is a genuine word in his mouth? It may be hard to resist such a conclusion, especially if the sound resembles a structured word rather than a mere cry, but have we as yet any reason to regard his uttering of that sound as of any greater significance than any other physiological reaction that might take place when he is in such a situation? When he is confronted with danger there will be other bodily changes which take place—a tensing of muscles, an increased flow of adrenalin, a prickling of the scalp—but we should not regard these as being in any way linguistic.

So far the man's utterance of 'perygl' is merely to be classed among his reactions generally. What more is required to make the sound an element of language? Well, suppose that the man's fellows look frightened and take flight on hearing him utter the sound. We are close to seeing 'perygl' as a linguistic sign if it plays such a role, but still not there, since they could equally take note of some physiological reaction, such as the man's hair standing on end, interpreting it as a sign of imminent danger, but this would not make either event describable as 'linguistic'. There is meaning here, but only in the way that clouds mean rain.

But suppose that the man not only produces this sound, but produces it in order to bring about this effect, the scattering of his fellows in the dangerous situation. That, it might seem, makes for a crucial difference. But how is the effect to be produced? Not merely causally, if it is to be a matter of a communicative use of language. That is, the man could make use of the sound 'perygl' to spur the others to action, but he might achieve this, not by exploiting the sign status of the word, but by making use of its acoustic properties: he galvanizes them into action by shouting the word. For there to be a genuine use of language we should require, it would appear, that he be trying to get his fellows to act in virtue of their understanding of what it is exactly that the word symbolizes, their knowledge of the kind of situation with which the word is customarily associated; their knowledge, in short, of what the word means.

A question arises here of the further involvement of intention both in the act of warning and in word-meaning, but first a clarification of what has just been concluded. The argument implies that, when I warn someone, my expectation is that they will do as I advise in virtue of understanding what I say. However, this is open to misinterpretation. It is as a result of hearing my utterance that they will, I hope, take action. There is on my part a tacit assumption that they understand what I say, but not a claim that this understanding will be a causal link in the chain leading to the desired action. It is against this background, of known understanding, that I can exploit the words for my purpose of eliciting action, and I should normally not be able to make use of the words for this purpose if they were not understood. So, understanding is a condition for the possibility of using words to warn, and my intention is that, on hearing my words—which I know them to understand— they shall take action, rather than that I intend that their understanding should be in any sense a cause of or reason for their action. Their understanding constitutes a necessary condition for the success of my warning, and, in another sense, their being physically able constitutes such a condition, but my intention is not that they should act because they understand any more than that they should act because they are able. In requiring, then, that the speaker should intend his audience to respond in virtue of their understanding of what he says, we are using a form of words which might carry this mistaken emphasis: the phrase 'in virtue of' may cover the right possibility; it certainly covers the wrong one. In general, then, one who is warning, urging, suggesting, imploring, and so forth, will perforce say what he says with a certain intention, but his intention can bear only upon factors over which he has some control. That his audience should act in virtue of understanding what he says is not something that he might intend; it is rather that such understanding is a presumed framework for him to consider it worthwhile trying to achieve his purpose by a use of language.

To the extent that circumstances and the sense of the words do not make it plain, reference to an appropriate intention will have to be incorporated in a full description of any utterance that is to count as a warning. However, for a Gricean analysis, still more is required. It is not just that the speaker says what he says with the intention of producing a certain effect in his audience, but he must intend that effect to be produced by means of the audience's recognition of that intention. That this complexity is mandatory for the case of warning is not clear. Awareness of the speaker's intention is important when it means awareness of his belief that there is danger, and when his having that belief gives his hearer some reason for acting. But while someone may fail to be warned by failing to appreciate what exactly someone is trying to tell him, if he is in fact apprised of the danger by hearing what he hears, perhaps in the most important sense he can be said to have been warned, however he envisages the intention behind the utterance. The model of the closed door in its first interpretation, not its second, may be appropriate enough.

A clearer case would be that of complaining. I say to a neighbour, 'Your boy has been teasing our cat', intending this as a complaint, not merely as an item of information which might be of interest to my neighbour. I shall certainly want this to be recognized as a complaint, since it may only be if it is seen in this light that I shall stand any chance of achieving what I want to achieve by imparting the information. However, an intention that one's intention be recognized is not an essential feature of speech acts generally. My intention may actually be thwarted by such recognition if I am trying to cajole, flatter, or impress.

The recognition of intention is put forward by Grice as a condition involved in meaning something by or when uttering certain words, as when one utters P meaning that such-and-such is the case, or that such-and-such is to be done. Consider the explanation, 'When I said "Term has begun" I meant that the *school* term had begun'. In Grice [1957] the speaker would here be held to intend his utterance to get his audience to believe that the school term had begun by means of a recognition of that intention. Following Grice [1968] we should specify the intention differently, the speaker now intending that his audience should think that he believes that the school term has begun, again as a result of recognizing that intention. However, it does not appear that either form helps with the central problem of meaning. The original explanation paraphrases fairly closely as 'When I said "Term has begun" I wished to be taken as saying that the *school* term had begun', the emphasis being surely on how I wished my words to be understood; it is the identity of my remark, as meaning this rather than that, that is being clarified; or at least, it is this dimension of meaning that has priority, the further questions— what I wish my audience to infer about my beliefs, what beliefs or responses I hope to induce—clearly presupposing an understanding, a grasp of the meaning, of what I have said. An account of the meaning of one's words is not given by an account of what it is to mean what one says, yet it is only on the latter that this style of analysis appears to have any bearing. In Grice [1968] it is recognized that the notion of correlation has a part to play, but it seems not to be appreciated just how far the explanation of meaning shifts in this direction, away from the original formulae in terms of intention.

With individual words intention appears to be secondary to convention as far as meaning is concerned: to intend a word in one meaning rather than another presumes a conventional association of the word with certain conditions, or whatever, that define its meanings, just as putting a word to use in warnings, suggestions, and so forth, presumes such an association. However, it is also worth pointing out that incorporability of a vocable within a speech act is necessary if it is to be a genuine word. The exclamation 'ouch!' provides a suitable illustration. We should not, I suggest, class this as a proper word, and yet it is construed as a sign, a sign that the speaker has been hurt. It occurs, however, as an involuntary cry in many cases, not as a sound which is conventionally used to indicate to an audience that the speaker has been hurt. Of course, a speaker might by uttering 'ouch!' induce in his audience a belief that he has been hurt, and he might do so intentionally, but his knowledge of the generally involuntary character of utterances of 'ouch!' stands in the way of his claiming an intention that his audience should recognize that he *wants* them to know that he is in pain as a result of hearing him say what he says.

For a contrast, we may look to the expletive 'damn' or the interjection 'boo'. I regard these as more properly linguistic, because they can be used to communicate annoyance or displeasure—can be used to this end, and do not merely function as signs thereof.

While this connection with an intentional use appears necessary to a vocable's being a genuine part of a language, I think that, at the same time, we should be reluctant to move far from the view that the properly linguistic use of words, their use in speech acts, is dependent on their having meaning in a way that can be grasped without any hypotheses as to speaker's intentions. Certainly, this appears to be essentially correct as far as descriptive vocabulary is concerned. Thus, a child might come to associate 'bottle' with its bottle, 'doll' with its doll, and so forth, thereby coming to a recognition of these words as signs, but without discerning any intention on the part of the speaker. There is at this stage no appreciation of the words as belonging to a language, but the priority of words as, roughly, natural signs, has considerable appeal in the way it takes a large dimension of meaning out of the realm of the mental. Indeed, scepticism about meaning, especially in connection with the indeterminacy of translation, may well derive from a failure to give sufficient weight to the consideration that what can be meant by a word is limited by the regularities of usage with respect to that word, regularities of a kind which keep us essentially at this level of words as natural signs. On the other hand, this claim for priority is quite resistible with terms of other types; it is surely too inflexible if it demands that appreciation of the sign values of words of a given type should always precede an understanding of speech acts into which they might enter: an understanding of 'Come!' as an order and of its connection with a more specific action might surely develop together.

If I am on course with my general approach, we can say that linguistic meaning involves both specific sign value—what differentiates 'fly' from 'flea'—and incorporability within a speech act. The speech act need not be that of assertion, so there is not an inevitable connection with truth in an explanation of meaning or of sameness of meaning, but so long as we have the required constancies we can have character as a sign, and so long as we can have an association with speech acts of one kind or another, we have the meaning proper to language.

Differences in parts of speech make for a complication of this simple scheme, but it does seem that a general conception of meaning applies equally to words which we might hope to elucidate in terms of their contribution to truth value, and words which enjoy another role. What we have, for words of whatever class, are, as I say, the regularities which confer upon a word its character as a sign. This dimension is, of course, not without its own difficulties. Consider the way in which a word may be associated with a large number of conditions, as those pertaining to something to which a common noun, as 'home' or 'garden', might be applied. Because of the known co-occurrence of a variety of such conditions, we meet with problems of definition, of essence, with the risk that we shall import a determinacy, a rigidity, where none is present once we seek to associate a word with a set of necessary and sufficient conditions for its application. Further uncertainty may come with changes in what we know. Suppose it becomes common knowledge that things to which w is applied have a certain feature, f, as metallic objects are found to be good conductors of electricity, or very hot objects found to be painful to the touch. It need not be any part of a speaker's intention to convey by his use of w that something is f, but to the extent that he knows that those listening to him will make this inference—and will know that he will be aware that they will—it may become difficult to exclude this implication from what is meant. We saw earlier a comparison between problems of assigning meaning and problems of identifying cause–effect relations, and the comparison applies again when it is a question of singling out just what does and what does not relate to meaning among the given correlations.

51. Parts of speech and their meanings

I have already shown some sympathy towards the model of sign and thing signified in explanations of meaning. This is not necessarily, I suggest, a model to fight shy of—no one could take exception to the claim that 'birch' is the word for trees of a certain kind—but it has in some cases been thought crude with good reason, the grammar of many simple statements of meaning providing an obstacle to this approach at its very starting-point. Thus, such a sentence as *'saepe* means "often"' does not associate the Latin word with a *significatum,* a non-linguistic item with which it is to correlate, and there appears to be no reformulation of the sentence which would show it to conform to this pattern. It is true that, if the grammar allows, the meaning of some words may be more directly specified, as when we say that by 'saffron' is also meant the colour of the substance that goes by the same name, and it is also true that such sentences as 'The meaning of "tuberculosis" is a certain disease' can be given an acceptable interpretation, despite their awkwardness. The failure of the inference to 'Many people used to die of that meaning' reflects the peculiar grammar of 'meaning', but it does not cast doubt on the truth or intelligibility of such statements of meaning.

It may be claimed that phrases like 'means a certain disease' present us with a special use of 'means', more akin to 'refers to' than to the use in '"presently" means "soon"'. Perhaps, but the difference may reside in what follows either. Still, it is the latter style of formula that is the more general and that has proved so difficult to analyse, despite its apparent simplicity. We note that, while there looks to be symmetry between the two words here in quotes, we cannot put 'the word' in front of the second: the word 'presently' means 'soon', but it does not mean the *word* 'soon'. It is sometimes suggested that 'means' in these formulae is used with the sense of 'means the same as'. This is implausible on general grounds, and two more specific objections can be raised. First, if 'means' did come to 'means the same as', then we *could* insert 'the word' where in fact we cannot. Second, 'w means the same as v' can be in place when we are ignorant of the meaning of each of w and v, whereas 'w means v' is generally used only when it is supposed that one's audience understands v. A person can know that 'olid' means the same as 'fetid' without having the faintest idea what either means, but we should hesitate to say without qualification that he knew that 'olid' meant 'fetid'.

What this may suggest is that the expression following 'means' in these formulae is one that we are in some way *using,* in which case the question becomes one as to the kind of use involved, a question which our earlier analysis of *oratio recta* equips us to answer. The impossibility of inserting 'the word' before '"soon"' in '"presently" means "soon"' is matched by the impossibility of adding 'the words' to the citations in 'He replied: "I have been unwell"' or '"I have been cheated", he complained'. The two cases draw still closer together if, taking the Romance languages as our guide, we paraphrase 'means' as 'wishes to say'. So, 'By "presently" he meant "soon"' becomes 'By "presently" he wished to say "soon"', or, making use of the other paraphrase suggested, 'When he said "presently" he wished to be taken as saying "soon"'.

There is one respect in which the comparison with direct speech breaks down. A phrase like 'he protested' purports to characterize the speech act implicit in the accompanying words, whereas 'he meant' performs no such role: '"Go!", he meant', is not a way of reporting a speech act. However, with such a sentence as '"Gang!" means "Go!"' or 'By "Gang!" he meant "Go!"' we do meet with a comparable use of '"Go!"'. It does not fall to 'means' to identify a speech act, but '"Go!"' is none the less envisaged as a phrase uttered with a certain force; it does not function here as a report of an actual utterance, but a hypothetical association with a speech act is intended—not merely a word thought of as a bare sequence of sounds or letters, but a word uttered as an imperative. This gives us a *use* of the quoted word which complements the intransitivity of 'means' and which makes for an obstacle to inserting 'the word' on a par with what we found in the case of '"I have been cheated", he protested', despite the difference between 'means' and 'protested'. Similarly with words making up less than a complete utterance, as in '"fractious" means "peevish"'. We should perhaps affirm this equation with an eye to a larger context from which the words might have been excerpted or in which they might be used, as ' "He is fractious" means "He is peevish"'. At all events, it is a live use of the words, the words as uttered, that we envisage, and it is the notion of *use* as thus explained which seems to me to yield a construal of the formula more plausible than any appeal to a species of referential use. This perhaps also explains why a reformulation of '*w* means *v*' as '*w* means the same as *v*' is

not necessarily accurate—though I might add that the difference that keeps the two apart is not such as to lend comfort
to anyone who feels that the latter somehow makes meanings
out to be elusive, identifiable only to one who already knows
them. We shall have more to say on this topic.

Any use of 'w means v', with v enjoying some kind of referential role, is limited, and not a possibility on which I wish to
rely in justifying my conception of meaning in terms of a relation between words and non-words. This is a relation that I
understand in fairly broad, but I hope innocent terms: among
others, it is to cover the case of a word being the word for
things of a certain kind, and the rather different case where a
word is used to convey that a certain condition obtains. To
see more of what is involved we shall now look at some of
the various parts of speech, beginning with nouns and verbs.
   When discussing subject and predicate I granted the possibility of giving explanations of noun and cognate verb which
differed only on those general features that make for nominal
and verbal character respectively. This will be so when what
is characterizable by the noun—'shout', say—is an act or event
that can be reported from a different perspective by the verb—
'He shouted'. The meaning of either can be explained by
reference to the same phenomenon, a loud vocal sound,
though, having regard to their different grammars, we might
say that 'shout' as a noun can be true of a shout, whereas 'shout'
as a verb can be true of a shouter. The earlier discussion of
subject and predicate continues to be relevant to elaborating
this distinction. The conception of a sentence as a series of
words with their associated meanings gives no indication of
the unity of a sentence, as opposed to a mere list of its constituents. The concept/object combination tries to give us
items for which the desired union is possible, but it is to the
roles of subject and predicate that we turn to see how phrases
hang together in a way that transcends a mere listing: it is a
matter of P being affirmed of something designated by S, not
a mere juxtaposing of the meanings proper to either. An elucidation of the more general classes of noun and verb can take
something from this account, especially with respect to the
latter.

In passing, it is sometimes said that indications of tense and number, for instance, have merely grammatical meaning. However, whatever that means, it remains true that at one level the pattern of explanation is as for other elements of the language. So, for example, the past tense ending, '-ed', allows of an explanation which places it among other indexicals, such as 'now', and a child learning the meaning of 'buns' will come to connect the termination '-s' with a plurality just as it comes to connect 'bun' with a certain edible object. There is no staying within language with either termination, despite the importance of each to grammar.

The association of adjectives with properties, traits, states, and so forth, is comparatively straightforward, so long as we steer clear of approaches that would have us associate a special kind of entity, perhaps an entity in a special sense, with an adjective—as opposed to, say, a noun. Once more, what correlates with the one part of speech can equally correlate with the other; features of the world are not to be read off features of language, so that we might pair adjectives with adjectival entities—the kind of picture which Frege's account of concepts encourages; which has, perhaps, been the most obfuscating aspect of that account. Absolutely anything can be described by a noun; the real difference just is the difference at the level of words, adjectives being dissociated from an index of number, or, if you wish, from a criterion of identity.

What of adverbs? These constitute a complex class, with no single form of explanation being of use at a specific level. One broad division which makes some sense is that between adverbs which do, and adverbs which do not signify a way of V-ing, V a verb. So, adverbs which do would be those in 'talk rapidly' and 'smile nervously', while those which do not would embrace modal terms, as 'possibly' and 'probably', and their near relations, as 'undoubtedly', 'definitely' and 'barely', together with those many adverbs which serve in various ways to qualify the whole utterance, as 'however', 'seriously', 'honestly', 'clearly', 'ideally', 'at least', 'besides', 'all in all', and so forth. With the former class we tend to look to actions or events having certain characteristics, as rapid talking or a nervous smile, and we should thereby find the element common to the meaning of both adverb and cognate adjective; indeed, the difference

between the two may be minimal, the explanation of meaning
that holds for the adjective being what is central for the adverb
as well, which is little more than the form taken by the adjective when it qualifies a verb.

Adverbs of the second class are often more complex, though
here too help may come from a cognate adjective, usually in
application to an assertion. So, understanding 'Frankly, you
are being foolish' is a matter of appreciating that the speaker
wishes to convey to us that the rest of the statement has a
certain character—that it is, of course, frank. Once more, the
adverbial form is not used to *assert* that the statement is so,
but again we can make sense of appropriateness and inappropriateness here, such words as 'frankly', 'seriously', and 'finally'
often being recognized as quite inappropriate in view of what
follows. In other cases, the involvement of an assertion or
assertions may be more roundabout, but none the less real:
thus those many words and phrases whose appropriate use
calls for contrasts of various kinds between the accompanying
assertion and something else, as 'anyway', 'however', 'besides',
'all the same', and 'none the less'. Coming to learn the meaning of such words is coming to recognize the specific relation
which makes their use appropriate, so again we connect words
with the circumstances of their use in the way the general
thesis requires. Similarly with conjunctions, as 'while', 'since',
and 'because', a class which has been very poorly served by the
largely inapplicable notion of a truth-functional connective.

Even if some parts of speech tie up with circumstances in
a way that is hard to make plain, the leading idea in the present
argument is simple enough. A child does not learn a word in
a vacuum, but, supposing he does not have its meaning explained to him verbally, he will come to appreciate that things
are thus rather than so when the word is used. I do not mean
that the child need have a prior conception of the relevant
circumstances, nor that any simple ostensive model is in place.
Even with nouns, what is learned may not be anything that
mere pointing could convey, as we saw earlier with indexical
expressions, such as 'you', whose understanding requires
appreciation of a relation, and with words like 'nevertheless',
any questions of pinning the term on an ostended object is
out of the question. All the same, however broadly we con-

strue it, there must be something that occurs as a regular con-
comitant of the use of a word if that word is to come to have
a definite meaning for the learner.

52. Force

In focusing on the extralinguistic connections of words I have
largely ignored the involvement of intentions. However, I did
claim that incorporability within a linguistic act was essential
to a word's being such, and in some cases a certain speech act
may be intimately involved in the meaning of a word. For
instance, we might explain 'this' in terms of an intention to
single something out—thus bringing in its general role as a
demonstrative—together with a condition on the side of what
is picked out, viz. that of being in proximity to the speaker,
which takes us to the more specific meaning whereby the word
is distinguished from 'that' and other comparable terms. There
would be some appeal in a scheme which defined parts of
speech in terms of the speech acts with which they were
minimally associated; we can go some distance towards such
a scheme, but its completion would require an unaccustomed
division of parts of speech.

One category which will have to make essential reference
to intention is that of *force*, and to this we now turn. It is
natural, and I think right, to ascribe a central place to the
declarative sentence form. Indeed, the more important features
of this form may be retained with a more specific choice: that,
namely, of the affirmative declarative sentence in the present
or past tense. We can qualify, or depart more radically from
this form in a number of ways. Thus, such a sentence as 'The
rocks were submerged' may be negated, qualified by an adverb
such as 'possibly' or 'probably', and subject and predicate may
be reconnected in an interrogative or imperative construction.
What we are disposed to reckon as different *moods* will no
doubt be influenced by the range of specific forms which our
language offers. In English we think principally in terms of
indicative, imperative, conditional, and a vestigial subjunctive;
there is no call to speak of a special negative mood, or one
indicative of mere probability, since adverbs in conjunction
with the standard forms serve to cover this case. However, we
can easily imagine a language in which a distinct form of the

verb might be invoked to express what English conveys in this analytic way; indeed, for practically any adverbial phrase— 'not', 'it is hoped', 'supposedly'—a corresponding mood makes sense, and in various languages various possibilities are realized, the Eskimos, for instance, using a different form of the verb depending on whether what is reported is reported on the basis of hearsay or as a result of using one's eyes.

Even with English verbs there are complexities. Should we regard 'will' as on a par with present or past, or is it better set against these and ranked along with modal auxiliaries such as 'may'? A little reflection on its connections with truth and evidence soon brings to light its relevant affinities with each category, and the problem of classification that comes with them. Then we have the further complication introduced by the difference between a mere prediction and an expression of intention: should these be regarded as distinct moods, despite the common form that we give to them?

However, my concern here is not so much with problems of detail with moods as with the problem of characterizing that use of language which has some claim to be considered primary, namely the assertoric. We have in fact already given some indication of what constitutes assertion when discussing truth, but the question is one that merits a closer look. If I actually assert, 'There is a fly in your soup', and am not just offering the sentence as a grammatical illustration, let us say, then I do more than just give voice to these words. What more? I must, it is true, mean what I say—or, making allowance for lying, must intend that people should take me to mean what I say—but to say this still leaves us with a reliance on the notion of a declarative form of words, since the question whether I mean what I say can arise equally with a command, such as 'Trump it!'. The problem of characterizing assertion is sometimes seen as one of determining what makes for a serious use of language—as opposed to joking, or speaking one's lines in a play—but the more specific contrasts, as that between assertions and commands, are at least as important. Bringing in truth and falsity, however, enables us to exclude these un- wanted forms; so we have the claim, as in Dummet [1973], p. 298, that the more required is that one should intend what one says *as true*. Again, of course, this must be amended to cope with lying: in uttering 'There is a fly in your soup' I may still make an assertion even if I know that your soup is devoid of insect life; so, perhaps what we need is: intend as true or intend to be taken as intending as true.

But what does 'intend as true' mean? The intention in question is not, evidently, an intention to utter just any true sentence, as if it were truth at all costs, not the content of one's assertion that mattered. But then, once this is ruled out, it is not clear what is left for us to intend. It is the particular utterance, 'There is a fly in your soup', that is intended as true, but how can this be? I cannot intend that the actual statement I make should be true, since it does not lie within my power to make it such, I can only *hope* that it is true. I can intend to *say* something—which is, or which I take to be true—but again this is not what is wanted: the intending is presumably to relate to the truth of what I say as much as to the saying of it, and truth just does not seem to be an appropriate object of one's intentions in a relevant way.

Performative utterances present a further difficulty for the appeal to truth. We may well doubt whether 'true' applies directly to many of the phrases thus categorized, but that is not, surely, to doubt their status as assertions, there being at least *a* sense in which such an utterance as 'I apologize' allows of this characterization despite not being strictly true, or false. There is a difference, in that the speaker cannot be said to have asserted that he apologized, but he does *assert*, 'I apologize'. I think it must be acknowledged that some sentences can count as assertions without truth value, but perhaps the offending locutions can simply be regarded as revealing an oversight in the categorization of the intended class. What has traditionally been of concern here just is that subclass of assertions for which we have truth and falsity; a circle threatens, but at least it is reasonable to hold that this picks out the assertoric form in its primary use.

We could leave it at this: assertions, in the relevant sense, just are those utterances which can be appraised as true or false. However, these appraisals very much suggest some *aim* which we have in making assertions and which should be made clear if assertions, and therewith the declarative sentence form, are to be more clearly recognized for what they are. We

saw that intending as true or intending to say something true
was unhelpful, but something related is surely what is wanted.

Let us go back to that primitive situation in which for the
infant's benefit we try to get across an association between
'water' and water, 'teddy bear' and teddy bears, and so forth.
How are we to recognize when the child has a grasp of assertions? After appropriate exposure to words and world, the
child may come to form the right expectations with respect
to 'all gone', let us suppose, said of its meal, and this surely
puts it well on the way to an appreciation of the character
of the utterance as an assertion. If the child is to come to an
understanding of the phrase, and a grasp of its character as
an assertion, it is in either case necessary that utterances of
the phrase should be accompanied by some indication of what
it is intended as applying to. Proper names give a sharper illustration of the point. If I call out 'Jim' to summon someone
not in view, I say nothing true or false; I do not *assert* that
anyone is Jim, but for that the name must be coupled with
a further identification, either implicitly, or in a form as
explicit as 'That is Jim'. As just contended, an assertion will
involve this duality—some person, place, thing, or whatever,
with respect to which something is affirmed—something
knowledge of which is presumed by the given atttribution
and of which we can continue to have knowledge even if the
words do not fit. Once the name is uttered in the known
presence of the person, it begins to make sense to treat it as
an identification that can be right or wrong.

The necessary components of an assertion are seen most
clearly with subject–predicate sentences, where the subject
term makes explicit the requisite identification or presentation of something, while the predicate adds an informational
increment. Essentially the same pattern remains with a more
general form of subject, as in 'Foxes like hens', where our
earlier characterization of completeness and incompleteness
applies, the intended application of the predicate being de-
limited by that of the subject. A much broader pattern is
displayed when the affirmation is made with respect to a
region of space, adverbially indicated, as with 'Here is a pin',
or where the context of utterance is indicated as the time and
place with respect to which the affirmation is to apply, as with

'It is dark'. In all cases, however, it would appear that we can speak of an affirmation intended with respect to something, some object, person, place, or time, even if 'with respect to' takes on a slightly different interpretation when we leave subjects behind. Even when, as with statements of existence, we are saying only that a description is satisfied somewhere, there is still this duality; not the duality of statement and fact as envisaged by the correspondence theory of truth, but what should be put in its stead.

Whether explicit or otherwise, an identification provides a fixed point for an affirmation to hinge upon, and it is of course the term that is coupled with an identification, or more generally the verbal phrase, that provides the point at which assertion enters, where we have a contrast with the negative form and with other adverbial qualifications of force. So what, we ask, is the intention that should be brought in at this point? Could it be said that the conveying of information is what gives the primary intention behind assertions? This will certainly often be to the fore, but of course it cannot be our intention if it is quite evident to all that the person addressed already has the information in question—a not uncommon situation and no bar to a standard use of an assertion. What does seem more plausible, if not glaringly obvious, is the claim that in coupling a predicative term with an identification our intention will typically be to give an applicable description of what has been identified. There will be an intention to characterize (certain) things faithfully or accurately, to represent or depict things as they are—or, in the case of lying, to be taken as saying what one says with that intention. Putting it thus makes clear the aim of assertions in a way which brings in that idea which talk of 'intending as true' almost, but not quite, captured—a phrase which does not, incidentally, signify a type of speech act. In saying 'This branch is rotten', it is not that I intend what I say to be true—something with respect to which I am powerless—nor is it merely that I have an intention to say something true—an intention which could be fulfilled simply by saying what day it was—but I do intend to say something true about a certain thing, an object singled out by a phrase occurring in my assertion. Similarly, while one's intention may be to get a conversation going when one says 'It has been exceptionally mild lately', the intention that is central to this as an assertion is an intention to say something true about the weather.

For a child to come to a grasp of assertions it will, then, be necessary for it to develop an appreciation of this intentional aspect, to realize that failure has a place, that the speaker sometimes does and sometimes does not succeed in what he intends. A basis for this understanding will be provided by the child's grasp of word meaning: the expectations generated by regularities of usage will presumably result in the child's having some conception of a word as being the word for a certain state, class of thing, and so forth, enabling it to understand success and failure in terms of (an intended) conformity to and (an unintended) divergence from the established pattern.

What of those utterances which we have set to one side, namely, performative utterances which, like 'I apologize' and 'Thank you', are lacking in truth value? Here again there is an intention to *do* something which defines the meaning, but not an intention to give a true report or a correct characterization of something. With 'I apologize' or 'Thank you' the intention is to convey one's apologies or thanks, and there can be misrepresentation in that one may use words which do not have this role, do not give expression to this intention. However, the words are not on that account deemed false, even if a related notion of incorrectness is in place. Imagine a foreigner who has confused 'I apologize' and 'I sympathize', coming out with the latter when the former was what he wished to say. We could say that he used the latter incorrectly, in that it was not appropriate to the intention he had, that intention being, of course, to make an apology. Similarly, a person makes correct use of the assertoric form if he intends to make a statement, rather than, say, ask a question. Correctness does not, needless to say, mean truth, and it is in this further dimension of success and failure that the difference between the two forms of assertion is to be found. If I cannot fail to do something when I say 'I apologize'—viz. apologize—I equally cannot fail to do something when I say 'I feel fine'—viz. make a statement—but the success which comes with mere understanding falls short of what is required for truth.

There is at first sight some difficulty in finding a place for the notion of a strict performative. Words are signs for something beyond themselves, and performatives surely cannot be reckoned exceptions; there must be something which goes with their utterance and which the learner comes to recognize, yet character as a strict performative appears to dispense the utterance from this requirement, just as it is dispensed from being judged in terms of truth and falsity. When, as with 'I feel fine', there is performance but no performative, the matter is less puzzling. How do we know that one who utters this is making a statement or assertion? The short answer is that we know him to be using a form of words which he knows will be taken as such, but ultimately the intention definitive of assertion is one that is recognized in a desire to get things right, shown by, for instance, the way in which the speaker adjusts what he says to changes in circumstances. With performatives such as 'I concede', 'I bet you lose' and 'I endorse that plan', we have again the short answer, but ultimately the intention which defines the performative is made apparent through its expression in other ways in conjunction with a use of the performative—as when the chess player who says 'I concede' ceases playing and agrees that his opponent has won.

Imperatives and interrogatives are worth a brief look. The imperative mood figures in a variety of speech acts: commands and orders perhaps come first to mind, but we also have requests—'Pass the jam, would you?'—pleas—'Do let me try'—instructions, suggestions, and exhortations—'Connect the green wire to the earth terminal', 'Take one tablet every mile', 'Enjoy a break away from the children', and 'Save energy'. Here it seems that something like Grice's approach is in order, the intention in uttering an imperative being to get one's hearer to (form the intention to) act as a result of his recognition of one's intention—though 'desire' might be preferred to 'intention' at its last occurrence, and again we should not overlook the presupposed correlation of words and intentions which defines the mood and which the speaker exploits on a given occasion, not to mention the other correlations definitive of the terms which may also occur outside the imperative.

What of the interrogative? A person can be said to understand this form if he realizes that the intention in using it is to ask someone something, but he has a proper understanding of that only if he is aware of the standard intention in asking, viz. to elicit words of a certain form—an answer, of course—the specific form being dictated by that of the question. This gives us the framework in which to explain particular interrogative terms, such as 'what', 'how', 'when', and 'why'. We could say that a person understands 'Why are we waiting?', say, if he knows that in uttering this a speaker is asking for a reason, justification, or explanation of the reported waiting. More informatively, we can say that the usual intention of one who utters 'Why is it that P?' is to elicit a statement of the form 'P because Q', or, more generally, to elicit a statement Q which would ostensibly explain P. Here we note a likeness to commands, these being aimed at eliciting action, questions being aimed at eliciting something more specific, an answer.

To go briefly over the main point of the preceding discussion, there is a sense of 'meaning' in which words can be said to have meaning in much the same way as we say this of natural signs: smoke can be a sign of fire, and so too can an utterance of 'fire'. When looking at words from this perspective we can play down any intentional dimension, even if this cannot be completely excluded; however, that dimension comes to the fore once we look at words as part of language, as being used for various purposes, in such speech acts as asserting, warning, questioning, and suggesting, acts which in general presume that the meanings of constituent words have been secured at the level of natural signs. This is not to say, however, that recognition of assertoric or interrogative status, for instance, rests on a radically different basis: such status will frequently be linguistically marked, and recognition of a marking as such is again recognition of symbolic character, grammatical forms coming to be appreciated as signs, but as signs of an intention definitive of the form or the correlative speech act. We connect words with intentions in that *some* intention, some speech act, is necessary for properly linguistic occurrence, but there is also the special case where an intention is to be introduced into an account of what is actually meant by a form of words.

The reference to intention brings in an aspect not adequately catered for by explanations of meaning of the simple form, '*w* means *v*', and shows the advantage of an explanation in terms of use which I hinted at when introducing the latter notion. Saying '*hic* means "this"' explains the Latin word to one who knows the English, but without any indication of the common role—to single out something in the neighbourhood of the speaker; that remains beneath the surface, so to speak, something it is assumed the hearer will already appreciate. I said above that consideration of statements of meaning led some to regard the meaning of a word as somehow ineffable, and it is certainly true that instances of the form '*w* means *v*' are not suited to imparting information about this important dimension of meaning. That is not to say, however, that something remains to be explained once, by explaining how the word is used, we do justice to this intentional aspect.

53. Sentence meaning

The account of assertion treated of one element of importance in sentence meaning, but there are other issues to be tackled under this heading, some of which I shall now approach via the use of 'means' in which it compares with the psychological verbs examined earlier.

In 'I mean, there must be some way I can help', we have a parenthetical use of 'I mean' in which it indicates that what follows is uttered in clarification of some previous remark, and the intransitivity of the verb in this occurrence is shared by 'meant' in 'He meant that there was enough for everybody'. As mentioned, phrases like 'wish to say' and 'wish to be taken as saying' give a reasonable paraphrase in this connection. The clausal context is not the most usual for noun or verb, though the customarily intransitive character of a verb before such a clause is worth pointing out with respect to 'mean', and is also relevant to a correct construal of 'His meaning was that there was enough for everybody', which, if 'meaning' is improperly assigned an identifying use, might be taken to introduce a most bizarre object as the man's meaning. The observation also bears upon the interpretation of '"*P*" means that *P*', and similar uses of conjunctive 'that' which have enjoyed some recent philosophical vogue.

To expand on this last point, consider the following pair of sentences:

(1) 'The pound will fall' means 'The value of the pound will decrease'

(2) 'The pound will fall' means that the value of the pound will decrease

The first, it is commonly thought, simply gives a translation of the sentence, 'The pound will fall', thus staying within language in its explanation of meaning. (2) is sometimes viewed with suspicion, because of a supposed commitment to propositions or facts, but it, or the simple '"The pound will fall" means that the pound will fall', may also, and for the same reason, be considered of some importance: they seemingly perform a vital task in bridging words and world, in giving a more direct specification of meaning than is provided by (1). In this it may appear—as in Dummett [1975], p. 104— that declarative sentences enjoy a notable advantage over the more recalcitrant words and phrases whose meaning eludes a more direct specification. However, while it is right to see a difference in the commitments of (1) and (2), the difference is not as supposed: (2) does not bear the desired interpretation, but is at best false.

To explain. There are two uses of 'mean' with a following noun clause, depending on whether or not a person is the subject. In the sentence, 'The Liberals have won the by-election. This means that the Government no longer has a majority', the phrase 'this means that' has the force of 'in consequence', clearly committing the speaker to the truth of what follows. We can similarly say that current speculation in the money markets means that the value of the pound will decrease, but the sentence or statement, 'The pound will fall', is powerless to have such a consequence—at least in general, though a particular utterance might be endowed with this capability. Such an interpretation, in which (2) is more than likely to be false, is the only one that the words will bear, and then only with some strain, but there is a related formulation in which the sentence is relativized to a speaker and his meaning then specified. So, 'By "The pound will fall" he meant that the value of the pound would decrease', or 'When he said "The pound will fall" he meant that the value of the pound would decrease'. But now, in this more acceptable replacement for (2), there is not the contrast intended. We can rewrite as 'When he said "The pound will fall" he meant: the value of the pound will decrease', and it makes no significant difference if we enclose the sentence after the colon in inverted commas or not. It would, for instance, be wrong to say that use of quotes is in order only if the words quoted are understood by the speaker. We can say 'By *Mai scrive* she meant "He never writes"', without attributing to the Italian speaker a knowledge of English, and if any difference is signalized by the absence of quotes, it concerns the speaker's intention rather than any question of reference, the clausal form not being favoured if it is thought that the speaker did not mean what she said.

The idea that (2) somehow takes us from words to world, that 'means' here projects sentences onto corresponding states of affairs or other non-linguistic items, is an idea which embodies misconceptions similar to those underlying the belief that (2) provides an occasion for mysterious propositional objects to make an entry. In both cases the transitivity of 'means' is taken for granted, and the appearance of a clause rather than quoted words is regarded as a sign that we have somehow gone beneath language to find a fitting object for the propositional attitude. Suppose, then, we subtract the implication which makes for the falsity of (2), the implication that the sentence following 'means that' is true. What this would leave us with, I suggest, is a sentence that is essentially equivalent to (1). Not a natural interpretation for the version with 'means that', but this is the best I can do for it. Certainly, I do not see a third possibility, one which might be indicated by the appropriate insertion of 'fact', 'possibility', 'situation', or whatever, before 'that'. On the contrary, the awkwardness consequent upon such expansions surely testifies to the intransitivity here of 'means': what sense can be made of '"The pound will fall" means the fact or the possibility that the pound will fall'?

Consider now one use commonly made of the formula, '"*P*" means that *P*', its use within the context of a hypothetical 'theory of meaning'. Such a theory is charged with specifying the meaning of the individual expressions in a language, and

is to cope with the indefinite number of possible meaningful
combinations of words by specifying further the rules for
their combination and the sense of such combinations. The
result is to be a procedure which would enable us to determine
the meaning of an arbitrary sentence of the language in
question.

In passing, a plea for a more sober approach to the 'infinity'
and 'novelty' of language. There is nothing excitingly novel
about the sentence, 'The missing tickets turned up in Aunt
Agatha's slipper', even if it makes its appearance for the first
time on this page: the sentence combines non-novel words in
a non-novel way. True, you can find grounds for speaking of
a novel result, a sentence never before encountered, but that
should not be allowed to obscure the more numerous respects
in which what we have is thoroughly familiar. Again, it is true
that an understanding of the plural termination, '-s', is not to
be explained in such a way as to imply a restriction of its use
to just those nouns in current use, and that any account which
failed to observe a proper degree of indifference to the particular would clearly be at fault. However, it is not easy to fall
foul of this requirement, and the infinity here, as in language
generally, is a pretty poor thing.

Returning now to our theory of meaning, what it is supposed this would enable us to do is complete 'The meaning
of "P" is . . .' for an arbitrary sentence, P. It would seem,
however, that the manner of completion is important, mere
provision of a synonymous form of words being unsatisfyingly
indirect. The original question was, in effect, 'What is the
meaning of "P"?', rather than 'What has the same meaning as
"P"?', and answers of the form '"P" means that P' are accordingly more suitable than those in which a translation, 'The
meaning of "P" is "Q"', is provided. So, while '"P" means
that P' may look less informative than the version with the
cited translation, the different use to which the two occurrences of 'P' is put is seen as making for an advantage which
counts decisively in favour of the former—though, of course,
any advantage attaching to either version can be preserved in
the form '"P" means that Q', 'P' and 'Q' distinct but synonymous sentences. At all events, it is insisted, there is nothing
trivial about the formulation instanced by '"Gold is a metal"

means that gold is a metal': a person can significantly be said to appreciate that this is what the sentence means; it is not something that he will grasp simply through grasping the truth of '"*P*" means "*P*"'. To make the point it perhaps helps to invoke a mixture of languages, as with '*O ouro é um metal* means that gold is a metal', but the point holds, it will be maintained, without the assistance of such formulations.

On my account, the objection is not that '"*P*" means that *P*' is trivial. It is simply false, and has a sense that is quite inappropriate to the general topic. Furthermore, the attempt to salvage something from this falsehood takes us to a version which is either trivial, as '"*P*" means "*P*"', or significantly true, as with '"*P*" means "*Q*"', appropriately filled in, but not what is desired. What it seems is wanted is a statement of what a given sentence means and a theory of meaning which explains how the speaker, who perhaps has never encountered the particular sentence before, none the less realizes that the sentence means just that. But it is the specification of the *that* that poses the problem. *O ouro é um metal* is the same in meaning as 'Gold is a metal', but one who understands the former does not necessarily know what is meant by the latter, or by anything else specifiable in different but synonymous terms.

But the speaker may well know what the given sentence means, so there is surely something here to be elucidated. What is it exactly that he does know? He must, of course, know the meanings of the individual words, their mode of combination, and the force appropriate to them. Is that all? I should say it is. Once we have appreciated that the grammar does not foist propositions or facts upon us as the meanings of sentences, there seems no reason to look beyond this simple scheme, all the word–world correlations having now been exhausted. This is particularly clear when the sentence is a question, as 'Who goes there?', an extralinguistic reference for the whole being not at all inviting, but it is only the superficial grammar that makes us think otherwise with declarative sentences. However, if the referential urge cannot be contained, opportunities offered by, most notably, phrases within the sentence can be exploited. With 'One who says *O ouro é um metal* is classifying gold as a metal' we surely engage satisfactorily with the world.

Those who require that a theory of meaning must show how the meanings of whole sentences are composed out of the meanings of their parts may feel that I have not done justice to the notion of overall sentence meaning, that the meaning of a sentence has an identity that is something more than that of its parts in combination. Is this not forced upon us by the consideration that two sentences may agree in meaning even though the meanings of their constituent words may differ? There is some validity in this point, but I do not think that it calls for any significant modification to the simple scheme. Identity of sentence meaning is fundamentally a matter of agreement in meaning between matching parts and grammatical dependencies of the two sentences being compared. This may or may not be adequate to covering agreement in force; to the extent that it is not, we must specify agreement here as well, force being a dimension which allows for some relaxation of what may otherwise be an excessively restrictive condition. Thus, we may grant sameness of meaning if we have agreement within a general frame which the two sentences can be said to exemplify: perhaps they both amount to saying of someone that he is so-and-so, or telling someone to do such-and-such. However, as soon as the two forms of words cease to be closely comparable, talk in terms of sameness of meaning is less certain, the notion of a *deductive equivalence* perhaps being more useful as well as more general. We may hesitate to say that 'John loves Mary' has exactly the same meaning as 'Mary is loved by John', and we should certainly not allow that 'Yesterday was Monday' meant the same as 'Tomorrow is Wednesday'; however, we could agree that each member of the pair could be deduced from the other. Again, we can say that, with certain assumptions, 'Neither P nor Q is true' and 'P and Q are both false' can be said to 'come to the same thing', but deductive equivalence rather than synonymy would appear to be the relation involved. The line is not sharp, but there is some conflict between the claim that two propositions are the same in meaning and the acknowledgement that this identity is arrived at by argument. A model for the sentence is that of a mixture rather than a compound: properties of the whole are properties of the elements in combination, with no call to recognize a unity which a word-by-word explanation of meaning, general force, and relations of grammatical dependence fail to capture.

There is one point on which my argument calls for refinement. I do not claim that knowledge of the meaning of a phrase or larger unit is invariably given with knowledge of its constituents. Such a claim would not make sufficient allowance for idioms, which frequently violate this scheme. I contend, rather, that there is no call for anyone's theory to show how the meaning of the larger unit is *derivable* from the meanings of its constituents—and their structural relations—and, *a fortiori*, that there is no call to seek an 'effective method' whereby the meaning of a sentence might be thus derived. Either we take the words one by one, elucidating each in turn and explaining how they combine, or we find that certain words have to be taken in groups. So, in 'They made up after their quarrel', there is nothing to be gained by giving independent explanations of 'made' and 'up' with a view to elucidating the verbal phrase, 'made up', but this can be treated as if it were a single word.

Attempts at explaining the meaning of a sentence by specifying when it is true may founder on such examples as 'Yesterday was Monday' and 'Tomorrow is Wednesday': even when necessary, agreement in truth is not sufficient. In explaining the meaning of a sentence there is no substitute for taking it apart and detailing the individual meaningful elements, put together in the particular way in question. Of course, if we do pay due regard to structure, an explanation of meaning may take the form of explaining when a sentence is true, as when we say that, for instance, knowing the meaning of 'Whitlam is a Prime Minister' or '101 is a prime number' is a matter of knowing what it is for the person or number specified to be as stated. This must, of course, be taken in a specific way—as stated *in these terms*—if it is to be adequate to conveying what is involved in knowledge of the meaning of the given sentences. Similarly, a person can be said to know when a mathematical proposition is true if he knows that it is the outcome of correct calculation, or is established by logical inference from true premisses, but he can know this of a given proposition without knowing its meaning. One can go off course here in much the same way as with the attempt to characterize assertion in terms of an intention to say something true, a more specific formulation being needed to avoid the objection that any true proposition would satisfy that intention.

The thesis that meaning is to be understood in terms of a correlation between words and non-words appears impossibly crude, a reversion to that unsatisfactory empiricism which had Russell examining his psychological states in search of a suitable item to pair with 'or', for instance—cf. chapter 5 in Russell [1940], where feelings of hesitation and indecision are selected for this role. We can go some distance with the simple model in terms of words like 'cup' and 'saucer', but there is surely nothing in our experience that answers in a relevant way to 'or', 'since', 'hardly', 'however', 'always', and so forth. Hence, of course, the attraction of *use,* which appears to liberate us from this narrow scheme. However, there is reason to think that switching to use merely defers the problems which 'means' forces us to confront, and in any case there is something non-accidental about the way the simple account applies in the favoured cases, as when we say that it is by coming to appreciate that 'saucer' is used of things having a certain form and function that a child comes to an understanding of its meaning. And is there an alternative in the general case? It is surely the progressively more accurate use of words in the right circumstances, with respect to the right things, that takes place as the child's mastery of the language develops quite generally, as its usage comes into line with our own. Knowledge of meaning is, after all, knowledge of more than just properties intrinsic to a word, and even with a term like 'since' there must be extralinguistic constancies of use which a child comes to recognize as it gets a grip on the meaning; if a particular character or identity for the word is to take shape, if its utterance is not to be quite arbitrary, there must be something distinctive about the situations in which the word is used, at least often enough for its utterance to generate relevant expectations. More will have to be said about words whose meaning is communicated purely by verbal explanation, and it is true that with a word like 'since', a word which may be said to correlate with a certain *condition*, there is a departure from more straightforward parts of speech, in that it often appears appropriate to call upon a clausal unit in giving a specification of the condition. This complexity may imply an order of acquisition, a child not being able to understand a word like 'since', 'while', or 'because' until it is capable of having certain beliefs, but there is no influx of mysterious items as correlates of such words. To say that w correlates with a certain condition, for instance, is to say no more than that use of w is appropriate when such-and-such is the case. I did allow that 'means' might be followed by terms which behave referentially, but I do not have to make out a case for such function in order to express the claim that, say, 'in', 'under', 'to', and 'from' connect with certain spatial positions and directions.

10

MEANING AND VERIFICATION

Sameness of meaning is a topic on which we have so far more questions than answers, and I shall now try to reduce the imbalance as a preliminary to commenting on the controversial distinction between analytic and synthetic propositions. I should also like to say a little on the notion of verification. What I have to offer here is woefully inadequate to such complex issues as those of sentience in others and the relation of verifiability to observability, but in view of preceding arguments there are two matters in particular that I feel are due some attention, these being the differences in obstacles to verification and the verifiability of general statements.

54. Sameness of meaning

There is at least one respect in which making sense of sameness of meaning is inextricably bound up with making sense of meaning: if you claim to have been using a word in, say, its literal meaning, I may reply that I understood it as having *that* meaning, and we can continue to use the word in the *same* meaning; so long as a word has a meaning, we are assured of the possibility of a condition in terms of which we can give substance to a use of 'same'. There is something more to defend if it is a question of two different words having the same meaning, since there is conceivably no room for distinct words to be identical in this respect. However, if there is any exclusivity here, something other than the demand for consistency is responsible for it: if the search for exact synonyms is doomed to failure, this will be because, for instance, languages do not tolerate redundancy in this respect, and even then this is not a point that will apply across languages.

Approaching meaning via use naturally leads us, at least with many words, to explain sameness of the former in terms of sameness of what a word is used of, sameness of application, but such formulae are in need of further refinement to be satisfactory. The adjectives 'suggestible', 'mystified', and 'divorced' may be used of persons and persons alone, but of course we wish to connect them with particular traits or conditions, if in indicating what they are used of we are to indicate their meaning. It will be the further qualification that does the work, as when we say that 'divorced' is used of persons in so far as their marriage has been dissolved. Similarly, if all and only sugary objects taste sweet, 'sugary' and 'sweet' will enjoy an identical application, but we can discern a difference in meaning in that we can connect the one with taste, the other with an ingredient substance. When words are as close as this there is always the possibility that they should become interchangeable, and to keep them apart we must be able to invoke at some level a difference in their extralinguistic connections— as characterizing objects of different senses, for instance—even if at another level we have agreement.

When trying to establish whether two terms w and v diverge or converge in meaning, the customary starting-point is to consider the impact which substitution of v for w has on the truth value of a sentence in which the latter occurs. Provided the context is one in which the word is being genuinely used rather than mentioned, any alteration in truth value will point to a difference in meaning, and if we find the kind of *de facto* agreement shown by such pairs as 'aerated' and 'fizzy', or 'creature with heart' and 'creature with kidneys', the context to consider is one in which the merely *de facto* character of the agreement disqualifies the substitution. So, if whatever is sweet is sugary, and vice versa, we can say that a person likes sweet things only if he likes sugary things, that sweet things are bad for you only if the same goes for sugary things, and so on, whereas with 'Anything sweet is necessarily sweet' we lose this freedom to substitute, at least one of 'Anything sugary is necessarily sweet' and 'Anything sweet is necessarily sugary' having to be rejected. Or, at least, there could be an interpretation on which we had falsity for one or both; it depends on the grounds for the introduction of the qualification 'necessarily'. The actual coincidence of the sweet and the sugary at the level of objects or substances could provide one basis, and one which would justify the qualification; if the necessity is to fail, it must be such as to require, precisely, sameness of meaning. If we know that only sugary things are sweet, we can say 'Since this is sweet, it has to be sugary', but the basis of this necessity is not as required for the satisfactoriness of the test.

This suggests that we should refuse to give the contexts featuring modal terms a crucial role. Not because there is something suspect about such terms; it is rather that the grounds for their introduction are of more immediate concern, grounds which, as we have just observed, are not always sure to be relevant, and which perhaps cannot be specified as relevant without circularity. That modal considerations are secondary is also clear from their inapplicability to words which make no contribution to truth value, as 'moreover', but it is useful to see their inadequacy even with the favoured class of word.

It is not, of course, only modal contexts that might be invoked to provide supposedly suitable non-extensional settings for the troublesome pairs. It might be said that 'Francis thinks he has eaten something sweet' could be true, but 'Francis thinks he has eaten something sugary' false. Such contexts may be thought derivative because of their nearness to quoted speech; certainly, whilst they are available to us once the difference in meaning has been assured, they would appear to present no more than peripheral reflections of differences in meaning, offering no indication as to what makes for such a difference. There are indefinitely many ways in which we may draw out the consequences of a non-identity, matching affirmations in respect of one term with denials in respect of the other. However, as our earlier treatment of identity indicated, some such conditions are more basic than others, and what we should like is a condition that is not merely not satisfied by v and w when these differ in meaning, but is such that its satisfaction by v and w is *sufficient* for identity of meaning on their part. We shall see shortly that the non-extensional contexts just sampled do not meet this demand.

It might be that whenever someone described something as 'sweet', he could with equal truth have called it 'sugary', but the applicability of the latter need not be something of which he is aware. If, then, we are to draw the two apart, should we look to a difference, not in when the words apply, but in our possible knowledge of their application? So, we might say: a person can know that something is sweet without knowing that it is sugary; or: you can be in a position to tell that something is sweet without being in a position to tell that it is sugary. Again, however, to the extent that what we have here is correct, it has the status of a theorem rather than an axiom, a simple consequence of non-identity of meaning, but not a consideration which throws light on that notion.

Still, we are perhaps coming closer to the exit from language that I have implied to be necessary, as we see on considering the related claim that a difference in method of verification makes for a difference in meaning. This thesis is plausible in so far as the former difference implies the possibility of conclusive grounds for the applicability of w at a time when one has no more than inductive grounds for v. That just is to acknowledge the logical possibility that w should apply when v does not, which does indeed ensure that they differ in meaning. So, if a liquid is aerated we can certainly suppose it fizzy, but the two properties connect with different methods of verification: it makes sense to suppose that while a liquid is known to be aerated, our tongues should reveal it not to be fizzy. This gives us a more direct indication of the kind of difference which underlies the more derivative indications of a difference in meaning, just as with my suggestion that we can discern a difference in meaning between 'sweet' and 'sugary' in so far as we connect the one with just taste, the other with the constitution of a substance. Put this more generally—each has different extralinguistic connections— and what we have is quite trivially a sufficient condition for a difference in meaning, but it is surely to differences at this level that we must trace back any differences in truth value.

More complex is the question whether identity of application makes for identity of meaning. When discussing sentence meaning I pointed out that 'Yesterday was Monday' and 'Tomorrow is Wednesday' do not have the same meaning, even though the one is of necessity true if the other is. We spoke instead of the two as being *deductively equivalent,* a notion which we might extend to such pairs as 'half empty' and 'half full', 'not everything is . . .' and 'something is not . . .', 'equilateral triangle' and 'equiangular triangle', '100' and '$1^3 + 2^3 + 3^3 + 4^3$'. The line between synonyms and deductive equivalents is uncertain, but it seems reasonably clear on which side these examples lie, despite the necessity which attaches to the equivalences. Again, while *Kurzstreckenläufer* is the German for 'sprinter', we could say that there was a divergence in meaning, however minor, because of the explicit way in which the notions involved in the former—'short-distances-runner'—are exhibited. Similarly, while English 'walk' and French *se promener* may describe the same action, use of the reflexive pronoun could be said to involve a different way of looking at that action, to pick out an aspect that is generally ignored in English, and so to debar the two verbs from being exactly synonymous. More difficult cases will arise when there is only limited appreciation of the structure of a word. There is a match in our terms between 'hippopotamus' and *Flusspferd*, but few English speakers think of the former as translating 'river horse', a breakdown which is quite apparent to a German speaker with respect to his word. On the other hand, to the extent that nothing is ever made of this breakdown by German speakers—so that they do not think of hippopotami as a species of horse, for instance—to that extent there ceases to be any ground for distinguishing the two, given their identity of application. Compare German *ver-* and *zer-*, which are readily recognizable as having independent senses—even though they are not separable from their verbs—with the English 'wr-'—as in 'wring', 'wrench', and 'wrestle'—which would not now be felt to convey a common meaning in the words in which it occurs.

I suggest, then, that it is not unreasonable to take strict sameness of meaning as requiring both matching structure and matching parts, to as fine a level as is commonly recognized to have meaning. Certainly, if two terms agree in their extralinguistic connections, if they show themselves to be interchangeable in their use, then we can speak of a difference in meaning only if there is in some way something different for us to understand in either case, and this can be so only if their structures are different, combining different elements; conversely, I claim, if there is something different to understand, then we have a divergence in meaning: '$\sin^2 + \cos^2$' may be interchangeable with '1', but there are operations to be mastered with the former, stages *en route* to an understanding of the formula, that are quite absent in the case of the simple numeral. In these terms we can distinguish the different expressions on either side of a correct equation, and more generally we have a rationale for keeping apart equivalent phrases or sentences whose equivalence is seen as the outcome of an argument—though once more, the more minimal the deduction required, the less inclined we shall be to insist on a difference in meaning, an insistence which in many cases would rightly be considered pedantic.

What I have been saying echoes Carnap [1947] and Lewis [1944], in particular with respect to the notion of *intensional isomorphism* in the former. However, difficulties that are perhaps peculiar to the present approach arise with words which have no internal complexity, and for which I hold that identity of application—understood aright—suffices for synonymy. So, if 'kine' and 'cattle' satisfy this condition, then, in view of the absence of any differences in their respective constitutions which make for something to be understood with respect to the one but not the other, we are obliged to reckon them synonyms. Much of the appeal of this conception resides in its promise of an extensional account of meaning in the basic cases, a promise held out by a notion, agreement in application, which comes close to that of agreement in reference. It is, however, the difficulties rather than the advantages of this approach that are likely to be found most striking. Must we reject as not strictly synonymous such hallowed pairs as 'bachelor' and 'unmarried man', 'oculist' and 'eye-doctor', or 'vixen' and 'female fox'? Simplicity of structure is surely not an inevitable bar to a representation of a word's meaning that is exact yet combines two or more morphemes. Think, after all, of the well-known difficulties confronting a semantically based morphology. The form 'walked' can be seen to combine 'walk' with a past-tense inflection, but how are we to deal with 'went' and 'ran'? We are surely restricting analysis intolerably if we are not permitted to go beyond superficial form.

Consider the pair, 'vixen' and 'female fox'. Here the following possibilities suggest themselves. First, it would seem possible, even if unlikely, that a person should come to a practical grasp of the word 'vixen' without having in any way isolated the notion of being a female; or, he may have such a notion, but it could conceivably come as a discovery to him that vixens were female, other factors, such as size, being what had guided him in his use of the word. Whereas the '-ess' ending in 'tigress' and 'lioness' is recognized as indicating the female of a species, the '-en' in 'vixen' is not, even though etymologically its contribution is the same—the entry for '-en' in *The Shorter Oxford English Dictionary* lists its occurrence in 'vixen' as the only surviving instance. The notion of being female has become submerged in the form of the word, and this could be reflected in a man's learning. And could he then be said to understand the word? We, of course, brought up on dictionaries, may regard him as ignorant of the word's true definition, but this objection threatens to introduce an element of artificiality: words do not have actual definitions merely through having meaning; they are given the former in an equation which, because of its extra precision and explicitness, is liable to be imperfect.

Of course, it remains true—and this is the second possibility—that the meaning of 'vixen' may be learned not by coming to recognize distinctive features of whatever it is that the word is applied to, but by being given an initial explanation in terms of the phrase 'female fox', in which case it is almost inevitable that the single word should be treated as interchangeable with the larger phrase. With names for the female of a species, something like a definition is a common route to their acquisition, the role being one that is familiar in the language and often made quite explicit, as with 'she-wolf', 'lioness', and other words with which 'vixen' can be brought into comparison—as we might compare 'went' with 'walked'.

It does not require the existence of dictionaries for there to be commonly accepted explanations of meaning having the role of definitions. On the other hand, below the ideal of the explicit definition there lurks a large number of facts of usage whose definitional status is difficult to evaluate. We can safely acknowledge a generally recognized intention to exclude males when speaking of *wives, mothers, daughters,* and *sisters,* and we can correspondingly say such things as 'Being female is necessary to being a sister', 'No male could literally or correctly be or count as a daughter', and so forth. However, the involvement of gender is atypical in its clarity. Certainly, it seems quite unrealistic to think of the general run of words as accurately paraphrasable in terms of a statement of necessary and sufficient conditions for their application. It is not at all apparent whether, when told that birds have wings, say, a child is being given information relevant to the question of what counts as a bird, or simply a general truth about birds. He is being told what a bird is, and that covers both; once we cast around for stricter conditions we may have to address ourselves to unfamiliar possibilities, discussion of which may terminate in a *decision* rather than uncover an underlying pattern of usage.

What comes first, I suggest, is agreement in application; this can exist, making for a sufficiently determinate usage with respect to a given word, even though different individuals make use of different criteria for the application of that word. Some criteria become highly natural, given that they are obvious to everyone—perhaps even such that one could not be in ignorance of them and yet able to apply the word correctly—and their general recognition may suffice to give them definitional status. Criteria which are not thus to the fore cannot be as safely extracted from actual usage, and may attain definitional significance only if we decree as much. There may accordingly be doubt as to the possibility of providing, without some distortion, a deductive equivalent for a given word, let alone a strict synonym. Furthermore, so long as a condition is not explicitly marked in a word, that word may have in this respect a degree of freedom it would otherwise lack, a freedom to extend to things which do not satisfy that condition without its being clear in general that we should speak of a change in meaning. Again, what is important is to avoid appeal to supposed conceptual connections which have no reality from the point of view of what a knowledge of usage can disclose.

As an illustration of these points, take the game of cards known as 'patience', among whose distinctive features is a general restriction to a single player. We should not wish to deny that 'patience' is applied on the basis of criteria; it is just that these may not be the same for all speakers; the criteria constitute a cluster, and it is not clear which are dominant. Enough of the game may be deemed to survive adaptation of a standard form to two players, enough for us to continue to speak of 'patience'—as is acknowledged in *The Shorter Oxford English Dictionary* definition as: 'a game of cards of which there are many varieties; usually for one player'. But now consider 'solitaire'. Because of the feature which this highlights, it will surely be less easy to speak of 'two-handed solitaire'.

This discussion takes us back to earlier observations on proper names and sense, where again what was dominant was what was determinate, viz. agreed application. If the word is one which is used in accordance with an explicit definition, or can be treated as thus used, then general criteria for its application can be given, criteria which we can claim to be bound up with the meaning of the word. This may hold both with respect to a common noun and, the point about meaning apart, with respect to a proper name, but equally it is possible that any relevant criteria should vary from individual to individual, in which case they of course have no place in an account of what is generally understood by the word. My earlier argument against ascribing meaning to proper names was naturally taken as offering a contrast with common nouns, but we could also argue that agreed reference—i.e. application—was paramount for the latter, criteria of application being capable of varying among speakers without revealing a difference in understanding with respect to 'hay' as much as to 'Hay'.

If the argument has been on the right lines, there is little to support the suggestion that two simple terms may enjoy an identical application yet expand into non-equivalent paraphrases. I do not rule this out as impossible, but the onus is surely on one who thinks this so with a given pair of words to show how the case of explicit definition gives a suitable model. To take an example from the realm of fantasy, Quine has suggested that a word which we were naturally inclined to translate as 'rabbit' might with equal justice be rendered as 'undetached rabbit part', as far as conformity with the data is concerned (Quine [1968]). Given that the sense of the word 'part' does not favour its application to a whole rabbit—so that we might speak of undetached rabbit parts as prolific breeders—the example is not as persuasive as it might be. That in pointing to the one we shall be pointing to the other is not the only consideration. Still, we can allow that, with a shift in sense, 'part' could come to apply to the whole, giving us an alternative rendering of the original word in much the same way as 'gin and tonic without the tonic' is interchangeable with 'gin'. Now it is true that in either case mere consideration of the range of application will not allow us to detect a difference in meaning, but this is not to say that we can with equal justice take the word in one way or the other. If it is possible to discern the appropriate complexity in the word or phrase, if our knowledge of other words in the language enables us to identify the relevant structure, the less straightforward reading becomes a possibility; failing such support, however, such an interpretation appears quite gratuitous.

55. Meaning and application

If we think of meaning on the model of sign and thing signified, there is a problem as to how meaning is to be understood if there neither is, nor ever has been, anything answering to a given word. Similarly in terms of application: if having meaning is having application, then the mere existence of a meaningful word will entail the existence at some time or other of an extralinguistic item of an appropriate kind. This objection can be met by expanding 'application' to 'possible application', a move which also accommodates words having different meanings but null extensions, words which could be said to differ in so far as their possible applications diverged. Once more, however, the modal term does not provide a satisfactory stopping-place, since it is the grounds for its introduction that furnish the more specific information which we seek: we wish to know how, precisely, that possibility is founded in the actual application or use of words.

In defining a word we commonly aim to provide another word or combination of words whose meaning is already known; knowing the meanings of the latter and understanding the way they are put together we can arrive at an understanding of how the word in question would be used, even if an occasion for using it—with actual reference to something—has never presented itself. It is a function of words whose meanings are already secured. The mode of combination here will typically be that involved in delimiting a general term, so the kind of operation seen in conjunction, or in the association with a relative clause. Thus, we have never perhaps had occasion to speak of a 'computerized metronome', but the linguistic possibility of such a device is clearly founded in actual usage, the individual terms being ones which we have had occasion to apply and the mode of combination being of the most elementary kind. That we can formulate such linguistically acceptable possibilities and recognize them as such prior to any actual application of the whole phrase to anything cannot be a matter for dispute, even if we can also devise combinations whose intelligibility is dubious.

Suppose we have a word which cannot be defined by appeal to other combinations of words—a word for an unusual smell, let us say. We can come by an understanding of such a word by being trained in its use, where such training involves the development of a recognitional capacity: we learn when or of what the word is correctly used. Can it be said that there is yet another alternative? It seems impossible that we should attain a grasp of the meaning of the word without recourse to one or other procedure, and indeed impossible even to ascribe a meaning to the word in the absence of both of the following possibilities: either the word has its meaning conferred upon it by its employment in circumstances which endow it with symbolic status, or else it can be defined in terms of words which are, ultimately, of this type—this latter being a possibility which we have reason to think exceptional. We loosen the former connection by allowing for the notion of a merely possible application, but not at the expense of severing a non-linguistic grounding of the terms which might enter into its definition. It may seem easy to divorce the notion of having a meaning from any extralinguistic facts, but this is to overlook the need for a backing which even a possibility demands. The only alternative is a mentalistic conception of meaning, the mind somehow conferring upon a sequence of sounds the kind of role which we have sought in an association with circumstances of utterance—as if we could dispense with the extralinguistic links definitive of meaning. However, I do not mean to reject the view in question as *logically* impossible; understanding is something we could have been born with. I do wish to stress the gulf which in fact exists between mental supply and linguistic demand; perhaps what we connect a word with is a property, but a universal is no less real, no more a creature of the mind, for being individuated on the basis of different principles from those pertaining to physical objects.

What is true is that the linguistic determination of meaning will have to be construed fairly broadly. Consider words which have their homes in stories. Sometimes an explanation which approximates to a definition may be offered—as with J. R. R. Tolkien's characterization of a *hobbit* at the beginning of *The Hobbit*—but perhaps our understanding of such words as 'elf', 'troll', 'leprechaun', and the rest is built up in more piecemeal fashion as the stories in which they occur develop. And perhaps we cannot really make that much sense of some of them at all; enough to get quite a lot out of the story, but if, say, a leprechaun is something with intelligence, a personality, can become invisible and get inside a watch, then the word does not appear to mean anything very coherent. There is no more than a presumption of sense in such cases. How much too, we may wonder, is the uncertain meaning of 'ghost' a reflection of the uncertain status of the phenomena which have prompted its use?

Which brings us to another obvious objection. I say that, although a word may in fact be applicable to nothing, its meaningfulness can be secured if it can be displayed as a function of terms whose applicability is not in doubt. Should we also say that an ostensibly descriptive phrase that *cannot* apply to anything is therefore meaningless, as my case would appear to require? Why not? If such expressions as 'goes on for ever', 'plane defined by two points', 'irresistible force meeting immovable object', 'time without change', and so forth, really do allow of no consistent or coherent interpretation, then there is no reason why we should not follow familiar usage and brand them as 'meaningless'.

The pressure against this move has two sources: the meaningfulness of the individual terms may be clear, and the denial of meaning may seem to challenge the legitimacy of proofs by *reductio ad absurdum,* or more generally, the intelligibility of larger contexts in which the phrase may occur. On the first point, however, we can simply say that so long as it is made clear that we are not casting doubt on the meaningfulness of the component expressions when we label the phrase as a whole 'meaningless', nothing is condemned that we should wish to see reprieved. The answer to the second point falls in line with this: an unintelligible mark figuring in a proof may well make nonsense of the proof, but the constituent expressions can play a role therein in accordance with their meanings even though their combination expresses an impossibility and so merits the epithet 'meaningless'. Again, there is no reason why we should not find an asymmetry between, say, 'This is a square circle' and 'This is not a square circle', calling the former meaningless, or nonsense, but not the latter. In their ordinary acceptation, both 'meaningless' and 'nonsense' are quite consistent with 'false'.

56. Analyticity

If asked to give a characterization of propositions which are necessarily or analytically true, many philosophers would think in terms of propositions which are true in virtue of the meanings and modes of connection of their constituent words, propositions for which the supposition of a change in truth value means a supposition that at least one of the words has undergone a change in sense. We have provided support for this approach in two ways. First, we have revealed the groundlessness of fears that use of 'meaning' will bring with it a commitment to problematic entities. Second, we have broken the 'intensional circle' in our treatment of synonymy, neither 'necessarily' nor any kindred notion being found indispensable, or even particularly useful, in this connection, no more useful than a modal term would be in explaining truths which depended on identity of reference. On the other hand, we have also seen that questions of meaning and questions of fact—or, as I should prefer, *other* questions of fact—are not always easily separable, a consideration which has been thought to count against the intelligibility of a division of sentences or statements into the analytic and the synthetic. We shall now look further at some aspects of the issue, beginning with the way in which analyticity is seemingly attained by excluding factors which make for variability in truth value.

Such a synthetic proposition as 'The shops are closed' may be true on one occasion of its utterance, false on another, without our having to assign a matching difference in the interpretation of any of its terms, though even with a synthetic proposition there is a sense in which a difference in what is meant must be involved if there is any change in truth value. If the sentence, 'The shops are closed', is true at a given time, then the speaker will have had in mind certain shops, and by 'are closed' will have meant 'are closed now, Christmas Day 1965', let us say. To suppose a change in truth value is to suppose a change in what is thus meant—leaving aside the more radical changes in meaning possible, as with the interpretation of 'shop', which are relevant to preservation of analyticity as well—and is of course to imply that the sentence contains terms which may have different such intentions associated with them. It is an important, if obvious fact about languages, that differences in the time and place of utterance, along with differences in the identity of objects of which we speak, do not have to find expression in the words used, but can be inferred from the context, thus ensuring the variability in truth value, or contingency, of those sentences that are non-committal in these respects, sentences which are 're-usable' despite a change in circumstances. The dependence of truth on meaning is quite general, not something that only analytic truths can generate, though it is perhaps most obviously to the fore with the latter. Thus, philosophers who find it easy to say that a truth such as 'Anyone taller than a given man is taller than anyone shorter than that man' could become false without any accompanying change in meaning, leave nothing which might explain the difference between truth at one time, falsity at another, a position that is no more plausible than that which would allow 'The baby is asleep' to vary in truth value without the speaker coming to intend a different baby or a different time.

The appropriate characterization of analytic propositions emerges readily enough from this contrast. We simply require that P be free of those factors which make for a possible variation in truth value, so a proposition whose terms bear a constant meaning and which cannot be interpreted with respect to different persons, places, times, and things from occasion to occasion of its utterance. If, then, P is true, it is analytically or necessarily true, if false, then analytically or necessarily false. The kinds of truth which will be most plainly analytic will be those from which any such variable reference is patently absent, and prominent among borderline cases will be such sentences as 'The tallest giraffe is the tallest giraffe', sentences which may be quite trivial, given that the description or name has application, but which we should not be prepared to assert without qualification if we did not think that the existence condition was satisfied. That is, there may still be some deictic element involved, and not the total indifference to the particular that ensures non-contingency.

It is not difficult to see the analyticity of mathematical truths in the terms suggested. Thus, geometrical propositions are understood in an idealized way, difficulties which might be encountered in any actual construction of a figure being simply ruled out, along with other conceivable sources of error, such as the disappearance of a line or its alteration in some respect. Arithmetic is similar. The ordering of the natural numbers is not thought to be subject to change: if a number lies between two other numbers, that is where it stays; if $2^{13} - 1$ is a prime, then it is so of necessity, in that this is not a feature that can vary with time, so give way to a different possibility when conditions change. Of course, to ensure the requisite static character some tidying up of usage may be required, though in the case of arithmetic, not very much. Again, even if we include possible changes in meaning among the allowable variable factors in such a way as to prevent us from labelling any proposition as analytic, this does not count against another usage according to which the possibility of such changes does not make for contingency. Either usage is equally possible.

The transition from an empirical proposition to a geometrical idealization, or other species of necessary truth, by a gradual elimination of possible sources of error, is an intelligible development, but it may be wondered how anything of substance can survive such purification. How do we avoid thereby divesting a proposition of all sense or content? It may

seem that no claim is made without a contrasting pole of
falsity, a genuine possibility to exclude, but that, I suggest, is
to look at the question of a contrast from the wrong perspective: we attach significance to a true statement about a number, not because a conflicting possibility remains to be taken
seriously after truth has been established, but because of the
contrast with what can be truly said of other numbers. Once
more, focusing on bare truth and falsity rather than more
specific features of a mathematical proposition leads to a distorted account of such propositions.

On the other hand, there are grounds for regarding the phrase
'necessarily true' as a misnomer, or at least as highly misleading. Calling a proposition *necessarily* true is like saying that it
is invariably true, like it in that it suggests that the truth of
the proposition is put to the test on repeated occasions. It is
as if we pretended that a given analytic proposition was of
a kind which it was not, that a possibility arose for it as for
a contingent proposition which might or might not hold in
certain circumstances, but whereas the latter could well fail,
that the analytic proposition was endowed with a special
virtue which enabled it to emerge triumphant on every such
occasion. There is a conventionalist strain in my account of
necessity, in so far as the emphasis is on the exclusion of
possible sources of error rather than on the necessary proposition as equipped to defy all attempts at falsification. Compare the description of an abstract object as 'indestructible',
which suggests a resistance to all efforts aimed at its destruction, when it is rather that the notion of destruction has no
clear sense in this instance.

Consider the contrast between 'A theodolite is an instrument for measuring horizontal and vertical angles' and 'All
theodolites make use of lenses'. Supposing that an instrument
would count as a theodolite even if it did not contain lenses,
the latter is liable to refutation should we come across a theodolite which is exceptional in this respect, whereas the former
is not thought of as at the mercy of findings in particular cases.
There is, of course, an underlying empirical regularity, a regularity in the usage of 'theodolite'—the term commonly being
deemed applicable only in so far as a given instrument is as
specified—but given that this regularity is established, there

need be no further risk involved in a projection to unexamined cases. There is a question here of degree, of indeterminacy in meaning allowing for different lines of usage to fall out, but there is a great difference in a speaker's treatment of the two forms, in his attitude towards future possibilities: if P is empirical, then he will leave open the possibility that inspection will favour one alternative over the other; if P is not empirical, the matter can be decided in advance: an instrument simply will not count as a theodolite if it does not satisfy the conditions given. Compare too the way our attitude may differ to the proposition, 'Horses do not come in herds', depending on whether this is taken as reporting a discovery—'Horses come only in ones and twos'—or as vouched for by usage, the term 'herd' not being applied to horses.

Analytic truths are sometimes characterized as truths which we refuse to give up, whatever the circumstances. As well as suggesting a misconception about the way such propositions might be put to a test, this characterization is unduly narrow. There is no reason why a form of words should not be understood at a certain time and by a certain group of people in such a way that it is deemed analytic, even though other interpretations have been favoured in the past or will become accepted in the future. Suppose, for instance, that for the customs officers, 'A pamphlet is a book' is analytic, even if in ordinary usage this is not so. Something like this limited analyticity is common in legal, commercial, and scientific discourse, but it would be quite inappropriate to liken this to the case where a strongly confirmed empirical proposition is involved, a proposition which we could give up only with great reluctance and in the face of findings which left us no choice. I suppose a person might hold to 'A pamphlet is a book' with some passion, but his strength of feeling would not, one would hope, blind him to the fact that what he was clinging to was no more than a way of using a word, and a way that is not even sanctioned by general usage. The view being criticized makes it sound as though analyticity were necessarily difficult to establish, that, as with an empirical generalization, the proposition had to stand the test, at least of our attitudes towards its assertibility, over indefinitely many occasions, when all that may be necessary is knowledge of speakers' intentions for a limited period.

Part of the confusion here is due to the habit of speaking of *the proposition* P in abstraction from particular circumstances. That is, it is the proposition P that we are asked to consider for analyticity, and which it is said we might or might not consider abandoning, but a person might well wish to hold that P, as uttered and understood on one occasion, could, because of the way it was intended, simply not be abandoned or rejected, whereas on another occasion of its use it need not be thus invulnerable. Talk of P's never being abandoned, come what may, suggests, as I say, that P is continually being put to the test, or at least that relevant situations continually arise, some of which might lead to its revision, but this does not apply if we are thinking of a proposition as individuated by spatio-temporal considerations. The character of such a proposition as analytic is not determined by considering the extent of the speaker's preparedness to revise that proposition, but by considering the kind of support that he considers appropriate. If he thinks it irrelevant to do anything describable as putting himself into a position to judge of the matter, but regards word usage as decisive, then his understanding of the words is as analytic, and it matters not one bit whether he will continue to use them in this way. Subsequent revision of usage will not show that the proposition which he uttered on that occasion was not analytic. There is no doubt that we do consider it appropriate to support different propositions in these different ways, that we so intend them that considerations of the two kinds are differently relevant to their truth, and this aspect of the distinction can be dissociated from hypotheses as to how in future we might propose to employ the key words.

The case I have been considering is rather straightforward, the hypothetical speaker not being supposed to think he must answer to a more generally established usage; there is an area of indeterminacy as regards the relations between the two words 'book' and 'pamphlet', an area which makes it reasonable to stipulate that a pamphlet is a book, or conversely that it is not. Someone who legislates in this way can be criticized for arbitrariness in his appropriation of a word, but he does not have to establish that usage favours him on borderline cases. When it is not a question of such stipulation, the support appropriate to an analytic interpretation of a form of words of this simple kind will make reference to general usage. Here, of course, the risks are greater, though there need be no demand that every usage agree with that required to make the sentence analytic. As long as there is *a* generally accepted usage in which it has this status, all is well. Doubts about the analytic/synthetic distinction are of little interest if they merely exemplify a form of scepticism about the existence of regularities in word usage, which in many instances are not even relevant. And it is only scepticism, surely, only a disregard for standards of credibility that would normally be accepted without question, that could lead someone to pretend that such a proposition as 'I'm not as young as I used to be' could, if understood literally, be anything other than true.

For those whose doubts derive from suspicions bearing upon meaning, in particular upon sameness of meaning, there is perhaps no really significant difference between the two kinds of case—that in which general usage is thought to provide a foundation for the analytic truth, and that in which legislation is dominant—difficulties in establishing sameness of meaning which require extensive knowledge of actual usage perhaps being thought secondary to the question of what it is that such researches establish, a question that is just as much to the fore if I stipulate that anything describable as w is to be reckoned a v, and vice versa. This would be a curious position. There is no denying the intelligibility nor the necessity of the notion of meaning, and therewith a resolve to use a word with a certain meaning, or with the same meaning as a given word. There are general reasons why we should not expect exact synonyms to abound, but there is no more than a general expectation that any two words in active use will be found to differ in meaning, however slightly. In speaking of one word as being a synonym of another we can set aside any nonsense about criteria of identity appropriate to 'entities', and in any event there is no need to concentrate on the extreme case of synonymy. With sentences of the form 'An F is a G', sentences which may figure in any genus plus difference definition, there may be nothing as strong as this required, no implication both ways. Furthermore, there is a rich yield of analytic truths from non-synonyms, most true statements of the form 'An F is not a G' being non-accidentally true. Just let F be the name of any insect, G the name of any kitchen appliance.

But what of those cases where, as I acknowledge, it is difficult to draw the line between support from language and support from non-linguistic facts? What, if I may use such a term, are we to *infer* from the existence of such instances? First, my impression is that we are not so much confronted with unresolvable cases, as with cases which, perhaps unexpectedly, are usually to be declared synthetic. Consider the proposition, 'Bananas are fruit'. On the one hand, such species–genus generalizations may initially be reckoned analytic; on the other hand, perhaps what is at work in creating this impression is the familiarity of the truth together with a certain dictionary mentality. After all, it would on reflection seem possible that we should have been able to identify bananas as such without having any conception of them as fruit, their character in this respect coming as a discovery. Similarly, with 'Whales are mammals' I should regard synthetic status as winning out—if only by a slim margin—at least as regards ordinary, non-technical usage.

Second, while there may be room for uncertainty once we move away from explicit definitions, or from areas where we have seen to it by stipulation that falsity is excluded, it does not appear that this uncertainty makes for significant obscurity, let alone unintelligibility, in the given characterization of the analytic/synthetic distinction. Is is obscure to say that an analytic truth is one that is true in virtue of the meaning of its constituent words and their mode of combination? As far as I can determine it is not, any apparent obscurities generally proving to be on the side of particular sentences to which we might seek to apply the characterization. But if there are, as there no doubt will be, occasions on which the obscurity is on the side of 'analytic', that does not spell the end of its usefulness. *Any* distinction is liable to be uncertain in its interpretation from time to time, and it would be wrong to condemn the present dichotomy for failing to come up to a standard which workable distinctions quite generally fail to meet. Whatever our theoretical doubts, we must in practice continue to maintain a lively concern with such questions as whether, for instance, 'effect' is intended in such a way that 'an uncaused effect' is inconsistent for a certain speaker, even if in non-philosophical contexts our concern is almost exclusively with truth, rather than with the exact grounds for what is said. What we do find, unsurprisingly, is that those analytic truths are clearest whose character as instances of logical laws is clearest, and least open to question are the general formulations of such laws. Why? Well, showing a truth to be analytic usually just is a matter of showing it to be an instance of a more general logical principle; furthermore, with descriptive vocabulary it is often possible to lay less than normal emphasis on one strand in a word's usage and still be left with something to say: play down the connection of 'bachelor' with 'male', so that we may speak of a 'bachelor girl', and the residue given by 'unmarried' leaves us with some content to the word, whereas with words like 'if' and 'not' we tend not to meet with a cluster of criteria which can be treated in comparable fashion. This is, of course, not to say that we can escape an appeal to meaning in giving an account of the logical vocabulary; there is no lessening of the dependence on that concept.

57. Indeterminacy of translation

A similar storm in a similar teacup is the debate over the indeterminacy of translation, a debate which I shall now very briefly join. Over the years speakers of a language come to a common grasp of subtle nuances in meaning which may be extremely difficult to convey to a non-native speaker. We do make a distinction between the members of such pairs as 'almost' and 'nearly', 'likely' and 'probable', 'if . . . not' and 'unless', but it may be obscure just what conditions have been operative in dictating the divergent patterns of usage. The question becomes of particular theoretical interest in connection with the problem of mastering an undocumented language. So, by what features do we recognize a certain term as expressing negation? How is a past tense to be identified as such? We know that words and the circumstances of their use, reinforced perhaps by explanations, furnish the data for an adequate answer to these and other questions of meaning—a native speaker, one whose mastery of the language is not in doubt, has, after all, access to nothing further—but in particular cases the correct identification of a word as having a certain meaning may prove complex, certain terms having to be assumed to have certain interpretations before we can assign a meaning to the given word. This is not quite the problem that confronts the child learning his mother tongue: he is not in a position to formulate hypotheses about the meanings of words he does not as yet understand. Nor does it mean that the point will not be reached where we, learners of a second language, are able to fit together the pieces unambiguously, the earlier assumptions having now been discharged, or recognized as erroneous. The fact that languages are mastered shows that we have nothing to fear from what has seemed to some a theoretical possibility: that the combination of words and the circumstances of utterance, however extensively envisaged, can fail to determine one interpretation of the language from among an indefinite number of genuinely distinct alternatives. It is true that in particular cases it can be difficult to show precisely how the correct interpretation excludes all its rivals, and some degree of indeterminacy of sense must always be granted. However, the fact that a shared understanding is recognizable, that indeed a difference in meaning or understanding which could not show itself in usage would be unintelligible, this is enough to show that there is no basis for scepticism in the consideration that various alternatives may remain open for some time in the initial stages of learning a language; it may be difficult to say when we have reached a point when our usage is substantially the same as that of the native speakers, but that—a like usage—is all that a common understanding demands, and the difficulty of drawing a line and the unsystematic character of our progress towards this state of understanding cast no doubt on its reality. Appeal may be made to the empirical character, and hence revisability, of any hypothesis about meaning, but all this does is counter one who believes that the point can be reached where doubt is *logically* excluded. It does not show that there is a realistic alternative to what has been established by experience, that doubts on this score are to be taken seriously.

In adopting the perspective of one learning a second language we risk distortion by placing ourselves in a disadvantageous position. Thinking of ourselves as observers, as concerned to put various interpretive hypotheses to the test, suggests exclusion from the situation in which we react unthinkingly with the right words in the right circumstances. When learning a language, a stage to get past as quickly as possible is that in which we say what we say as a result of reasoning, of applying rules. The native speaker, who constitutes the ideal, does not say what he says on any such basis, but his linguistic responses are what may be used to test a rule, to show it to be or not to be a satisfactory recipe for instructing a learner. It was not the Ancient Romans who had to go about saying, in Latin or in mentalese, such things as 'From *nemo* let me never say, *neminis* or *nemine*', and if some rather backward centurion had to admonish himself with such reminders, he would be making use of a rule which was derivative upon established regularities and in no way their source. Again, our intonation patterns show regularities of various kinds, but given that we may be quite unaware of any rule that might be used to regulate our speech so as to produce the appropriate patterns, the (intentional) notions of applying or following a rule appear misplaced. A foreigner may have to make a conscious effort to remind himself of the way in which we modulate questions, say, and he reaches a more authoritative position when he is no longer dependent on a rule, when he has been brought to the stage which we reached without any such help, giving unthinking responses which match those of the native speaker.

It is the unreasoned responses that go with a firm grasp of a language, with a genuine feeling for the use of words. If our proposer of a hypothesis as to meaning has not attained this stage, he is hardly equipped to pronounce definitively upon such a hypothesis. If he has, then there can be no doubts on his part as to what the words in question mean, whatever the difficulties met with in finding adequate equivalents in his mother tongue. *What w means* is not the same as *how w translates*; or: learning a foreign language is one thing, translating it another. There is no expectation that mapping sentences from one language onto those from another will invariably prove possible, but the difficulty in finding a good fit gives no support to the claim that genuinely distinct interpretive hypotheses are always possible—or not in any interesting sense. If a given term, w, does not have a close match, we might say that equating it with u is no better and no worse than equating it with v; they are equally far out. But this is not a matter of a hypothesis that w may mean u or it may mean v, we simply cannot tell. We can tell: it does not mean either. Indeterminacy of translation is bound to exist, but it shows no more than a looseness of fit between languages at some point. Indeterminacy of meaning is also inevitable, but only in the sense that native speakers may respond differently in the same situation, some deeming a given word in place, others not. Such indefiniteness is not the ground for distinct accounts of what the word *really* means.

It is sometimes supposed that our everyday beliefs can be treated as having the character of hypotheses, hypotheses which we might choose to retain or not, depending on the pragmatic value which adherence or rejection might have. This open character is difficult to reconcile with the seemingly mandatory character which such beliefs possess. As a person looks about him he thinks what he thinks willy-nilly, quite without regard to his wishes or intentions; if what he thinks, without reservations, is that he is climbing a hill, he can at best pretend to believe otherwise, and to say that *logically*, none the less, other alternatives are possible, is only to say that there is room for alternatives only so long as he is prepared to discount what, as it happens, he cannot but believe; or, if conflicting alternatives are to be described as 'logically' possible, that is only to say that, whatever excludes them, it is not pure logic; it is not to give sense or substance to an alternative in any real way.

Scepticism about meaning is likewise difficult to take seriously so long as language is not viewed abstractly, as some kind of formal, combinatorial system, but is taken in conjunction with circumstances of utterance, circumstances which of necessity impose a constraint on the interpretation of what is said. After all, if they do not, what grounds have we for regarding the sounds we hear as belonging to a language, as constituting meaningful signs? It may be argued, however, that lying and error can be called upon to make the extralinguistic

connections untraceable, to destroy the constancies determinative of meaning. And indeed they can, but only with respect
to a fragment of linguistic behaviour. First, we note that consistent misuse of words, as might be expected from speakers
anxious to prevent others from arriving at an understanding of
their speech, may soon defeat the misusers by conferring a
new meaning on the words, which rapidly become reliable
signs of their originally inapposite correlates. Regularly use
'fish' for 'pig' and that is what the word will come to mean,
and be taken to mean, in your mouth. Use the word according
to no pattern, and of course you will cease to be saying anything. My claim is that, while allowance must always be made
for indeterminacy of sense, coherent speech is not susceptible
of genuinely opposed alternative interpretations; the claim is
not that we can decipher nonsense. Second, and more important, the supposition that the speakers can embark upon the
less wild use of language, but that they should endeavour in
various ways to thwart the learner by making the connections
between words and world quite opaque, this presupposes an
earlier normal period when the associations were set up, the
language given shape and learned. After all, if he cannot learn
the language in the given conditions, there is no reason to
suppose that the native speakers could have fared any better
had they been exposed to like conditions, and nothing more.
If we are excluded from knowledge of this earlier period, the
exclusion is only contingent and of no theoretical interest.
Both error and lying involve a recognizable divergence from
constancies already established, and we can make no sense of
them in the absence of data that are adequate for our understanding in a way which lying and error were supposed to
threaten.

One final point. It is sometimes supposed that indeterminacy
of translation becomes more acute as we move to the more
theoretical reaches of a science. I should have thought that,
on the contrary, the propositions which arise here would be
much easier to deal with, since by the time we are in a position
to tackle them we shall presumably have mastered the basic
elements of the language, the necessary quantitative, spatio-
temporal, and other concepts which give us the framework in
which to ask questions about what scientists think they are

up to. Explaining the difference between 'atom' and 'molecule' is not obviously more difficult than explaining the difference between 'think' and 'believe', or any other more homely words. Perhaps it is supposed that, while we can acquire some understanding of less sophisticated propositions by considering what is taking place when they are uttered, this procedure will let us down once we move away from our observational base. That is no doubt true. It is also extremely difficult to work out the rules of a card game just by watching people playing, and in either case we can consider ourselves fortunate that the role of silent spectator, never requesting a word of elucidation, is not one to which we are inevitably restricted.

58. Verifiability

My account of meaning has been of a distinctly verificationist cast, and I should like now to set forth briefly some points in elucidation and defence of this involvement, at the same time carrying some earlier discussions a stage further and indicating how the sceptic might be tackled. I shall begin with fairly 'untheoretical' problem cases, such as that of statements about the past, and then proceed to general propositions and propositions about subatomic particles. All very sketchily.

Arguments in favour of verifiability, as necessary for any proposition which we can say is either true or false, often take the form of arguments for conclusive verifiability, and it is this development which, as much as any, threatens to make the insistence thereon appear unreasonable. To outline that development, we have that if some phenomenon, A, can be considered evidence for B, as smoke is for fire, this must seemingly be because the joint occurrence of the two has been observed. Since the two are logically independent, there is no other way in which the association might have been learned except through experience, which implies that B has been independently ascertained, so ascertained without the assistance of A, and ultimately, without the assistance of any indirect indications such as A. Some kind of direct ground appears necessary if we are to have a fixed point against which the evidential value of various signs and indications can be assessed. In short, it appears that a termination in conclusive verification is demanded. Against this demand, on the other hand, we can perhaps set the consideration that doubt is never logically excluded: however careful and thorough our investigations, however extensive the confirmation of others, we can make sense, it would seem, of the possibility that some relevant consideration has been overlooked, that future findings will in some way force retraction of our claim.

Verification is to be conclusive only if no reliance is placed on mere signs or evidence. Does admitting the possibility of error mean that we can never have more than evidence? The sceptic, of course, thinks that the data which we consider to furnish evidence are in fact the most we can hope for: however vivid our seeming memories, the truth of our beliefs about the past is never guaranteed; however detailed our knowledge of a person's behaviour and physiology, his sensations and state of mind remain conjectural. In presenting the problem to us in such terms, the sceptic is taking a stand on the question of what can be justifiably asserted, and at the same time putting forward a framework of *proof* in terms of which his challenge is to be met. It is supposed that anything more than a non-committal report of memories, for instance—non-committal with respect to what has taken place earlier—is not strictly warranted. Consequently, acceptance of what he considers an assured starting-point means that success at meeting his challenge will have to be at the expense of consenting to some form of reductionism—in this case, of past to present. To counter the sceptic, then, we might reject his conception of what qualifies as a warranted assertion in the circumstances, and/or reject the use which he wishes us to make of the notion of proof.

Both these rejections look reasonable. So, if asked by the sceptic to prove an empirical claim which strikes us as incontrovertibly true, we may be at a loss to know how to proceed. To take one of his more basic targets, we may be sure beyond any shadow of a doubt that there is a strong smell in the room, but just saying or believing this does not make it so; appealing to others will not give the conclusiveness which the sceptic demands: he will find nothing amiss with the idea that our error should become more widespread, the result perhaps of an hallucination affecting everyone in these circumstances.

And in general, since anything which might have the truth of our claim as a consequence will be at least as vulnerable, we can be sure in advance that our cause is lost if it requires us to furnish a premiss that is satisfactory to the sceptic. And if our claim relates to the past, hopes of success are even dimmer. I am quite certain that I coughed a short time ago, but I am fortunate if I can get independent corroboration from a witness, so fortunate if I can get even as far as the inconclusive position which I have *vis-à-vis* the present smell.

When we have apparent certainty but no clear idea as to how our claim might be proved, it is worth remembering that proof must come to an end. It is in general quite artificial to think of a belief about a present smell or a recent action as being arrived at by reasoning, but in any case justification cannot always consist in tracing one belief back to another on which it depends; at some point justification, if it is to be had, must take a different form. However, if it is easy to recognize the limitations in the notion of proof as applied to empirical propositions, it is less easy to see how we can make sense of justification in its absence. What we must do is abandon the procedure which takes mathematics as its model and which makes it appear that a proposition is without support so long as it is without the backing of a proof; for propositions of the kind in question, anything that would count as a proof, whether deductive or inductive, is very much secondary. What we have first and foremost—the beginning of the language game—is agreed forms of judgements in certain circumstances, circumstances in which it is difficult to understand the possibility of error in any concrete way until it has been shown to be consistent with things' seeming to us as they do.

What does it mean to say that I might be wrong? If I make a prediction, saying that we shall find the light on in the cellar if we look, my being wrong is easily understood in terms of the relevant expectations not being fulfilled when I find myself appropriately placed to judge. If, however, the relevant expectations are satisfied as far as I am concerned, then one form of falsification is excluded. If, now, further investigations by me and by others continue to confirm the initial report, then the area in which a falsification might be found has contracted still more, and we are soon in a position where possible sources of error are difficult even to specify, insubstantial possibilities which merely reflect our concession that verification can never be described as logically conclusive. If that is the point we reach, there is no call to qualify our assertion in deference to such possibilities: to say merely that this is *probably* a dagger that I see before me—with the implication that there is a chance worth recognizing that my hand should pass right through it—would in most circumstances be to accord too great a weight to a possibility which is no more than fantasy.

The appeal to circumstances is clearly important, rationality often being simply a matter of proportioning one's confidence to the character of the circumstances in which one's judgement is made. Identifications of fast-moving distant objects made in a poor light are generally not to be trusted as much as those made in good light with respect to a motionless object near at hand. Indeed, it is our unfamiliarity with error in the latter kinds of circumstance that makes for our bewilderment when the sceptic voices his doubts—and for our frustration at not being able to force him to acknowledge what we find inescapable.

As another example, suppose we refuse to abide by the sceptic's judgment as to what qualifies as a fully warranted assertion with respect to a person's sensations, offering the disputed proposition—'This man has hurt himself', let us say—as something that we are perfectly entitled to assert in the circumstances. Sometimes, no doubt, this will be rash, by ordinary standards as well as by the sceptic's, but there surely are occasions when we can assert with justifiable confidence that another is in pain, even if on reflection we should allow that, in view of general human fallibility, doubt is abstractly conceivable.

The sceptic will allow that this characterizes our attitude in real-life situations, but he will hold that our failure to doubt is of merely psychological interest; logically, there is always room for doubt whatever the extent of the evidence at our disposal. However, the claim that we are fully warranted in what we say can be sustained to the extent that we can appeal to the proven reliability of such a judgement made in such circumstances. In these terms, our certainty that a man who has just struck his thumb with a hammer has hurt himself is not in the slightest misplaced. When have we ever had cause to retract such a judgement? When have we found that it is not confirmed by subsequent developments, that it has met with anybody's dissent? People have occasionally deceived us by pretending that they have injured themselves, but we may suppose that hammer and thumb have been observed to come into contact, that the flesh has been seen to be damaged and a loud cry heard to follow. By contrast, consider the reactions of a footballer after a seemingly hard tackle: his groans and writhings indicate pain, but his subsequent behaviour—the remarkable recovery once a penalty has been awarded against the opposition and the failure of the playback to show that the man had received a serious knock—soon dispose us to treat these performances with a degree of warranted scepticism.

The question now arises how an established record of success is to be taken; more specifically, whether such a record constitutes inductive grounds for the claim at issue. This is certainly a status it can have, but only if there is something further which remains to be checked and for which it offers positive support. If checking and re-checking have left us unable to know where error might lie, there may be no further investigation of a more decisive character whose outcome can be reasonably predicted on the evidence of our past successes. Given the lack of scope for any more clinching verification, there is not much we can usefully take the evidence as evidence for, though we might perhaps take it as increasing the likelihood that some unusual source of error will not reveal itself. So, we may never go wrong in stating the whereabouts of streets in our neighbourhood, this unblemished record giving support to a present judgement, but if the latter is verified by following up the claim with a direct verification *in situ,* our history of past successes becomes superfluous, its only possible relevance being in giving us further grounds for supposing that our apparent verification will not turn out to be only apparent.

A reliance on the notion of turning out to be true, as is made by an appeal to evidence, again takes us back to the more important non-inductively based assertion. This is where the problems lie. With respect to the example of a person in pain, we must determine what counts as excluding all realistic forms of error in such a way as to leave us with a claim that makes no presumption as to the evidential value of our data. The question is notoriously complex and will not be pursued here, but I venture to say that we may have to give greater attention than is generally realized to the question of the precise way in which the body is affected if we are to circumscribe pain adequately. This seems counter-intuitive, as our concept of pain appears to be essentially a concept of something that is not known of by observation. However, Wittgenstein's private language argument indicates that we cannot stop here, and while that argument is only indirect—implying that the meaningfulness of talk of sensations requires public criteria of correctness, but without telling us what those criteria are in any specific way—I suggest that the general argument might be reinforced with a characterization of painful sensations which will connect these, not merely with aversive behaviour, but with bodily disturbances of a detectible kind: damage to bodily tissue in the first instance, and perhaps even less obvious physiological considerations relevant to distinguishing pains from other unpleasant sensations, such as those of nausea, vertigo, or intense cold, such considerations becoming more important when there is no visible injury. We are inclined to regard an avowal of pain, made with sincerity and understanding, as guaranteeing its truth, and thereby to be independent of the public criteria which make for the vulnerability of, say, perceptual judgements. A claim that there was a loud bang can compete with the judgements of others, and does not necessarily win out in cases of conflict; by contrast, a claim to have a pain in the knee does not appear to generate expectations with regard to what must at least be possible for another to discover. However, answerability to public criteria does come in via the condition of understanding. It is not automatically assured that a person's use of 'pain' is backed with understanding, any more than his use of any other word, and establishing that it is involves finding it to be used in conditions which are standard for speakers of the language. Exactly what those conditions are is a question for further investigation, and it is not clear *a priori* where exactly such investigation will lead us.

Other aspects of the general problem can be illustrated by statements about the past. It is often thought that such statements cannot be verified, the assumption being that verification would require us to revisit the past, that the past is as would be revealed to one who had it in his power to go back in time and inspect the scene remembered, so not necessarily as our memories, written records, and so forth, would have it be. This is a misconception, but it does draw attention to the possibility that a statement about the past may be uncertain, simply because the speaker had not made a sufficiently careful check at the earlier time. The degree of certainty in this respect will vary from case to case, but the central problem concerns doubts about past-tense statements which bear just on their past-tense character, statements for which, it would be said, the reality which makes them true is no more. However, I suggest that we can still speak of verification, still draw a suitable direct/indirect contrast, the role of a direct, non-inductively based judgement being filled by just those statements having that role with respect to the present, only with the tense of the verb altered. The statement, 'I can see the traffic', would not normally be regarded as based on evidence, and the same status can be claimed for the form adjusted to reflect the lapse in time, namely, 'I was able to see the traffic'. Similarly, 'There was a debate in progress' may compare with 'There is a debate in progress', just in so far as both may be based on indirect indications.

I think of evidence in these terms, rather than say that a statement about the past is based on evidence just through being a report of what is *remembered*, as opposed to currently witnessed. This is like regarding one's present preparedness to say 'I can see the traffic' as evidence for its truth; not impossible, but highly unusual, especially for the speaker himself. However, he could be looking forward to possible confirmation from others, or, in other instances, to what might be found by looking again, and in either case we can make some sense of evidence in relation to such a further development, a development which the present judgement gives reason to anticipate. If an individual's memory thus offers only evidence, at least in regarding it as such we come to specify what counts as more final verification. What I do not allow is that memory reports should be considered less than final because of the supposedly unfavourable comparison with what might be disclosed to one who could travel backwards in time. More generally, the important consideration is not that *A* rather than *B* should be characterized as indirect, but that any characterization of evidence as such should be supplemented by an indication of how the respects in which it is wanting might be made good.

Equally confusing is the converse characterization of memory reports in general as those which give direct verification, so are to be excluded from the category of indirect evidence. I have already indicated the distinction that is thereby conflated, but to run again over the different cases, suppose we have a past-tense proposition, as 'The dog was whining'. A person who can report hearing the dog in question whining could be said to provide verification of that proposition, which could be held to be less directly confirmed by recollection of what indirectly confirmed it at the time, as uncertain hearsay. With a more favourable example we could also have indirect evidence in the form of present findings which lent some probability to the proposition. Finally, an individual's report could be said to be verified by like reports of others.

I set forth these mundane observations simply to make plain the parallel between past-tense and present-tense assertions. Influenced by a particular conception of how the notion of *evidence* must be understood, we readily see an asymmetry in place of the essential likeness. It is not as if all our judgements about the past had to be regarded as indirectly based, as resting on no more than evidence, with the consequent difficulty in understanding how they could be recognized as having any evidential value at all. The direct/indirect contrast can follow the same lines in either case, the difference coming in with the difficulty, perhaps impossibility, of making amends now for only casual observation or incomplete inspection at the earlier time. However, so long as our inability to determine the truth value of a past-tense proposition is due to nothing more than the contingent lack of observations on an earlier occasion, or of memories or records dating from that time, there is nothing to cast doubt on the framework in which we make sense of past-tense propositions and their evidential relations.

It is sometimes said—as in Waismann [1945]—that, because their truth requires fulfilment of an infinite number of conditions, empirical propositions cannot be conclusively verified. This surely cannot mean that, understanding such a proposition as 'This is a hand', I thereby appreciate that an infinity of conditions await my checking before I am assured of its truth. There may be no limit to the number of different descriptions one might give of a putative hand, but since a vast number of these will be indifferent to the question whether this appendage to my arm is a hand, there appears to be no support for the thesis from this consideration in the way Waismann thinks. Furthermore, if non-fulfilment of a condition can be taken as a disproof of the original proposition, this connection is one which must have a foundation in actual usage, something which is not possible if the number of such conditions is infinite. The thesis becomes more plausible if 'infinite' is replaced by 'of indeterminate number', but on that reading verification is not necessarily precluded: we may not be able to set a precise upper bound to the number of conditions to be satisfied—admittedly an artificial way of looking at most empirical propositions—but this does not mean that the point cannot be reached where we have more than enough to say that the proposition has been established beyond any reasonable doubt.

There is no case for regarding 'This is a hand' as a proposition with a meaning to which only an infinity of conditions could do justice, but there is in principle no limit to the number of factors which might adversely affect a seeming verification of such a proposition. So, returning to memory, a person might seemingly recall an incident with clarity and conviction, but his recollection be in error as a result of some disordered state of his brain; at this level it is not possible to specify the number of different factors which might be found to distort our memories, or other judgements. However, as long as our judgements remain dependable, squaring with other evidence and with the judgements of others, we can safely disregard any facts or conjectures about the workings of our nervous system. Particular conditions of the brain, drugs and so forth, are not identified as interfering factors simply through being abnormal, through introducing new causal factors, but their distorting influence, if any, is recognized in the departure from truth for which they are responsible. This order is important. Suppose, for instance, that, while under hypnosis, a person is given details of an incident which he had witnessed but subsequently forgotten, items of information which he then advances as actual memories. In such a case it might be said—has been said in Martin and Deutscher [1966]—that the causality was not as it should be for this to be a matter of genuine memory. However, if the subject does not claim to remember events which did not happen, even when the odd inaccurate detail has been fed to him under hypnosis, then we have as yet no good reason for not taking what he says at its face value. Perhaps nothing short of hypnosis will succeed in reawakening his memory; that at least is where it stands until we can say that information implanted about events outside his experience is sometimes offered as a personal memory at a later stage, or some other connection with falsehood shows the hypnosis to be a distorting influence. If, conversely, there are causal relations that are necessary to genuine memory, they are to be discovered by research into the factors present and prior to agreed verification.

Although the supposition may be without foundation in a given case, it seems always to make sense to suppose some kind of malfunction or other aberrant condition to have vitiated an individual's ostensible verification of a proposition; we cannot tell *a priori* what might not have this effect, and new interfering conditions can continue to come to light. Such conditions do not, however, relate to the meaning of the relevant propositions; they do not constitute checkable implications of these propositions, implications which have gone unfulfilled or at least untested, but they are conditions attendant upon one's assertion or thought that *P*. As apparently always possible, they show why verification can never be logically conclusive, but with no repercussions for our understanding of *P*. There is not, however thorough our checking, an inevitable falling short of what our understanding of

P enables us to recognize as a condition which its truth requires to be satisfied. We still have a contrast between the error that can arise through an ostensible verification's being in some way flawed, and the inadequacy of a condition which, given its meaning and that of *P*, is recognized to lend at most inductive support to *P*.

With this approach I preserve the appeal to recognition which made for the involvement of verification in my account of meaning. Let me summarize and explain. One of the principal reasons for an insistence on verifiability is provided by the practice of regarding certain findings as giving inductive support to certain conclusions, our justification for treating the former in this way appearing to presuppose the possibility of a more direct verification of the latter. Such a possibility is rejected by the sceptic, whose challenge is one which some would hope to meet by showing that the relevant knowledge rests, or can be made to rest, on foundations that are incorrigible, or in some way self-justifying. I do not adopt this approach, since propositions which make any kind of substantial claim, as do those under consideration, transcend any basis in incorrigible judgements. Now, however, it is not clear how I can admit that the logical possibility of error is always with us yet hold that we can have verification that deserves to be reckoned as final.

My answer to this is to distinguish the finality which can be achieved when there is only a limited number of conditions, each of which can be described as checkable, from the finality which would require that verification of such conditions might not prove only apparent. Otherwise put, we can distinguish two ways in which a seeming verification might be faulted. First, it could be that certain conditions have not been investigated, conditions which we shall appreciate as relevant given that we as much as understand the proposition in question. So, I may mistakenly identify a tomato as a plum if I judge something to be the former just on the basis of its size, shape and colour. Second, we may make the checks which an understanding demands, but things may for some reason appear to us other than they are: because of the unusual state of my tongue, the tomato actually tastes like a plum. It is trivial to say that possibilities of the latter kind do not cast doubt on one's understanding, but it would also appear that there is no loosening of the relevant concepts' ties with experience. Inconclusiveness of verification in this respect leaves essentially undisturbed the kind of extralinguistic relation that gives content to a word.

59. Verification and generality

To grant that verification can be inconclusive in the way indicated is not to defend those who think that, because we can never finally establish a hypothesis, it is a matter of choice what hypothesis we do accept. Nor, of course, does it support an interpretation of general propositions which would require satisfaction of an actual infinity of conditions for their truth. This is flatly at odds with what considerations of meaning demand, even if with some propositions we can speak of an indefinite number of conditions to be satisfied. The case is worth considering further, since it is thought that such propositions are both the stuff of science and proof of the futility of any general insistence on verifiability. The propositions in question are not to be thought of on the lines of the unquantified generalizations mentioned earlier, sentences of the form 'As are B' which await further determination in various ways, but it is universal generalizations, as 'Every body perseveres in its state of rest or of uniform motion in a straight line, unless it is compelled to change that state by impressed forces', that are at stake, where the intended application is to each and every thing of the kind in question that ever has existed or will exist. Here, it is said, we have the possibility of finding false, but no matching possibility of finding true.

Attempts at treating verification and falsification asymmetrically are liable to come to grief when negation is considered: if falsification seems from some point of view the more important notion with respect to P, the relevant virtues are likely to transfer to verification with respect to not-P. In the present instance, however, the case for asymmetry is at first sight persuasive: an A which is not B falsifies 'All As are B', but there is no question of finding each and every A to be B, as verification would demand.

There is certainly an asymmetry here, but, as with our earlier example concerning memory and evidence, there is also a suggestion that it may be of our own making. After all, we should not overlook the sense in which we can speak of verifying a general hypothesis by the discovery of confirming instances. Schoolboys in laboratories across the world are no doubt constantly verifying the propositions 'Acid turns blue litmus paper pink' and 'Magnets attract iron filings'. We can understand 'verify' in terms of finding true in the particular case, just as we take 'falsify' in terms of finding false in the particular case, and the symmetry is restored. Any reservations we have had concerning logically conclusive verification do not extend to the ordinary, non-sceptical uses of the notion, and this is one such familiar use.

'But you cannot *really* verify the hypothesis, since you cannot say in advance how all the particular cases will turn out'. Not only can we not say this in advance, we cannot say it at any time; but then we cannot say that we are presented with a genuine possibility which we should take into account in specifying a coherent interpretation of the hypothesis. To say that we cannot verify generalizations makes it appear as if we were under some constraint or limitation, when it is just that nothing counts as verification in the way intended: there never is any such totality as that of *all As* for these generalizations, but they are to be considered open-ended, not as propositions which equate to an infinite conjunction of singular propositions, as though there were already in some sense a vast body of individual truths or facts against which, ideally, they were to be measured.

Given that we should prefer to have a use for the notions of verification and falsification which did not make nonsense of either, the incoherence of the intended application of the former is an argument against eliminating the asymmetry in the other obvious way, namely, by taking 'falsify' to mean 'find false in *all* cases'. But, even if we stay with the reading of 'verify' which I propose, it may still be felt that there is an asymmetry between verification and falsification. After all, however many times we have verified a hypothesis, there is always the possibility that a falsifying instance will turn up, in which case we lose interest in the hypothesis;

falsification has a definitive character which contrasts with the provisional character of verification, in my sense. However, a falsified hypothesis is not a totally worthless hypothesis; falsification does not simply take us back to our starting-point, but it makes for an anomaly to be explained if it follows upon a succession of verifying instances in a variety of circumstances. A breakdown is not necessarily something which we cheerfully accept as simply negating what the preceding data had shown to be true in many cases, but we take it as indicative of the presence of novel conditions, as a pointer to the need for a further refinement of the hypothesis. What was secured by the successful verifications is not lost, but incorporated in an amended version. And, so long as our hypothesis remains empirical, there is in theory no limit to the number of revisions that changes in circumstances might require.

Generalizations such as Newton's laws of motion are not reports summing up a totality of observations of the behaviour of bodies in, for each such, an indefinite number of circumstances. Nor can they be taken as anticipating an infinity of future judgements, in the sense that they will be seen to be true when the time comes when all the individual findings are in. There clearly is no such time. Does this make it appropriate to treat such propositions as if they were procedural rules, as in F.P. Ramsey's analysis? No. We make a retreat from the superficial interpretation, in that we refuse any assimilation to a report and any association with truth conditions which lie outside anything we can ever know. However, this requires only that we take care in our interpretation of the notion of verification, not that we forsake the given form of words for one appropriate to a rule, so for something to which the notion of verification has no application whatsoever.

It is useful to compare empirical generalizations with those occurring in mathematics. Let us ask whether induction has any place here—not mathematical induction, of course, but induction as it is said to occur in the natural sciences. So, we find that the first 200 consecutive even numbers verify Goldbach's Conjecture, and we infer that the conjecture is correct for all even numbers. But that will not do, it will be said, since it could conceivably turn out that the very next even number to be considered refuted the conjecture. But then why cannot the same objection be raised in the empirical case? All roses so far examined have been found to have stamens, but it could certainly turn out that the next rose examined was lacking in this respect. However, there is a difference, a possibility that is fundamental in the mathematical case being of less importance with empirical statements. So, it is held that the 200 numbers which I have found to verify Goldbach's Conjecture do not raise the probability of that conjecture, 200 over infinity being no better than 2 over infinity; neither makes a significant inroad into the number of individual cases to be checked. However, the individual cases have or can have probative value in so far as they give us grounds for expecting a proof to be forthcoming, *not* as cutting down the number of falsifying cases, cases to be checked for conformity with the hypothesis. In these terms, 200 might be a significant number. We might learn by experience that with such problems essentially new possibilities were unlikely to arise after that point. So, the favourable cases do not lead us to make a direct transition, a mindless transition from quantity to quantity, to an infinite number of particular cases, but the data may, in the light of our experience, give us grounds for supposing that a pattern will be extracted, a pattern which will in turn be usable for generating an indefinite number of particular equations.

Our understanding of empirical generalizations is distorted by attempts to fit them into the framework commonly associated with first-order predicate logic, a framework which introduces determinacy in a number of unwanted ways. Most notably we have the excessively rigid truth conditions, a generalization being assertible if and only if each individual instance is so-and-so without exception. If 'all' is endowed with this degree of strictness, well and good, but our commoner unquantified generalizations are not of this kind. Second, we have determinacy with respect to existence of the particular cases: the quantifier is thought of as 'ranging over' a given totality of objects. We have seen how both these conceptions may lead us astray with empirical generalizations, but even in the mathematical case there is a similar possibility of distortion. In mathematics, a counter-example to a generalization is to be taken to refute that generalization, not by revealing that a given totality is not uniformly of a certain character—the model which is suggested by the case of empirically given totalities of objects, such as the cups in a cupboard—but by showing something, namely the establishment of the desired generalization, to be impossible. The counter-example is to be taken in a way appropriate to its connection with a general proposition whose truth is to be recognized in a certain way—to wit, by a proof; it is to show the impossibility of such a proof, but not in the way in which it would show the impossibility of a prediction, where confirmation or refutation is dependent solely on what future experience turns up.

60. Verification and observability

Our final topic is that of the status of electrons and other submicroscopic particles, a topic important both because of the connection with verification and because of the role of such particles in providing a common model for questions of existence in other areas, including even numbers and like abstractions.

Two opposing general theses often met with here are

(1)   that subatomic particles are no more than convenient fictions, theoretical entities with no real existence,
(2)   that such particles do exist, quite literally, though we can have no more than indirect evidence for their existence.

The notion of postulation appears more at home with (2) than with (1). If, as (1) presumably implies, it makes no sense to assert the literal physical existence of subatomic particles, then it makes no more sense to suppose that they might exist; as mere fictions they make no pretence to be capable of location in physical space, and since they are supposedly introduced with explicit recognition of this status, it is hardly appropriate to speak of 'postulating' them, as if we wished to leave room for the possibility that after all, they might not enjoy any real existence, even though they could sensibly be supposed to exist. I shall not press the point, but it is worth mentioning the difficulties of this nature which (1) faces, and the unreality of the position when confronted with a physicist's natural way of speaking. Consider the proposition, 'If a filament is heated to a high temperature, electrons are emitted which can produce fluorescence on a screen'. The strain on the notion of the electron as a theoretical entity becomes immediately apparent when it is considered that such a proposition would be advanced by the working physicist as a literal, elementary truth. There can be idealizations, such as the notion of point-mass, but given the kinds of context into which a term like 'electron' enters, it is difficult to see how both it and its contexts are to be rewritten in line with the claim that it does not apply to anything in the natural world. If the fluorescence is not strictly produced by something physical, then what does bring it about? Do we have here an uncaused event? How could an electron have any explanatory value, let alone any specifically causal role, unless it actually existed?

Consider now (2). If we are to think of subatomic particles and their properties as perpetually conjectural, then we shall take the world of the physicist to be highly mysterious, a conception which scientists themselves may not be loath to encourage. We seemingly observe effects or manifestations of the fundamental physical entities, but their real nature is hidden from us; any understanding we may have is only what can be yielded by a model or an analogy; we can never have more than such derivative and inadequate aids, and we can only dimly apprehend the reality that is there. The mystery in this realm is quite other than what may be attributed to many other disciplines of which we have little knowledge. Mathematics, medicine, economics, these may seem somewhat mysterious so long as we have no more than a smattering of the relevant knowledge, but the impression steadily diminishes as we become familiar with the required vocabulary, techniques and agreed facts. With physics, however, it is sometimes felt that the mystery remains however much the frontiers of the subject are advanced; it is as if successive discoveries of conventional kinds made no real impression on our ignorance, but that, try as he might, the physicist could never push through to the realm which was his main concern.

In order to rid oneself of this illusion of a real but undiscoverable residue standing in the way of genuine knowledge it is necessary to take seriously the inapplicability to submicroscopic phenomena of many of the descriptions which make perfectly good sense when used of the macroscopic world. The inapplicability of terms relating to colour and visible shape, for instance, should not be construed as making for the applicability of terms from different but analogous genera—whatever these could be—terms which would define features rendering electrons observable in something like the way coloured tangible objects are observable, only not in such a way as to leave them observable to us. An electron's lack of a given macroscopic property is not to be seen in a more positive and perplexing light, as if such a negative consideration meant that there was more to an electron than had been supposed, that we had grounds therein to surmise the presence of a property which the particle really did have but which, unfortunately, we could never directly perceive.

There is, of course, mystery in the matter of properties as yet undiscovered, as well as, in an equally harmless sense, mystery in what we already know. But there is no cause to think that our knowledge must inevitably fall short of genuine knowledge. We may think otherwise if we misconstrue the breakdown of our familiar descriptive vocabulary as indicative of the presence of other properties which superior observational powers might bring to light and which define the true but impenetrable nature of the physical world. However, discarding this picture does not leave us deprived of 'mass', 'spin', 'charge', and other terms which we might reasonably hope to invoke in a more sober and literal explanation of the meaning of the relevant hypotheses.

Whether or not we can speak of actually observing electrons, or only of observing their tracks or other traces, I suggest that observation can furnish us with adequate grounds for affirming their existence. Of course, the tracks in a cloud chamber may be consistent with the presence of some particle other than that which we conjecture to be there, and in such circumstances we may be able to speak only of signs or indications of an electron, say, of making an inference to the probable presence of such a particle. But what is needed to confirm the conjecture is not the making of an observation which is beyond our powers, but, roughly speaking, more of the same; more data which, in association with the findings which by themselves do not enable us to decide between the various possibilities, add up to a justification of the claim that we have to do with a particle of one kind rather than another. Initially we have to do with a conjecture, more or less well founded, but it is within experience that it is to be confirmed.

Looking at the matter from a rather different perspective we might ask why anyone should wish to define *electron* in such a way that the existence of electrons cannot be verified; not merely defining the term so as to leave room for the possible ascription to electrons of properties as yet unknown, but actually excluding, by definition, knowledge of their existence. However, this prompts a very natural objection. It can be agreed all round that affirmations of existence are always based on observable data in some way or other; it will be maintained on one side, however, that any such data invariably have the status of, at best, *effects* of the phenomena to whose existence they point. It is not mythical properties that define the shortfall between what there is and what is disclosed to observation, but such a gap is (logically) required by the role which physical particles play in explaining the phenomena which lead us to postulate their existence. If we are to have the verification which I suggest is possible, we need something more than putative effects inclining us to postulate a cause.

This objection can be countered in the following way. Suppose we note a series of changes suggestive of the passage of a particle; think here of the tracks thought to be made by an electron, or, on a larger scale, of the way in which a medium of some sort might be observed to part and rejoin as if in response to the movement through it of some object. In the former case we do not take ourselves to have, without certain assumptions, sufficient grounds for saying that we have learned of the passage of an electron; if that sufficed, then there being an electron in the relevant region would mean no more than that changes of this nature could be observed, whereas there clearly is more to that particular species of particle than is disclosed by such a series of changes. Similarly, in the example of the medium parting it is conceivable that we have witnessed no more than a moving hole, that there is nothing of substance forcing the medium apart, but just a succession of changes brought about in some other way or ways and which gives the impression of a physical object passing through.

So long as our data are thus incomplete it is appropriate for us to entertain various causal hypotheses with respect to what we have observed; and, of course, if there is in addition something that would count as actually seeing one of the objects which we might thus postulate, there is a highly satisfactory way of passing beyond the stage at which we have no more than a hypothesis. Closer inspection of our moving hole may reveal a visible surface, or, even if nothing is seen, the presence of a body might make itself known to our sense of touch. By bringing the senses of sight or touch into play in this way we can bring to an end speculation about the reality of the putative cause of the changes we have observed, but even when, as with the electron, there is nothing that would count as seeing or touching, at least in any comparably simple sense, it is, I suggest, still possible for us to extend our observations to the point where the existence of the relevant particle can be affirmed, not now as a causal hypothesis, but as a proposition that is fully warranted by the data accumulated. Or, if anything stands in the way of such verification, it relates to certain contrary-to-fact conditions, conditions which circumstances have prevented us from ascertaining, but which relate to findings on a par with those we have actually made.

The macroscopic case, with the possible object, possible hole, gives support to this claim. To establish materiality of the phenomenon in the medium we should wish to verify its power to displace and/or be displaced by other physical things. We have prima-facie evidence of this in the changes described, and if we observe sufficient changes of this and similar kinds, and if too we can eliminate other explanations of how the changes come about, we can eventually conclude that we have to do with something more than a moving hole. As I say, if we can actually discern a surface, or if the thing can be felt, we may be able to dispense with further such investigations, but even without visibility or felt solidity we may arrive at essentially the same conclusion, even if the route to this conclusion is now less direct. I do not claim that what counts as a sufficient variety and number of the relevant observed changes is sharply defined, but the point can be reached when we can reasonably pass from a causal hypothesis to a redescription affirming the existence of what was conjectured, a transition which does not prevent us from saying that what has been shown to exist was the cause of the changes in question. Think here of the wind. We could come to know of the wind's existence without relying on our experience of feeling it, needing only to eliminate the alternative possibility that leaves, smoke, and so forth, are moved about by causes within them. Physical phenomena can be known through their impact on us, but the impact they have on one another can also lead to their detection.

What I have said here seems to apply readily enough to submicroscopic particles. They may not be strictly observable, but the availability of data analogous to the above renders strict observability superfluous: visibility is not just what is needed to transform the purely theoretical into the concrete; it simply adds another dimension to what could be shown to be real by other considerations. With electrons, protons, and so forth, there is of course a complexity which is generally absent from the macroscopic case, though explanations of meaning with respect to the former are more like those appropriate in the latter than they are like those required by words signifying fictions or idealizations. But again, this complexity is not to be made into an obstacle to verification by incorporating the false picture of inaccessible properties lying beyond a perceptual veil. The invocation here of an incoherent condition to show that ostensible verification is inevitably no more than that provides a striking parallel to the treatment of universal generalizations which I rejected, though in the present instance the problems of sense are more pervasive: any description we might think to apply to the submicroscopic world has to be certified as warranted by the data. It has seemed natural to use such a term as 'particle' with every confidence, as if we could simply take the planetary model and compress it, leaving everything intact, even if reduced below the level of observability; but, as came to be realized, *particle* is not a merely formal universal; it is a word that makes a distinction of a certain sort and whose use accordingly stands in need of justification, of an empirical rather than an *a priori* character. Similarly, questions of location at a point and of identity over time may be open in a way that is not appreciated so long as our thinking is dominated by concepts whose initial application is to macroscopic bodies.

The way in which our everyday concepts may hamper understanding is shown by worries over the notion of action at a distance. How, given the spatial separation of moon from earth, can the former influence tides on the latter? The boundaries of a body are fixed by what is disclosed to the senses of sight and touch, but we might imagine an extended notion of a body according to which it could be deemed present in so far as certain forces were operative, forces which radiated from the body, as currently understood. Compare the medieval idea that a spirit is where it acts. Moon and earth would thus be thought of as spread out in overlapping spaces, and not as discrete spheres completely cut off from one another; a departure, obviously, from our normal conceptions, but a liberation which does not amount to a refutation of what we normally think. Similarly, Eddington's table with its vast areas of space and negligible bulk is easier to comprehend if the picture of particles with well-defined surfaces, like billiard balls, is replaced by a conception of fields of force with particular concentrations at certain points, a conception which gives the more literal content of the relevant descriptions.

Perhaps the most likely objection to my position is the kind of objection to be expected from one who finds indeterminacy of translation logically inescapable. At a given stage in the development of our knowledge we may be able to say that such-and-such an observation establishes the existence of electrons only under the assumption of several other hypotheses, hypotheses which are in turn associated with further *ifs*. I wish to say that we may, little by little, reduce the number of uncertainties, that in principle the point may be reached where there can be no real doubt about what observation decides. In the case of learning a foreign language, where alternative hypotheses may be open for some time, we have the advance assurance that success is possible, just by dint of knowing that we are dealing with an established form of communication. With scientific hypotheses, however, there is not only no similar assurance, but we must acknowledge that dramatic shifts in outlook have taken place over the years. There is a difficult line to draw here. Since we are dealing with empirical propositions, we do not wish to lay emphasis on the possibility of verification to the point that we close the door on future discoveries, that we constrain in advance the further development of science. On the other hand, to the extent that scientists have been scrupulous in their use of language, to that extent there must be a body of knowledge that remains to be built upon rather than completely overthrown by developments which lie ahead. My position is plausible so long as it is or becomes possible to see that descriptions which come to be faulted could have been recognized at the time as not strictly justified by the data, perhaps through an unwitting importation of concepts with a clear interpretation only in respect of macroscopic phenomena. So long as any revisions, however drastic, merely exploit the gap between what was strictly warranted and what the truth of the supposedly verified hypotheses implied, we are entitled to see in this area too the kind of connection between words and world which my account of meaning found plausible in the more familiar cases.

Throughout this work the sceptic has been one of the main targets, and in this final chapter the object of a more sustained attack. The sceptic about meaning may well be guilty of a form of philosophical arrogance: his failure to give an acceptable account of this indispensable concept is taken to show the concept rather than his analysis to be defective—whatever that might mean with respect to the former. Such failure in turn makes for a deepening of doubts about the analytic/synthetic distinction, when any uncertainties here belong more properly on the side of the data to which the distinction is applied. The Fregean striving for determinacy of sense—so that we might be able to decide definitely about every object whether it falls under a given concept or not (Frege [1884], § 74)—is a striving for a totally impossible ideal, but no such extreme is required by a workable distinction between the two kinds of proposition. Nor is there a rational doubt to trouble translators in the alleged possibility that there inevitably are distinct but equally allowable alternatives to translations of a foreign tongue.

If it is held that a hypothesis can never be finally verified or falsified, it is important to know what precisely is supposed to make for this impossibility. Problems posed by a failure to check relevant conditions, whether by oversight or because the circumstances happen to rule this out, do not present a serious challenge to an empiricist account of meaning. It is not like the case where the very meaning of a hypothesis is thought to preclude either verifiability or falsifiability. To some extent conjectures about the submicroscopic world have for this reason been thought to lie outside the realm of the verifiable, and to a much greater degree this has been the basis for thinking general propositions to be unverifiable. Even though this latter conclusion has been the outcome of nothing more than an insistence on using 'verify' in a certain inappropriate fashion, this has not stood in the way of those who would build a whole philosophy on the supposed asymmetry between verification and falsification. None of this is to deny the existence of deeper perplexities involving meaning and verification. A few philosophical clouds have been condensed into drops of grammar, but there are many others on the horizon.

BIBLIOGRAPHY

Wherever applicable, page references in the text are to articles as reprinted

AUSTIN, J. L.
  [1946]   'Other Minds', *Proceedings of the Aristotelian Society*, Supp. Vol. xx (1946), reprinted in Austin [1970].
  [1954]   'Unfair to Facts', in Austin [1970].
  [1970]   *Philosophical Papers*, ed. J. O. Urmson and G. J. Warnock, Oxford, Clarendon Press, 2nd edn.

BEARDSLEY, M. C.
  [1975]   'Actions and Events: The Problem of Individuation', *American Philosophical Quarterly*, xii.

BELL, J. M.
  [1973]   'What is Referential Opacity?', *Journal of Philosophical Logic*, ii.

BENACERRAF, P.
  [1965]   'What Numbers Could Not Be', *Philosophical Review*, lxxiv.

BOAS, F.
  [1911]   'Handbook of American Indian Languages', i, *Bureau of American Ethnology*, Bulletin 40, Pt 1.

BOLINGER, D.
  [1967]   'Adjectives in English: Attribution and Predication', *Lingua*, xviii.
  [1972]   *That's That*, The Hague, Mouton.

BROAD, C.D.
  [1923]   *Scientific Thought*, London and New York, Kegan Paul, Trench & Trubner.

CARNAP, R.
  [1947]   *Meaning and Necessity*, Chicago, University of Chicago Press.

CARTWRIGHT, R.
  [1971]   'Identity and Substitutivity', in *Identity and Individuation*, ed. M. K. Munitz, New York, New York University Press.

CASTANEDA, H-N.
  [1966]   ' "He": A Study in the Logic of Self-Consciousness', *Ratio*, vii.

CHANDLER, H. S.
  [1975]   'Rigid Designation', *Journal of Philosophy*, lxxii.

COHEN, L. J.
  [1966]   *The Diversity of Meaning*, London, Methuen, 2nd edn.

DAVIDSON, D.
   [1967]   'The Logical Form of Action Sentences', in *The Logic of Decision and Action*, ed. M. Rescher, Pittsburgh, University of Pittsburgh Press.

DONNELLAN, K. S.
   [1966]   'Reference and Definite Descriptions', *Philosophical Review*, lxxv.

DRETSKE, F. I.
   [1975]   'The Content of Knowledge', in *Forms of Representation*, ed. B. Freed, A. Marras, and P. Maynard, Amsterdam, Oxford, and New York, Elsevier North-Holland.

DUMMETT, M.
   [1959a]   'Truth', *Proceedings of the Aristotelian Society*, lix (1958–9), reprinted in *Truth*, ed. G. Pitcher, New Jersey, Prentice-Hall, 1964, and in Strawson [1967].
   [1959b]   'Wittgenstein's Philosophy of Mathematics', *Philosophical Review*, lxvii.
   [1967]   'Frege, Gottlob', in *Encyclopedia of Philosophy*, vol. iii, ed. P. Edwards, New York, Macmillan.
   [1973]   *Frege: Philosophy of Language*, London, Duckworth.
   [1975]   'What is a Theory of Meaning?', in *Mind and Language*, ed. S. Guttenplan, Oxford, Clarendon Press.

FILLMORE, C. J.
   [1970]   'Subjects, Speakers, and Roles', *Synthèse*, xxi.

FØLLESDAL, D.
   [1965]   'Quantification into Causal Contexts', in *Boston Studies in the Philosophy of Science*, vol . ii, ed. R. S. Cohen and M. W. Wartofsky, New York, Humanities Press, 1965, reprinted in *Reference and Modality*, ed. L. Linsky, Oxford, Clarendon Press, 1971.

FREGE, G.
   [1884]   *The Foundations of Arithmetic*, trans. by J. L. Austin, Oxford, Blackwell, 2nd revised edn., 1953.
   [1891]   'Function and Concept', in *Translations from the Philosophical Writings of Gottlob Frege*, ed. and trans. by P. T. Geach and M. Black, Oxford, Blackwell, 2nd revised edn., 1960.
   [1892a]   'On Sense and Reference', in *Translations from the Philosophical Writings of Gottlob Frege*.
   [1892b]   'On Concept and Object', in *Translations from the Philosophical Writings of Gottlob Frege*.
   [1918]   'The Thought: A Logical Inquiry', trans. by A. M. and M. Quinton, *Mind*, lxv (1956), reprinted in Strawson [1967].

GEACH, P. T.
   [1950a]   'Russell's Theory of Descriptions', *Analysis*, 10.4.
   [1950b]   'Subject and Predicate', *Mind*, lix.
   [1962]   *Reference and Generality*, Ithaca, New York, Cornell University Press, 2nd revised edn.

[1965]   'Assertion', *Philosophical Review*, lxxiv.
[1972]   *Logic Matters*, Oxford, Blackwell.
[1975]   'Names and Identity', in *Mind and Language*, ed. S. Guttenplan, Oxford, Clarendon Press.

GIVON, T.
[1973]   'Opacity and Reference in Language: An Inquiry into the Role of Modalities', in *Syntax and Semantics*, vol. 2, ed. J. P. Kimball, New York and London, Seminar Press.
[1976]   'Topic, Pronoun, and Grammatical Agreement', in Li [1976].

GRICE, H. P.
[1957]   'Meaning', *Philosophical Review*, lxvi (1957), reprinted in Strawson [1967].
[1968]   'Utterer's Meaning, Sentence-Meaning, and Word-Meaning', *Foundations of Language*, iv (1968), reprinted in *The Philosophy of Language*, ed. J. R. Searle, Oxford, Clarendon Press, 1971.

GRIFFIN, N.
[1977]   *Relative Identity*, Oxford, Clarendon Press.

HARE, R. M.
[1952]   *The Language of Morals*, Oxford, Clarendon Press.

JACOBS, R. A., and ROSENBAUM, P. S.
[1968]   *English Transformational Grammar*, Massachusetts, Blaisdell.

JESPERSEN, O.
[1927]   *A Modern English Grammar on Historical Principles*, Heidelberg, Carl Winters Universitätsbuchhandlung.

JONES, O. R.
[1968]   'In Disputation of an Undisputed Thesis', *Analysis*, 28.4.

KEENAN, E. L.
[1976]   'Towards a Universal Definition of "Subject"', in Li [1976].

KEENAN, E. L., and EBERT, K. H.
[1973]   'A Note on Marking Transparency and Opacity', *Linguistic Inquiry*, iv.

KIPARSKY, P., and KIPARSKY, C.
[1970]   'Fact', in *Progress in Linguistics*, ed. M. Bierwisch and K. E. Heidolph, The Hague and Paris, Mouton.

KIRSNER, R. S.
[1976]   'On the Subjectless "Pseudo-Passive" in Standard Dutch and the Semantics of Background Agents', in Li [1976].

KITELEY, M.
[1964]   'The Grammars of "believe"', *Journal of Philosophy*, lxi.

KRAMSKY, J.
[1972]   *The Article and the Concept of Definiteness in Language*, The Hague, Mouton.

KUNO, S.
[1972]   'Functional Sentence Perspective: A Case Study from Japanese and English', *Linguistic Inquiry*, iii.

LEECH, G.
[1974]   *Semantics*, Harmondsworth, Penguin Books.

LEWIS, C. I.
[1944]   'The Modes of Meaning', *Philosophy and Phenomenological Research*, iv (1944), reprinted in *Semantics and the Philosophy of Language*, ed. L. Linsky, Urbana, University of Illinois Press, 1952.

LI, C. N.
[1976]   ed. *Subject and Topic*, New York, San Francisco, and London, Academic Press.

LI, C. N., and THOMPSON, S. A.
[1975]   'The Semantic Function of Word Order: A Case Study in Mandarin', in *Word Order and Word Order Change*, ed. C. N. Li, Austin and London, University of Texas Press.

MARTIN, C. B., and DEUTSCHER, M.
[1966]   'Remembering', *Philosophical Review*, lxxv.

PERLMUTTER, D. M.
[1970]   'On the Article in English', in *Progress in Linguistics*, ed. M. Bierwisch and K. E. Heidolph, The Hague and Paris, Mouton.

PRIOR, A. N.
[1963]   'Oratio Obliqua', *Proceedings of the Aristotelian Society*, Supp. vol. xxxvii.

QUINE, W. V.
[1960]   *Word and Object*, Cambridge, Massachusetts, M.I.T. Press.
[1961]   'Reference and Modality', in *From a Logical Point of View*, Cambridge, Massachusetts, Harvard University Press, revised edn.
[1968]   'Ontological Relativity', *Journal of Philosophy*, lxv (1968), reprinted in *Ontological Relativity and Other Essays*, New York and London, Columbia University Press, 1969.

RATNER, J.
[1935]   'The Correspondence Theory of Truth', *Journal of Philosophy*, xxxii.

RIVERO, M.-L.
[1975]   'Referential Properties of Spanish Noun Phrases', *Language*, li.

RUNDLE, B. B.
[1968]   'Transitivity and Indirect Speech', *Proceedings of the Aristotelian Society*, lxviii (1967-8).
[1969]   'Is Natural Deduction Natural?', *Proceedings of the Aristotelian Society*. Supp. vol. xliii.
[1972]   *Perception, Sensation, and Verification*, Oxford, Clarendon Press.

RUSSELL, B.
[1905]   'On Denoting', *Mind*, (1905), reprinted in *Logic and Knowledge, Essays 1901-1950*, ed. R. C. Marsh, London, Allen & Unwin, 1956.

[1912]   *The Problems of Philosophy*, London, Oxford University Press.
[1918]   'The Philosophy of Logical Atomism', *Monist*, xxviii (1918), reprinted in *Logic and Knowledge, Essays 1901-1950*.
[1940]   *An Inquiry into Meaning and Truth*, London, Allen & Unwin.
SCHACHTER, P.
[1976]   'The Subject in Philippine Languages: Topic, Actor, Actor-Topic, or None of the Above', in Li [1976].
SELLARS, W. F.
[1960]   'Grammar and Existence: A Preface to Ontology', *Mind*, lxix (1960), reprinted in *Science, Perception and Reality*, London, Routledge & Kegan Paul, 1963.
SMULLYAN, A. F.
[1948]   'Modality and Description', *Journal of Symbolic Logic*, xiii (1948), reprinted in *Reference and Modality*, ed. L. Linsky, Oxford, Clarendon Press, 1971.
STAMPE, D. W.
[1968]   'Toward a Grammar of Meaning', *Philosophical Review*, lxxvii (1968), reprinted in *On Noam Chomsky: Critical Essays*, ed. G. Harman, New York, Doubleday Anchor, 1974.
STRAWSON, P. F.
[1949]   'Truth', *Analysis*, 9.6 (1949), reprinted in *Philosophy and Analysis*, ed. M. Macdonald, Oxford, Blackwell, 1954.
[1950a]   'On Referring', *Mind*, lix (1950), reprinted in Strawson [1971].
[1950b]   'Truth', *Proceedings of the Aristotelian Society*, Supp. vol. xxiv (1950), reprinted in Strawson [1971].
[1959]   *Individuals, An Essay in Descriptive Metaphysics*, London, Methuen.
[1964]   'Identifying Reference and Truth-Values', *Theoria*, xxx (1964), reprinted in Strawson [1971].
[1967]   ed. *Philosophical Logic*, Oxford, Clarendon Press.
[1971]   *Logico-Linguistic Papers*, London, Methuen.
[1974]   *Subject and Predicate in Logic and Grammar*, London, Methuen.
THORNTON, M. T.
[1969]   'Rundle on Referential Opacity', *Analysis*, 29.4.
TOULMIN, S. E.
[1958]   *The Uses of Argument*, Cambridge, Cambridge University Press.
URMSON, J. O.
[1952]   'Parenthetical Verbs', *Mind*, lxi (1952), reprinted in *Essays in Conceptual Analysis*, ed. A. Flew, London, Macmillan, 1956.

URMSON, J. O. (*cont.*)
[1968]   'Criteria of Intensionality', *Proceedings of the Aristotelian Society*, Supp. Vol. xlii.

WAISMANN, F.
[1945]   'Verifiability', *Proceedings of the Aristotelian Society*, Supp. vol. xix (1945), reprinted in *How I See Philosophy*, ed. R. Harré, London, Macmillan, New York, St. Martin's Press, 1968.

WHITE, A. R.
[1972]   'What We Believe', in *Studies in the Philosophy of Mind*, *American Philosophical Quarterly*, Monograph Series, ed. N. Rescher, Oxford, Blackwell.

WITTGENSTEIN, L.
[1956]   *Remarks on the Foundations of Mathematics*, ed. G. H. von Wright, R. Rhees, and G. E. M. Anscombe, trans. by G. E. M. Anscombe, Oxford, Blackwell.

INDEX

abstract entities, abstractions, *see* universals, numbers, *and* nouns, abstract

action, 312-3

at a distance, 478

adjectives, 19-20, 29, 237-8, 258-9, 288, 308-11, 350, 413-4

adverbs, adverbial qualifications, 28-9, 58, 103-4, 114-5, 133-4, 167, 169-70, 200, 300, 302, 310, 318-19, 333-4, 391, 401, 413-6

aleph-zero, 271-3

'all', *see* generality

ambiguity, 13-18, 22-25, 89, 122

analyticity, 444-52

'and', 12, 28, 392-3, 398-401

application, 10, 121-2, 127-8, 131, 142-3, 205, 227, 372, 376, 385-6, 390, 432-3

appropriateness, 392-7, 401, 414, 420

article, definite, 12-13, 35, 50-71, 204-9, 402, *see also* descriptions, definite

indefinite, 7, 31, 35, 74, 83-92, 120-32, 207, 224, 226-7

assertion, assertoric force, 28, 105-9, 134, 282, 303, 332-3, 361-5, 368-9, 371, 375, 393, 414, 416-20

attitudes, 387-8, *see also* propositional attitudes

attributive use, construction, 29, 258-66, 288, 309

Austin, J. L., 301, 320, 325-7, 380

awareness, 247-8

Beardsley, M. C., 312-3

'because', 184-5, 370, 394

belief, 158-60, 280, 283, 287, 294-9, 330

Bell, J. M., 247

Benacerraf, P., 258, 263

Berkeley, 187, 191-2

Boas, F., 41, 45

Bolinger, D., 29, 292-3

Broad, C. D., 3

'but', 392-4, 398-9, 402

Cantor, 271

Carnap, R., 437

Cartwright, R., 150

Castañeda, H-N., 164

category mistakes, 55

causality, 40, 236, 316, 331-2, 337-9, 381, 475-7

Chandler, H.S., 218

ChiBemba, 83

Chinese, 96, 123

Chomsky, N., 22

clauses, 19, 136, 153, 186, 238-9, 252, 270, ch. 7 *passim*, 424-5

Cohen, L. J., 178

collections, 256-8, 261, 268, 270

completeness, *see* incompleteness

componential analysis, 384

concepts, 32f., 98-101, 109-10, 113, 142, 231, 255, 351, 412-3

conditionals, 107, 326, 352-7, 370

conjunctions, 322-3, 370, 414

co-ordination, 285, 299, 301-2

conventionalism, 447

copula, *see* 'is'

correctness, 376, 392, 394-7, 401, 420

counting, 255-7, 263-4

Davidson, D., 27

declarative sentence, 243-5, 391, 400, 415-21, 424

deductive equivalence, 428, 435-7

deep structure, 18-26, 132

demonstratives, 43f., 58, 60-2, 283-5, 394, *see also* 'this' *and* 'that'

Descartes, 46

descriptions, definite, 35, 50-71, 77-9, 165-7, 177-8, 234-5, 269, 391, 394, 401-2

indefinite, 83-92, 120-32

theory of, 51f., 119

desires, 381
determinacy, 61f., 88, 93-4, 123-4,
    471
Deutscher, M., 466
direct speech, 35, 281-2, 297-8, 304,
    375, 411
disjunction, 12, 106-7, 357, 430
Donnellan, K.S., 69
Dretske, F.I., 184
Dummett, M., 30, 109, 219-22, 231,
    352, 393, 398, 416, 424
Dutch, 116

Ebert, K.H., 64
Eddington, A., 478
electrons, 472-80
ellipsis, 26, 232, 290-1
'entity', 188-90, 194-9, 203, 243,
    249, 377-84, 450
equality, 261-2
equivalence relation, 171, 174, 181,
    211f., 254, 261, 265, 268
Eskimo, 41, 45, 416
essentialism, 176, 216-8
events, 27, 189, 193-5, 197, 312-3,
    326-7
evidence, 458, 461-5
existence, 2, 52f., 63f., 85, 116-9,
    125-6, 134-6, 163, 165-7 ch. 5
    passim, ch. 6 passim, 279, 305-
    6, 321, 401, 419, 472-80
    and predication, 7, 9-11, 30f., 136-
    45
extensionality, 69, 148, 150, 160-1,
    163, 165, 179f., 210, 247, 249,
    287, 312, 379, 434, 437

facts, 19, 244-6, 284, 311f., ch. 8
    passim, 381, 424-5, 427
fallacy of subtraction, 192-3
falsification, 459, 468-72, 480
falsity, 53-5, 58, 358, 374, 397
fiction, 65, 72, 79, 247-8
Fillmore, C. J., 18
Finnish, 123
Føllesdal, D., 184
force, 396, 403, 411, 415-23, 427-8
fractions, 262
Frege, 2, 26, 30, 32f., 47-50, 75,
    79, 82, 109-11, 127-8, 142,
    153-5, 164-6, 170-1, 174, 185,
    231, 254f., 270, 351, 380, 390,

392, 398, 401, 413, 480
    the Frege argument, 179-85
French, 61-3, 130, 264, 337, 352, 436
Geach, P. T., 53, 105-6, 108, 126, 174,
    211-3
general form of proposition, 363-5,
    374-5
generality, generalizations, 2-3, 15, 62,
    93, 126-7, 132, 204-9, 226, 229-
    30, 308, 326, 468-72
generative semantics, 22
generic 'the', 62, 204-9
German, 63, 166, 436
Givón, T., 83, 118
'good', 14, 29, 108-9
Grice, H. P., 403, 406-7, 421
Griffin, N., 215

Hare, R. M., 108
'however', 392, 394, 402
hypostasis, 192, 209

'I', 44-6, 174
identification, 45, 56, 60, 66-70, 73,
    75-6, 90, 97f., 112, 140-1, 144,
    162, 173-4, 225, 239f., 249, 334,
    418-9
identity, 13, 62, 67-70, 75-6, 118-9,
    149, 171-3, 181, 202-3, 209-18,
    231-50, 236-7, 239f., 261-2, 268,
    352, 379-80, 434
    criterion of, 81, 204f., 213f., 246,
    264-5, 382
    relative, 211f.
'if', see conditionals
imperative, 20, 52, 402, 408, 421-2
incompleteness, 32, 97, 109-15, 418
indeterminacy of translation, 408,
    452-8, 478-9
indexicals, 43-51, 413-4
indirect speech, 35, 147-74, 185-6, ch.
    7 passim
individuation, 59, 62, 77-8, 173, 205,
    219, 225, 231-3
Indo-European, 45, 64, 100
induction, 470-1
infinitive, 65-6, 107, 135, 169, 306-9
infinity, 271-7, 426, 465f.
intensional isomorphism, 437
intention, 17-18, 25, 47-50, 91, 312-
    3, 386, 397, 403-9, 416-23
intentionality, 36, 82, 135, ch. 4 passim,
    278, 305

interrogative, 52, 108, 243-5, 306-8, 378, 421-2
intuitionism, 389, 399-400
'is', 10, 13, 130, 140-4, 166
'it', 8-9, 27, 117-19, 290-1, 297, 313f., 330, 333-4

Jacobs, R. A., 19-20, 26-7
Japanese, 96, 104, 398
Jespersen, O., 285
Jones, O. R., 361

Kant, 30
Keenan, E. L., 64, 95, 116
kind, 37, 263, 270-1
Kiparsky, P. *and* Kiparsky, C., 19
Kirsner, R. S., 116
Kiteley, M., 302
knowledge, 284, 330-2
Krámský, J., 51, 64
Kuno, S., 104

Lahu, 96
Latin, 7, 307, 332
law of excluded middle, 277, 357
Leech, G., 13-14
Leibniz's Law, 210-6
Lewis, C. I., 437
Li, C. N., 96, 116, 118, 1: 318
Lisu, 116
logical form, 8, 10, 32, 139

Malagasy, 64
Malayan, 122
Martin, C. B., 466
mass terms, *see* nouns
matter, 219-22
meaning, 12f., 34, 47, 71f., 132, 189, 191-2, 247, 252, ch. 9 *passim*, ch. 10 *passim, see also* synonymy of sentences, 423-31, 435
theory of, 425-9
meaninglessness, 371, 443-4
memory, 463-6
metaphor, 387
middle verbs, 378-9
modality, 17-18, 78-9, 107, 125, 134, 146, 167, 175-9, 217-8, 250, 278, 333, 416, 433-4
mood, 415-6
Moore, G. E., 145

names, 35, 67, 71-82, 100, 139, 154, 165, 172, 198, 260-3, 266-8, 287, 391, 440
necessity, 175-9, 186, 217-8, 250, 433-4, 444, 447, *see also* analyticity
negation, negatability, 54-6, 102-5, 114-5, 276, 310, 346, 355-8, 391, 394, 401
nominalism, 232f., 246, 248, 264, 268, 351
nominalizations, ch. 6 *passim*, ch. 7 *passim*, 326, 344-8
Norwegian, 98
nouns, abstract, 51, 63, 66-7, 204-9, 225, 229-30, ch. 6 *passim*, 321
count, 51, 62, 72, 90, 92-9, 100, 202-3, 218-30, 383, 412
mass, 51, 62-3, 90, 94-5, 100, 130, 192, 202, 206, 218-32, 235, 237, 244, 383
'now', 43, 46
numbers, 37f., 176-9, 188, 190, 193, 231, 254-77, 446
numerals, 264-6

objects, 109, 136, 239, 254-5, 280-99, 305, 330-1, 425
observability, 472-80
ontological commitment, 5, 85, ch. 5 *passim*
opacity, 82, 152, 164f., 241-2
'or', *see* disjunction
oratio obliqua, see indirect speech
oratio recta, see direct speech
ordinary language, 39-40, 188-9, 196-7
Otomí, 400

pain, 322, 460-2
'particle', 478
'particular', 85, 89
passive, 111, 116, 280, 287, 290-1, 297, 378-9
past, 458-9, 463-5
performatives, 19, 301-2, 375, 417, 420-1
Perlmutter, D. M., 132
Philippine languages, 115
philosophical theses, 1-4
possible worlds, objects, 271-4
postulation, 4, 189-90, 201, 203, 269, 342, 382, 472

pragmatism, 4, 190, 271, 339, 455
predicates, predication, 6f., 30f., 68,
  ch. 3 *passim*, 137f., 184, 235-7,
  240-4, 248-50, 258, 279, 308,
  329, 374, 391
predictions, 17-18, 275-6
prepositions, 201-3, 288, 309, 335-6,
  390, 431
presupposition, 53f., 129, 394, 401
Prior, A. N., 287
probability, 146-7, 242, 389, 395-6
proof, 458-9, 471-2
properties, 111-2, 213, 243, 257f.,
  380, 474-5
propositional attitudes, 69-71, 147-74,
  ch. 7 *passim*, 425
propositions, 108, 250-4, 279, 293-8,
  303, 305, 317, 328-33, 362, 368,
  424-5, 427
psychological verbs, 298-306, 318, 322

quantification, 93, 111, 141, 175-6,
  190, 198-200, 272, 471
questions, 243-4, 378, 380, *see also*
  interrogative
Quine, W. V., 120, 149, 176, 184, 192,
  440
quotation, 168-9, 267, 281-2, 382-3,
  410-11, 425

Ramsey, F. P., 470
Ratner, J., 343
realism, 231, 234-7, 245-6, 350-1
reasons, 337-9
reductive analyses, 200-4, 245, 348
reference, 6f., 30f., ch. 2 *passim*, ch.
  3 *passim*, ch. 4 *passim*, 187-8,
  206-7, 239f., 280, 310, 313-23,
  333-4, 379-83, 427, 437
  covert, 86f., 123-7
revisability, 448-9, 453
'right', 365-6
Rivero, M.-L., 166
Romance languages, 411
Rosenbaum, P. S., 19-20, 26-7
rules, 454
Rundle, B. B., 235, 352
Russell, 33, 48, 51-2, 60, 115, 119,
  274, 298-9, 345, 391, 430

scepticism, 408, 450, 453, 455, 457f.,
  479-80
Schachter, P., 115
scope, 125, 132, 165, 167
Sellars, W. F., 111
semantic objects, 384
semantic paradoxes, 213, 371
semantic syntax, 22
sense, 35, 47-50, 71f., 153-5, 165,
  171-2, 174, 401, 403
sentences, 251, 423-31, 435
sets, 180-3, 270-1
Smullyan, A. F., 175
'so', 367-9, 374
'some', 125-6, 204
'something', 138-9, 199
Spanish, 65, 107, 166
speech acts, 251-2, 281-2, 363, 372,
  395, 406-8, 411, 415, 419, 422
Stampe, D. W., 378
statements, 241, 250-4, 319-20
states of affairs, 327-8, 343-4
stating, 66, 241, 252, 325, 379-80
Strawson, P. F., 53-5, 96f., 319, 360f.
subatomic particles, 472-80
subjects, subject-predicate distinction,
  6f., 30, ch. 3 *passim*, 133f., 257-8,
  286-7, 289-93, 320-1, 329, 373,
  412, 418
subjunctive, 64-6, 107-8, 165-8, 177-8,
  185-6, 238, 279, 299, 306-8,
  353-4
substitutivity, 69, 148, 175-86, 247,
  386, 433-5
synonymy, 26, 385-7, 389, 390, 392,
  426, 428, 432-41, 450

tense, 41-2, 46, 98-9, 157, 182-3, 413
'that', 65, 155, 283f., 307, 314-6, 423
'there is', 129-30, 137-45, 192-5,
  197-9
'thing', 196, 364
'this', 43-5, 47-50, 165, 217, 402, 415
Thompson, S. A., 96, 116, 118, 123,
  318
Thornton, M. T., 178
Tibetan, 116
time, 3, 41, 194, 196, 230, 274-6
token-reflexivity, 42f.
tone, 392-403
Tongan, 116
topics, 96, 116, 118, 318
Toulmin, S. E., 395-6

transitivity, 118, ch. 7 *passim*, 423, 425
truth, 53-5, 124, 131, 167, 301, 319,
 328-9, 353-5, 391-3, 399-402,
 416-7, 429-30, 433, 445
 correspondence theory of, 339f., 361,
  363-4, 372, 419
 redundancy theory of, 361f.
 truth-functionality, 28, 179-85, 390-
  1, 399-401, 414
 truth value gap, 53-5
Turkish, 122
type, 37, 110, 204, 207, 234, 254

undecidability, 276-7
understanding, 48-9, 72, 173, 405,
 430, 462
uniqueness, 52f.
universals, 1-2, 26, 97, 99, 101, ch. 6
 passim, 279, 348-52

Urmson, J. O., 156, 299
use, usage, 16, 18, 21, 25, 383-9, 411,
 430, 432-3, 453

verbal noun, 309-12, 315-6, 346
verbs, 19-20, 46, 100, 228, 238, 412-3
verification, verifiability, 353-4, 357,
 383, 395, 435, 457-80

Waismann, F., 465
'what', 306-7, 378
White, A. R., 295
Wittgenstein, 1, 30, 384, 390, 462

'you', 48-9, 122, 156, 163, 414

Zeno, 180